Guide to the thesaurus

Look at the sample word groups on the opposite page. They have been marked with directions which will help you find your way through the thesaurus.

Keyword
This word gives you an idea of the overall meaning of the word group. It will usually be a word you already know. For example, the keyword **crooked** tells you that this is the group to look at if you want to find other words which express the idea 'curved or not straight'.

Definition
Only one meaning of the keyword is given. You can see that this is where a thesaurus is different from a dictionary in which all the meanings of a word are listed next to that word. In the first sample **crooked** has been used with the group of words which mean 'curved or not straight'. Now look at the second sample. **Crooked** has been used here too, with its second meaning, 'dishonest'.

Related words
These words are related in meaning to the keyword and also to each other. You may prefer to use one of these because it expresses your idea more precisely, or is a more interesting or unusual word than the keyword. The information following each related word will help you decide which one to use.

What the word means
This is rather like a definition. It explains the similarities and differences between the related words and the keyword. With this information you will be able to choose a word with precisely the meaning you want.

Word use
This tells you if the word is a legal word, a formal word or one you would use in everyday language.

Illustrative sentence
This is just one example we have thought of to show you how to use the word. You can probably think of many more examples yourself.

Cross-references
Similar words are other keywords which are rather like the words in this group. For example, **illegal** is the keyword of a group consisting of these words: *illicit, criminal, felonious, fraudulent, contraband.* You can see that they have been put into their own group, separate from **dishonest,** because they have a different shade of meaning.
Contrasting words are keywords which are unlike the words in this group. For example, **honest** is the keyword of a group consisting of these words: *truthful, honourable, upright, sincere, scrupulous.* All of these express an idea which contrasts with **dishonest.**

The Collins School Thesaurus

The Collins School Thesaurus

General Editor
Linsay Knight

Collins Educational

First published in Australia 1986 by
THE JACARANDA PRESS

This edition published by
COLLINS EDUCATIONAL
8 Grafton Street
London WIX 3LA

Printed in Singapore
Reprinted in Singapore 1988

ISBN 0 00 313318 4

Contents

Editorial staff

General Editor Linsay Knight, M.A., Dip.Ed. (Macquarie)

Executive Editor Susan Butler

Editors Jessie Terry
Leah Bloomfield

Indexer Leah Bloomfield

Writers Ann Atkinson
Virginia Stuart-Smith
Diana Terry
Jessie Terry

Computer Coordinator William E. Smith

Computer Programmers Robert Mannell
William E. Smith

Editorial Assistants Kristine Burnet
Jenny Cant
Maureen Leslie
Anne Teong

Editorial Committee, The Macquarie Dictionary

Editor in Chief: A Delbridge, M.A.(Lond.), B.A., Dip.Ed.(Syd.)
Professor of Linguistics and Director of the Dictionary Research Centre, School of English and Linguistics, Macquarie University

J.R.L. Bernard, B.Sc., B.A., Ph.D., Dip.Ed.(Syd.)
Associate Professor in Linguistics, Macquarie University

D. Blair, M.A.(Syd.)
Lecturer in Linguistics, Macquarie University

W.S. Ramson, M.A.(N.Z.), Ph.D.(Syd.)
Reader in English, Australian National University

Executive Editor: Susan Butler, B.A.

Collins Educational wish to express their thanks to Ginny Lapage who adapted the Thesaurus for the English edition and to John McIlwain who checked the proofs and made many helpful suggestions.

Preface *... for teachers and parents*

This Thesaurus is designed for children to use in their last years of primary school and early years of secondary school.

We have written the entries and arranged them on each page in a way which is clear and simple, and have provided extra information which adults will find unnecessary. By supplying this extra information we have been able to do away with the abbreviations and codes which can be baffling and distracting to a young reader. This means that the thesaurus is ideally suited for teaching children what thesauruses do and how they can be useful. Young readers will be able to progress naturally to more adult thesauruses in their own time, secure in the knowledge that they understand how they work and what sort of information they are likely to contain.

Since people use thesauruses to find alternatives to the easy or well-used words they already know, our policy has been to include hard words at the expense of those easy ones that a young reader wouldn't bother to look up. Interesting colloquial words, legal and more formal words, but above all, words having the same or nearly the same meaning as others in the language have been chosen to form groups covering the large range of concepts that children in the middle years of their education will find useful.

Words which are very closely related such as *nice, pleasant, enjoyable, lovely, acceptable* and *welcome* as well as words which are more loosely related such as *lesson, lecture, seminar, sermon* and *course* have been grouped together, each under a **keyword** which reflects the overall meaning of the whole group. These keywords appear in alphabetical order in the thesaurus and each has its part of speech, definition and an illustrative sentence to show how it is used. Its **related words** are arranged under it in an order which has been carefully considered. Words most similar to the keyword come first, followed by words which may be less similar in meaning or usage. Instead of just listing those related words, we have provided extra information and comments as to meaning and usage. We have also provided an illustrative sentence which is, after all, the most interesting way of showing how a word is used, in each case.

Each group of related words is confined to five or six words, as any more would be too much for the young reader to consider at once. Each group covers only one particular meaning of the words. Thus, a word might be used several times in the thesaurus, but in a specific sense each time.

At the end of a group of related words there may be a cross-reference if it is relevant. The reader will find groups of similar or contrasting words which may be useful to look up for extra information.

Linsay Knight.

Introduction *. . . for young readers*

What is a thesaurus?

Have you ever been stuck for a word and felt very annoyed because you knew it was lurking somewhere but you just couldn't bring it to mind? Well, Peter Mark Roget often had just this problem so he wrote down lists of similar words for his own use over the years. He was a doctor and often lectured to students at the Manchester Medical School, so he needed to use just the right words to express his meaning. In 1849, when Roget was 70, he began to write these lists so that they could be published. He called this treasure trove of words his 'thesaurus'.

Roget put together in the same group all the words and phrases which expressed a particular idea. For example, in a group called *force* in a thesaurus you might find *power, strength, might, muscle* and *vigour*. These five words refer to some aspects of the idea of *force* but they are not the same as it and so they do not define it. Roget did not want his book to be like a dictionary with definitions of every word. Rather, he wanted to gather in each group the words you might think of when a particular topic is being discussed. They are related to one another by being in the same area of meaning but they do not necessarily mean exactly the same thing.

Roget's thesaurus was so useful to people trying to write letters, essays, speeches and so on, that it was very, very successful. Twenty-eight editions were published in Peter Roget's lifetime. His son, John Lewis Roget, and his grandson, Samuel Romilly Roget, kept his good work alive by bringing out updated versions with his original publisher.

Other publishers brought out their own versions. Some have just been called 'Thesaurus', while others were called 'Roget's Thesaurus' even though they didn't come directly from Roget himself. Gradually, the word 'thesaurus' has ceased to refer to one book and is now defined in dictionaries as a 'book of words arranged in groups which have similar meaning'.

The Collins School Thesaurus

The Thesaurus is arranged in two sections — the word groups, and the index.

Word Groups

In the first section you will find over 940 word groups. Each group consists of five or six words or phrases that are closely related to one another. There is also some information about what each word means and how it can be used. This will help you make your writing and conversation more interesting and precise and also expand your vocabulary.

Inside the front cover there are instructions telling you how to use the Thesaurus.

Index

The back section is the index which is printed in green to help you find it more easily. This is a list of all the keywords and related words in the thesaurus arranged in alphabetical order. You can use the index to look up any word in the thesaurus to find which word group it is in and which page it is on.

Inside the back cover there are instructions telling you how to use the index.

What's in a word?

Andrew and Joanne had never been away from England before. When they arrived in Australia they each sent a postcard to their grandparents describing the journey.

'It was really *exciting*, yet a bit scary to *soar* so high above the *ocean.* I realised that our *aircraft* was *zooming* further and further from our *home.* Never fear, the meals were *terrific*', wrote Andrew.

'Well, I had a *great* time *flying* over here. I couldn't see the *sea* from the plane as it was too dark. The food was *delicious.* I knew we were travelling far from our *native land*', wrote Joanne.

These two children managed to describe the same incident and never used the same words. There is a wealth of meaning in each word in the English language. It is very important to learn to use words so well that you know which is the right one to express exactly what you mean.

Try browsing in this thesaurus and you will certainly come to appreciate the value of words. You will meet some words that are old friends and some that are new and exciting. You will always need your dictionary to help you as well — a dictionary and a thesaurus go hand-in-hand.

abduct *verb*

to take someone away by force. *The terrorists **abducted** the president as he was walking to his car.*

kidnap To **kidnap** means to abduct someone and hold them prisoner until a ransom is paid, or some other condition is met. *Some criminals kidnapped the millionaire's daughter.*

shanghai To **shanghai** can mean to take someone away and force them to join the crew of a ship. *In times of war soldiers used to go from town to town looking for men to shanghai into the navy.*

poach To **poach** can mean to take animals or fish from someone's property without permission. *Our chickens keep disappearing so we think someone is poaching them.*

rustle To **rustle** can mean to steal cattle or horses. *The dishonest cowboy rustled livestock from nearby ranches.*

similar words: **capture, steal**

abrupt *adjective*

rude and quick-tempered. *He gave an **abrupt** answer.*

short **Short** can mean rudely brief in your way of speaking. *She was very short with me when I asked her the time.*

curt **Curt** means rudely brief in your speech or manners. It is very similar to **short**. *His curt reply hurt me.*

brusque **Brusque** means abrupt and impolite. *His brusque manner upset me.*

terse **Terse** means using few words, often in an impolite way. *Her terse comment showed plainly what she meant.*

blunt **Blunt** can mean plain and direct in your way of speaking. *They gave a blunt refusal to our request.*

similar words: **rude**
contrasting words: **talkative**

abundant *adjective*

more than enough. *The canteen had an **abundant** supply of sausage rolls.*

ample — **Ample** means more than enough in size or amount. *There was ample space for us all to fit in the car.*

plentiful — **Plentiful** means great in amount or number. *The coach always had a plentiful supply of bandages at the football matches in case anyone was injured.*

bountiful — **Bountiful** can mean generous in number or amount. *The rains produced a bountiful harvest.*

copious — **Copious** means large in quantity. *We took copious notes during the lesson because our teacher was revising the term's work before the exam.*

prolific — **Prolific** means producing plentifully. *We have a prolific orange tree in the backyard and always have enough oranges for our family and friends.*

similar words: **numerous, sufficient**
contrasting words: **scant, insufficient**

accidental *adjective*

happening unexpectedly or by accident. *Don't get angry with him for breaking the window because it was purely **accidental**.*

chance — **Chance** means not due to any known reason. *I came across this valuable old vase by a chance visit to a junk shop.*

coincidental — **Coincidental** means happening at the same time by accident or chance. *It was coincidental that we both went to the movies yesterday.*

random — **Random** means not following a pattern or method. *The police stopped us for a random breath test.*

haphazard — **Haphazard** means not planned, or happening by chance. *He made many errors because he worked in such a haphazard way.*

fluky — **Fluky** means obtained by accidental advantage or a stroke of good luck rather than by skill, especially in relation to sport. It is more suited to everyday language. *That fluky goal in the basketball match was thrown by their shortest player.*

contrasting words: **deliberate**

acclaim *verb*

to praise someone with sounds of approval. *The crowd **acclaimed** the footballer with shouts and clapping.*

applaud To **applaud** means to praise someone or express approval of them, especially by clapping your hands or calling out. *The audience applauded the boy at the end of his song.*

clap To **clap** means to show approval or enjoyment of someone or something by striking your hands together. *They clapped the funny clown after he had performed some clever tricks.*

cheer To **cheer** means to greet someone with shouts of approval. *We cheered the winner as he crossed the finishing line.*

toast To **toast** means to express your approval of someone by having a special drink in their honour. *We toasted the new president of the club.*

honour To **honour** means to show your admiration and respect for someone or something. *The Queen honoured the great scientist by making him a knight.*

similar words: **praise**
contrasting words: **scold**

accompany *verb*

to go or be with someone. *I am going to **accompany** my parents on their overseas trip.*

partner To **partner** means to take part in something with someone. *He promised to partner his sister for the next dance.*

escort To **escort** means to go along with someone as a mark of respect or to guard them. *The police escorted the prime minister back to his hotel.*

chaperone To **chaperone** means to accompany someone to make sure they behave properly. *The teachers will chaperone the children at the school dance.*

associate with To **associate with** means to spend time with someone. *She only associates with girls from her own class.*

hang around with To **hang around with** means to spend your spare time with someone. This is more suited to everyday language. *She hangs around with bikers.*

accomplish *verb*

to carry something out successfully. *Congratulations! You have **accomplished** a difficult task.*

achieve	To **achieve** can mean to accomplish something or bring it to a successful end. *You will have to work hard to achieve your ambition to be a musician.*
attain	To **attain** means to reach or complete something by trying hard. *He attained his goal of coming first in English.*
fulfil	To **fulfil** means to carry something out. *He fulfilled his promise to repay the debt.*
carry through	To **carry through** means to finish or complete something. *She carried her plan through with great courage and determination.*
bring off	To **bring off** is an informal way of saying to **accomplish**. *The escape was dangerous but they managed to bring it off.*

accuse *verb*

to blame someone openly for doing something wrong. *He **accused** the boy of cheating in the test.*

denounce	To **denounce** means to speak out against something or someone. *The leader of the revolution denounced the traitors.*
frame	To **frame** can mean to make someone seem to be guilty of something. *I didn't do it your honour, he framed me.*
allege	To **allege** means to declare something without having proof of it. This is rather a formal word. *The shopkeeper didn't see the girl steal the book but he alleges it.*
charge	To **charge** means to accuse or blame someone for something. This can be a legal word. *The police charged her with speeding.*
book	To **book** can mean to record someone's name in order to accuse them of doing something wrong. *If you break the law again I'll have to book you.*

contrasting words: **forgive**

achievement *noun*

something you gain by hard work. *They praised him for his **achievement** in completing the marathon.*

accomplishment An **accomplishment** is something you achieve through hard work. It is similar to **achievement**. *Winning the cup two years in a row was a great accomplishment.*

effort An **effort** is something done by trying. *The teacher thought my project was a good effort.*

success A **success** is a very good result. *Our team had a great success in the chess competition.*

feat A **feat** is something you do using great skill, strength or courage. *It was a great feat to climb to the top of Mount Everest.*

contrasting words: **failure**

actual *adjective*

existing in fact. *Mum gave me the **actual** prayer book she carried on her wedding day.*

real **Real** means true or actual. *We have a real Swiss cuckoo clock at home.*

concrete **Concrete** can mean existing as an actual thing, not just an idea. *The sports club Kate formed for blind children like herself was a concrete example of her courage.*

tangible **Tangible** means able to be touched or felt. *Mr Williams gave the sports club a large donation as tangible proof of his support.*

material **Material** means existing in a form you can touch. *Her big house and car are the material signs of her success.*

physical **Physical** can mean having to do with **material** things in the world rather than spiritual things. *We need money to buy things for our physical needs.*

contrasting words: **shadowy, imaginary**

add *verb*

to join something on to something else in order to increase it in size or number. ***Add** another bead on to the necklace to make it longer.*

supplement To **supplement** something means to add to it. *She supplements her pocket money by babysitting.*

throw in To **throw in** means to add something as an extra. *They threw in some extra drinks in case they met up with some friends.*

append To **append** means to join or add as an extra part. *We appended the cheque to the letter.*

tack on To **tack on** means to add something on to something else. *They tacked another room on to the shed.*

attach To **attach** means to fasten or join something to something else. *Let's attach the party lights to the tree.*

similar words: **enlarge, insert**
contrasting words: **subtract, remove, reduce**

admit *verb*

to agree that something is true. *I **admitted** that I had broken the vase.*

confess To **confess** means to own up to something you have done. *I confessed that I had not listened when she told me to be careful.*

blurt out To **blurt out** means to tell something suddenly or without thinking. *I meant to keep it a secret but then I blurted it out.*

acknowledge To **acknowledge** means to say that you realise something is true. *I acknowledged that it was kind of her to forgive my carelessness.*

unburden To **unburden** can mean to ease yourself or your mind by telling or confessing something. *I felt better after I unburdened myself and told her what I had done.*

betray To **betray** can mean to give away a secret without meaning to. *The empty space on the mantelpiece had betrayed my clumsiness.*

similar words: **reveal**
contrasting words: **hide**

adult *adjective*

grown-up or fully grown. *The **adult** birds are quite a different colour from their young.*

mature — **Mature** means adult or fully grown. *He can make up his own mind now that he's a mature man.*

elderly — **Elderly** means old. *Sometimes we visit elderly people in special homes and read the newspapers or talk to them.*

aged — **Aged** means very old. *The aged man had many stories to tell about how different things were when he was a boy.*

geriatric — **Geriatric** means having to do with old people. *When great-grandfather became ill he went to a geriatric hospital where he could have extra care.*

senile — **Senile** means weak in your body or mind because of old age. *The very old lady was senile and needed to be looked after carefully.*

contrasting words: **young**

advance *verb*

to move or go forward. *She **advanced** to the front of the room.*

progress — To **progress** can mean to advance or move forward. *The circus parade progressed slowly down the road.*

make headway — To **make headway** means to progress or move forward. *The car made little headway in the heavy rain.*

proceed — To **proceed** means to move or go forward, especially after stopping. *We drove carefully over the gravel road because the sign said 'Proceed with caution'.*

push on — To **push on** means to continue or go forward, usually with difficulty. *The weary travellers pushed on from one town to the next.*

forge ahead — To **forge ahead** means to move forward with great effort. *The explorers forged ahead through the thick bush.*

contrasting words: **reverse**

advise *verb*

to tell someone what you think should be done. *The doctor* ***advised*** *his patient to get more exercise.*

guide To **guide** can mean to advise, lead or direct someone in the way you think they should go. *His mother guided him in his decision to stay at school.*

suggest To **suggest** means to put forward the idea of doing anything. *My tennis coach suggested that I practise my backhand.*

propose To **propose** means to put forward or **suggest** something. *She proposed a good method of raising money.*

recommend To **recommend** means to **suggest** something as being good or worthwhile. *The librarian recommended this book to me.*

advocate To **advocate** means to speak in favour of something. *Our dentist advocates brushing your teeth after every meal.*

similar words: **warn**

adviser *noun*

someone who tells you what they think you should do. *She is a very wise* ***adviser*** *so I usually do what she suggests.*

guide A **guide** is someone whose suggestions and advice you usually follow. *I let him be my guide when I'm not sure what to do.*

mentor A **mentor** is an adviser who is very wise and whom you trust. *Her father has been her mentor for many years.*

counsellor A **counsellor** is a person who is specially trained to help people solve problems or difficulties. *The careers counsellor helped me to decide what I should do.*

guru A **guru** is a wise and powerful teacher or **guide**. *Many people listened to the guru and tried to do everything he taught them.*

similar words: **teacher**

aggressive *adjective*

likely to attack others. *He is only **aggressive** if you tease him.*

combative	**Combative** means ready or eager to fight. *She has a combative nature and seems to enjoy fighting.*
belligerent	**Belligerent** means angry and wanting to fight. *Her belligerent behaviour towards her friends surprised us.*
pugnacious	**Pugnacious** means likely to quarrel or fight. *He is so pugnacious that the others have stopped trying to be friends with him.*
hostile	**Hostile** means acting like an enemy. *Her hostile reply to our invitation upset us.*

similar words: **argumentative, warlike**
contrasting words: **submissive**

agile *adjective*

lively and active. *The **agile** gymnast did the most difficult exercises with ease.*

athletic	**Athletic** means physically active and strong. *Our runners are very athletic, which is why our school won the cross-country race.*
sprightly	**Sprightly** means lively and merry. *He played a sprightly tune on the recorder.*
nimble	**Nimble** means able to move quickly and easily. *Her nimble fingers made playing the piano look easy.*
spry	**Spry** means **nimble** or active. *He is a spry old man and climbs all the stairs to his flat.*
light	**Light** can mean agile or **nimble**. *He was very light on his feet when he danced.*

contrasting words: **clumsy**

agree *verb*

to say yes or to have the same opinion as someone else. *I **agreed** to his plan.*

concur To **concur** means to agree with something. *I concur with your decision.*

assent To **assent** means to agree to something. *The council members assented to the suggestion to build a new school.*

see eye to eye To **see eye to eye** means to have the same opinion as someone else. It is more suited to everyday language. *My sister and I see eye to eye on which TV programmes we like to watch.*

shake hands To **shake hands** can mean to clasp hands with someone as a sign that you agree about something. *I wanted to buy his car so we shook hands on the deal.*

contrasting words: **disagree**

agreeable *adjective*

pleasing or to your liking. *She is a very **agreeable** person to be with.*

good-natured **Good-natured** means having a pleasant nature and being easy to get on with. *He's so good-natured everyone wants to be on his team.*

likeable **Likeable** means easy to like. *The new girl was very likeable and fitted into the class easily.*

amiable **Amiable** means agreeable and friendly. *I rang my friend and we had an amiable conversation.*

charming **Charming** means having the ability to please and attract people. *He is a charming boy and is sure to be class captain.*

similar words: **nice, friendly**
contrasting words: **nasty**

alert *adjective*

watching things carefully and quick to react. *The guards were **alert** to any danger.*

watchful — **Watchful** means alert or careful to notice what is going on. *She was always watchful when her children were swimming.*

observant — **Observant** means alert or quick to notice things. *The observant girl noticed where the biscuits were kept.*

attentive — **Attentive** means watching carefully. *Only the most attentive people saw how the trick was done.*

awake — **Awake** can mean alert or ready for anything that might happen. *They were awake to the dangers of walking home in the dark.*

similar words: **inquisitive**
contrasting words: **dreamy**

allow *verb*

to let someone do something. *Will your parents **allow** you to come?*

permit — To **permit** is so similar to **allow** that you can usually use either. *The law does not permit you to leave school before you are fourteen.*

authorise — To **authorise** means to agree or consent to something officially. *The principal has authorised this excursion.*

license — To **license** means to give official permission to someone. *The council has licensed this shop to sell wine and beer.*

tolerate — To **tolerate** means to allow something, although not very willingly. *I will tolerate his presence in the house, but I'm not happy about it.*

suffer — To **suffer** can mean to allow or **tolerate** something. It is a rather old-fashioned meaning of this word. *Today I'll suffer his company on the way home, but never again.*

contrasting words: **refuse, prevent, ban**

ancestor *noun*

someone related to you who lived long ago. *What country did your **ancestors** come from?*

forebear — **Forebear** is so similar to **ancestor** that you can usually use either. *Our forebears fought at the Battle of Hastings.*

forefather — **Forefather** is so similar to **ancestor** and **forebear** that you can usually use any of them. *Some of our forefathers mapped unexplored areas of the world.*

antecedents — **Antecedents** can be your line of ancestors. *Horse trainers think that it is important to know the antecedents of a thoroughbred horse.*

predecessor — A **predecessor** is someone who has gone before you, especially in a job or position. *Our new head teacher is younger than her predecessor.*

contrasting words: **offspring**

anger *noun*

a strong feeling of annoyance caused by thinking that something wrong has been done to you. *He could not control his **anger** when he saw the broken window.*

wrath — **Wrath** is anger or revenge. It is a rather old-fashioned word. *When I'm naughty, I bring upon myself the wrath of my parents.*

ire — **Ire** is very similar to **anger** and **wrath**. Like **wrath**, it is a rather old-fashioned word. *My ire increased as the next-door neighbour's party became noisier and noisier.*

rage — **Rage** is violent anger. *When he was in a rage everyone was frightened of him.*

fury — **Fury** is a violent feeling, especially one of anger. It is very similar to **rage**. *He smashed the door in his fury.*

temper — **Temper** can be an angry or resentful mood. *She's often in a temper when she's had a bad day at work.*

anger *verb*

to make someone or something annoyed or violent. *When the visitors teased the monkeys it **angered** the zoo-keeper.*

incense	To **incense** means to make someone angry. It is a more formal word than **anger**. *The accused man's lawyer incensed the judge with his interruptions.*
enrage	To **enrage** means to make someone very angry. *Her cheeky questions enraged the teacher.*
infuriate	To **infuriate** is so similar to **enrage** you can usually use either word. *The workers infuriated their boss when they refused to work overtime.*
drive someone up the wall	To **drive someone up the wall** means to annoy someone very much. This is more suited to everyday language. *That noise you are making is really driving me up the wall.*

similar words: **irritate, annoy**
contrasting words: **pacify**

angry *adjective*

very annoyed because you think that something wrong has been done to you. *She gave me an **angry** look when I was rude to her.*

indignant	**Indignant** means angry about something which you think is unfair. *I arrived on time so I was indignant when I was accused of being late.*
offended	**Offended** means feeling displeased or hurt. *They were offended when their friend ignored them.*
irate	**Irate** means very angry. *The customer was irate when he wasn't served in his turn.*
furious	**Furious** means extremely angry. *She was so furious that she began to shout.*
livid	**Livid** means almost uncontrollably angry. It is similar to **furious**. *He was livid when we told him we had scratched his car.*

similar words: **grumpy, annoyed**
contrasting words: **glad, happy, joyful**

annoy *verb*

to irritate someone or make them crotchety. *Very loud music **annoys** me.*

aggravate	To **aggravate** can mean to annoy or provoke someone. *Don't aggravate the teacher by shuffling your feet.*
exasperate	To **exasperate** means to annoy someone very much. *Kevin exasperated us with his stubbornness.*
hassle	To **hassle** means to worry or annoy someone. It is more suited to everyday language. *Don't hassle me when I'm tired.*
rub up the wrong way	To **rub up the wrong way** means to annoy or irritate someone. It is more suited to everyday language. *That girl always rubs me up the wrong way with the silly questions she asks.*
get on someone's nerves	To **get on someone's nerves** means to irritate or annoy someone. It is more suited to everyday language. *He gets on my nerves when he complains all the time.*

similar words: **irritate, upset**
contrasting words: **please**

annoyed *adjective*

irritated or made cross. *The **annoyed** customer demanded that the shop should replace the faulty toaster.*

crotchety	**Crotchety** means bad-tempered or cross. It is more suited to everyday language. *Alec was really crotchety when his car had a flat tyre.*
infuriated	**Infuriated** means made very angry or annoyed. *Dad was infuriated when the careless driver ran into his new car.*
vexed	**Vexed** means made annoyed or irritated. It is a rather old-fashioned word. *Grandma said she was vexed by the shopkeeper's rudeness.*
fed up	**Fed up** means annoyed with, or tired of something. This is more suited to everyday language. *We were fed up with camping after a week of rain.*

similar words: **grumpy, angry, dissatisfied**
contrasting words: **glad**

annoying *adjective*

likely to make you angry. *This rain is so **annoying** because I wanted to go to the beach.*

irritating — **Irritating** means causing anger or impatience. *'Your irritating chatter will have to stop', their teacher said.*

exasperating — **Exasperating** means very annoying. *It is exasperating when you can't think of the exact word you want to use.*

trying — **Trying** means annoying or **irritating**. *The way he keeps talking about himself is very trying.*

infuriating — **Infuriating** means causing very great anger. *My little brother's constant interruptions were infuriating.*

maddening — **Maddening** is so similar to **infuriating** you can usually choose either word. *It's maddening! — I'm sure I put my book on my desk but now I can't find it.*

contrasting words: **nice**

answer *verb*

to acknowledge a question, request, letter, and so on, using actions, words, or in writing. *She **answered** the question with a shake of her head.*

respond — To **respond** means to answer, using actions or words. *People responded generously to the clothing appeal.*

reply — To **reply** means to give an answer or response. *Did you reply to the letter?*

retort — To **retort** means to give a quick or sharp answer. *When I said that she was late, she retorted by saying that I was lucky she had come at all.*

react — To **react** means to act in answer to something. *We all react to danger in different ways.*

return — To **return** can mean to answer or **retort**. *When they tried to make friends she returned by snapping rudely.*

contrasting words: **question**

apathetic *adjective*

having no feelings for, or interest in things that other people find interesting or exciting. *The people passing by seemed to be **apathetic** about the demonstration.*

indifferent — **Indifferent** means showing no interest or concern. *He was indifferent to my pain.*

half-hearted — **Half-hearted** means not showing much willingness or interest. *He made a half-hearted attempt to join in the party.*

lukewarm — **Lukewarm** means not very enthusiastic. *The proposal to erect a statue of the mayor received a lukewarm response at the council meeting.*

passive — **Passive** means letting things happen without taking any action yourself. *He would be no good as a leader because he is too passive.*

similar words: **lethargic**
contrasting words: **enthusiastic**

appear *verb*

to become visible. *The sun **appeared** over the horizon.*

come — To **come** can mean to appear. *There's something wrong with the TV — the picture comes and goes.*

emerge — To **emerge** means to come out into view. *She emerged from behind the trees.*

loom — To **loom** means to appear, often in a large or frightening form. *The man suddenly loomed in front of me out of the shadows.*

show up — To **show up** means to appear or be seen, often unexpectedly. *I was glad that my library book showed up when I tidied my room.*

materialise — To **materialise** means to appear in a physical shape. *Her figure materialised out of the mist.*

contrasting words: **disappear**

appearance *noun*

the way something or someone looks or seems on the outside. *His bushy black beard gave him a fierce **appearance**.*

aspect — **Aspect** is the way a thing appears or seems. *We were shocked by the burnt aspect of the land after the forest fire.*

air — **Air** can be the way something looks or seems. It is very similar to **appearance** and **aspect**. *The rich business woman has an air of success.*

complexion — **Complexion** can be very similar to **appearance** and **aspect**. It can usually be used in the same way. *A fresh coat of yellow paint gave the room a completely different complexion.*

presence — **Presence** can mean your personal appearance or your way of doing things. *The grand presence of the princess made us feel very unimportant.*

similar words: **manner**

approve *verb*

to like something and agree to it. *We **approved** the idea of having a holiday on the farm.*

endorse — To **endorse** means to approve of or to support something. *Do you endorse the cutting down of trees in the rainforest?*

sanction — To **sanction** means to give approval or support to something. This is rather a formal word. *The headmaster sanctioned our plan to hold a fete to raise money.*

advocate — To **advocate** means to speak favourably about something. *In my speech I advocated peace not war.*

bless — To **bless** means to approve something and to wish it every success. *He blessed our decision.*

hold with — To **hold with** is to approve of or agree with something. *I don't hold with the new rule.*

similar words: **praise**
contrasting words: **disapprove of, fault**

argue *verb*

to disagree, often in an angry way. *We **argued** about what colour car we should buy.*

quarrel — To **quarrel** can mean to argue angrily. *We quarrelled over who would have the first ride.*

squabble — To **squabble** means to argue angrily, but usually for a short time, about something unimportant. *Children often squabble during card games.*

row — To **row** means to argue angrily and noisily. It is more suited to everyday language. *The new neighbours rowed so much someone called the police.*

clash — To **clash** can mean to disagree angrily about something you consider to be very important. *They clashed over what school the children should go to.*

conflict — To **conflict** means to disagree or be in opposition to one another. It is similar to **clash**. *Our ideas conflict about that because we are so different.*

similar words: **disagree**

argument *noun*

a disagreement, especially a noisy one. *We had an **argument** about who had won the race.*

quarrel — A **quarrel** is an angry argument. *You don't have to have a quarrel every time you disagree.*

dispute — A **dispute** is an argument or **quarrel**. *They had a dispute over who was the better singer.*

difference — A **difference** can mean a disagreement or **quarrel**, especially between two people who usually get on well. *I had a difference with Felicity about what to do on Saturday.*

controversy — A **controversy** is an argument or a difference of opinion. *There has been a public controversy over where the new airport should be built.*

altercation — An **altercation** is an angry **dispute** or disagreement. *They had an altercation over who was to blame for the traffic accident.*

similar words: **conflict**

argumentative *adjective*

liking to argue. *Some people are **argumentative** if they are criticised.*

quarrelsome — **Quarrelsome** means likely to quarrel easily. *The children were quarrelsome because they were bored.*

cantankerous — **Cantankerous** means bad-tempered and likely to pick a fight. *The cantankerous bus driver told off the children for singing.*

stroppy — **Stroppy** means annoyed and wanting to argue. It is more suited to everyday language. *She was stroppy because she couldn't have her own way.*

contrary — **Contrary** can mean always disagreeing or purposely taking the opposite view. *He is sure to be contrary no matter what we suggest.*

similar words: **defiant, aggressive**
contrasting words: **submissive**

arrange *verb*

to put something in order. *She **arranged** the books on the shelf so that she could find them easily.*

group — To **group** means to gather things or people together because they are thought to be connected in some way. *The sports teacher grouped the children according to age for races at the Sports Carnival.*

sort — To **sort** means to arrange according to type or kind. *We sorted the washing into piles for each member of the family.*

grade — To **grade** means to arrange according to a stage or step on a scale of positions, quality or value. *A wool classer grades wool into bundles of fine or coarse texture.*

classify — To **classify** means to arrange according to quality or likeness. *This book classifies plants into different groups according to where they come from.*

file — To **file** can mean to put or arrange something in a file. *The librarian filed all the index cards so that we could find them easily.*

similar words: **list**
contrasting words: **disorganise**

ask *verb*

to put a question to someone. *I'll **ask** my father to help me with this problem when he gets home.*

request To **request** means to ask for something in a formal way. *The judge requested the public to be silent during the court case.*

beg To **beg** means to ask someone for something in a humble way. *I beg you to forgive me.*

implore To **implore** means to ask someone for something in an earnest or urgent way. *Don't go, I implore you!*

entreat To **entreat** means to **implore**. These two words are so similar you can often choose either of them. *We entreat you to help us escape.*

beseech To **beseech** means to ask anxiously for something. *I beseeched him for news of the missing fishermen.*

similar words: **demand**

assemble *verb*

to come together. *We **assembled** in the playground before going on the excursion.*

gather To **gather** is so similar to **assemble** that you can usually use either. *A crowd gathered to watch the fight.*

meet To **meet** means to come together for discussions or a shared activity. *The club meets at 9 o'clock every Friday in the church hall.*

congregate To **congregate** means to come together in very large numbers. *A huge crowd congregated to see the fireworks.*

turn out To **turn out** means to come along. *All her friends turned out for her wedding.*

rally To **rally** means to come together for a common cause or purpose. *The people rallied behind their leader.*

associate *noun*

someone who is connected with you and shares your interests. *My father's accountant is a business **associate**.*

comrade A **comrade** is a very close friend or mate. *My father and my uncle have been comrades since being in the army together.*

partner A **partner** is someone who takes part in something with you. *You should always go skindiving with a partner.*

colleague A **colleague** is someone who does the same sort of work as you. *People can learn a lot by talking to their colleagues.*

collaborator A **collaborator** is someone who works with you on a special task or job. *The two friends were collaborators in writing a play.*

similar words: **friend, helper**

astonished *adjective*

filled with sudden and great wonder. *We were **astonished** when we saw how red the sunset was.*

surprised **Surprised** means filled with a feeling of shock and wonder at something unexpected or very unusual. *I was surprised by her sudden outburst of anger.*

amazed **Amazed** means completely overcome with astonishment. *I was amazed that I had managed to complete the marathon.*

astounded **Astounded** means completely overcome with astonishment. *We were astounded when we discovered gold on our land.*

flabbergasted **Flabbergasted** means shocked or greatly astonished. *I was flabbergasted when she spoke to me so rudely.*

stunned **Stunned** means astonished and very shocked. *News of the president's death stunned the world.*

astonishing *adjective*

causing great surprise or wonder. *It was* ***astonishing*** *to see the slow tortoise beat the hare.*

amazing — **Amazing** means causing surprise and astonishment. *It was an amazing finish to the race.*

astounding — **Astounding** means causing complete surprise. *The astounding result shocked the hare.*

remarkable — **Remarkable** means very unusual and worthy of notice. *It was a remarkable effort for the tortoise to trick the hare.*

staggering — **Staggering** means causing shock and wonder. *Soon everyone had heard the staggering news that the tortoise had beaten the hare.*

stupendous — **Stupendous** means astonishingly good. *The tortoise's stupendous feat would be remembered for a long, long time.*

similar words: **wonderful**

attack *noun*

the use of force or weapons against a person or group of people. *The soldiers loaded their rifles ready for the* ***attack****.*

assault — An **assault** is a violent attack. *They made an assault on the enemy city.*

onslaught — An **onslaught** is a fierce rush or attack. *The sudden onslaught left many people wounded.*

ambush — An **ambush** is a sudden attack from a hidden place. *Our enemy's ambush caught us by surprise.*

blitz — A **blitz** is a sudden attack. *The people ran to the air-raid shelter for cover during the blitz.*

foray — A **foray** is a raid or attack in order to steal something. *We made a foray into the enemy's camp in the hope of capturing some hostages.*

contrasting words: **defence**

attack *verb*

to use force or weapons against a person or group of people. *They **attacked** the enemy with all their strength.*

assault — To **assault** means to attack someone or something violently. *The thugs assaulted the old man and he had to be taken to hospital.*

charge — To **charge** means to attack someone or something by rushing violently at them. *The bull charged us and we just managed to escape in time.*

mug — To **mug** means to attack and rob someone. *Someone mugged her in the lonely park at night.*

beat up — To **beat up** means to attack someone and hurt them.This is more suited to everyday language. *She cried when the bully beat her up.*

let fly — To **let fly** means to attack someone energetically. This is more suited to everyday language. *She let fly at the bully and scratched his face.*

contrasting words: **protect**

attempt *noun*

a try to complete or do something. *This will be our final **attempt** to reach the top of the mountain.*

effort — An **effort** is a serious attempt. *Our effort to reach the top took all of our strength.*

endeavour — An **endeavour** is a try or an attempt to do something that is worthwhile. *We knew our endeavours had been worthwhile when we finally reached the peak.*

crack — A **crack** can be an attempt that may not be successful. It is more suited to everyday language. *After I tried to take the lid off, he had a crack at it.*

stab — A **stab** is an attempt that hasn't much chance of succeeding. It is more suited to everyday language. *Can you make a stab at the answer?*

bash — A **bash** is a casual or unenthusiastic try or attempt. It is more suited to everyday language. *I don't really want to climb this tree but I'll have a bash.*

attempt *verb*

to make an effort to do something. *I will **attempt** the yacht race next year.*

try To **try** means to make an effort or attempt to do something. *It seems easy until you try it.*

undertake To **undertake** means to attempt or say that you will do something. *I will undertake the job tomorrow.*

tackle To **tackle** means to take on and struggle with something or someone. *Let's tackle the problem together.*

attack To **attack** can mean to go to work on something strongly. *We shall have to attack the next difficult task now.*

work towards To **work towards** means to make an effort to achieve something. *We have to work towards a fair solution to the argument.*

attract *verb*

to make someone pay attention or come near, especially by being interesting or pleasing. *The new television show **attracted** the whole family.*

draw To **draw** can be so similar to attract that you can usually use either. *Her cries drew me to the scene of the accident.*

lure To **lure** means to attract or tempt someone by seeming to be very pleasant or exciting. *Promises of good things to eat lured them towards the strange house.*

magnetise To **magnetise** can mean to attract someone so strongly that their whole attention is taken up. *The way she danced at the disco magnetised us.*

pull in To **pull in** can mean to attract or **draw** someone, usually a large group of people. *The final match pulled in the biggest crowd.*

similar words: **charm**
contrasting words: **repel**

attractive *adjective*

pleasing or appealing. *Going to the beach instead of studying is an* ***attractive*** *idea.*

magnetic — **Magnetic** can mean strongly attractive. *The new compere of the TV show had a magnetic personality.*

irresistible — **Irresistible** means not able to be resisted or withstood. *The chocolate cake in the fridge was so irresistible that I had to have some.*

tempting — **Tempting** means inviting or enticing. *The clear, blue water of the lake looked very tempting on such a hot day.*

seductive — **Seductive** means enticing or captivating. *The film star looked seductive in her low cut dress.*

charismatic — **Charismatic** means having special personal qualities that give someone influence over a large number of people. *The charismatic leader had a large following.*

avoid *verb*

to keep away from something or someone. *We went another way to* ***avoid*** *the traffic jam.*

miss — To **miss** can mean to avoid or fail to attend something. *I missed that film because I thought it would be boring.*

evade — To **evade** means to avoid doing or taking notice of something. *He manages to evade the school rules.*

elude — To **elude** means to avoid in a clever way someone who is looking for you. *The robber eluded the police.*

shirk — To **shirk** means to avoid doing a job or a duty. *They were very clever at shirking the hard work.*

steer clear of — To **steer clear of** means to avoid something or someone very carefully. *We steered clear of the deepest part of the river.*

contrasting words: **seek**

bad *adjective*

nasty or unpleasant. *There's a **bad** smell coming from that factory.*

atrocious — **Atrocious** means very bad or lacking in taste. *I can't put up with her atrocious behaviour.*

abominable — **Abominable** means hateful or disgusting. *Slavery was an abominable practice.*

abysmal — **Abysmal** means so bad that it could not be worse. *Her exam results were abysmal.*

monstrous — **Monstrous** means frightful or shocking. *The monstrous creatures on the advertisement for the film put us off going.*

rotten — **Rotten** means bad or dishonest. It is more suited to everyday language. *It was a rotten trick to sell him the bike you didn't even own.*

similar words: **nasty, pathetic**
contrasting words: **nice, good**

ball *noun*

something with a round or roundish shape, like the toy which you can bounce or kick, catch, or hit in games. *Throw me the **ball**.*

sphere — A **sphere** is something completely round in shape. *All the planets are spheres.*

globe — A **globe** is anything shaped like a ball, particularly a round map of the world. *Turn the globe around so that we can see Australia.*

orb — An **orb** is a ball-shaped object. It is used in poetry to mean a planet, the sun or the moon. *The sun is the orb of the day.*

globule — A **globule** is a very small ball-shaped object, especially a drop of liquid. *Globules of sweat ran down his forehead.*

ban *verb*

to forbid something. *Our teacher* ***banned*** *bleeping digital watches from the classroom.*

bar To **bar** can mean to forbid or prevent something or someone. *They barred that particular glue from being sold to children.*

outlaw To **outlaw** means to forbid something by law. *In Great Britain, the government has outlawed owning a gun without a licence.*

censor To **censor** means to prevent someone from seeing, hearing or reading things that are considered objectionable for any reason. *The Board censored the film because it was too violent.*

disqualify To **disqualify** can mean to prevent someone from getting something, or make them unsuitable to receive certain rights, or something similar. *His large income will disqualify him from getting a pension.*

boycott To **boycott** can mean to stop buying or using something, as a means of frightening or forcing someone. *We boycotted the new soap powder in an effort to stop the manufacturer from polluting the river.*

similar words: **prevent, exclude**
contrasting words: **allow**

bandit *noun*

an armed robber. *A gang of* ***bandits*** *broke into the bank.*

highwayman A **highwayman** was someone who held up travellers on highways and robbed them, usually on horseback. *People travelling from town to town in England in the olden days were scared of highwaymen.*

brigand A **brigand** is a robber who lives with a gang of other robbers in hidden mountain or forest areas. *Beware of brigands when you get to that lonely mountain road.*

pirate A **pirate** is someone who attacks and robs ships at sea. *The captain kept a lookout for pirates.*

buccaneer A **buccaneer** is a more old-fashioned word for a **pirate**. *There are many exciting stories about buccaneers who lived long ago.*

similar words: **thief, criminal**

bare *adjective*

having no covering. *I like to feel the warm sun on my **bare** skin.*

exposed — **Exposed** can mean uncovered or bare, especially something which should be or is usually covered. *When the mountain climber lost his gloves his exposed hands became icy cold.*

naked — **Naked** means having no clothes on. *The naked baby chuckled as she splashed in the bath.*

nude — **Nude** means unclothed, **naked** or without your usual clothes or coverings. *Nude bathers are allowed on some beaches.*

bald — **Bald** means not covered with hair, or any other natural growth. *Dad always wears a hat in the garden to keep the sun off his bald head.*

bay *noun*

a sheltered part of the sea or a lake formed by a curve in its shore. *The sailing boats were anchored in the **bay**.*

bight — A **bight** is a bend or curve in the shore of the sea. *The Great Australian Bight is a very wide bight in the southern coast of Australia.*

gulf — A **gulf** is a part of an ocean which is partly bounded by land. *The Gulf of Mexico is the biggest gulf in North America's coastline.*

inlet — An **inlet** is a small narrow bay. *The smugglers rowed to an uncharted inlet from their ship moored in the harbour.*

cove — A **cove** is a small bay or **inlet**. *There was room for just a few cottages and a shop along the shore of the cove.*

estuary — An **estuary** is the mouth or lower part of a river which is affected by the tides. *The launch had to wait for high tide before it could cross the bar at the estuary.*

similar words: **lake**

beat *verb*

to hit something or someone again and again. *The cruel man **beat** his dog without mercy.*

smack To **smack** means to hit someone with your open hand. *She smacked her son for disobeying her.*

punch To **punch** means to strike someone or something with your fist. *The two boys punched each other until a teacher broke up the fight.*

thump To **thump** means to strike someone heavily. *He thumped me excitedly on the back when I won the race.*

hammer To **hammer** can mean to hit something forcefully over and over again. *She hammered the table with her fist.*

bang To **bang** is to hit or beat something noisily. *The children banged the pieces of wood together in time with the music.*

similar words: **hit, thrash**

beautiful *adjective*

pleasing and enjoyable to hear, look at, touch, smell or taste. *The choir sang a **beautiful** song at the wedding.*

lovely **Lovely** is so similar to **beautiful** that you can usually choose to use either. *My friend has a lovely face.*

exquisite **Exquisite** means finely and delicately beautiful. *The bride's veil was made of exquisite lace.*

gorgeous **Gorgeous** means richly beautiful, especially in colouring. *The peacock spread his gorgeous tail.*

stunning **Stunning** means beautiful in a way that surprises you or captures your attention. It is more suited to everyday language. *It was such a stunning dress that everyone in the room turned to look at her.*

similar words: **pretty**
contrasting words: **ugly**

become extinct *verb*

to no longer exist on the earth. *Dinosaurs **became extinct** millions of years ago.*

die out To **die out** can mean to become extinct or no longer live on earth. *Cockroaches are insects that have existed for millions of years and never died out.*

vanish To **vanish** can mean to cease to exist. *Some species of plants have vanished during the last century.*

pass To **pass** can mean to cease to be or exist. *The glories of the Roman Empire have passed.*

be no more To **be no more** means to cease to exist. It is usually used in poetic or important-sounding language. *The days of my youth are no more.*

similar words: **die**
contrasting words: **live**

befriend *verb*

to aid or be friendly towards someone. *She **befriended** the new boy at school because he didn't know anyone.*

defend To **defend** can mean to support someone or something by speaking on their behalf. *He defended me when they said I was a bully.*

champion To **champion** can mean to **defend** or fight for someone. *She championed her sister in the playground.*

stand by To **stand by** can mean to help or support someone loyally. *Friends should stand by each other in times of need.*

stick up for To **stick up for** means to **defend** or support someone. *Thanks for sticking up for me when the others started disagreeing with what I'd said.*

side with To **side with** means to be on the side of a person or a group of people in support of a particular issue. *He always sided with his friend in an argument.*

similar words: **help**

begin *verb*

to take the first step in something. *Please **begin** work now.*

start To **start** is so similar to **begin** that you can usually use either. *I am going to start my project tonight.*

commence To **commence** is so similar to **begin** and **start** that you can usually use any of them. *The builders have commenced the additions to our house.*

embark To **embark on** means to begin something that is going to be long or important. *He is embarking on a new job tomorrow.*

set about To **set about** means to begin doing or **start** preparing something. *I will set about cooking dinner.*

open To **open** means to begin or **start** something. *He opened the batting with four runs.*

similar words: **initiate**
contrasting words: **finish**

behave *verb*

to act in a particular way. *Please don't **behave** badly when the visitors are here.*

conduct yourself To **conduct yourself** means to behave in a certain way. *He conducted himself well even though his brother teased him.*

carry yourself To **carry yourself** means to behave, walk or stand in a particular way. *Everyone else was shouting but she carried herself calmly.*

perform To **perform** means to behave. It can be used about people to mean they behave badly. It can also be used about machines or vehicles. *She really performed when she didn't get her own way. The car performed well on our holiday.*

acquit yourself To **acquit yourself** means to show what you can do in a particular activity. *He will acquit himself well in the debate.*

contrasting words: **misbehave**

believable *adjective*

likely to be true or able to be believed in. *Your story is strange but **believable.***

credible **Credible** is so similar to **believable** that you can usually use either. *I thought what happened in that film was quite credible.*

plausible **Plausible** means seeming to be true or reasonable. *She had a plausible excuse.*

probable **Probable** means likely to be true. *She gave a probable account of the accident.*

possible **Possible** means maybe true, although there may be knowledge to the contrary. *It is possible that ghosts exist.*

conceivable **Conceivable** means able to be imagined, although maybe unlikely. *It is conceivable that her story is true.*

similar words: **possible, likely**
contrasting words: **unbelievable, impossible**

believe *verb*

to think that something is right or true. *I don't **believe** your story.*

accept To **accept** can mean to believe something to be true. *I accept that what you say really happened.*

credit To **credit** is so similar to **believe** and **accept** that you can usually use any of them. *I can hardly credit that he would do such a thing.*

trust To **trust** means to believe or have confidence in something. *I trust what you tell me.*

take for granted To **take for granted** can mean to believe something without questioning it. *I take it for granted that she really committed the crime.*

assume To **assume** means to believe something without proof. *I assume you're the cause of this.*

similar words: **think**
contrasting words: **doubt**

bend *verb*

to turn something in a particular direction. *Please try not to **bend** the cards when you are playing snap.*

flex	To **flex** means to bend something, especially a part of your body. *You have to flex your spine when you lean over and touch your toes.*
deflect	To **deflect** means to bend or turn something aside. *I tried to hit the ball straight but the tree deflected it and it bounced into the creek.*
curl	To **curl** means to bend something into a curved or twisted shape. *I like the way you have curled your hair.*
curve	To **curve** means to bend something into a rounded shape. *The carpenter curved strips of wood to make the arms of the chair.*
loop	To **loop** means to bend something into an oval or circular shape. *You can make a knot if you loop the rope around twice and pull the end through.*

similar words: **turn**

best *adjective*

higher than the rest in quality or importance. *She is the **best** runner in our team.*

star	**Star** means the most brilliant or well-known. *She is our star runner.*
top	**Top** can mean the most excellent. *He is the top student in the class.*
leading	**Leading** means the most important or chief. *She is the leading dancer in the ballet company.*
head	**Head** can mean being in the position of leadership. It is similar to **leading**. *You had better ask the head librarian.*
principal	**Principal** means highest in position or importance. It is similar to both **leading** and **head**. *He is the principal actor in the film.*

similar words: **excellent, good, great, superior, main**

betray *verb*

to be unfaithful or disloyal to someone. *The spy **betrayed** his country.*

doublecross	To **doublecross** means to betray someone by promising one thing and doing another. *She said she would keep my secret but she doublecrossed me.*
sell out	To **sell out** means to betray someone. This is more suited to everyday language. *He would sell out his friends if he thought he could get himself out of trouble.*
give up	To **give up** can mean to inform against someone. *I had to give up you up because they threatened to tell my parents otherwise.*
report	To **report** can mean to complain or give information about someone or something. *We reported our neighbours to the council for having an unfenced pool.*
sneak	To **sneak** means to betray or report someone. *You can't trust that girl because she sneaks on her friends.*

similar words: **blab**

big *adjective*

great in size or amount. *We made a **big** cake so that everyone could have a piece.*

large	**Large** means of more than the usual size, amount or extent. *An elephant is a large animal.*
bulky	**Bulky** means **large** and awkward to manage because of its size and shape. *It was difficult to hide the bulky present.*
substantial	**Substantial** means very great in size or amount. *The treasure hunters found a substantial fortune hidden away.*
generous	**Generous** can mean big or bigger than you needed or expected. *Grandma gave us generous helpings of ice-cream and chocolate sauce.*
ample	**Ample** can mean large or well filled out. *She has an ample figure.*

similar words: **huge**
contrasting words: **small**

blab *verb*

to tell or reveal a secret without thinking. *She was angry when I **blabbed** the name of her boyfriend to everyone.*

let slip To **let slip** means to say or reveal something without meaning to. *You just let slip all the information about my secret experiments.*

spill the beans To **spill the beans** can mean to blab or tell a secret, or something similar. It is more suited to everyday language. *Don't trust him next time because he has just spilt the beans about our last conversation.*

let out To **let out** can mean to tell a secret, or something similar. *How dare you let out the fact that my parents have just got a divorce.*

give away To **give away** can mean to let a secret be known. *You have just given the hiding place away and now they will find the sweets.*

similar words: **reveal, betray**

black *adjective*

without any colour or brightness. *She wore **black** stockings to match her dress.*

dark **Dark** can mean giving out very little light. *Her dark hair matched her dark clothes.*

pitch-black **Pitch-black** means very black or **dark**. *The pitch-black clouds loomed on the horizon.*

inky **Inky** means as black as ink. *He disappeared completely into the inky shadows.*

jet-black **Jet-black** means of a deep, glossy black colour, like the shiny coal of the same name. *He groomed Black Beauty until his jet-black coat shone in the sun.*

ebony **Ebony** means black, like the valuable wood of the same name. *The cat stared at me through its large, ebony eyes.*

block *verb*

to be in the way of someone or something. *The accident **blocked** the traffic.*

obstruct To **obstruct** means to block or close off something. *A landslide obstructed the road.*

barricade To **barricade** means to block or defend something with a barrier or a wall which has usually been built in a hurry. *The protesters barricaded themselves in the building and wouldn't let anyone in.*

blockade To **blockade** means to close a port, harbour and so on, using ships or soldiers to stop supplies going in or out. *The enemy ships blockaded our main port and food became very scarce.*

bar To **bar** means to stop or prevent someone or something. *The guards barred them from entering the building.*

close To **close** can mean to block something off. *Heavy snow closed the road.*

similar words: **prevent, hinder**
contrasting words: **further**

blue *adjective*

having the colour of a clear sky. *We searched anxiously for signs of rain clouds in the **blue** sky.*

azure **Azure** means having a sky blue colour. *I'm going to use that azure glaze on my pot.*

navy **Navy** means having a very dark blue colour. *When I go to Guides I'll wear a navy skirt and hat.*

aquamarine **Aquamarine** means having a light blue-green colour. *Boats bobbed up and down on the aquamarine sea.*

sapphire **Sapphire** means having a deep blue colour. *As evening approached the lake took on a sapphire hue.*

boast *verb*

to speak with too much pride about your own affairs. *He* ***boasted*** *about winning the tennis tournament.*

brag	To **brag** is so similar to **boast** that you can usually use either. *No one likes him because he brags about how rich his family is.*
crow	To **crow** can mean to boast or talk loudly of any success or victory you may have. *She wouldn't stop crowing about the way her team won the debate.*
bluster	To **bluster** is to boast in an empty way. *I don't know what he has to bluster about.*
blow your own trumpet	To **blow your own trumpet** means to praise or say that you admire yourself. This is more suited to everyday language. *She isn't interested in what I do because she's too busy blowing her own trumpet.*
flaunt	To **flaunt** means to display possessions very obviously so people think you are more important than you really are. *She flaunted her expensive dress at the party.*

boil *verb*

to cook something by heating it in a bubbling liquid. *We* ***boiled*** *the potatoes in their jackets.*

poach	To **poach** means to cook something in a liquid that is just below boiling point. *Poach the eggs while I make the toast.*
coddle	To **coddle** means to cook something very slowly in water. *I coddled the eggs so they would still be soft and runny.*
simmer	To **simmer** means to cook something slowly in a liquid that has only a few bubbles rising. *Put all the ingredients for the soup in a big saucepan and simmer them gently for two hours.*
stew	To **stew** means to cook something slowly in a gently boiling liquid. *I stewed some apples in a little bit of water to eat with ice-cream for dessert.*
braise	To **braise** means to fry something quickly in a pan, then **stew** it gently in a covered pot. *I love the delicious gravy you get when you braise chops with lots of onions and tomatoes.*

similar words: **toast**

bold *adjective*

rude or not showing respect. *That was a **bold** thing to say to a teacher.*

cocky — **Cocky** can mean not showing respect, especially in the way you speak to someone. *Don't be cheeky to me, you cocky young man!*

pert — **Pert** means bold or impudent. *I don't like your pert way of speaking.*

saucy — **Saucy** means quite cheeky. It is more suited to everyday language. *That's a saucy answer to give your mother.*

brazen — **Brazen** means shamelessly rude. *Her brazen behaviour embarrassed us all.*

forward — **Forward** means behaving boldly in order to make people notice you. *She was so forward in front of the visitors that her parents sent her from the room.*

similar words: **rude, unashamed**
contrasting words: **shy, polite**

book *noun*

a number of pages bound together inside a cover, for writing in or for reading. *We borrow **books** from the library each week.*

manual — A **manual** is a book which tells you how to do or use something. *We looked at the manual to see how to fix the car.*

textbook — A **textbook** is a book setting out the information for a course of study in a subject. *We had two textbooks for science.*

anthology — An **anthology** is a collection of poems, plays or short stories by various authors or from various books. *We studied several of the poems in the anthology at school.*

volume — A **volume** is a book, especially one of a series. *There were twenty volumes of the encyclopaedia.*

diary — A **diary** is a book in which you write down daily events or thoughts. *I kept a diary while we were on holiday.*

similar words: **publication**

bored *adjective*

feeling dull or tired because you aren't interested in what you are doing. *It rained all afternoon and the children complained that they were **bored**.*

blasé — **Blasé** means so used to doing exciting things that they no longer interest or excite you. *My aunt is blasé about going to Australia again.*

tired of — **Tired of** means bored with or no longer interested in something. *We are tired of playing Monopoly.*

sick of — **Sick of** means very bored with or feeling that you have had enough of something. *I'm sick of my job.*

fed up — **Fed up** means very bored, annoyed or frustrated with something. *I'm fed up with having nothing to do all day.*

contrasting words: **excited**

boring *adjective*

uninteresting or wearying. *This book is so **boring** that I don't think I'll finish it.*

dull — **Dull** can be so similar to **boring** that you can usually use either. *The characters in it are all very dull.*

tedious — **Tedious** means long and boring. *The hero often makes tedious speeches about being well-behaved.*

stale — **Stale** can mean uninteresting because it has been used so many times before. *The author has used a stale plot in his novel.*

monotonous — **Monotonous** means boring because it is always exactly the same. *A postman's job must be a monotonous one.*

humdrum — **Humdrum** means boring because it is ordinary and doesn't change. It is similar to **monotonous**. *I'm going to try and change my humdrum life by finding an interesting hobby.*

contrasting words: **exciting**

boss *noun*

someone who employs and directs people in their work. *Our* ***boss*** *is very fair and makes sure no-one is overworked.*

foreman A **foreman** is a worker who is placed in charge of skilled or semi-skilled workers. *The factory foreman said the men would not do overtime.*

supervisor A **supervisor** is someone who directs or watches over people who are working. *The supervisor at the exam told the students to stop writing.*

overseer An **overseer** is someone who supervises or is in charge of a group of workers. *The factory overseer was in charge of training the apprentices.*

chief A **chief** is the head person in a group. *We elected her as the chief of the committee to talk to the manager about our complaints.*

master A **master** is a man who directs others, or is in charge of animals, or is a teacher in a school. *The master of the local stable had once been a master at my school.*

similar words: **manager**

bossy *adjective*

wanting to order other people about. *The little girl was* ***bossy*** *when she played with younger children.*

overbearing **Overbearing** means bossy, arrogant and expecting other people to do as you say. *I hate her overbearing way of taking over our games.*

imperious **Imperious** means **overbearing** or ruling over people in a severe and bossy way. *She's an imperious class captain and nobody likes her.*

autocratic **Autocratic** means ruling without caring about, or regard for, other people. *'What an autocratic king he is', groaned his subjects.*

dictatorial **Dictatorial** means **overbearing**, or tending to order about other people. *The manager's dictatorial manner made him unpopular.*

authoritarian **Authoritarian** means acting without considering people's freedom. *His father was very authoritarian and wouldn't let him watch TV.*

similar words: **tyrannical**
contrasting words: **submissive**

bottom *noun*

the lowest or deepest part of something. *I signed the letter at the* ***bottom*** *of the page.*

floor The **floor** is the lowest flat part of a room or other space. *The floor of the cave was quite dry.*

foot The **foot** can be the bottom part. *We camped in the valley at the foot of the mountain.*

base The **base** is the bottom part of anything which gives support. *We stood at the base of the huge tree and gazed upwards.*

bed The **bed** can be the foundation or **base.** *We found the wrecked ship on the sea bed.*

contrasting words: **top**

brave *adjective*

ready to face danger or pain whether you are afraid or not. *The* ***brave*** *shopkeeper showed no fear of the armed robber.*

courageous **Courageous** means able to do or face something you find frightening. It is similar to **brave**. *The courageous girl swam across the flooded river to get help.*

fearless **Fearless** means not feeling fear even in dangerous situations. *The fearless lion tamer put his head between the lion's jaws.*

bold **Bold** means withour fear or ready to take risks. It is similar to **fearless**. *His bold deed was admired by everyone.*

heroic **Heroic** means brave or acting in the daring way a hero does. *The heroic fireman carried the woman from the burning house.*

valiant **Valiant** means brave or showing great courage. *Her valiant efforts saved her friend's life.*

contrasting words: **fearful**

break *noun*

a gap or open space in something. *The cattle got out through the **break** in the fence.*

split — A **split** is a long narrow break or division in something. *My jeans were so tight I got a split in them when I bent over.*

crack — A **crack** is a slight opening. *There was a crack in the cup and the tea leaked out.*

fissure — A **fissure** is a long narrow break, usually in something hard or solid. *There was a deep fissure in the ground after the earthquake.*

rift — A **rift** is a long narrow opening made by something breaking or dividing. *The violent explosion caused a rift to appear in the earth.*

crevice — A **crevice** is a **crack** or cleft that forms an opening in something. *I quickly pushed the secret map through the crevice in the rock to hide it.*

similar words: **cut, hole**

brief *adjective*

using few words. *There was a **brief** report of the accident in the newspaper.*

short — **Short** can mean fairly brief or not as long as usual. *I had a short letter from my penfriend.*

concise — **Concise** means using few words to tell a lot. *She gave a concise account of what had happened.*

abridged — **Abridged** means made briefer by leaving out some parts. *I enjoyed the abridged version of the novel and then went on to read the complete edition.*

condensed — **Condensed** means expressed in fewer words than before. *I haven't much time to listen so give me a condensed version of what happened.*

contrasting words: **lengthy**

bright *adjective*

giving out a strong light. *He drew a picture of a **bright** sun and a pale moon.*

light — **Light** means not dark. *My bedroom is always light because it has wide windows.*

illuminated — **Illuminated** means having been lit up. *The city buildings were illuminated at night during the festival.*

brilliant — **Brilliant** can mean shining with a bright light. *They enjoyed the display of brilliant fireworks.*

dazzling — **Dazzling** can mean shining with a light that almost blinds you. *Drivers should not look at the headlights of other cars because they are too dazzling.*

glaring — **Glaring** can mean being so bright that it is uncomfortable to look at. *She sheltered her eyes from the glaring sunlight.*

similar words: **shining**
contrasting words: **dark**

broad-minded *adjective*

able to accept other people's ideas and ways. *When you start to meet different sorts of people you learn to be **broad-minded** and enjoy the things that are different about them.*

liberal — **Liberal** means broad-minded or able to accept a wide range of ideas. *Mr Wilson's liberal attitude towards teenagers made him a very good youthleader.*

tolerant — **Tolerant** means showing or having respect for, or patience with other people's opinions or ways of doing things. *I try to be tolerant of her untidiness even though we have to share a room.*

indulgent — **Indulgent** means willing to give in to the wishes or feelings of others. *He is an indulgent father in most things but he insists on obedience.*

permissive — **Permissive** means allowing people freedom to do as they wish, especially in sexual or moral matters. *Some people are very upset by our modern permissive society.*

similar words: **unconventional**
contrasting words: **strict, narrow-minded**

broke *adjective*

out of money. This word is more suited to everyday language. *I can't pay you back till next week because I'm **broke**.*

impecunious — **Impecunious** means not having any money. This is rather a formal word. *The impecunious young man gambled his last few pounds at the races.*

destitute — **Destitute** means not having any money or the belongings that are necessary for everyday living. *The whole family was destitute after the fire destroyed their home.*

ruined — **Ruined** can mean having lost everything you own. *Many people were ruined by the disastrous floods.*

bankrupt — **Bankrupt** means unable to pay the money you owe to other people. *He was bankrupt after his business failed.*

insolvent — **Insolvent** means having more debts than you can pay. It is very similar to **bankrupt**. *Because he was insolvent he could only pay half of what he owed people.*

similar words: **poor**
contrasting words: **wealthy**

brown *adjective*

having the colour of earth. *I want to ride that **brown** horse over there.*

beige — **Beige** means having a very light brown colour, like natural wool. *We learned how to spin the undyed wool to make warm, beige jumpers.*

fawn — **Fawn** means having a pale yellowish-brown colour. *Gently I stroked the soft, fawn coat of the young Jersey calf.*

tan — **Tan** means having a yellowish-brown colour. *I rubbed and polished the tan leather saddle until it shone like new.*

brunette — **Brunette** means having a rich dark brown colour. *She tied her thick, brunette hair into a long ponytail.*

sepia — **Sepia** means having a dark brown colour, like that used in drawing or photography, especially in very old photographs. *My great-grandmother has a sepia photograph of her wedding day.*

build *verb*

to make something by joining parts together. *The little girl **built** a tower with the blocks.*

construct To **construct** is so similar to **build** that you can usually use either. *He constructed a play house with the wood.*

erect To **erect** means to build something up. *They have erected a house on the block next to our school.*

put up To **put up** is so similar to **erect** that you can usually use either. *My father put up a fence at the back of our house.*

shape To **shape** means to give definite form, shape or character to something. *The potter carefully shaped his pots.*

fashion To **fashion** means to form something. *The carpenter fashioned a doll out of the piece of wood.*

similar words: **make**

bungle *verb*

to do something badly. *He **bungled** the whole job.*

botch To **botch** means to spoil or bungle something. *She botched the cake by using too much sugar.*

fumble To **fumble** means to handle something clumsily. *The wicket-keeper fumbled the ball and dropped it.*

muff To **muff** means to miss or bungle something. It is more suited to everyday language. *I muffed my chance of being in the team when I dropped the ball.*

muck up To **muck up** means to make a mess of something. This is more suited to everyday language. *He was cross when his little brother mucked up his stamp collection.*

fluff To **fluff** means to fail to do something properly. This is more suited to everyday language. *The actress fluffed her lines.*

busy *adjective*

fully occupied. *My mother was **busy** painting my bedroom.*

active	**Active** means continuously busy. *My grandfather leads an active life even though he is eighty.*
hard-working	**Hard-working** means always willing to work hard. *He does well in his job because he is hard-working.*
industrious	**Industrious** can mean willing to work hard. It is very similar to **hard-working.** *She is an industrious student.*
hectic	**Hectic** can mean full of activity and busyness. *We had a hectic weekend moving house.*
flat out	**Flat out** means so busy that you haven't time to stop. *The farmers were working flat out trying to harvest the wheat before the storm.*

similar words: **energetic**
contrasting words: **lazy, lethargic**

buy *verb*

to get something by paying money. *I am saving up to **buy** a new bike.*

purchase	To **purchase** is so similar to **buy** that you can usually use either. *My parents have purchased some shares in British Telecom.*
reserve	To **reserve** means to buy something by paying a deposit and collecting the item when you can pay for it in full. *I am going to ask the shop if I can reserve that lovely blue dress that I saw today.*
hire	To **hire** means to pay money for the use of something. *We hired a boat for the day.*
rent	To **rent** means to pay money regularly for the use of something, usually a place to live in. *We are renting a house near the school.*
redeem	To **redeem** can mean to get back something by paying. *Thank goodness I managed to redeem the watch that I pawned.*

contrasting words: **sell**

buyer *noun*
someone who buys or pays money for something. *I am a regular **buyer** of that magazine.*

purchaser A **purchaser** is so similar to a **buyer** that you can usually use either. *The purchaser of our old house loves it.*

customer A **customer** is someone who buys goods from another person. *The shopkeeper was anxious to please his customer.*

shopper A **shopper** is someone who is visiting a shop with the intention of looking for and buying something. *The shopper didn't see anything she liked so she went to another store.*

patron A **patron** is someone who regularly spends money at a shop, hotel, theatre, and so on. *The local cinema has a lot of patrons on Sundays.*

consumer A **consumer** is someone who buys and uses goods or services, as compared with a producer. *Advertising encourages consumers to buy more.*

contrasting words: **seller**

calculate *verb*
to work out something using mathematics. *He took out his ruler and **calculated** the area of the square.*

compute To **compute** means to calculate or work out something using maths. *She computed the time it would take for light to reach earth from the sun.*

figure-out To **figure-out** means to work out or calculate something. *I figured-out that the cost will be £150 and if we save carefully we can buy the bike by Christmas.*

make To **make** can mean to add something up to a certain amount. *How much do you make it?*

derive To **derive** means to get the answer to a problem by working it out. *I derived the answer by adding the numbers together.*

reckon To **reckon** means to calculate or count something up. *I reckon the amount we made at the cake stall to be £100.*

similar words: **count, measure**

callous *adjective*

showing no concern for someone else's feelings. *It was **callous** of them not to visit their lonely grandmother.*

hard-hearted **Hard-hearted** means having no kind feelings towards others. *The hard-hearted landlord refused to allow the widow any more time to pay the rent.*

unfeeling **Unfeeling** is so similar to **hard-hearted** that you can usually use either. *'Too bad', was her unfeeling reply.*

insensitive **Insensitive** can mean lacking in feeling but not necessarily meaning to be cruel. *Teasing him for being short showed how insensitive she was.*

stony **Stony** can mean refusing to be moved by kind feelings. *I begged her for help but she had a stony heart.*

cold-blooded **Cold-blooded** can mean having no feelings, especially of pity. It usually describes a more callous person or action than **hard-hearted** or **unfeeling**. *The cold-blooded murderer shot the shopkeeper.*

similar words: **cruel**
contrasting words: **kind**

calm *adjective*

not getting excited or upset. *He always stays **calm** when there is trouble.*

cool **Cool** means calm or not excited. *She was quite cool although everyone else was shouting.*

poised **Poised** means calm, confident and self-possessed. *She is always poised when she meets visitors.*

relaxed **Relaxed** means feeling at ease and unworried. *You will be able to think better if you are relaxed.*

placid **Placid** means calm and peaceful. *Mary is a placid person and isn't upset by little things.*

composed **Composed** means feeling calm in your body and mind. *I know you are upset now, but after a good sleep you may feel more composed.*

similar words: **peaceful**
contrasting words: **excited, upset, frightened, nervous**

cancel *verb*

to put an end to the operation or effectiveness of something. *I wish we could **cancel** all the school rules and make new ones.*

dissolve — To **dissolve** can mean to bring something to an end. *The Queen dissolved Parliament and called an election.*

break off — To **break off** can mean to put a stop to something. *I decided to break off our friendship.*

abolish — To **abolish** means to put an end to something altogether. *A law was passed to abolish slavery.*

annul — To **annul** means to put an end to something, such as a law or a marriage. *Parliament annulled the law against wearing bikinis.*

repeal — To **repeal** means to put an end to something legally and officially. It is similar to **abolish**. *The government repealed the tax on books.*

similar words: **finish**
contrasting words: **initiate**

capture *verb*

to take someone or something by force. *The soldiers **captured** the village.*

arrest — To **arrest** means to take someone prisoner. *The policeman arrested the thief.*

apprehend — To **apprehend** means to take someone or something into keeping. *The police apprehended the burglar as he ran down the road.*

trap — To **trap** means to catch birds or small animals in a snare or to catch someone by surprise. *We trapped the bully who stole our toys.*

pick up — To **pick up** can mean to capture someone you are looking for, especially a criminal. *They picked up the escaped convict as he tried to flee across the border.*

hijack — To **hijack** means to seize something, using threats or violence. *The terrorists hijacked the plane and forced the pilot to fly to another country.*

similar words: **grab, abduct**
contrasting words: **free**

careful *adjective*

putting time and effort into your work. *She is a **careful** writer.*

diligent — **Diligent** means paying careful and unceasing attention to what you are doing. *The diligent worker was promoted to foreman.*

conscientious — **Conscientious** means being particularly careful and thorough in what you have to do. *The conscientious nurse was praised by the doctor.*

attentive — **Attentive** means paying careful attention to someone. *The attentive pupils learned a lot from the teacher's diagrams on the board.*

fussy — **Fussy** means being very careful in what you are doing, sometimes in an irritating way. *She was such a fussy worker that she was the last one to finish.*

contrasting words: **careless**

careless *adjective*

done without taking enough care or paying enough attention. *His **careless** driving caused the accident.*

thoughtless — **Thoughtless** means doing or saying something without thinking carefully about it. *Her thoughtless remark hurt his feelings.*

casual — **Casual** can mean doing something without giving it enough thought. *His casual attitude to his work caused him to fail.*

lax — **Lax** means careless or not strict. *She was lax in keeping discipline in the class.*

negligent — **Negligent** means not paying any attention to what you should be doing. *He was negligent in carrying out his duties.*

irresponsible — **Irresponsible** means not careful or reliable, sometimes in a dangerous way. *Her irresponsible behaviour alarmed us.*

contrasting words: **careful**

carry *verb*

to take something from one place to another. *The ship **carried** its cargo across the sea.*

transport To **transport** is very similar to **carry**. *We hired a truck to tranport our furniture to our new house.*

transfer To **transfer** means to carry or move something from one place to another. *A helicopter transferred the sailors from their sinking ship to the rescue boat.*

convey To **convey** means to carry something from one place to another. *A bus conveyed the passengers from the airport into town.*

deliver To **deliver** means to carry something and hand it over to someone else. *The postman delivers the mail every day.*

run To **run** can mean to carry or **transport** someone to a particular place. *If you're ready now I'll run you to school.*

similar words: **send**

catch *verb*

to capture something, especially after a chase. *The police **caught** the thief by forcing his car off the road.*

trap To **trap** means to catch an animal in a device made for this purpose. *They trapped the foxes and then decided to let them go.*

snare To **snare** means to catch birds and small animals with a device usually consisting of a noose. *The gamekeeper caught the poacher who had snared the pheasants.*

ambush To **ambush** means to attack something or someone after lying in wait in a hidden place. *The highwayman ambushed the stagecoach and robbed the passengers.*

waylay To **waylay** means to lie in wait for someone or something, especially in order to attack, rob or capture them. *They waylaid him outside his house and kidnapped him.*

take by surprise To **take by surprise** can mean to come upon something or someone suddenly and when they least expect it. *The crocodile watched the zebra drinking at the river and took the animal by surprise when it surfaced nearby.*

cause *verb*

to bring something about or to make it happen. *Her forgetfulness* ***caused*** *a lot of trouble for us all.*

provoke To **provoke** can mean to cause something or to stir it up. *His constant teasing provoked an angry response.*

induce To **induce** can mean to cause something or to bring it on. *This drug induces sleep.*

produce To **produce** can mean to bring something into being. *The rich soil produced good crops for the farmers.*

inspire To **inspire** can mean to **produce** or awaken a feeling or thought in someone. *His happy and kind nature inspires love in all his friends.*

evoke To **evoke** means to **produce** something or to give rise to it. *The soft music evoked a feeling of calm.*

centre *noun*

the middle and most important part of something. *There are many shops in the* ***centre*** *of the city.*

hub A **hub** can be a busy or important centre. *The main street was the hub of activity in the town.*

heart The **heart** can be the most important part, especially of an argument or situation. *We got straight to the heart of the matter and found out what the problem really was.*

core The **core** can be the central, middle or main part of anything. *The core of this lesson is that everyone is equal.*

nucleus The **nucleus** can be the central and most important part or thing around which other parts are grouped. *The drummer was the nucleus of the new rock band.*

focus The **focus** can be the main point of interest or attraction. *The new girl in the class was the focus of attention.*

similar words: **inside**
contrasting words: **outskirts**

change *verb*

to make something different. *Darren* ***changed*** *his story so it would have a happy ending.*

alter To **alter** means to make something different in some way. *They altered their plans so I could come too.*

adapt To **adapt** means to change something to make it better suited to your needs. *We adapted the play so everyone could have a part in it.*

vary To **vary** means to **alter** something a little bit. *I varied my lunch today by bringing a banana instead of an apple.*

convert To **convert** can mean to change something completely. *With a wave of her wand the fairy godmother converted the pumpkin into a glass carriage.*

transform To **transform** means to change the form or appearance of something. *New wheels and some bright red paint transformed the old go-cart.*

contrasting words: **keep**

charm *verb*

to attract, win over or delight someone. *She* ***charmed*** *me with her sense of humour.*

fascinate To **fascinate** means to attract and hold the interest of someone completely. *She fascinated us with her stories.*

entice To **entice** means to attract or tempt someone, especially by promising money, enjoyment or some other gain. *The luscious cakes in the window enticed us into the shop.*

beguile To **beguile** means to attract or enchant someone. *Her big blue eyes and winning ways beguiled him.*

bewitch To **bewitch** means to charm someone as if under a spell. *The wonderful music and dancing bewitched the audience.*

mesmerise To **mesmerise** means to hold the attention of someone completely. *The beauty of the scenery mesmerised us.*

similar words: **attract**
contrasting words: **repel**

cheap *adjective*

of low price. *You can buy **cheap** fruit at road-side stalls.*

inexpensive — **Inexpensive** means not costing very much money. *We want to stay at an inexpensive hotel.*

reduced — **Reduced** means being of lower price than usual. *The furniture was reduced because there had been a fire.*

discount — **Discount** can mean selling things at a cheaper price than usual. *We bought a washing machine at a discount store.*

no-frills — **No-frills** means being cheap because you don't pay for any luxuries. *We travelled second class and stayed at cheap hotels on our no-frills holiday.*

dirt-cheap — **Dirt-cheap** means very **inexpensive**. It is more suited to everyday language. *The bicycle was dirt-cheap.*

contrasting words: **dear**

cheat *verb*

to take something belonging to someone else dishonestly or by tricking them. *He **cheated** me out of all this week's pocket money.*

swindle — To **swindle** means to cheat someone out of something, especially money. *The dishonest businessman swindled his client out of nearly all her savings.*

defraud — To **defraud** means to cheat or deceive someone so as to get their money, property and so on. It is usually used in more formal language. *He was fined because he defrauded the Taxation Department.*

fleece — To **fleece** means to cheat someone out of all or nearly all of something. It is usually used in less formal language. *They fleeced him of every penny he had.*

rip off — To **rip off** means to cheat someone by making them pay too much for something. It is usually used in less formal language. *She ripped us off by charging us £10 for that junk.*

similar words: **trick, deceive**

chew *verb*

to bite and crush food with your teeth. *Babies must have their food mashed because they cannot **chew** it.*

munch To **munch** means to chew something noisily. *The cows were munching grass.*

chomp To **chomp** means to chew noisily. It is similar to **munch**. *Don't chomp your food when you eat.*

nibble To **nibble** means to chew or bite in little bits. *She nibbled her biscuit.*

masticate To **masticate** means to chew in order to digest. It is a more formal word than **chew**. *He always masticates his food thoroughly.*

similar words: **eat, drink**

chic *adjective*

attractive and stylish. *Your hair is very **chic**.*

elegant **Elegant** means graceful or stylish. *She's a very elegant woman, especially in the way she dresses.*

smart **Smart** can mean neat and keeping up with the latest fashion. *That's a smart new suit you have.*

dapper **Dapper** means very neat and **smart** in a slightly showy way. *He's very dapper in his spotless white shirt and new bow-tie.*

fashionable **Fashionable** means in keeping with the style of clothes and appearance that most people think is attractive. *Pierced ears are very fashionable.*

all the rage **All the rage** means very up-to-date and stylish. *The clothes I bought for the disco were all the rage.*

contrasting words: **old-fashioned**

choice *noun*

something or someone you have chosen or picked out from a number of things or people. *The blue one is my* ***choice.***

selection A **selection** can be a thing or things chosen carefully. *Bring your selection to the cashier.*

option An **option** is something you have chosen or which you may choose. *My option is to spend the day at a funfair.*

preference A **preference** is something that you choose or like better than another. *My preference is to travel there by plane.*

alternative An **alternative** is one of two or more choices. *We had to decide on one out of a whole list of exciting alternatives.*

dilemma A **dilemma** is an almost impossible choice. *The boy was in a dilemma when his play rehearsal clashed with his piano lesson.*

choose *verb*

to settle on something or someone above all the others in a group. ***Choose*** *a number between one and ten.*

select To **select** means to choose something or someone carefully. *Have you selected a record yet?*

pick To **pick** means to choose or **select** something from amongst a number of things. *Pick your favourite colour.*

take To **take** can mean to choose something from more than one alternative. *We lost our way after we took the wrong road.*

decide To **decide** can mean to choose between various alternatives. *I decided that the sensible thing to do was to go to the party.*

fix To **fix** can mean to settle on or determine. *I've fixed the price now and it's not too high and not too low.*

similar words: **prefer**

city *noun*

a large or important town. *Thousands of people work in the many offices and factories in the **city**.*

metropolis A **metropolis** is a large important city. *London is the biggest metropolis in Great Britain.*

capital A **capital** is the main city of a country or state and is where the government is situated. *Paris is the capital of France.*

suburb A **suburb** is a district of a city with its own shopping centre, school and so on. *We would rather live in a waterside suburb.*

big smoke The **big smoke** means the city. It is an expression often used by country people. This is more suited to everyday language. *Let's go to the big smoke for a holiday.*

concrete jungle The **concrete jungle** means the city. It is an expression used to show that you think some things about cities are unpleasant, such as crowding and tall buildings. *My parents say they want to leave the concrete jungle when they retire and live in the country.*

contrasting words: **the country**

civic *adjective*

having to do with a city, or the people who live in it. *The council buildings are usually in the **civic** centre.*

urban **Urban** means having to do with a city or town, or living in that city or town. *Most of the urban population work in offices and factories.*

metropolitan **Metropolitan** means having to do with a very large city, or the people who live in it. *The metropolitan area spread for miles.*

suburban **Suburban** means having to do with, or living in an area which is often quite far from the city centre. *It is quicker to go to our suburban cinema.*

contrasting words: **country**

clean *adjective*

not having any dirt or stains. *We wore **clean** clothes to the party.*

spotless — **Spotless** means free from stains, marks, spots or any other similar blemishes. *I washed my handkerchief until it was spotless.*

immaculate — **Immaculate** means free from spots or stains. *Your uniform must be immaculate.*

hygienic — **Hygienic** means clean and free from dirt and germs. *We are taught to be hygienic and always wash our hands before meals.*

spick-and-span — **Spick-and-span** means clean and neat. This is more suited to everyday language. *The spick-and-span soldier saluted the general.*

pure — **Pure** can mean clean and **spotless.** *She has a lovely, pure complexion.*

contrasting words: **dirty**

clean *verb*

to remove the dirt from something or someone. *She **cleaned** her shoes.*

wash — To **wash** means to wet and rub someone or something, usually with soap or detergent, in order to remove the dirt. *He washed his face and hands before dinner.*

scrub — To **scrub** means to rub someone or something hard with a brush, soap and water in order to remove the dirt. *He had to scrub his nails because they were filthy.*

cleanse — To **cleanse** means to make something clean and pure. *We cleanse our skin every night.*

sterilise — To **sterilise** means to destroy the germs in something, often by boiling it. *Mum sterilised the baby's bottle.*

mop up — To **mop up** means to clean or wipe up dirt and so on with a mop or something similar. *Mop up the paint you spilled!*

contrasting words: **dirty, spoil**

clear *adjective*

easily understood. *Give us some **clear** examples.*

plain — **Plain** can mean clear to your mind. *It's plain that you don't really want to come.*

obvious — **Obvious** means so clear that no explanation or thought is needed. *The answer to this question is obvious.*

evident — **Evident** can mean quite clear to your understanding. *It's evident you don't know what you're talking about.*

straightforward — **Straightforward** can mean not difficult or complicated. *I would rather you gave me a straightforward explanation.*

explicit — **Explicit** can mean fully set out or expressed in a clear way. *This bike comes with a booklet of explicit instructions.*

contrasting words: **confusing, vague**

clergyman *noun*

someone who is a priest or minister of the Christian church. *He is studying to be an Anglican **clergyman**.*

minister — A **minister** is a clergyman who conducts services in a church. *The minister of our church preaches very good children's sermons.*

parson — A **parson** is a clergyman or **minister**. It is mostly used about Protestant clergymen. *The Baptist parson opened his Church's annual fete.*

priest — A **priest** is someone whose job is to perform religious ceremonies, especially in the Roman Catholic or Anglican churches. *The priest always wears his cassock in church.*

vicar — A **vicar** is a **priest**, especially one in charge of an Anglican parish. *Our vicar visits people who are sick at home and can't come to church.*

chaplain — A **chaplain** is a clergyman who works in a school, hospital, or the armed forces. *The hospital chaplain gave great comfort to the sick man and his family.*

clever *adjective*

good at thinking or learning quickly. *She is **clever** at maths.*

intelligent — **Intelligent** means having good mental ability. *He is an intelligent boy who succeeds in whatever he does.*

brainy — **Brainy** means having the ability to learn and understand easily. It is a less formal word than **clever** or **intelligent**. *She is so brainy she remembers everything she reads.*

smart — **Smart** means clever or **intelligent**. *Our dog is smart and has learned to open doors.*

bright — **Bright** can mean good at learning and understanding. *My friend is bright and explains problems I don't understand.*

brilliant — **Brilliant** can mean very, very clever. *Our most brilliant pupil won a scholarship when he went to university.*

similar words: **shrewd, sensible**
contrasting words: **stupid, silly**

climb *verb*

to move up something. *The fireman **climbed** the ladder.*

ascend — To **ascend** is so similar to **climb** that you can usually use either. *Jack and Jill ascended the hill.*

mount — To **mount** means to go up something. *I heard my mother begin to mount the stairs.*

scale — To **scale** means to climb up or over something, as if you were using a ladder. *She scaled the wall.*

clamber up — To **clamber up** can mean to climb something with difficulty, using both feet and hands. *As they clambered up the steep path that led to the castle, they nearly fell several times.*

shin up — To **shin up** means to climb something by holding fast with your hands or arms and your legs and pulling yourself up. *The boy shinned up the palm tree to get a coconut.*

cloth *noun*

a substance formed by weaving, knitting or pressing fibres like wool, hair, silk or cotton together. *The factory made many different kinds of **cloth** and sold them to the shops.*

fabric — **Fabric** is any woven, knitted or felted cloth. *I bought some cotton fabric to make a sundress. The nursery animal mobiles were made of felt fabric.*

material — **Material** is cloth that has been or is capable of being woven. *The curtain material has a pretty floral pattern.*

textile — A **textile** is any woven cloth. *Silk, wool and cotton are natural textiles. Nylon is a synthetic textile which is used to make parachutes.*

stuff — **Stuff** can be cloth or **fabric**. This word is not often used nowadays. *The pioneer woman bought some strong, woollen stuff to make clothes for her family.*

---

clothing *noun*

the articles or garments that you wear on your body. *I always wear old **clothing** when I work in the garden.*

apparel — **Apparel** is clothing, especially the type worn on the outside. It is a rather formal word. *This shop specialises in wedding apparel.*

attire — **Attire** is clothing for a special occasion, usually rather rich or splendid. *The guests at the opening night of the play wore formal attire.*

dress — **Dress** can mean a particular style of clothing. *Susan did a project on the dress of the Middle Ages.*

garb — **Garb** is clothing of a particular style, especially if if shows your job, hobby or is rather eye-catching. *You have just enough time to change into your football garb before the match starts.*

wardrobe — Your **wardrobe** is your entire supply of clothing. *I've grown so much since last year that I need a whole new summer wardrobe.*

---

cloudy *adjective*

not sunny because of clouds. *The sky has been **cloudy** for days.*

overcast — **Overcast** is so similar to **cloudy** that you can usually use either. *The game was cancelled because of the overcast weather.*

dull — **Dull** can means cloudy and grey. *A dull day with a lot of rain is forecast for tomorrow.*

misty — **Misty** means not bright or sunny because of a covering or cloud of mist. *The mornings are often misty in the mountains.*

foggy — **Foggy** means dark because of fog. *The motorists turned on their headlights because it was foggy.*

hazy — **Hazy** means not clear because of a thin mist or cloud of dust. *You can't see much of the view today because it is too hazy.*

similar words: **dreary**
contrasting words: **fine**

club *noun*

a group of people organised together to share a particular interest, sport or hobby. *We started a chess **club** at school.*

association — An **association** is a group of people organised for a common purpose. It is similar to **club**. *My father belongs to an association of stamp collectors.*

assembly — An **assembly** can be a group of people gathered together for the same purpose. *The Prime Minister made a speech to the assembly of workers.*

congregation — A **congregation** is a group of people gathered together in a church. *Our church has a large congregation each Sunday.*

lobby — A **lobby** is a group of people who try to get public and political support for a particular cause. *He is the leader of the lobby for more government funding for schools.*

similar words: **group**

clumsy *adjective*

unskilful in the way you move about or do things. *The **clumsy** boy knocked the vase over.*

awkward	**Awkward** means clumsy or not graceful. *The actor's awkward movements on stage spoiled the play.*
gangling	**Gangling** means tall and thin and moving awkwardly. *The gangling child was all legs and arms.*
all thumbs	**All thumbs** means not being skilful with your hands. *I was all thumbs when I tried to knit.*
accident-prone	**Accident-prone** means likely to have a lot of accidents. *He is so accident-prone no-one was surprised when he fell down the stairs.*
heavy-handed	**Heavy-handed** means clumsy with your hands. *She is too heavy-handed to be trusted to wash the good china.*

similar words: **incompetent**
contrasting words: **agile, competent**

coat *verb*

to cover something with a substance. ***Coat** the chicken with breadcrumbs before you cook it.*

spread	To **spread** can mean to cover something with a layer. *Don't spread the bread too thickly with butter.*
daub	To **daub** means to coat something with a soft or sticky substance. *They daubed mud all over the clean wall.*
smear	To **smear** can mean to rub or **spread** something with grease, oil, paint or dirt. *We smeared our faces and hands with charcoal so no-one would see us in the dark.*
plaster	To **plaster** can mean to cover something thickly, as if with plaster. *He plastered his hair with gel to make it lie flat.*
pave	To **pave** means to cover a road, path or something similar with stones, tiles, bricks or concrete to make a flat hard surface to walk on. *We paved the area around the pool with blue tiles.*

coating *noun*

a covering of some substance spread over a surface. *I put a **coating** of batter on the fish before frying it.*

veneer A **veneer** is a thin layer of wood or other material used to cover the surface underneath. *The maple veneer on the pine table made it more attractive.*

skin A **skin** can be a surface layer. *I peeled the skin off the apple. I lifted the skin off the milk.*

crust A **crust** can be a hard outer surface. *A crust of blood formed over the wound to protect it from germs.*

glaze A **glaze** is a smooth shiny coating or surface. *The potter put a beautiful blue glaze on his vase.*

film A **film** can be a thin layer or coating. *A film of oil covered the water where the boat had sunk.*

---

coil *noun*

a loop or series of loops twisting around. *We tied the end of the rope into a **coil** and threw it out to the drowning man.*

loop A **loop** is a round or oval shape twisted in a piece of ribbon, string or something similar. *Make a loop with the string big enough to fit around the bundle of pencils.*

spiral A **spiral** is a curve or series of curves winding around away from a centre. *The staircase went up in a spiral, twisting around and around to the very top of the tower.*

curl A **curl** can be something that has a spiral or curved shape. *The waves made huge curls in the ocean.*

twist A **twist** is something that is curved or bent around. *The bus crawled through all the twists in the road.*

---

cold *adjective*

having or feeling a lack of warmth. *It's a very **cold** night. My feet are **cold**.*

nippy — **Nippy** means very chilly or cold. *In the late afternoon the breeze at the beach can be nippy.*

freezing — **Freezing** means extremely cold. *I'd better wear a coat in this freezing weather.*

frigid — **Frigid** can mean very cold in temperature. *The frigid temperature in Antarctica makes life difficult for the scientists who work there.*

sharp — **Sharp** can mean very cold or piercing. *The sharp wind blew right through our jackets.*

icy — **Icy** means cold like ice. *Let me rub your icy hands.*

frosty — **Frosty** means very cold or freezing. *We wore our scarves because it was such a frosty day.*

similar words: **wintry**
contrasting words: **hot**

colour *verb*

to put colour onto something. *The dawn **coloured** the sky with beautiful shades of pink.*

dye — To **dye** means to change the colour of something. *I dyed my old white curtains a pretty blue.*

tint — To **tint** means to colour something slightly. *The cook tinted the icing on the cake to a pale pink.*

stain — To **stain** means to colour something made of wood with a liquid which soaks into it. *He stained his pine desk to show up the grain of the wood.*

paint — To **paint** means to cover something with a liquid colouring substance. *We are going to paint my bedroom.*

highlight — To **highlight** means to colour something so that it stands out against the background. *The artist highlighted the flowers in her painting.*

colourful *adjective*

having many colours. *The opening of the Olympic Games was a* ***colourful*** *sight.*

bright — **Bright** means being strong, clear and easy to see. *The artist used bright blue to paint the sea.*

vivid — **Vivid** means dazzling or very **bright**. *The vivid colours of the Christmas lights delighted the children.*

gay — **Gay** can mean cheerful and **bright**. *The dancers in their national costumes presented a gay scene.*

rich — **Rich** can mean having fine, wonderful colours. *The rich velvet cloak looked lovely over her evening dress.*

garish — **Garish** means being brightly-coloured in an unattractive or unusual way. *The clown's garish suit made us all laugh.*

similar words: **gaudy**
contrasting words: **colourless, drab**

colourless *adjective*

lacking in colour. *A shower of rain brought the* ***colourless*** *desert to life.*

pale — **Pale** means whitish or not having much colour. *His face was pale with fright.*

pastel — **Pastel** means having soft **pale** colours. *Pastel colours suit most fair people.*

neutral — **Neutral** can mean having no particular colour that stands out. *Everything about her appearance was neutral.*

faded — **Faded** means having lost its colour. *The faded curtains made the room look shabby.*

bleached — **Bleached** means having had the colour taken out. *The shirt had been washed so often it was bleached.*

contrasting words: **colourful**

combine *verb*

to mix or put things together. *The Education Department **combined** the two schools.*

assemble To **assemble** means to bring or put things together to make a whole. *We painted the model plane after we assembled the parts.*

blend To **blend** means to mix things together so that they can't be separated. *You can blend flour and water to make glue.*

fuse To **fuse** means to join two things together by melting them. *He fused the two metals by heating them.*

merge To **merge** means to unite or bring two or more things together. *There was an accident where the two motorways merged.*

amalgamate To **amalgamate** means to join two or more things together so as to make one. It is very similar to **merge**. *The board of directors decided to amalgamate the two companies.*

similar words: **mix, join**
contrasting words: **separate**

come *verb*

to get to a place you have been moving towards. *We will **come** to you in the morning.*

arrive To **arrive** means to come to the end of a journey. *We set out early and arrived at dawn.*

reach To **reach** means to get to or arrive at. *We were very glad when we reached there after our long journey.*

turn up To **turn up** means to come or **arrive**. *She turned up late at the party.*

berth To **berth** means to tie up at a dock or wharf. It is only used about ships. *When the ship berthed we saw our friends standing on the deck.*

surface To **surface** can mean to **arrive**. It is more suited to everyday language. *We all thought he wasn't coming but he finally surfaced.*

contrasting words: **leave**

comfort *noun*

a lessening of sadness and worry. *I gained great **comfort** from her visits when I was in hospital.*

consolation — **Consolation** can mean comfort or cheer in your distress. *His optimism when the mountaineers were missing was a great consolation.*

solace — **Solace** means comfort in a time of sorrow or trouble. *The two sisters found solace by being together when their parents were so ill.*

relief — **Relief** means freedom from pain, unhappiness or worry. *What a relief to see them again!*

ease — **Ease** is freedom from any problem, discomfort or pain. *He lived a life of ease after he won first prize in the lottery.*

similar words: **pity**

comfort *verb*

to cheer someone up or make them feel less sad or worried. *He **comforted** the baby by cuddling her.*

soothe — To **soothe** means to calm or comfort someone. *The soft music soothed me.*

ease — To **ease** means to give someone relief or comfort. *The news that the doctor was coming eased her mind.*

relieve — To **relieve** means to make someone free from pain, unhappiness or worry. *The news that they were safe relieved us.*

alleviate — To **alleviate** means to make something easier to bear. *Talking to my parents alleviated my worry.*

lighten — To **lighten** can mean to make something less hard to bear. *Getting a new dog lightened Peter's sadness at losing Blackie.*

similar words: **pacify**
contrasting words: **upset**

comment *noun*

a short note or statement that gives an opinion or explanation. *The reporters asked the Prime Minister if he would make a* ***comment****.*

remark A **remark** is a brief expression of your opinion. It is usually spoken. *Have you got any remarks to make about my suggestion?*

observation An **observation** is a comment made about something you have noticed, usually not of great importance. *I said that she looked a little pale, but it was only an observation.*

interjection An **interjection** is a comment made to interrupt a conversation or a speech. *I will stop speaking if there are any more interjections.*

exclamation An **exclamation** is something said or cried out suddenly in pleasure or fright. *She gave an exclamation of surprise when she opened his present.*

commotion *noun*

a wild or noisy disturbance. *There was a great* ***commotion*** *in the playground when two dogs started fighting.*

fuss A **fuss** can be a noise or disturbance. *Everyone made a fuss because the bus was late again.*

hullabaloo A **hullabaloo** is a loud noisy disturbance. *She made a great hullabaloo when he accidently tripped her.*

tumult A **tumult** is a noisy violent disturbance or uproar, often made by a huge crowd. *A tumult of cheering burst from the hundreds of waiting fans.*

turmoil A **turmoil** means a commotion or a condition of wild disorder. *The house was in turmoil when we were packing to move to another state.*

riot A **riot** is a disturbance of the peace by a group of people. *When the two rival gangs met there was a riot in the street.*

similar words: **noise**

compete *verb*

to set yourself against one or more people to gain or win something. *Ben and James **competed** for the running trophy.*

race — To **race** means to compete with someone in a contest of speed. *The drivers raced around the track.*

run — To **run** means to compete or take part in a race. *The horses ran against each other in The Grand National.*

vie — To **vie** means to compete against or try to beat someone. *The boys vied with each other in games.*

contest — To **contest** means to compete with or struggle against someone. *The rivals contested with each other for his friendship.*

---

competent *adjective*

skilful at a particular thing. *She is a **competent** driver.*

able — **Able** means having enough skill to do a particular job. *He is a very able mechanic.*

capable — **Capable** means knowing the right way to do something and doing it well. It is very similar to **competent**. *He is a capable cook.*

expert — **Expert** means having a lot of special skill or knowledge. *He is an expert pilot.*

proficient — **Proficient** means skilled or **expert**. *She is a proficient nurse.*

good at — **Good at** means being able to do something well. It is a less formal word than **capable**. *She is good at telling stories.*

similar words: **experienced**
contrasting words: **incompetent, inexperienced, clumsy**

competition *noun*

a contest or a situation in which you try to do better than anyone else. *Jan won first prize in a poetry* ***competition****.*

game A **game** is a competition with set rules. *Let's have a game of marbles.*

match A **match** is an official competition. *The cricket match was a draw.*

race A **race** is any kind of competition which is always a test of speed. *We had a race to the end of the street.*

championship A **championship** is a contest between the best in any sport or game. *Clare has entered in the 800 metre running championship.*

bout A **bout** is a contest, especially a boxing or wrestling **match**. *The boxers were exhausted after their bout to decide who would be world champion.*

complain *verb*

to tell about your troubles, illnesses, pains or any of the things you are not satisfied with. *However much I try to please her, she always* ***complains****.*

grumble To **grumble** means to complain crankily, usually in a low voice. *He grumbled about the dirty fingermarks on his book.*

whinge To **whinge** means to complain continually in an annoying way. *I certainly will not buy you that toy if you keep whingeing about it.*

whine To **whine** can mean to complain in an annoying, high-pitched voice. It is similar to **whinge**. *That child is always whining at his mother.*

nag To **nag** can mean to keep on complaining or finding fault. *My grandmother has started to nag more as she has grown older.*

gripe To **gripe** means to complain continually and bad-temperedly. It is more suited to everyday language. *Please stop griping about how cold the weather is.*

complicated *adjective*

having many related or entangled parts. *This material has a **complicated** pattern.*

elaborate	**Elaborate** means having great detail. *We worked out an elaborate plan.*
intricate	**Intricate** means having fine details or puzzlingly entangled parts. *We had to follow an intricate maze of paths.*
fiddly	**Fiddly** means so complicated that it needs a lot of care and practice. *This toy is very fiddly to assemble.*
involved	**Involved** means lengthy and going into great detail. *She gave an involved reply to my simple question.*
convoluted	**Convoluted** means too lengthy, complicated and difficult to understand. *She gave a convoluted answer when I invited her to dinner and I didn't know if she was coming or not.*

contrasting words: **easy**

compose *verb*

to create literature or music. *Would you please help me **compose** this limerick?*

write	To **write** can mean to create or produce something using words, musical notes or other symbols. *I hope to write a novel one day.*
draft	To **draft** can mean to **write** or draw the outline or plan of something. *I still have a lot of work to do on my essay because I have only drafted it.*
pen	To **pen** means to **write** down something using a pen, usually a song or poem. This word is not often used as it can sound rather pompous. *Can you pen a few lines to go with this catchy little tune?*
dash off	To **dash off** can mean to **write** something in a hurry. *I must remember to dash off a thankyou note to my aunt for the birthday present she sent me.*
set down	To **set down** can mean to put something down in writing. *I must set down my memories of our overseas trip before I forget them.*

conceited *adjective*

too proud of yourself and your own importance and abilities. *Carl was so* ***conceited*** *he thought he could do everything better than anyone else.*

vain — **Vain** means too proud of yourself in any way. *The vain man was always boasting about his important job.*

narcissistic — **Narcissistic** means loving yourself too much, especially your appearance. *She was so narcissistic she kept looking in her mirror.*

egotistic — **Egotistic** means always thinking and talking about yourself. *The egotistic boy told us all about his holiday but didn't ask about ours.*

stuck-up — **Stuck-up** means thinking you are better than everyone else. It is more suited to everyday language. *She's too stuck-up to even talk to us!*

big-headed — **Big-headed** means conceited or **vain**. *Emma is so big-headed now that she has an older boyfriend that she won't speak to her old friends.*

similar words: **proud, pompous**
contrasting words: **humble**

concentrate on *verb*

to fix your mind on something. ***Concentrate*** *on learning to spell those words.*

focus on — To **focus on** means to concentrate or centre your thoughts on something. *Focus on solving this puzzle.*

consider — To **consider** can mean to think carefully or direct your thoughts towards one particular thing. *Please don't rush me because I need to consider before I reply.*

take notice of — To **take notice of** means to pay attention to something or someone with interest. *You should take notice of her advice.*

attend to — To **attend to** means to give something or someone your full attention. *Attend to your work!*

mind — To **mind** can mean to pay close attention, especially to what you are doing or to what is happening around you. *Mind that you don't trip.*

similar words: **ponder**
contrasting words: **daydream**

concert *noun*

a public performance by musicians or other performers. *The audience applauded when the choir came on stage to begin their* ***concert****.*

eisteddfod An **eisteddfod** is a competition of singing, playing music and reciting poetry. *Our recorder group hopes to win a prize in this year's eisteddfod.*

jam session A **jam session** is an informal meeting of jazz musicians, usually to play for their own enjoyment. *Everyone had brought along their instruments so we decided to start playing a tune we all knew and have a jam session.*

promenade concert A **promenade concert** is an informal concert at which people sit on the floor or stand around. *We pushed all the seats aside for the promenade concert.*

soiree A **soiree** can be a small gathering of people in the evening, usually in someone's home, to listen to a musical performance or poetry. *They held a soiree every Saturday night so their friends could hear different musicians play.*

conclude *verb*

to decide something after thinking about it. *After reading the book carefully she* ***concluded*** *that the murderer was not a member of the victim's family.*

deduce To **deduce** means to work something out by reasoning. *We deduced from all the information we had that he would be late.*

infer To **infer** means to form an opinion about something after considering all the facts and information. *He inferred from the spy's report that the enemy would attack early in the morning.*

gather To **gather** can mean to understand something as a result of things you have heard. *I gather that you had a wonderful time at the picnic.*

reason To **reason** can mean to decide something by sensible argument. *They reasoned that the river would flood because of the rain and the cattle should be moved to higher ground.*

similar words: **think, solve**

concoct *verb*

to think up something, such as a story or an excuse. *He **concocted** a story to explain why he was late.*

make up To **make up** means to invent something for a particular reason. *It is no good making up excuses.*

cook up To **cook up** means to concoct something or to invent it in order to mislead or deceive someone. It is more suited to everyday language. *They have cooked up an explanation between themselves.*

hatch To **hatch** means to concoct or arrange something, often in secret. *They hatched a clever plan.*

contrive To **contrive** means to invent or plan something in a clever way. *She contrived a way to stay out of trouble.*

similar words: **invent, create**

confine *verb*

to keep or shut someone in a place. *The warders **confined** the unruly prisoner in her cell for two days.*

imprison To **imprison** means to shut someone up against their will, usually in a prison. *The kidnappers imprisoned their victim in an old farmhouse.*

jail To **jail** means to put someone in prison. *The judge jailed him for five years.*

lock up To **lock up** means to shut someone in a place fastened with a lock, such as a prison. *The constable locked up the suspect in a cell until he could be taken before a judge.*

restrain To **restrain** can mean to take away someone's freedom. *Some people want the government to make laws to restrain anyone who frequently commits crimes.*

intern To **intern** means to keep someone in an enclosed and guarded area, especially during wartime. *The government interned any German tourists who were in England when war was declared in 1939.*

contrasting words: **free**

conflict *noun*

a fight, struggle or disagreement. *We want to avoid a **conflict** between nations so that there will be peace in the world.*

feud A **feud** is a bitter, long-lasting quarrel, especially one between two families. *We had never met his cousin because of the family feud.*

row A **row** is a noisy quarrel or fight. *I can't concentrate while you are having a row.*

disagreement A **disagreement** is a failure to agree. *We are having a disagreement over whom to invite to the party.*

bust-up A **bust-up** is a fight or quarrel, often leading to a parting between friends. It is more suited to everyday language. *I had a bust-up with my boyfriend last week.*

similar words: **argument, fight**

confuse *verb*

to mix up your mind or your thoughts. *Susan and Diana both tried to show me how to play the game but they only **confused** me.*

muddle To **muddle** means to make someone confused in their mind or unable to think clearly. *So many people told us how to get there they only muddled us.*

fluster To **fluster** means to make someone nervous and confused. *The boss flustered me when she said I only had ten minutes to finish typing the letter.*

distract To **distract** means to make someone confused by drawing their attention away from what they are doing. *The TV will distract you while you are doing your homework.*

befuddle To **befuddle** means to confuse someone especially by talking cleverly or too quickly. *You befuddle me when you use those big words that I don't understand.*

bamboozle To **bamboozle** means to confuse or deceive someone. This word is more suited to everyday language. *She bamboozled us by sending us a message written in secret code.*

similar words: **puzzle**
contrasting words: **explain**

confused *adjective*

feeling unsure or mixed up. *I am so **confused** that I do not know what is the right thing to do.*

puzzled — **Puzzled** means confused or bewildered. *She gave a puzzled frown as she read the strange letter.*

nonplussed — **Nonplussed** means completely confused and **puzzled**. *I can't think sensibly at the moment because I am nonplussed by his strange behaviour.*

undecided — **Undecided** means unsure or not having made up your mind. *I am undecided as to whether I like your new dress.*

ambivalent — **Ambivalent** can mean uncertain or doubtful, because you can't make up your mind. *I have an ambivalent attitude to riding horses and I don't know whether I will continue having lessons.*

contrasting words: **sure**

confusing *adjective*

hard to understand. *I couldn't follow the **confusing** instructions.*

bewildering — **Bewildering** means so confusing that you don't know what to do. *He couldn't find his way out of the bewildering maze.*

perplexing — **Perplexing** means confusing and troubling, especially by being difficult to understand or answer. *This is a perplexing problem.*

mysterious — **Mysterious** means full of mystery or difficult to explain. *No-one can explain her mysterious disappearance.*

puzzling — **Puzzling** means difficult to explain or find an answer to. *It took me a long time to finish the puzzling crossword.*

ambiguous — **Ambiguous** means confusing or **puzzling** because it has more than one meaning. *He gave an ambiguous reply.*

contrasting words: **clear**

continue *verb*

to keep on. *They **continued** to walk in the rain.*

last — To **last** means to go on or continue. *This lesson will last for half an hour.*

endure — To **endure** can mean to last well. *This car goes so well it should endure for years.*

hold out — To **hold out** means to **last** or continue. *I hope you can hold out until help comes.*

survive — To **survive** can mean to keep going or remain in existence, especially in the face of some difficulty or change. *The singer's popularity has survived through many music fads.*

persist — To **persist** can mean to go on and on. *Her toothache persisted even though she had taken an aspirin.*

contrasting words: **stop**

continuous *adjective*

going on without stopping. *The **continuous** rise and fall of his chest showed that the lifesavers had successfully revived the man.*

constant — **Constant** means continuing all the time. *His success was a constant source of pleasure to his family.*

steady — **Steady** can mean continuous and regular. *She made steady progress in learning to play the violin.*

persistent — **Persistent** means going on and on. *Her persistent grumbling spoilt our holiday.*

endless — **Endless** can mean seeming to have no end. *The endless ringing of the burglar alarm brought the police who arrested the thieves.*

interminable — **Interminable** means as if without an end. It is very similar to **endless.** *Lessons on the hot summer afternoon seemed interminable.*

similar words: **permanent**
contrasting words: **erratic**

cool *verb*

to make someone or something pleasantly cold or less hot. *The gentle breeze **cooled** us when we sat down after our hot walk.*

fan To **fan** can mean to cool or refresh someone with, or as if with, a fan. *It was so hot in the assembly hall that I fanned my face with a piece of paper.*

air-condition To **air-condition** can mean to cool air with a machine that keeps the temperature of a room at a comfortable level. *We'll have to air-condition this office because it's too hot for the computers, as well as the workers.*

chill To **chill** means to make something cold. *I chilled the drinks quickly with ice-cubes.*

freeze To **freeze** means to turn something to ice. *We froze our orange drinks.*

refrigerate To **refrigerate** means to make or keep something cold or frozen. *Mum refrigerated the leftover meat and we had it for lunch the next day.*

cooperate *verb*

to work or act together. *The two councils **cooperated** to build a new library.*

collaborate To **collaborate** means to work together, especially on a job. *Alice and James collaborated in writing the book.*

team up To **team up** means to work together for a particular reason. This is more suited to everyday language. *Nathan and Simon teamed up so their sandcastle would be the biggest.*

combine To **combine** means to join or act together. *The two boys combined to finish building the model aeroplane.*

unite To **unite** means to join or work together as one. *The whole town united to save the whales.*

contrasting words: **argue**

copy *noun*

something which is made the same as something else. *The secretary took my letter and made two **copies**.*

duplicate A **duplicate** is something which is exactly the same as something else. *I have made a duplicate of my essay so that I can give one to the teacher and keep one for myself.*

replica A **replica** is an exact copy. *He made a small replica of the rocket.*

model A **model** can be a small copy. *My brother gave me a model of an aeroplane for my birthday.*

likeness A **likeness** is something which is similar to something else but not exactly the same. *There is a definite likeness in my family so that you can tell we are all related.*

effigy An **effigy** is a representation of something, usually a picture or a statue of a person. *There is an effigy of the Queen on the back of all our coins.*

copy *verb*

to do or make something the same as something else. ***Copy** this spelling list from the blackboard.*

duplicate To **duplicate** means to make an exact copy of something. *The secretary duplicated the letter.*

reproduce To **reproduce** means to make a copy or strong likeness of something. *The artist reproduced the famous painting.*

photocopy To **photocopy** means to make an exact copy of a page of writing or pictures on a machine using a special camera with paper which reacts to light. *He photocopied his birth certificate.*

trace To **trace** means to copy something by following the lines of the original on transparent paper placed over it. *Anna traced the map of Australia.*

match To **match** can mean to make something similar to or like something else. *Try to make your drawing match mine.*

correct *verb*

to make something right by removing the mistakes or faults. *I **corrected** my letter carefully before I sent it.*

rectify To **rectify** means to put something right. *He soon rectified the situation.*

remedy To **remedy** can mean to correct a wrong or an evil. *You have been treated unjustly but we will soon remedy it.*

revise To **revise** means to check or correct something in order to make it better. *I decided to revise my story after reading it through.*

amend To **amend** means to correct or change something for the better. *You need to amend the rules of this game.*

reform To **reform** means to improve something by correcting and changing the mistakes or bad parts. It is similar to **amend**. *It was decided to pass a law to reform the education system.*

similar words: **improve, repair**

council *noun*

the governing body of a small area such as a city or a shire. *Our local county **council** has to keep the roads in good repair.*

parliament A **parliament** is a group of people elected to make the laws for a country or state. *We decide who will sit in parliament at a general election.*

senate A **senate** is one of the decision-making bodies in the government of some countries. *A person who is elected to a senate is called a senator.*

committee A **committee** is a group of people who meet to organise, make decisions about or investigate some activity. *The football club was run by a committee of eight members.*

congress A **congress** is a meeting of people to discuss ideas of interest to them all. *A congress of health workers was held here last week.*

board A **board** is a group of people in charge of a business or organisation. *The board of the golf club is holding a meeting next week.*

count *verb*

to use numbers to find the sum of a collection of things. *She **counted** the apples to see if there would be enough for everyone.*

add up — To **add up** means to find the sum of a number of things. *Who can add up these three numbers?*

total — To **total** means to find the sum or whole amount of something. *Please total the excursion money to see if any is missing.*

tally — To **tally** means to count up or calculate something. *Will you tally my bill and tell me how much I owe you.*

number — To **number** means to count something, often saying the numbers one by one. *Sam numbered his birthday presents and found that he had five.*

similar words: **calculate**

countless *adjective*

too many to count. *I'm surprised that they haven't broken that window because their football has hit it **countless** times.*

untold — **Untold** can mean more than can be counted or measured. *He was a man of untold wealth.*

umpteen — **Umpteen** means having to do with something that is unknown, especially a very large number that can't be counted. *I have told you umpteen times not to put your feet on the lounge.*

myriad — **Myriad** means of a very great but unknown number. *There are myriad stars in the night sky.*

infinite — **Infinite** can mean **endless** or never seeming to run out. *There are an infinite number of grains of sand on the beach.*

endless — **Endless** means having or seeming to have no end. *There seemed to be an endless number of chocolates in the tin.*

similar words: **numerous**

country *adjective*

coming from, or having to do with the land outside the towns and cities. *It's fun visiting our **country** friends on their farm.*

rural — **Rural** means having to do with the country or with farming. *There is a special government department to look after rural matters.*

agrarian — **Agrarian** means having to do with farming. *Do you think agrarian work is more healthy than working in an office?*

pastoral — **Pastoral** can mean having to do with farming, particularly the grazing of animals. *This is rich pastoral land.*

rustic — **Rustic** means having to do with, or living in the country, especially living a simple and peaceful life as opposed to a hectic city existence. *I spend my days in rustic pastimes such as milking cows.*

wilderness — **Wilderness** means the most remote parts of the world where there are very few living things to be found. *The Antarctic is a wilderness of snow and ice.*

contrasting words: **civic**

country *noun*

an area of land separated from other areas. *France and Germany are two **countries** in Europe.*

nation — A **nation** is a large group of people living in one country and under one government. *There are over one hundred nations in the British Commonwealth.*

kingdom — A **kingdom** is a country ruled over by a king or queen. *When the king died the young prince became the new ruler of the kingdom.*

realm — A **realm** is the same as a **kingdom**. *He ruled his realm wisely and fairly.*

republic — A **republic** is a **nation** which has an elected president, not a king or queen. *They elected a new president to be the leader of the republic.*

power — A **power** can be a strong country that is able to control or influence other countries. *Leaders from the major world powers met to discuss their differences.*

course *noun*

the way along which anything moves. *The map showed the course that the captain of the ship had plotted.*

path — **Path** can mean a way from one place to another. *The small boat hurried out of the path of the ship.*

route — A **route** is a regular line of travel. *The bus takes the long route home.*

track — A **track** is a rough **path** or trail. *The pond is at the end of the track.*

beeline — A **beeline** is a direct line, like the course bees take when returning to the hive. *The children made a beeline for the food.*

orbit — An **orbit** is the curved **path** or line of flight followed by a planet or satellite around the earth or sun. *The astronomers carefully studied the satellite's orbit around the earth.*

---

cover *verb*

to lie over or be spread over something. *A fine layer of dust **covered** all the furniture.*

blanket — To **blanket** can mean to cover something with a layer or covering. *Crisp, white snow blanketed the ground.*

envelop — To **envelop** can mean to surround something completely. *The heavy fog soon enveloped the whole town.*

wrap — To **wrap** can mean to surround someone or something, often as if with folds. It is similar to **envelop**. *The night wrapped us in its mantle of darkness.*

wreathe — To **wreathe** can mean to surround or cover something in curving or curling masses. *Mist wreathed the mountains and valley.*

shroud — To **shroud** can mean to cover something completely, causing a feeling of mystery. *Darkness shrouded the old gold mine.*

similar words: **enclose**

coward *noun*

someone who acts badly or weakly out of fear. *The* ***coward*** *let his friend take all the blame for writing on the wall.*

chicken A **chicken** is a coward. This word is more suited to everyday language. *He is too much of a chicken to admit that he was in the wrong.*

sissy A **sissy** can be a fearful or cowardly person. This word is more suited to everyday language. *He is too much of a sissy to go camping.*

scaredy-cat A **scaredy-cat** is someone who lacks courage. This word is more suited to everyday language. *When the dog barked she ran away showing what a scaredy-cat she really is.*

cry-baby A **cry-baby** is someone who cries more often than is usual or necessary, or who shows weakness easily. This word is more suited to everyday language. *They called her a cry-baby for whimpering when they shouted 'boo'.*

cower *verb*

to shrink away in fear. *We* ***cowered*** *among the trees as the snarling lion came into the clearing.*

quail To **quail** means to shrink with fear or lose courage when in a difficult or dangerous position. *We quailed at the thought of the lion catching sight of us.*

flinch To **flinch** means to draw back suddenly from something dangerous or unpleasant. *A twig snapped under my foot and we all flinched at the sound.*

waver To **waver** can mean to act uncertainly, sometimes because of fear. *Our brave guide did not waver as he took aim with his rifle.*

chicken out To **chicken out** means to back out or go away because you are scared. This is more suited to everyday language. *Surprisingly, the lion chickened out and leapt back into the forest.*

create *verb*

to make, using your own ideas or imagination. *Danielle **created** a beautiful pattern.*

design — To **design** can mean to invent and then draw up plans for something. *Dad designed our house.*

develop — To **develop** can mean to bring something into being. *The gardener developed a new kind of rose.*

compose — To **compose** means to create literature or music. *Justin composed the tune for this song.*

improvise — To **improvise** means to create or **compose** something on the spot. *Anthony improvised a tune for the song.*

similar words: **invent, concoct, make**

criminal *noun*

someone who is guilty of a crime. *The police were sure he was the **criminal** but they could not prove it.*

offender — An **offender** is someone who has broken the law in some way. This is a rather formal word. *Don't vandalise the railway cars — offenders will be prosecuted.*

felon — A **felon** is someone who has been convicted of a serious offence. *The judge sentenced the felon to life imprisonment.*

outlaw — An **outlaw** is someone who has broken the law and is wanted by the police. *There were pictures of outlaws on posters at the police station.*

gangster — A **gangster** is a member of a gang of criminals. *I saw three of the four gangsters get out of the car and go into the bank.*

hood — A **hood** can be a criminal, often a member of a gang. It is more suited to everyday language. *The hoods attacked the shopkeeper and stole all the money in the till.*

similar words: **crook, bandit**

crook *noun*

a dishonest person. This is more suited to everyday language. *I hope that **crook** goes to jail.*

rogue A **rogue** is a scoundrel or a dishonest person. *There are often rogues around at carnival time to take advantage of careless people.*

cheat A **cheat** is a dishonest person who tries to get things by deceit or trickery. *He was expelled from school for being a cheat.*

knave A **knave** is a dishonest and hateful man or boy. It is an old-fashioned word. *The king called him a knave for trying to cheat the trusting old man.*

fraud A **fraud** is someone who is not what they claim to be. *She said she was an expert dressmaker but she was a fraud.*

shark A **shark** can be a person who makes money dishonestly from other people, usually through false or unfair deals. *When you want to borrow large sums of money be careful of loan sharks.*

similar words: **criminal**

crooked *adjective*

curved or not straight. *The **crooked** man had a **crooked** stick.*

bent **Bent** means curved or made into an angled shape. *There was a bent spoke in the wheel of my bike.*

warped **Warped** means **bent** out of its usual shape. It is most often used about something straight and flat like timber. *The builder could not use the warped plank of wood.*

buckled **Buckled** means **bent,** or pushed out of shape. *My bike had a buckled wheel after the accident.*

twisted **Twisted** means pulled into curves and bends. *I used a piece of twisted wire to hold the chain together.*

distorted **Distorted** means crooked or pulled out of shape. *Her distorted face showed what pain she was in.*

cross *verb*

to go from one side of something to another. *The bridge* ***crossed*** *the river just near its mouth.*

traverse To **traverse** means to pass across or over something. *The hikers traversed the mountain pass as soon as the mist lifted.*

ford To **ford** means to cross a river where it is shallow enough to walk or ride across. *They had to wait for the flood waters to go down before they could ford the river.*

bridge To **bridge** means to make a bridge over something so that it can be crossed. *It was easier for the explorers to bridge the deep, narrow gorge than to travel around it.*

span To **span** means to extend or stretch across something. *The bridge spanned the river at its narrowest point.*

---

crowd *noun*

a large number of people or things gathered closely together. *Ann pushed her way through the* ***crowd*** *of children.*

throng **Throng** is so similar to **crowd** that you can usually use either. *A throng of people gathered to watch the parade.*

mob A **mob** is a large crowd which is sometimes rowdy or violent. It can also be a collection of animals like sheep. *An angry mob gathered outside The Houses of Parliament.*

flock A **flock** is a number of animals of the same kind, especially sheep, goats or birds, feeding or kept together. It can also be used to mean a crowd of people. *A shepherd looks after a flock of sheep.*

herd **Herd** is similar to **flock** but is usually used about cattle. *He drove the herd to a new pasture.*

pack A **pack** is a group of certain animals living and hunting together. Like **flock** and **herd** it can also be used to mean a group of people, especially criminals. *A pack of wolves lives in this forest.*

---

similar words: **group**

---

cruel *adjective*

likely or liking to cause pain or unhappiness. *Her **cruel** remark made me cry.*

savage — **Savage** can mean cruel or fierce. *Men, women and children were killed in the savage attack.*

brutal — **Brutal** means fiercely or extremely cruel. *It was a brutal blow when the flood destroyed all our crops.*

barbaric — **Barbaric** means extremely **savage** or cruel. *Everyone condemned the barbaric torture of prisoners.*

vicious — **Vicious** means very **savage**, cruel or harmful. *The vicious dog tried to attack the passers-by.*

ruthless — **Ruthless** means so cruel that you show no pity or mercy. *The ruthless dictator executed anyone who dared oppose him.*

similar words: **callous, violent**
contrasting words: **lenient**

crush *verb*

to break something into small pieces. *The machine **crushed** the huge rock and we were able to carry the pieces away.*

crumble — To **crumble** means to break something into small pieces, especially something that is soft. *The child crumbled the cake in her hand.*

grind — To **grind** can mean to crush something until fine particles are formed. *We ground the coffee beans and then percolated the coffee.*

mill — To **mill** means to crush something into fine particles using a machine. *You mill wheat to make flour.*

pound — To **pound** can mean to crush something into pieces or powder by beating it with something. *I pounded the herbs in the mortar with the pestle.*

pulverise — To **pulverise** means to crush something until it turns to dust or powder. *Superman pulverised the rock into sand.*

cry *verb*

to shed tears. *We all **cried** when our pet dog died.*

bawl To **bawl** means to cry loudly. *She bawled when she broke her leg.*

blubber To **blubber** means to cry noisily and usually with a lot of tears. *He blubbered for an hour because he wasn't allowed to watch TV.*

wail To **wail** means to give a long sad cry. *My mother wailed when she found that the thief had stolen her wedding ring.*

sob To **sob** means to cry, making a gulping noise as you breathe. *The little lost girl was sobbing when her father found her.*

whimper To **whimper** means to cry weakly. *The puppies whimpered when they were taken from their mother.*

contrasting words: **laugh, smile**

cunning *adjective*

able or likely to trick someone. *Here's a **cunning** plan to make them think we've gone away.*

crafty **Crafty** means cunning or clever in deceiving someone. *The hare was amazed that the crafty tortoise beat him.*

wily **Wily** is very similar to **crafty**. *The wily old fox escaped the hunters by swimming downstream.*

sly **Sly** means cunning in a clever or deceitful way. *His sly answer made us think he was innocent.*

devious **Devious** means tricky, usually not in a completely honest way. *Her devious behaviour lost her nearly all her friends.*

artful **Artful** means clever and cunning in getting what you want. *The artful football fans found a way into the sports ground without paying.*

similar words: **dishonest**
contrasting words: **honest**

cut *noun*

an opening in something made with a sharp object. *I have a **cut** on my finger.*

gash — A **gash** is a long deep cut. *The doctor had to stitch the gash in his leg.*

slit — A **slit** is a long straight cut or opening. *The nail has torn a slit in my skirt.*

incision — An **incision** is a deep cut, usually made for a particular reason. *The doctor started the operation by making a deep incision.*

score — A **score** can be a rough cut or deep scratch, especially on wood or metal. *Vandals had made a great score across the desk.*

notch — A **notch** is a small sharp cut. *There was a notch on the edge of the table.*

similar words: **break, opening**

cut *verb*

to separate or make something shorter using a sharp instrument. *I **cut** a piece of string.*

snip — To **snip** means to cut something using short quick strokes. *She snipped the roses off the bush.*

trim — To **trim** means to shorten something by cutting it. *The barber trimmed his hair.*

clip — To **clip** means to cut off or shorten something using scissors or shears. *She clipped the hedge.*

mow — To **mow** means to cut something off or down with a scythe or machine. *Dad mowed the lawn.*

shear — To **shear** means to remove hair or fleece from something using large scissors or something similar. *They sheared the sheep.*

similar words: **scratch, tear**

damage *verb*

to harm, injure or break a part of something. *He **damaged** the car when he backed into the tree.*

mar To **mar** means to damage or ruin something. *She marred the book by scribbling on it.*

sabotage To **sabotage** means to damage something on purpose or in order to cause problems for the owner. *The spy sabotaged the enemy planes.*

vandalise To **vandalise** means to deliberately damage or destroy something for no good reason. *Someone vandalised our school last night.*

ruin To **ruin** means to damage something so badly that you can't use it. *The hail storm ruined the harvest.*

wreck To **wreck** is so similar to **ruin** that you can usually use either one. *He wrecked the radio when he dropped it in the water.*

similar words: **destroy, hurt, spoil**
contrasting words: **repair**

dangerous *adjective*

likely to cause harm or injury. *Plastic bags are **dangerous** toys for very young children.*

perilous **Perilous** means dangerous because you are exposed to harm or injury. *We breathed a sigh of relief when we finished our perilous climb up the steep slope.*

hazardous **Hazardous** means dangerous because there is a possibility of harm or injury. *Most people agree that smoking is hazardous to your health.*

precarious **Precarious** means dangerous or not safe. *Robert pulled his brother away from his precarious position at the edge of the cliff.*

risky **Risky** means dangerous because there is a chance of injury or loss. *It would be risky to play on the road even though it's not very busy.*

dicey **Dicey** is very similar to **risky**. It is more suited to everyday language. *We decided that it was too dicey to cross the river while the current was so strong.*

contrasting words: **safe**

dark *adjective*

with little or no light. *I was frightened in the **dark** house.*

dim — **Dim** means without bright light, but not completely dark. *I could just see her shape moving in the dim passageway.*

shadowy — **Shadowy** means slightly dark or having light and shade. *We walked through the shadowy forest.*

murky — **Murky** means unpleasantly and gloomily dark. *We were trapped in the murky cave.*

obscure — **Obscure** can mean dark and out-of-the-way. *He hid in an obscure corner of the room.*

pitch-dark — **Pitch-dark** means completely dark. *The night was pitch-dark and we couldn't see where we were going.*

contrasting words: **bright**

darken *verb*

to make something have very little or no light. *Thick clouds **darkened** the sky.*

shade — To **shade** means to darken something by shutting out light. *Heavy curtains shaded the room.*

dim — To **dim** means to make something less bright. *She dimmed the lights in the sick child's bedroom.*

obscure — To **obscure** means to make something hard to see because of darkness. *A sudden thunderstorm obscured our view of the mountains.*

eclipse — To **eclipse** can mean to block the light of a heavenly body from the earth, thus causing darkness. *Sometimes the moon eclipses the sun and it becomes dark in the middle of the day.*

fog — To **fog** means to make something blurry or hard to see through. *Mist fogged the windscreen of our car.*

dart *verb*

to move suddenly and quickly. *I lost sight of him as he **darted** through the crowd.*

scurry To **scurry** means to move quickly and lightly. *She was too fast for us as she scurried around the corner.*

scamper To **scamper** means to run or hurry away quickly and lightly. *The rabbit scampered across the road and into its burrow.*

dive To **dive** can mean to move very quickly into something. *I dived into the carriage just before the door banged shut.*

scramble To **scramble** means to climb or move quickly and awkwardly. *Our feet slipped as we scrambled over the rocks to escape the huge wave.*

scoot To **scoot** means to dart or move along very quickly. It is more suited to everyday language. *I scooted down the stairs and along the path to see what the postman had brought.*

similar words: **speed, hurry**
contrasting words: **dawdle, walk, trudge**

dawdle *verb*

to waste time by being slow. *You'll never get there if you **dawdle** so much!*

dally To **dally** means to waste time or be very slow. *Stop dallying and do your work!*

delay To **delay** means to move or do something slowly. *If you delay we'll be late again.*

loiter To **loiter** means to stay in the one place or to move around in a slow aimless way. *I loitered near the park hoping to see someone to play with.*

linger To **linger** means to stay on in a place because you don't want to leave. *We lingered at the monkeys' cage because they made us laugh.*

tarry To **tarry** means to wait or be slow in starting to do something or go somewhere. *We tarried until it was almost too late to catch the train.*

contrasting words: **hurry, speed, dart**

daydream *verb*

to imagine pleasant things in a dreamy way. *I often **daydream** about being a film star.*

muse To **muse** means to think about something so deeply that you become dreamy. *I mused happily on what I would do over the weekend.*

be lost in thought To **be lost in thought** means to think about something so deeply that you do not pay attention to anything else. *I did not hear what she said because I was lost in thought.*

switch off To **switch off** means to lose interest in what is happening and think about something else.This is more suited to everyday language. *The lesson was so boring that I switched off and thought about the party.*

let your thoughts wander To **let your thoughts wander** means to stop concentrating on a particular thing. *I was meant to be working out the answers to the sums but I let my thoughts wander.*

contrasting words: **concentrate on, ponder**

dead *adjective*

no longer alive or useful. *In the autumn, **dead** leaves fall off deciduous trees.*

lifeless **Lifeless** can mean no longer having life. *They lifted his lifeless body into the ambulance.*

deceased **Deceased** means dead. It only refers to people. *Both my grandparents are deceased.*

departed **Departed** is very similar to **deceased**. It is a less common word. *My recently departed uncle left me some money in his will.*

late **Late** means having recently died. *The late Mr Jones was well-respected in our community.*

fallen **Fallen** can mean dead. It generally refers to those people who were killed in a war. *On Remembrance Sunday we remember the fallen soldiers of World War I.*

dear *adjective*

costing too much money. *Those jeans are* ***dear****.*

exorbitant — **Exorbitant** means being far more in amount than you think is reasonable. *Their prices are exorbitant.*

pricey — **Pricey** means costing more money than you think necessary. This is more suited to everyday language. *It is a pricey hotel.*

expensive — **Expensive** means costing a lot of money. *She bought an expensive dress for the party.*

costly — **Costly** means **expensive** or costing a great deal, usually because it is so precious or fine. *He gave her costly jewels.*

contrasting words: **cheap**

deceive *verb*

to trick someone by not telling the truth. *She* ***deceived*** *us by saying she'd found the money when she'd really stolen it.*

dupe — To **dupe** means to trick or deceive someone. *He duped them into believing he would pay them for working for him.*

hoodwink — To **hoodwink** is very similar to **dupe.** It is usually used in less formal language. *She hoodwinked us with promises she knew she couldn't keep.*

mislead — To **mislead** can mean to lead or guide someone wrongly, often on purpose. *You misled us when you said that paint would match our carpet exactly.*

delude — To **delude** means to trick or **mislead** someone. *He deluded them into thinking he was an honest person.*

take for a ride — To **take for a ride** means to trick or deceive someone. This is more suited to everyday language. *He certainly took you for a ride when he promised to come back with the money he borrowed.*

similar words: **trick, cheat**

decent *adjective*

acting in a way that is approved by most people. *We thought he was a **decent** man until we saw him cruelly beating his dog.*

proper — **Proper** can mean correct in behaviour. *It is not proper for children to sit in a bus while older people stand.*

right — **Right** means fair and good. *It was right for you to refuse to help him cheat in the exam.*

moral — **Moral** means acting according to the rules of what is thought to be right, especially in sexual behaviour. *She took a moral stand against their shoplifting.*

respectable — **Respectable** means good or worthy of respect, especially in the sense of being socially acceptable. *They are a poor but respectable family and their children are honest and reliable.*

ethical — **Ethical** means in agreement with the rules for **right** and **proper** conduct. *Our school expects high ethical standards from us.*

similar words: **honest**
contrasting words: **indecent, evil**

decrease *verb*

to become less. *The time I take to swim the length of the pool **decreases** the more I practise.*

diminish — To **diminish** is so similar to **decrease** that you can usually use either. *The number of dancers diminished as the competition became more fierce.*

abate — To **abate** means to become less in strength. *At last the storm abated.*

moderate — To **moderate** means to become less violent or severe. *The winds moderated as the cyclone moved out to sea.*

wane — To **wane** can mean to grow less gradually, especially in strength of feeling, power and so on. *Our enthusiasm waned when we realised how long it would take.*

peter out — To **peter out** means to become gradually smaller or weaker and then disappear or stop. *Our supply of food is petering out.*

contrasting words: **increase**

decrepit *adjective*

broken down or made weak by old age. *The **decrepit** house was almost beyond repair. The **decrepit** old man stumbled downstairs.*

infirm **Infirm** means weak in body or health. *She's infirm now that she's old, so you'll have to help her.*

timeworn **Timeworn** means worn with age or showing signs of disrepair because of long use. *The old lady got her timeworn photo album out of the drawer and looked at the faded pictures.*

moth-eaten **Moth-eaten** can mean in poor condition or worn out, usually with age. *The old, rather moth-eaten carpets will have to be replaced.*

threadbare **Threadbare** can mean worn and thin, usually with age. *What threadbare clothes he is wearing!*

crumbling **Crumbling** can mean decaying or disappearing bit by bit. *We looked sadly at the crumbling walls of our old house.*

similar words: **defective**

deed *noun*

something someone does. This is a rather formal word. *Going into the burning house to save the owner was a brave **deed**.*

act An **act** is something someone does. It can often be used instead of **deed**. *It was the act of a hero.*

action An **action** is so similar to **deed** or **act** that you can often choose any of these words. *The newspaper printed a report of her brave action.*

exploit An **exploit** is a notable and daring deed. *They told fascinating tales of their exploits in the jungle.*

move A **move** can mean something you do for a particular reason. *Saving his energy for the end of the race was a clever move.*

similar words: **achievement**

defeat *verb*

to overcome someone in a battle or contest. *The army **defeated** the rebels who didn't have enough ammunition.*

beat — To **beat** means to defeat someone, especially in a contest. *The visiting team beat our cricketers by ten runs.*

conquer — To **conquer** means to overcome someone by force. *The Allies conquered the Japanese in World War II.*

vanquish — To **vanquish** means to defeat someone, especially in battle. It is a more formal word than **defeat** or **conquer**. *The Roman army vanquished the Gauls.*

thrash — To **thrash** can mean to defeat someone completely or thoroughly. *Our soccer team trained very hard and thrashed the other team.*

lick — To **lick** can mean to defeat someone. It is more suited to everyday language. *They beat us at tennis but we licked them at cricket.*

defective *adjective*

having a weakness, mistake or blemish. *Dad replaced the **defective** car battery with a new one.*

faulty — **Faulty** means having weaknesses or mistakes. *Then we found that a tyre was flat because it had a faulty valve.*

unsound — **Unsound** means having defects or weaknesses. *The engine was unsound too, and had to be repaired.*

substandard — **Substandard** means below the normal grade or level, or not as good as it should be. *Dad was angry because the garage's work on the engine was substandard.*

shoddy — **Shoddy** means of poor quality or badly made. *He said the mechanic did a shoddy job.*

similar words: **inferior**
contrasting words: **perfect**

defence *noun*

something that keeps you safe from harm or acts as a protection against attack. *The moat was an important part of the castle's **defence**.*

protection — **Protection** is a form of defence from injury, danger or annoyance. *We keep an Alsatian dog for protection against burglars.*

security — **Security** is something that keeps you safe. *Staying together when we got lost in the forest was our greatest security.*

safeguard — A **safeguard** is something which helps protect or defend you. *Shark patrols are a safeguard for surfers.*

shield — A **shield** can be anything you use to protect yourself from harm. *She held her hands to her eyes as a shield against the sun.*

contrasting words: **attack**

defer *verb*

to put off something until later. *We'll have to **defer** making a decision about buying a new computer until we find out how much money we have.*

delay — To **delay** means to put off something until later, often because of an inconvenient interruption. *We can't delay the meeting just because Bob hasn't arrived.*

postpone — To **postpone** means to put off something until a future time. It is very similar to **defer**. *They postponed the game because of rain.*

adjourn — To **adjourn** means to put off something. It is often used about court cases, debates in parliament and other formal proceedings. *The judge adjourned the trial until the following week.*

suspend — To **suspend** can mean to defer something for some time, especially a punishment or law. *The magistrate suspended the car thief's sentence for twelve months.*

shelve — To **shelve** can mean to put off considering or thinking about something for a while. *That's such a tricky problem I'll have to shelve it until I find out more about it.*

defiant *adjective*

boldly going against someone or something in authority. *The **defiant** prisoners would not return to their cells.*

rebellious — **Rebellious** means openly or actively defiant. *The rebellious pupils were expelled from school.*

antagonistic — **Antagonistic** means disagreeing with and acting against something or someone. *She was antagonistic to any new ideas.*

recalcitrant — **Recalcitrant** means resisting authority or control. *The police had to use force because of the recalcitrant behaviour of the demonstrators.*

dissident — **Dissident** means disagreeing or differing, especially with a particular political system. *The dissident groups held a rally to protest against the harsh new laws.*

militant — **Militant** means fighting or ready to fight, especially for a cause. *My friends are militant supporters of nuclear disarmament.*

similar words: **argumentative, disobedient**
contrasting words: **submissive**

deliberate *adjective*

carefully considered and done on purpose. *Someone had made a **deliberate** attempt to set fire to the house.*

intentional — **Intentional** means done with a purpose or reason. *Her late arrival at the party was an intentional insult to the hostess.*

purposeful — **Purposeful** means having a set reason for doing something. *She set about her work in a purposeful way and soon finished it.*

premeditated — **Premeditated** means planned beforehand. *The judge said it was a premeditated crime and sent the murderer to prison for life.*

planned — **Planned** means done according to a plan. *Our planned fishing trip had to be postponed because of bad weather.*

contrasting words: **accidental**

delicious *adjective*

very pleasant to smell or taste. *That was a **delicious** dinner you cooked.*

luscious — **Luscious** means very pleasant or delicious to taste or smell. *What a luscious trifle!*

scrumptious — **Scrumptious** means very tasty or delicious. It is usually used in less formal language than **luscious**. *We had a scrumptious ice-cream while we were shopping.*

appetising — **Appetising** means so delicious that it makes you feel hungry. *The appetising smell of roast chicken wafted through the house.*

mouth-watering — **Mouth-watering** means looking or smelling so delicious that you want to eat it straightaway. *I stared at the mouth-watering cream cakes and fruit buns in the shop window.*

more-ish — **More-ish** means so tasty or delicious that you want to keep eating more. *Have you got another packet of those more-ish chocolate biscuits?*

contrasting words: **inedible**

demand *noun*

an urgent or forceful request or need. *Our **demand** for information must be met.*

claim — A **claim** is a demand placed on someone or something that is expected to be met even if it is difficult or unfair. *She became tired and ill because her job made too many claims on her.*

call — A **call** can be a demand or **claim** placed on someone or something. *I have so many calls on my time that I can never play games.*

ultimatum — An **ultimatum** is a final statement of terms or conditions which must be accepted. *His teacher gave him an ultimatum that if he forgot his homework again he would have to do it at lunch time.*

requisition — A **requisition** can be a formal or official request for something you need. *Our school put in a requisition for a new computer.*

levy — A **levy** is something, often a fee or tax, demanded from you by an official body. *The council imposed an extra levy on people using the car park at night.*

similar words: **order**

demand *verb*

to ask for something forcefully, as if it's your right. *He **demanded** an apology.*

order To **order** can mean to ask for or request something. *I'm going to order a milk shake.*

insist To **insist** means to demand something very strongly. *I insist that you come with me to see the doctor.*

require To **require** can mean to demand or **insist** on something. *The boss requires the finished report by this afternoon.*

ask To **ask** can mean to demand or expect something. *She is asking a high price for her skateboard.*

stipulate To **stipulate** can mean to demand something as an essential part of an agreement. *He stipulated an apology from me before he would agree to take me to the zoo.*

similar words: **ask**

dependant *noun*

someone who relies on or needs the support of another person. *Children are the **dependants** of their parents.*

protégé A **protégé** is someone who is protected or supported by someone else. This comes from a French word. *The musician's protégé was a young pianist who had a lot of potential.*

ward A **ward** is a young person who has been legally placed under the care or control of a guardian. *He was made a ward of court because his parents were not able to look after him.*

satellite A **satellite** can be something which depends on or is dominated by something else. *The new town will be a satellite of the capital city.*

hanger-on A **hanger-on** is someone who stays around or depends on someone whom they admire. *Pop stars have lots of hangers-on who follow them from one performance to another.*

parasite A **parasite** can be someone who lives on the money earned by other people without doing anything in return. You use this word about someone whose behaviour you don't approve of. *He was such a parasite that he always lived on his parents' money.*

descend *verb*

to go or come down. *The plane has started to **descend**.*

drop — To **drop** can mean to descend very suddenly. *The plane dropped when it entered an air pocket.*

sink — To **sink** can mean to descend gradually to a lower level. *The sun is sinking in the west.*

coast — To **coast** means to go down a hill on a bicycle without pedalling or in a car while it is not in gear. *The hill was so steep that they could coast all the way to the bottom.*

climb down — To **climb down** means to go down, usually using both hands and feet. *Their mother told them to climb down when she saw them at the top of the tree.*

describe *verb*

to give a picture of something or someone using words. *He **described** the accident and how it happened.*

represent — To **represent** can mean to describe or state something in words. *Does his novel really represent life in the Scottish Highlands?*

portray — To **portray** means to describe or explain something in words. *Her story portrayed the excitement she felt when she won the prize.*

depict — To **depict** means to describe or show something in words. *My grandmother tells me stories depicting life when she was a girl.*

illustrate — To **illustrate** can mean to make something clear by giving examples to help people picture or imagine it. *He illustrated his talk on bravery with stories about the first astronauts to go into space.*

express — To **express** means to put thoughts into words. *Try to express your ideas clearly so we all know what you mean.*

destroy *verb*

to wreck or damage something so completely that it does not exist any more. *The cyclone **destroyed** many houses.*

demolish To **demolish** means to knock down or destroy something. *The workman demolished the old house.*

wipe out To **wipe out** means to defeat someone or destroy something completely. *The hailstorm wiped out our garden.*

annihilate To **annihilate** means to destroy or defeat something completely. *They annihilated the enemy's army.*

exterminate To **exterminate** means to destroy something in order to get rid of it. *We exterminated the cockroaches in the kitchen.*

eradicate To **eradicate** means to root out or destroy something. *We want to eradicate crime in large cities.*

similar words: **damage**
contrasting words: **make**

deteriorate *verb*

to become worse. *The house **deteriorated** while it was not lived in.*

worsen To **worsen** means to become not even as good as it was before. *The condition of the house worsened after being empty for four years.*

degenerate To **degenerate** means to become bad or worse than before. *He degenerated into a lazy good-for-nothing while his parents were away.*

go to seed To **go to seed** means to get worse in your way of living. *The old man went to seed after he lost his job.*

decline To **decline** can mean to become worse or less. *His health has declined since he came here.*

waste away To **waste away** can mean to lose your strength or health, usually from an illness or disease. *Their bodies wasted away during the famine.*

similar words: **rot**
contrasting words: **recover**

die *verb*

to stop living. *My pet dog* ***died*** *last week.*

expire To **expire** can mean to die or give out your last breath. It is rather a formal word. *The old man expired on Christmas Day.*

breathe your last To **breathe your last** means to die. It is similar to **expire**. *The king breathed his last at half past two today.*

perish To **perish** means to die in an unnatural way, sometimes from violence or lack of food. *The explorers perished in the desert.*

pass away To **pass away** means to die naturally. People usually use it because they think it is less upsetting than using the word **die**. *I am ringing to tell you that your aunt passed away peacefully in her sleep.*

kick the bucket To **kick the bucket** means to die. This is only suited to everyday language. *Everyone in that television show ended up kicking the bucket.*

similar words: **become extinct**
contrasting words: **live**

difficult *adjective*

not easy to do or understand. *This is a* ***difficult*** *puzzle.*

hard **Hard** can mean difficult to do or explain. *It was a hard exam.*

complex **Complex** means difficult to understand or explain because it is complicated. *Maths is too complex for me.*

tough **Tough** can mean very difficult to deal with. *He has a tough job to do.*

arduous **Arduous** means needing a lot of hard work. *She was tired after an arduous day in the factory.*

demanding **Demanding** means needing a lot of time, hard work and energy. *Nursing is a demanding occupation.*

contrasting words: **easy**

dig *verb*

to break up, turn over or remove something, such as earth, using your hands or an implement. *Fido often* ***digs*** *the soil in the vegetable patch so he can bury his bones.*

scoop To **scoop** means to take something up or out, as with a spoon or your cupped hands. *We scooped sand out to make a moat around our sand castle.*

hollow out To **hollow out** means to make a hole in something by digging out the inside. *Kellie hollowed out a pineapple and filled it with strawberries and grapes for the party.*

excavate To **excavate** means to make a hole or tunnel by digging something. *The archaeologists excavated the ruined city hoping to find ancient pottery and coins.*

gouge To **gouge** means to dig out something roughly or crudely. *Heavy earth-moving machines gouged earth and rocks out of the side of the mountain.*

mine To **mine** means to dig something, such as earth, to get minerals, precious stones and so on. *In South Yorkshire thousands of men mine coal for power stations.*

dirty *adjective*

covered with dirt or stains. *We had* ***dirty*** *hands by the time we had finished cleaning our bikes.*

grubby **Grubby** means dirty, messy or untidy. *What a grubby room!*

grimy **Grimy** means very dirty, especially on the surface. *Underneath the grimy surface the walls were painted bright blue.*

grotty **Grotty** means dirty, nasty or unpleasant. This is more suited to everyday language. *It was a grotty old house.*

filthy **Filthy** means very dirty or unpleasant. *The beach was filthy where the sewage emptied onto it.*

polluted **Polluted** means made dangerously dirty or unfit to use. *The water was too polluted to swim in.*

contrasting words: **clean**

dirty *verb*

to make something unclean, or cover it with marks and stains. *Who **dirtied** the clean floor?*

soil To **soil** means to make something dirty or stained. *We soiled the new chairs with our muddy feet.*

smear To **smear** means to rub or spread dirty marks over something. *I didn't mean to smear paint on the walls.*

smudge To **smudge** means to mark something with dirty streaks. *He smudged his tear-stained face with his grubby hands.*

spot To **spot** means to mark or stain something. *You have spotted your jacket with ice-cream.*

similar words: **spoil**
contrasting words: **clean**

disagree *verb*

to fail to agree about something. *The two reports of the disaster **disagree** as to the number of casualties.*

differ To **differ** means to disagree or have different ideas or feelings about something. *The brothers differed as to which was the quickest way home.*

dissent To **dissent** means to disagree or have a different opinion. *Ten members of the club agreed to change the rules and two members dissented.*

dispute To **dispute** means to argue loudly and for a long time. *They spent the whole day disputing about anything and everything.*

bicker To **bicker** means to squabble or argue about little things. *The children have been bickering all day.*

wrangle To **wrangle** means to argue or quarrel noisily. *Don't wrangle with me!*

similar words: **argue**
contrasting words: **agree**

disappear *verb*

to go out of sight. *He **disappeared** around the corner.*

vanish To **vanish** means to disappear quickly. *With a wave of the magician's wand the rabbit vanished before our very eyes.*

dematerialise To **dematerialise** means to disappear without a trace. *Everything the Martian pointed his gun at dematerialised while we watched.*

fade To **fade** means to disappear slowly. *Her smile faded as her ice-cream fell to the ground.*

dissolve To **dissolve** means to disappear gradually. *The ghostly shape dissolved into the mist.*

melt To **melt** means to fade gradually and is very similar to **dissolve**. *He turned the corner and melted into the darkness.*

contrasting words: **appear**

disappointment *noun*

failure to have your hopes satisfied. *It was a great **disappointment** to me when it rained on my birthday.*

letdown A **letdown** is so similar to **disappointment** you can usually choose either word. *After all our hopes it was a letdown when we couldn't go to the toyshop.*

anticlimax An **anticlimax** is a disappointing end to something you expected to be very good or exciting. *We were excited about the fete and it was an anticlimax when rain caused it to be cancelled.*

blow A **blow** is a sudden shock or disappointment. *It was a blow when the clouds drifted away and the farmers didn't get the rain they needed.*

setback A **setback** is something which stops or slows down your progress. *It was a setback which was hard to overcome.*

washout A **washout** is an occasion when plans are spoiled by accident. *We had hoped to take a trip to the zoo, but the strike made it a washout.*

disapprove of *verb*

to have a bad opinion of something or someone. *My father* ***disapproves of*** *my punk haircut.*

frown on	To **frown on** means to disapprove or have a bad opinion of something. *Our parents frowned on our plan for a picnic in the rain.*
take a dim view of	To **take a dim view of** means to have a bad or unfavourable opinion of something. *Your mother and I take a dim view of the way you stayed out so late.*
take exception to	To **take exception to** means to object to something strongly. *I take exception to what you just called me.*
look down on	To **look down on** means to have no respect for someone or to regard them with scorn. *You've always looked down on us just because we don't live in the same suburb as you.*

similar words: **fault**
contrasting words: **approve, praise**

disaster *noun*

any sudden terrible happening which causes great suffering and damage. *The flood was one of the worst* ***disasters*** *we've had for years.*

catastrophe	A **catastrophe** is a sudden disaster. *What a catastrophe it was when the grandstand at the football match collapsed.*
calamity	A **calamity** is a terrible happening. *The newspaper said that the building of a road through the rainforest would be a national calamity.*
tragedy	A **tragedy** is any very sad or dreadful happening. *It was a tragedy when her brother died in the accident.*
debacle	A **debacle** is a dreadful disaster. *Their business venture proved to be a debacle in which they lost all their money.*

similar words: **misfortune**

discard *verb*

to throw something away because you don't need it any more. *We **discarded** all the clothes we'd grown out of.*

shed To **shed** means to cast off something. *The grass-snake shed its skin in our garden.*

jettison To **jettison** means to throw something off because you don't want or need it. *The pilot jettisoned most of the spare fuel before making the crash landing.*

scrap To **scrap** means to throw something away because it is useless. *We scrapped any broken toys that couldn't be mended.*

dump To **dump** can mean to throw something down or get rid of it. *They dumped the rubbish in a hole in the ground.*

ditch To **ditch** means to get rid of something. It is more suited to everyday language. *The murderer ditched the body in the river as soon as it was dark.*

contrasting words: **use**

discordant *adjective*

having an unpleasant combination of musical notes. *If the orchestra doesn't tune up properly the music will be **discordant**.*

dissonant **Dissonant** means sounding harsh and unpleasant. *We put our hands over our ears to block out the dissonant music.*

cacophonous **Cacophonous** means loud and lacking any pleasant musical qualities. *A cacophonous clatter and banging came from the workshop.*

atonal **Atonal** means not in any particular musical key, thus lacking the expected musical qualities. *Not everyone liked the atonal music she wrote.*

flat **Flat** can mean singing or playing too low or below the correct pitch. *'The violins are flat', shouted the conductor.*

sharp **Sharp** can mean singing or playing too high or above the correct pitch. *Don't blow your recorder too hard because the notes will be sharp.*

contrasting words: **musical**

discourage *verb*

to try to prevent someone from doing something. *He will **discourage** her from learning to hang-glide.*

dissuade To **dissuade** means to persuade someone not to do something. *We dissuaded him from leaving home.*

deter To **deter** means to prevent someone from doing something. *The fact that he doesn't want me to learn to hang-glide won't deter me.*

talk out of To **talk out of** means to argue with someone in order to stop them doing something. *My parents talked me out of spending all my pocket-money on sweets.*

advise against To **advise against** means to tell someone they shouldn't do something. *The sign advised us against taking a caravan on the mountain track.*

put a damper on To **put a damper on** means to discourage someone. It is more suited to everyday language. *The forecast for storms put a damper on our plans to go to the beach.*

contrasting words: **encourage, persuade**

disgust *verb*

to cause you to totally dislike something. *Cruelty **disgusts** me.*

horrify To **horrify** means to cause someone to feel great disgust and fear. *Hearing about that murder on the news horrified me.*

offend To **offend** can mean to displease someone or to affect them disagreeably. *It offends me when you kick your dog.*

sicken To **sicken** means to make you feel sick. *Violence on TV sickens me.*

nauseate To **nauseate** means to make you feel you want to vomit. *The idea of eating snails nauseates me.*

revolt To **revolt** can mean to make you feel sick and disgusted. *When I saw what the vandals had done it revolted me.*

contrasting words: **please**

dishonest *adjective*

likely to lie, cheat or steal. *The **dishonest** employee lost his job.*

deceitful — **Deceitful** means likely to lie or try to trick or mislead people. *No-one liked her because of her deceitful ways.*

shifty — **Shifty** means **deceitful** and looking as if you have something to hide. *We thought the man who was lurking near the school had a shifty look about him.*

hypocritical — **Hypocritical** means pretending to be better than you are. *I don't want a hypocritical friend who talks about me behind my back.*

crooked — **Crooked** can mean dishonest or likely to swindle people. It is more suited to everyday language. *The crooked businessman was jailed for ten years.*

shady — **Shady** can mean of doubtful honesty or lawfulness.It is more suited to everyday language. *He has been mixed up in some shady deals.*

similar words: **cunning, illegal**
contrasting words: **honest, frank**

dislike *noun*

a feeling of not liking, or a distaste for, someone or something. *I could not hide my **dislike** of him.*

hatred — **Hatred** means very strong dislike. *She looked at her enemy with hatred.*

aversion — **Aversion** means strong dislike, usually with a feeling of disgust. *I have an aversion to spinach.*

antipathy — **Antipathy** means a long-standing dislike or feeling of disgust. It is very similar to **aversion**. *She has an antipathy to strangers.*

hostility — **Hostility** means unfriendliness or the treating of someone as an enemy. *She met his attempts to be friendly with hostility.*

animosity — **Animosity** means a feeling of dislike or unfriendliness. It is very similar to **hostility**. *The party was spoilt by the animosity between the two families.*

disobedient *adjective*

refusing to obey. *The **disobedient** girl was punished.*

unruly — **Unruly** means disobedient and uncontrollable. *More police had to be called to control the unruly crowd.*

wilful — **Wilful** means obstinate and determined to have your own way. *The wilful boy wouldn't take any notice of the warning.*

delinquent — **Delinquent** means having broken the law. *She was sent to a home for delinquent girls.*

headstrong — **Headstrong** means hard to control and determined to have your own way. *He was so headstrong we weren't surprised when he ended up in trouble with the police.*

insubordinate — **Insubordinate** means not obeying your superiors. *The sailor was sent to the captain for insubordinate behaviour.*

similar words: **naughty, defiant**
contrasting words: **obedient, well-behaved, submissive**

disobey *verb*

to refuse to obey someone or something. *They were punished when they **disobeyed** the teacher.*

defy — To **defy** means to boldly refuse to obey someone. *Luke defied his mother when she told him to turn off the television.*

infringe — To **infringe** means to disobey rules or laws. *You must not infringe the school rules.*

flout — To **flout** means to show no respect for authority by being disobedient. *They flouted the drug laws by importing heroin.*

violate — To **violate** means to break a rule or law deliberately. *The United Nations censured the nation which violated the international treaty.*

transgress — To **transgress** means to **flout** or **violate**. It is usually used in connection with religious laws. *At our local church we were taught not to transgress the Ten Commandments.*

contrasting words: **obey**

disorganise *verb*

to throw something into confusion and disorder. *Unexpected visitors* ***disorganised*** *our plans and we didn't go to the concert.*

disrupt — To **disrupt** means to interrupt something and throw it into disorder. *The sound of the fire-engine going by disrupted the singing lesson and we had to start again.*

disturb — To **disturb** means to unsettle someone or something. *The unexpected news disturbed us and we didn't know what to do next.*

upset — To **upset** can mean to put something into disorder or confusion. *The rain upset our plans for a picnic.*

mess up — To **mess up** can mean to make something confused. *The train strike messed up our holiday plans.*

mix up — To **mix up** means to get something confused. *Douglas and Judith mixed up the time they were to meet and they missed the bus.*

contrasting words: **arrange**

display *noun*

a show or showing of something. *We went to a fireworks* ***display****.*

exhibition — An **exhibition** is a public showing of something made or done by people. *The handicraft club held an exhibition today.*

demonstration — A **demonstration** can be a public showing of something in order to advertise it. *The microwave cookery demonstration was very helpful.*

parade — A **parade** can be a gathering of troops, scouts or other people and things for inspection or display. *There was a parade of all the animals and their trainers before the circus began.*

pageant — A **pageant** is a colourful public show, often including a procession of people in costume. *Our town had a pageant to celebrate its centenary.*

preview — A **preview** is a private showing of a film or exhibition before the public is allowed to see it. *The mayor was invited to a preview of the film.*

disprove *verb*

to prove something is not true. *The new experiments **disproved** the old theory.*

refute — To **refute** means to prove something is false. *Mark quite easily refuted their accusation that he had been shoplifting because he was sick in bed on that day.*

rebut — To **rebut** means to show something is false by proof or argument. It is so similar to **refute** that you can usually choose either word. *Karen rebutted their claim by showing them the true information in her encyclopaedia.*

invalidate — To **invalidate** means to show something is not true or sensible. *The first flight to the moon invalidated the story that it was made of green cheese.*

contradict — To **contradict** means to be the direct opposite of something. *His happy face contradicted the story we heard that he was always miserable.*

demolish — To **demolish** can mean to put an end to something, such as a belief or claim. *We demolished their claim to be champions when we beat them so easily.*

contrasting words: **prove**

dissatisfied *adjective*

annoyed because your wishes or needs haven't been fulfilled. *She gave her presents a **dissatisfied** look.*

displeased — **Displeased** means annoyed or offended. It is very similar to **dissatisfied**. *I am displeased with your behaviour.*

discontented — **Discontented** means not feeling happy, pleased or satisfied. *He is discontented with his job.*

disgruntled — **Disgruntled** means made annoyed and sulky. *He is disgruntled because he has to leave for work so early.*

browned off — **Browned off** means extremely annoyed or fed up. It is more suited to everyday language. *It is no use talking to her when she is browned off.*

querulous — **Querulous** means dissatisfied and complaining. *'Why can't we leave now?' she grumbled in a querulous voice.*

similar words: **angry, annoyed**
contrasting words: **satisfied, glad**

distant *adjective*

far off. *The rocket travelled through space to a **distant** planet.*

faraway — **Faraway** is so similar to **distant** that you can usually use either. *I dream of visiting faraway lands.*

remote — **Remote** means very far off and out-of-the-way. *We visited a remote village in the mountains.*

outlying — **Outlying** means far from the centre of things. *The cows had wandered into an outlying paddock.*

isolated — **Isolated** means separated or apart from other people. *If you live on an isolated farm you can be very lonely.*

contrasting words: **near**

distinguished *adjective*

having an air or quality that impresses people. *What a **distinguished** gentleman he looks in his military uniform!*

aristocratic — **Aristocratic** can mean showing the finest qualities. *Our new black stallion looked aristocratic.*

noble — **Noble** means of a high quality that you admire. *Climbing the tallest mountain in the world was a noble feat.*

refined — **Refined** can mean without any coarseness or roughness. *Our dinner guest had very refined manners.*

genteel — **Genteel** means very polite and careful in your manners, speech and behaviour. *She is so genteel that she won't allow any swearing or bad manners in her presence.*

classy — **Classy** can mean **refined** or suited to those of high class. It is more suited to everyday language. *We enjoyed going to the classy restaurant even though it was expensive.*

similar words: **superior, grand**
contrasting words: **ordinary, inferior**

distribute *verb*

to give or share something out. *Santa Claus **distributed** gifts to the children.*

issue To **issue** means to give or send out. *The shopkeeper issued his accounts once a month.*

allot To **allot** means to hand out something. *Their father's will allotted equal shares of the farm to the two brothers.*

dispense To **dispense** means to deal something out. *The courts dispense justice.*

allocate To **allocate** means to set something apart for a special purpose. *The children allocated some of their money to buy sweets.*

ration To **ration** means to share out the fixed amount of something that is allowed to one person or group. *During the war, the authorities rationed food because it was in short supply.*

similar words: **share**

double *adjective*

having two parts. *I ate a **double** chocolate ice-cream.*

dual **Dual** means having to do with two or having two parts. *That book has a dual purpose — to teach you and to entertain you.*

two-piece **Two-piece** means having two parts that go together. This is usually used about clothing. *She was wearing her new two-piece swimming costume.*

twin **Twin** can mean having two things that match or look alike. *This plane has twin engines.*

duplicate **Duplicate** can mean double or having two parts that are similar or go together. *The couriers made out duplicate accounts, one for the customer and one to keep for themselves.*

contrasting words: **single**

doubt *verb*

to be uncertain or unsure of something. *I have reason to **doubt** her excuse for being late.*

distrust To **distrust** means to doubt or have no confidence in someone or something. *I distrust her claim that she won the race.*

disbelieve To **disbelieve** means to **distrust** or have no faith in something or someone. *I disbelieve anything he tells me.*

question To **question** can mean to doubt something and want to know more about it before you believe it. *I question the truth of that story.*

query To **query** means to doubt or ask questions about something. *You should query her story about her rich parents.*

take with a grain of salt To **take with a grain of salt** means to doubt something someone tells you. *I take the things he says with a grain of salt.*

contrasting words: **believe**

drab *adjective*

looking dull and uninteresting. *Those **drab** curtains spoil the look of the room.*

mousy **Mousy** can mean having a grey-brown or drab colour. It is used about the colour of hair. *She put a henna rinse in her mousy hair.*

sombre **Sombre** can means dull in colour. *She always wears sombre clothes, even to parties.*

dingy **Dingy** means not bright or new-looking. *They live in a dingy flat.*

gloomy **Gloomy** can mean dull and dark. *They were locked in the gloomy dungeon.*

similar words: **dull**
contrasting words: **gaudy, colourful, spectacular**

dreamy *adjective*

vague or lost in a dream thinking about something else. *He had a **dreamy** look on his face as he thought about his holidays.*

preoccupied — **Preoccupied** means completely taken up with your own thoughts. *I was so preoccupied I didn't hear a word you said.*

bemused — **Bemused** means lost in thought. *While our teacher read the story my friend had a bemused look on her face.*

half-asleep — **Half-asleep** means vague and **preoccupied.** *Because you were half-asleep you missed the joke.*

inattentive — **Inattentive** means not paying attention to what is going on around you. *You were certainly inattentive when I gave out the instructions.*

absent-minded — **Absent-minded** means being so vague that you forget things. *What an absent-minded person you are to put on different coloured socks!*

contrasting words: **alert, inquisitive**

dreary *adjective*

dull or gloomy. *It was a **dreary** afternoon with no sunshine.*

dismal — **Dismal** means causing a feeling of sadness or gloom. *The weather has been dismal for days.*

depressing — **Depressing** means causing a feeling of sadness or lack of energy. *It is depressing when it rains all day.*

cheerless — **Cheerless** means without brightness or warmth. *They spent the cheerless day trying to get warm.*

bleak — **Bleak** means cold and harsh. *It was a bleak winter's day.*

grey — **Grey** can mean dark and overcast. *Don't hurry to get up because it's a grey morning outside.*

similar words: **cloudy**
contrasting words: **fine**

drink *verb*

to take liquid through your mouth. ***I drink** eight glasses of water a day.*

sip To **sip** means to drink something in small mouthfuls. *Alison sipped her lemonade to make it last longer.*

imbibe To **imbibe** means to drink. It is a more formal word. *The Governor's guests imbibed excellent wine with their dinner.*

quaff To **quaff** means to drink thirstily. *We quaffed our fruit juice with gusto after winning the tennis match.*

guzzle To **guzzle** means to drink or eat greedily and noisily. *The louts at the bar guzzled their beer while talking loudly.*

swallow To **swallow** means to take liquid or food into your stomach through your throat. *Daniel swallowed his nasty medicine quickly and then had a piece of chocolate.*

similar words: **eat, chew**

drip *verb*

to let drops fall. *The tap **drips** all the time.*

dribble To **dribble** means to flow in small drops. *Saliva dribbled from the baby's mouth.*

trickle To **trickle** means to flow in a very small or slow stream. *Milk trickled out of the hole in the carton.*

seep To **seep** means to leak slowly or flow through something gradually. *Water seeped through the hole in the ceiling.*

ooze To **ooze** means to flow slowly, as if through small openings. It is very similar to **seep**. *Mud oozed through our toes as we walked in the rain.*

similar words: **flow**

drop *verb*

to allow something to fall or go to a lower position. *Careful! Don't **drop** the baby.*

lower To **lower** means to put something in a lower position. *We lowered a rope over the side of the cliff.*

let down To **let down** is so similar to **lower** that you can usually use either. *Mum had to let down the hem of my uniform because I had grown taller.*

dip To **dip** means to lower something briefly before lifting it again. *Dip the ladle into the soup.*

sink To **sink** means to make something go down to the bottom. *The destroyer sank the battleship.*

submerge To **submerge** means to put something under the surface of the water. *The captain submerged the submarine before attacking.*

contrasting words: **lift**

dry *adjective*

not wet or damp. *The lawn was very **dry** so we hosed it.*

arid **Arid** means dry and hot. *We carried plenty of water in our car when we drove across the arid desert.*

parched **Parched** means having become very dry. *The flowers died in the parched garden while we were away on holidays.*

dehydrated **Dehydrated** means having lost all its water or moisture, or having had it removed. *The sick baby was dehydrated because she couldn't drink without vomiting. Currants are dehydrated grapes.*

desiccated **Desiccated** means thoroughly dried. *We sprinkled desiccated coconut on the chocolate cake.*

contrasting words: **wet**

dull *adjective*

not bright, shiny or clear. *The top of this table was very **dull** before I polished it.*

flat — **Flat** can mean not shiny. It is mainly used about paint. *We used flat paint for the walls in the lounge room.*

matt — **Matt** means having a dull surface. *I prefer matt snapshots to glossy ones.*

lacklustre — **Lacklustre** means without brightness or lustre. *She looked unhealthy with her tired eyes and lacklustre hair.*

lifeless — **Lifeless** can mean dull and lacking vitality. *If you used brighter colours your picture wouldn't look so lifeless.*

similar words: **drab**
contrasting words: **shiny**

earth *noun*

the softer part of the dry land, rather than rocks or sand. *The toddlers made mud pies out of **earth** and water.*

clay — **Clay** is a dense earth which holds water and is used in making pottery and bricks. *I need to wet my clay before I make a vase.*

soil — **Soil** is earth, especially the kind in which you can grow plants. *The soil in our garden needs plenty of fertiliser.*

ground — **Ground** is earth or **soil**. *We dug a hole in the ground for the posts.*

dirt — **Dirt** is loose earth or **soil**. You usually think of dirt as being very dry. *I dropped my book in the dirt.*

loam — **Loam** is a loose **soil** made up of clay, sand and natural fertilisers. *Good fodder crops grow in the loam on the river flats.*

easy *adjective*

not difficult or hard to do or understand. *Swimming is **easy** once you have been taught.*

simple — **Simple** means easy to understand, do or use. *It was a simple explanation.*

uncomplicated — **Uncomplicated** means not hard to use or understand. *She gave me uncomplicated instructions.*

effortless — **Effortless** means done easily or without much effort. *He won the game with an effortless serve.*

foolproof — **Foolproof** means designed not to fail and to be easy to use even if you are inexperienced. *My mother has given me a foolproof method of making biscuits.*

contrasting words: **difficult, complicated**

eat *verb*

to take food into your mouth and swallow it. ***Eat** your ice-cream before you get into the car.*

taste — To **taste** means to eat just a small amount of something to see if you like it. *He tasted the soup to see if it needed more pepper.*

consume — To **consume** means to eat or drink something. It is a more formal word. *The chocolate biscuits were so delicious we consumed every one.*

devour — To **devour** means to eat something very hungrily. *I was so hungry I devoured nearly a whole loaf of bread.*

gobble — To **gobble** means to eat something very quickly without chewing it well. *We gobbled our dinner so we could go out to play.*

gulp — To **gulp** means to swallow something quickly, often a large amount at a time. *The large dog gulped his meat down in a minute and then looked for more.*

similar words: **chew, drink**

edge *noun*

a line, side or boundary, where two parts or surfaces meet. *The **edge** of the cardboard box was dented.*

border A **border** is the edge or side of anything. *I painted a design around the border of my drawing.*

margin A **margin** is the edge of something. *Grass grew around the margin of the lake.*

rim A **rim** is an outer edge, especially of a circular or round object. *The rim of the wheel is bent.*

brim A **brim** is the top edge of a container like a glass or basin. *He filled the glass to the brim.*

brink A **brink** is the edge of a steep or dangerous place. *They have put up a fence on the brink of the cliff.*

similar words: **outskirts**

educated *adjective*

having had a good education. *We need **educated** people in parliament.*

cultivated **Cultivated** means having had your mind and abilities developed and improved. *Cultivated people enjoy reading, music and going to the theatre.*

learned **Learned** means having a lot of knowledge from study. *Aunt Helen is a learned woman who likes to talk about books.*

erudite **Erudite** means having knowledge gained from study, especially in history or literature. This is rather a formal word. *The students enjoyed the lectures of the erudite professor.*

knowledgeable **Knowledgeable** means having knowledge or understanding, especially about a particular subject. *He is very knowledgeable about European wild flowers.*

well-informed **Well-informed** means having a wide general knowledge or knowledge of a variety of subjects. *My Uncle Daniel helped me with my current affairs project as he is a very well-informed man.*

similar words: **clever, shrewd**
contrasting words: **ignorant**

elastic *adjective*

able to be pulled out or extended and then go back to its original shape again. *The **elastic** sides of the boots stretch to go over my feet and then fit tightly around my ankles.*

stretchy — **Stretchy** means elastic or able to be extended. *This stretchy belt will fit almost anyone.*

springy — **Springy** means elastic or able to regain its shape after being stretched. *We jumped up and down on the springy mattress.*

bouncy — **Bouncy** means able to spring back into shape, or rebound as a ball does. *Look at her thick, bouncy hair.*

rubbery — **Rubbery** means soft and **stretchy**. *The rubbery clay was easy to push and pull into different shapes.*

resilient — **Resilient** means able to bounce back. *Rubber is such a resilient material that many children's toys are made of it.*

---

emphasise *verb*

to point out the importance of something. *The manager **emphasised** the necessity for everyone to get to work on time.*

stress — To **stress** is so similar to **emphasise** that you can usually use either. *The manager stressed the need for punctuality.*

accentuate — To **accentuate** means to make something seem important or noticeable. *He accentuated the main parts of his speech by thumping his fist on the table.*

highlight — To **highlight** means to make something stand out. It is very similar to **accentuate**. *I highlighted the important sentence by underlining it.*

labour — To **labour** can mean to develop something in too much detail, usually because you consider it very important. *She really laboured the point about how dangerous the trip would be.*

magnify — To **magnify** can mean to make something seem more important than it is. *They always magnify their troubles.*

---

contrasting words: **minimise**

---

empty *adjective*

containing nothing. *The children were disappointed when they discovered that the letterbox was **empty**.*

void — **Void** means completely empty or without contents. This is a very formal word. *This statement is void of meaning.*

blank — **Blank** means not written or printed on. *I couldn't think what to write on the blank page.*

finished — **Finished** means empty because everything has been used up. *We ate the chocolates until the box was finished.*

vacant — **Vacant** means not occupied by anyone. *The house has been vacant since the last owner died.*

deserted — **Deserted** means empty of people bcause they have all gone away. *There was an eerie feeling in the deserted town.*

contrasting words: **full**

enclose *verb*

to shut in or close in on all sides. *A wall **enclosed** the jail.*

box in — To **box in** means to enclose someone or something, as if in a box. *The tall hedges boxed me in and I couldn't get out.*

coop up — To **coop up** means to keep someone or something in a small place. *You shouldn't coop up all the rabbits in the one cage.*

confine — To **confine** means to shut or keep someone or something in. *I'll confine you to your room until you stop being cheeky.*

surround — To **surround** means to go around something completely. *A wooden fence surrounds our house.*

encircle — To **encircle** means to enclose something by making a circle around it. *A deep moat encircled the castle.*

similar words: **cover**

encourage *verb*

to cheer someone on. *We **encouraged** the team with shouts and flag-waving.*

urge To **urge** means to push or drive someone or something on. *I urged my brother to try again.*

inspire To **inspire** means to have an encouraging and uplifting effect on someone. *His bravery inspired the others.*

motivate To **motivate** means to give someone a strong reason for doing something. *My high class marks motivated me to study hard for the exams.*

set an example to To **set an example to** means to encourage someone by being a good model for other people to follow. *Her physical fitness set an example to everyone on the camp.*

similar words: **persuade**
contrasting words: **discourage**

end *noun*

the last or final point of something. *I fell asleep before the **end** of the television show.*

finish **Finish** is so similar to **end** that you can usually use either. *She ran the race to the finish.*

conclusion The **conclusion** is the point at which something comes to an end. *At the conclusion of the concert the curtain fell.*

close **Close** is so similar to **conclusion** that you can usually use either. *Stumps were drawn at the close of the cricket match.*

finale A **finale** is the special last part of a performance that comes just before the end. *We sang 'Land of Hope and Glory' as the finale of the concert.*

termination **Termination** means the bringing of something to an end. *She was sad because of the termination of their friendship.*

contrasting words: **start**

end *verb*

to come to the finishing point. *The storm **ended** almost as suddenly as it had begun.*

finish To **finish** means to come to an end. *The match finished when it grew too dark to see the ball.*

terminate To **terminate** can mean to end or **finish**. It is usually used in more formal language. *The concert terminated with a solo by the leading tenor.*

stop To **stop** means to **finish** or to come to a halt. *We stopped when the whistle blew.*

cease To **cease** is very similar to **stop**. It may be used in more formal language. *The canary's whistling ceased when I covered its cage.*

expire To **expire** can mean to come to an end. *Can you lend me 20 pence because the time limit on the parking meter has expired.*

similar words: **stop**
contrasting words: **start**

endanger *verb*

to put someone or something in danger. *They **endangered** their lives going fishing during the fierce storm.*

jeopardise To **jeopardise** means to put something in danger, or to chance its loss or harm. *Don't jeopardise all your good work by being careless now!*

expose To **expose** can mean to leave something open to danger or harm. *The soldiers exposed themselves to the enemy's fire as they made their attack.*

compromise To **compromise** can mean to lay something open to danger, or something similar. *He compromised our position when he told the enemy where we were.*

threaten To **threaten** can mean to be likely to cause damage or harm to something or someone. *The drought threatened our crops.*

put at risk To **put at risk** means to put something in a position or situation where it may be damaged or harmed. *Most doctors agree that smoking puts your health at risk.*

contrasting words: **protect, save**

endure *verb*

to bear something patiently or without making a fuss, usually for a long time. *The explorer **endured** many hardships before he finally reached civilization.*

put up with — To **put up with** means to endure something that you don't like or that is hard to do. It is more suited to everyday language. *I put up with her teasing for days.*

tolerate — To **tolerate** can mean to endure or **put up with** something. *I tried to tolerate the uncomfortable pillow but in the end I asked for another one.*

stick — To **stick** can mean to endure or **tolerate** something, even though you may be tempted not to. *If we can only stick the bad weather for the next few days I'm sure our holiday won't be spoilt.*

suffer — To **suffer** can mean to endure or **put up with** something that may hurt you very much. *She suffered their insults quietly.*

---

enemy *noun*

someone who hates someone else, or wishes to harm them. *He was a good man and had no **enemies**.*

foe — **Foe** is a rather old-fashioned word for an **enemy**. *The soldiers went into battle against their foes.*

antagonist — An **antagonist** is an enemy or someone you are striving against, often in an unfriendly way. *The antagonists fought to the bitter end as they each wanted to win the trophy.*

adversary — An **adversary** is someone you compete against or fight with. *The boxer's adversary weighed much more than he did.*

opponent — An **opponent** is someone who is on the opposite side to you in a contest or argument. *The opponents fought hard to win the last point in the tennis match.*

rival — A **rival** is someone who is aiming at the same thing as another person, or who tries to equal or outdo them. *She is my main rival for the championship.*

---

contrasting words: **friend**

---

energetic *adjective*

strong and active. *Puppies are very **energetic**.*

vigorous — **Vigorous** means strong, energetic and full of life. *We were hot after our vigorous game of football.*

dynamic — **Dynamic** means energetic and forceful. *The coach of the football team was a dynamic person.*

lively — **Lively** means full of energy and spirit. *The children in the playground are lively.*

spirited — **Spirited** means showing lively courage. *The spirited horse wouldn't let anyone ride it.*

full of beans — **Full of beans** means energetic. It is not used in formal speech. *I felt full of beans this morning so I went for an early swim.*

similar words: **busy**
contrasting words: **lazy, lethargic, tired**

enlarge *verb*

to make something bigger. *I am going to **enlarge** this photo and frame it.*

increase — To **increase** can mean to make something bigger, greater or faster. *We increased our speed as we drove out into the country.*

expand — To **expand** can mean to make something bigger or wider in scope. *She expanded her knowledge by reading.*

augment — To **augment** means to enlarge something by adding to it. *Dad began working at night to augment his income.*

amplify — To **amplify** can mean to enlarge something or make it greater. It is usually used about sound. *I used a loudhailer to amplify my voice.*

boost — To **boost** means to raise something or make it bigger or stronger. *Her win in the first heat boosted her confidence.*

similar words: **add**
contrasting words: **reduce**

entertainer *noun*

someone who sings, recites or amuses people in a public place, usually for payment. *He earns his living as an **entertainer** in clubs.*

performer A **performer** is someone who performs any skill or displays an ability in front of an audience. *She will have to be a good performer to be picked for the musical.*

jester A **jester** was a clown who entertained a prince or nobleman and his court in medieval times. *'Ask my jester to come and sing to us', shouted the king.*

comedian A **comedian** is someone who performs in plays, films or other entertainments that make you laugh. *The comedian was not the star of the play but we all liked him the best.*

player A **player** is a rather old-fashioned word for actor. It is also used for someone who plays a musical instrument. *The villagers were excited when they heard there was a band of strolling players coming.*

busker A **busker** is a musician who performs in the street hoping to get money from people passing by. *The busker played his guitar so well there was a lot of money in the box at his feet.*

enthusiastic *adjective*

having a lively interest in something. *She is **enthusiastic** about her new job.*

keen **Keen** means full of enthusiasm. *He's a keen fisherman and tries to go fishing every weekend.*

eager **Eager** means really wanting to do something. *She is eager to help us build the tree-house.*

anxious **Anxious** can mean sincerely and earnestly **eager**. *He was anxious to please his father.*

avid **Avid** means wanting to do something as often as possible. *She is an avid reader.*

willing **Willing** means being happy to agree to doing something. *He was a willing helper.*

contrasting words: **apathetic, unwilling**

equal *adjective*

being of the same number, value, or other quality as something else. *Everyone's share is **equal**.*

equivalent — **Equivalent** means of equal or matching value or rank. *An admiral in the navy is the equivalent rank to a general in the army.*

level — **Level** can mean at an equal standard. *Their abilities are level in all subjects.*

symmetrical — **Symmetrical** means having the parts arranged so that they are balanced or equal in size or shape. *The pattern on the wallpaper is symmetrical.*

uniform — **Uniform** means having the same appearance. *The packages were of uniform size and weight.*

similar words: **similar**
contrasting words: **uneven**

err *verb*

to make a mistake or be incorrect. *I know this sum isn't right but I can't see where I have **erred**.*

miscalculate — To **miscalculate** means to make a mistake in working out the amount of something. *I thought I bought enough flour for the cake but I miscalculated.*

go wrong — To **go wrong** is so similar to **err** that you can usually use either. *You have gone wrong in the second line of the sum.*

make a slip — To **make a slip** means to make a mistake. *We don't want to make a slip at the last moment.*

trip up — To **trip up** can mean to make a mistake or do badly at something. *I was doing well in the exams, until I tripped up on the last question.*

boob — To **boob** means to make a silly mistake. It is more suited to everyday language. *Oops, I've boobed again.*

erratic *adjective*

irregular or not steady in behaviour or movement. *The Coastguard went to investigate the boat because of its **erratic** course.*

unsteady — **Unsteady** means not constant or regular. *Fay's movements were very unsteady just before she fainted.*

intermittent — **Intermittent** means stopping and starting. *There was intermittent rain all day.*

sporadic — **Sporadic** means not very regular or frequent. *She makes sporadic attempts to learn to play the piano but doesn't like practising.*

fitful — **Fitful** means stopping and starting in a very irregular way. *The sick man's fitful sleep worried the nurse.*

irregular — **Irregular** means uneven in timing. *Her heartbeat was irregular until she recovered from fright.*

contrasting words: **continuous, repeated**

escapee *noun*

someone who has broken out of prison. *The newspaper said that the **escapee** might be dangerous.*

fugitive — A **fugitive** is someone who is running away, usually from the police. *The thief had to live as a fugitive so that he wouldn't be caught.*

absconder — An **absconder** is someone who runs away secretly, usually to avoid the law. *The police caught the absconder with a briefcase full of money.*

runaway — A **runaway** is someone who has escaped or run away, often a child who has left home. *The runaway wouldn't tell the police where she lived.*

truant — A **truant** is someone who stays away from school without permission. *She suspected that the boy on the train was a truant.*

refugee — A **refugee** is someone who escapes to another country for safety, especially during war. *The refugees had to live in camps because they had left their homes in a hurry.*

contrasting words: **prisoner**

evil *adjective*

breaking the laws of right or moral behaviour. *Snow White's* ***evil*** *stepmother tried to poison her.*

wicked **Wicked** means evil and causing great harm. *The wicked witch cast a spell on the prince and turned him into a frog.*

sinful **Sinful** means **wicked** or disobeying God's laws. *The Ten Commandments help us avoid sinful behaviour.*

black **Black** can mean evil or **wicked**. *The rebels soon lost support because of their black deeds.*

villainous **Villainous** can mean very **wicked** or vile. *The villainous gangsters kept hitting the bank manager until he gave them the keys to the safe.*

heinous **Heinous** means hateful and deserving severe punishment. *Kidnapping is a heinous crime.*

similar words: **indecent, dishonest**
contrasting words: **decent**

examine *verb*

to inspect or look at someone or something carefully. *The doctor* ***examined*** *me to make sure I was not hurt in the accident.*

analyse To **analyse** means to examine something in detail in order to find out or show its meaning or importance. *The jury analysed all the facts presented by the barristers and decided that the woman was guilty.*

study To **study** means to examine or look at something closely. *We studied our accounts to see whether we could buy a new washing machine.*

assess To **assess** means to work out the value of something by examining it in detail. *The mechanic assessed the amount of damage to my car.*

vet To **vet** means to examine or check carefully. *The personnel officer vets all the people who apply for a job.*

review To **review** means to examine something, especially in a formal or official way. *The admiral reviewed his fleet to see that all was in order.*

similar words: **investigate, test, inspect**

example *noun*

one of several things, or a part of something, which shows what the whole thing is like. *He gave us an **example** of what he wanted us to do.*

sample — A **sample** is a small part or piece of anything which is meant to show what the whole is like. *I have seen a sample of his art work and will be very happy to sell his paintings in my shop.*

model — A **model** is an example used for copying or comparing. *Her work was used as a model by the teachers.*

specimen — A **specimen** is a part of something, or a single thing, taken as being typical of a larger amount, or a whole group. *The doctor took a specimen of my blood for tests.*

guide — A **guide** can be anything that shows you the way to do something. *The gardening book served as a reliable guide when we planted the vegetables.*

pattern — A **pattern** can be a **model** that shows how something can be made. *When I asked my mother for a new dress, she gave me some material and a paper pattern!*

excellent *adjective*

remarkably good or of the highest quality. *Your schoolwork is **excellent**.*

outstanding — **Outstanding** means so good that it stands out from all others. *She is an outstanding tennis player.*

fantastic — **Fantastic** means extremely good or wonderful. *We saw a fantastic movie last week.*

terrific — **Terrific** means very good or excellent. *The team spirit before the match was terrific.*

sensational — **Sensational** can mean excellent or very pleasing. It is more suited to everyday language. *He always gets into the team because he's a sensational swimmer.*

exceptional — **Exceptional** means of unusually high quality or ability. *Only exceptional people win the Nobel prize.*

similar words: **good, great, perfect, superior, wonderful, best**
contrasting words: **bad, ordinary**

excess *noun*

an extreme amount. *He had an **excess** of food at the party and was sick afterwards.*

surplus A **surplus** is an amount that is more than is needed or used. *Because Year 5 is smaller than it was last year, we have a surplus of desks in our room.*

glut A **glut** is a very big **surplus**. *There was such a glut of beans on the market that they were very cheap.*

oversupply An **oversupply** is too large an amount of something that has been supplied to you. *The weary mother felt her toddler had an oversupply of energy.*

backlog A **backlog** is a piling up of things that need to be done. *I have a backlog of letters to answer.*

bellyful A **bellyful** is more than enough of something. It is more suited to everyday language. *I have had a bellyful of his complaining.*

contrasting words: **lack**

exchange *verb*

to give one thing in return for another. *I think I'll take this jumper back to the shop and **exchange** it for a smaller one.*

swap To **swap** means to exchange. They are so similar you can usually choose either word. *I swapped my apple for my friend's sandwich.*

replace To **replace** something means to renew it or put something else in its place. *I have to replace the cup I broke with a new one.*

substitute To **substitute** means to put something in the place of something else. *The thief substituted a fake for the diamond.*

stand in for To **stand in for** means to act in place of someone. *I will stand in for you while you have lunch.*

transpose To **transpose** means to make two or more things change places. *If you transpose the letters in the word 'on' you get 'no'.*

excited *adjective*

having the strong feelings you get when you are looking forward to something or enjoying something very much. *Jane was **excited** about going to the zoo.*

thrilled — **Thrilled** means very excited. *She was thrilled when she knew you were coming.*

exhilarated — **Exhilarated** means filled with energy and excitement. *They felt exhilarated after the ride on the roller-coaster.*

restless — **Restless** means unable to remain quiet and still. *Everyone in the class was restless because it was almost time for the play to begin.*

keyed up — **Keyed up** means excited with expectancy and nervousness. *The actor was very keyed up before his entry on stage.*

frenzied — **Frenzied** means wildly or furiously excited. *The dog began a frenzied barking when he saw his owner.*

contrasting words: **calm, bored**

exciting *adjective*

arousing feelings of eagerness or interest. *This book is so **exciting** I can't put it down.*

exhilarating — **Exhilarating** means filling you with energy and excitement. *I love the exhilarating feeling of zooming across the water in a speedboat.*

stimulating — **Stimulating** means stirring up interest and enthusiasm for something. *That stimulating film on surfing made me feel like racing straight down to the beach.*

rousing — **Rousing** means stirring into action and interest. *The troops sang a rousing song before marching into battle.*

thrilling — **Thrilling** means causing a tingling feeling of strong excitement. *I couldn't get to sleep after that thrilling movie.*

breathtaking — **Breathtaking** means causing excitement and admiration mixed with a little fear. *We had a breathtaking view of the volcano from the cable car.*

contrasting words: **boring**

exclude *verb*

to shut or keep something or someone out. *Blinds **exclude** light from rooms.*

preclude — To **preclude** means to rule out or exclude someone. *The new rules will not preclude women from becoming members of the club.*

leave out — To **leave out** means to exclude or fail to include someone or something. *When Jack chose the teams he left out his sister.*

drop — To **drop** can mean to exclude someone from a group. *The manager dropped her from the team after she hurt her arm.*

skip — To **skip** means to pass over something without reading or noticing it. *He often skips bits when he's reading.*

delete — To **delete** means to take out or wipe out something written. *Delete their names from the list.*

similar words: **ban, isolate**
contrasting words: **include**

expand *verb*

to express something in greater detail so as to make it longer, usually by adding more words. *She **expanded** her short story into a novel.*

develop — To **develop** can mean to expand or enlarge upon the detail of something. *She's trying to develop her ideas about nuclear disarmament before she gives her talk to the class.*

amplify — To **amplify** can mean to expand something by adding more details. *Please amplify your story so that I can understand what happened.*

embellish — To **embellish** means to make a statement or tale more interesting by adding details, mostly imaginary or exaggerated ones. *He embellished his story with a description of her screams.*

embroider — To **embroider** can mean to improve or make a story more interesting with untruthful additions. *My brother embroidered the tale so much that I could hardly believe the things he described had happened to him.*

pad — To **pad** can mean to fill out a speech or piece of writing with unnecessary words or information. *You padded your essay with too many trivial details.*

contrasting words: **shorten**

expect *verb*

to think that something is likely to come or happen. *I **expect** the storm will break in the next half hour.*

anticipate — To **anticipate** can mean to expect something will come to pass. *We anticipate the release of the prisoner tomorrow.*

foresee — To **foresee** means to expect or see something in advance. *I can foresee trouble as Mum looks very cross to me.*

count on — To **count on** means to depend upon or expect something. *The boss is counting on us being on time.*

bargain for — To **bargain for** means to expect or be prepared for something. *We didn't bargain for the crowd at the picnic ground.*

look forward to — To **look forward to** means to expect something with pleasure. *We are looking forward to our holiday.*

expel *verb*

to drive someone out or away with force. *I'm afraid I will have to **expel** you from the school.*

evict — To **evict** means to turn someone out of a place or remove them. *The landlord evicted the tenants for not paying the rent.*

banish — To **banish** means to send someone away as a punishment. *The king banished the evil magician from his country forever.*

exile — To **exile** means to force someone to leave their country. *The king exiled her for treason.*

deport — To **deport** means to send out of a country someone who is not a citizen of it. *The government deported the migrant who was selling illegal drugs.*

throw out — To **throw out** is an informal way of saying **expel**. *The doorman at the hotel threw out the noisy drunk.*

similar words: **isolate**

experienced *adjective*

skilful as a result of having done something many times. *She is an **experienced** hang-glider.*

professional — **Professional** means following an occupation to earn a living from it. *He is a professional golfer.*

qualified — **Qualified** means having passed examinations to enable you to do a job. *He is a qualified nurse.*

practised — **Practised** means being skilful at something because you have done it a lot. It is similar to **experienced**. *She bandaged his leg with practised ease.*

veteran — **Veteran** means having had many years of experience in doing something. *He is a veteran soldier.*

similar words: **competent**
contrasting words: **incompetent, inexperienced**

expert *noun*

someone who has a lot of skill or knowledge about something. *She is a skating **expert**.*

authority — An **authority** is someone who is a reliable source of information about something. *He is an authority on snakes.*

consultant — A **consultant** is an expert who charges you for advice. *The engineering firm called in a consultant to help plan the new bridge.*

specialist — A **specialist** is someone who has concentrated on a special area of study or work. *The heart specialist operated on my grandmother.*

ace — An **ace** is an expert who is usually quite famous. *Douglas Bader, the pilot, was an ace of World War II.*

prodigy — A **prodigy** is someone, usually a child, who has an extraordinary talent for something. *Mozart was a musical prodigy.*

explain *verb*

to make something clear, plain or easy to understand. *Can you **explain** what you mean?*

clarify To **clarify** can mean to make something clear or able to be understood. *Can you clarify your answer?*

elucidate To **elucidate** means to explain something by giving more details about it. *I can't give you an answer until you elucidate what you want.*

spell out To **spell out** can mean to explain something in a very simple way to make quite sure that nothing has been missed. *Tom is only five so you had better spell out the rules of the game.*

illustrate To **illustrate** can mean to explain something by giving examples of it. *He illustrated his theory about leadership with accounts of the lives of some famous explorers.*

interpret To **interpret** can mean to explain the meaning of something. *I never know what my dreams mean but my mother can interpret them.*

contrasting words: **confuse, puzzle**

extend *verb*

to reach or be drawn out over some distance. *The mountain range **extends** right down to the coast.*

cross To **cross** means to go or reach from one side or place to another. *They built the bridge to cross over the river.*

spread To **spread** means to extend or stretch out, especially over an area. *The flood waters spread over the farmland.*

stretch To **stretch** means to extend for a long distance. *The desert stretched to the horizon.*

run To **run** can mean to extend or continue. *A crack runs down the wall.*

extra *adjective*

more than usual or necessary. *There is always* ***extra*** *work to do in the garden when we come back from holidays.*

superfluous — **Superfluous** means more than is needed. *There were so many helpers that he was superfluous.*

surplus — **Surplus** means being more than is needed. *The British Government gave some of our surplus crop of wheat to the people in Africa suffering from a famine.*

excessive — **Excessive** means more than usual or proper. *The excessive rainfall this week caused the river to flood.*

redundant — **Redundant** means no longer needed because there is already enough. *Because there were no orders for tractors, my father was made redundant.*

unnecessary — **Unnecessary** means needless, or more than needed. *Her offer of help was unnecessary as we already had enough volunteers.*

similar words: **sufficient**
contrasting words: **scant, necessary, insufficient**

fail *verb*

to be unsuccessful or fall short in something. *He* ***failed*** *in his maths test because he could only answer a couple of questions.*

fall through — To **fall through** means to be unsuccessful or to fail. *Their plans fell through because they hadn't prepared well enough.*

collapse — To **collapse** means to fail suddenly. *The plans for the peace talks collapsed when one of the leaders said that he would not attend.*

fizzle out — To **fizzle out** means to fail after a good start. *The idea fizzled out even though everyone was enthusiastic to start with.*

miscarry — To **miscarry** means to fail to get the right result or decision. *The terrorist's plan miscarried when the bomb exploded too soon.*

founder — **Founder** can mean to sink into nothing. *Like the Titanic, his great plans foundered after a short while.*

contrasting words: **succeed, thrive**

failure *noun*

something or someone that doesn't succeed. *The artist felt that his exhibition was a **failure** because only a few people came to see it.*

disaster A **disaster** can mean a total failure. *The school play was a complete disaster because nearly everyone forgot their lines.*

fiasco A **fiasco** is an embarrassing or ridiculous failure. *The party was a fiasco because only half the guests turned up.*

flop A **flop** is something that is a failure. This is more suited to everyday language. *The critics said the play would be a flop because the acting wasn't very good.*

dud A **dud** is something that proves to be a failure. This is more suited to everyday language. *The car turned out to be a bit of a dud because it kept breaking down.*

write-off A **write-off** can mean someone who lacks skill and ability or is a complete no-hoper. This is more suited to everyday language. *Most people say she's a write-off because she keeps getting expelled from school.*

contrasting words: **achievement**

fair *adjective*

treating everyone equally and not showing favouritism. *He was a very **fair** judge of our projects.*

impartial **Impartial** means not taking one side against the other. *The judge in the trial was impartial.*

just **Just** means fair or rightly judged. *Most people agreed his decision was just.*

right **Right** means fair and good. *He was right not to judge you too harshly.*

objective **Objective** means being fair and not allowing your own opinions to influence you. *You need an objective mind to be a judge.*

similar words: **neutral**
contrasting words: **unfair**

faithful *adjective*

always staying true to a friend, or a leader, or to what you believe in. *I will be **faithful** to you until I die.*

loyal — **Loyal** means faithful and true. *He stayed loyal to me through all my trouble.*

devoted — **Devoted** means loving and **loyal**. *She is my devoted friend.*

trustworthy — **Trustworthy** means deserving trust or confidence by showing that you are faithful. *They were our trustworthy allies during the war.*

constant — **Constant** means unceasingly faithful. *Their constant love kept their marriage happy for 50 years.*

trusty — **Trusty** means faithful and able to be trusted. *My dog has been my trusty friend for 15 years.*

similar words: **reliable, steadfast**
contrasting words: **unfaithful**

fake *adjective*

made or done in such a way as to trick other people. *We were all fooled by the **fake** jewels.*

phoney — **Phoney** means not real or genuine. It is more suited to everyday language. *The phoney £20 notes were the hardest to detect.*

false — **False** can be so similar to **phoney** that you can usually use either. *He wore a false nose to the fancy-dress party.*

sham — **Sham** means not what it pretends or appears to be. *The army put on a sham battle for the visitors.*

counterfeit — **Counterfeit** means made to look exactly like something else in order to deceive people. It is usually used to describe something that is illegal. *Not even the police could pick the counterfeit money at first.*

bogus — **Bogus** means **counterfeit** or not real. It is more suited to everyday language. *The man was caught when he tried to use the bogus passport.*

contrasting words: **genuine**

fall *verb*

to come down suddenly from a higher to a lower position because of loss of balance or support. *The cup **fell** to the ground and smashed.*

slip To **slip** means to lose your footing and fall. *He slipped on the polished floor.*

topple To **topple** means to fall forward because of lack of balance. *The old man felt faint from the heat and toppled over.*

trip To **trip** means to fall over, or nearly fall, because you struck your foot against something. *I tripped over that toy.*

stumble To **stumble** means to fall, or nearly fall, when walking or running. It is very similar to **trip**. *She stumbled on the uneven ground.*

pitch forward To **pitch forward** means to fall forward very suddenly. *The leg of my chair broke and I pitched forward onto the carpet.*

similar words: **overbalance**

family *noun*

parents and their children. *The whole **family** went on a picnic.*

relatives **Relatives** are people who belong to your wider, or extended family, such as uncles, aunts, cousins and grandparents. *All our relatives came to celebrate our parents' wedding anniversary.*

kin **Kin** means all your **relatives**. This word is not used as often as **relatives** or **relations**. *Her mother's kin are Greek.*

relations **Relations** are your **kin** or **relatives**. These words are all so similar you can usually choose any one of them. *Most of Joshua's relations live in Israel.*

flesh and blood **Flesh and blood** means someone's children or other close **relatives**. This is often used by people who are feeling very emotional about the person they are talking about. *I didn't think my own flesh and blood would do such a thing.*

famous *adjective*

widely known. *The **famous** runner won his third gold medal.*

renowned — **Renowned** means very widely known and well thought of. *Not a sound was heard as we listened to the adventures of the renowned explorer.*

celebrated — **Celebrated** means so famous that you are publicly recognised and praised. *The celebrated author was surprised and pleased when we gave a dinner in her honour.*

noted — **Noted** means famous or honoured for a particular achievement. *The speaker at the conference was a noted expert on his subject.*

notable — **Notable** means important or worthy of being noticed. *He is a notable young writer who has had a lot of success.*

notorious — **Notorious** means famous or well-known for something bad. *Dick Turpin was a notorious highwayman.*

similar words: **important**
contrasting words: **insignificant**

fashion *noun*

a custom or way of doing things. *The **fashion** of entertaining at a barbecue is popular.*

vogue — A **vogue** is a fashion at a particular time. *Copying pop stars is in vogue among teenagers at present.*

fad — A **fad** is something that is popular for a short time. *Yoyos are a fad that comes and goes.*

craze — A **craze** is very similar to a **fad**. You can usually choose either word. *Haven't you heard about the latest craze for putting coloured gel in your hair?*

trend — A **trend** is a tendency or movement which leads to a fashion. *There is a trend towards buying smaller cars these days.*

rage — A **rage** is something that is very fashionable or popular at a particular time. This is often used in the phrase 'all the rage'. *Space adventure films are all the rage at present.*

fast *adjective*

able to move at a great pace. *She's a very **fast** runner.*

quick — **Quick** means fast or without any delay. *He was so quick he got away before we could catch him.*

rapid — **Rapid** means very fast or **quick**. *Linda's such a rapid worker she did twice as much as Sue.*

speedy — **Speedy** is so similar to **rapid** that you can usually use either word. *Even though her work was speedy she didn't make one mistake.*

swift — **Swift** means able to move very quickly and smoothly. *With one swift dive the bird grabbed my sandwich in its beak and flew off again.*

express — **Express** means very fast, without stopping or delaying. *We sent her present by express post so she would receive it as soon as possible.*

contrasting words: **slow**

fat *adjective*

weighing more that you should. *She said she was quite **fat** after her holiday.*

plump — **Plump** means rather fat and well-rounded. *The new puppies were plump and cuddly.*

tubby — **Tubby** means short and fat. *The tubby little boy ate too many chips.*

stout — **Stout** means rather overweight and often looking thick and heavy. *He is a stout man with a big, booming voice.*

portly — **Portly** means quite large and fat. *Santa Claus is said to be a very portly gentleman.*

obese — **Obese** means extremely fat. *Most people who are obese try to lose some weight.*

similar words: **stocky, heavy**
contrasting words: **thin, slight**

fatal *adjective*

causing death. *He suffered **fatal** injuries in the car accident.*

deadly — **Deadly** means likely to cause death. *Cyanide is a deadly poison.*

lethal — **Lethal** is so similar to **deadly** that you can usually use either. *Some household cleaners can be lethal if children swallow them.*

malignant — **Malignant** can mean **deadly** or tending to produce death, as a disease does. *My uncle died from a malignant tumour.*

terminal — **Terminal** can mean causing or happening at the end of your life. *The doctors told him that he had a terminal illness and only had a few months to live.*

fate *noun*

a fixed and inescapable plan for the whole of your life, supposedly designed by some unknown power. *It was due to **fate** that we should meet.*

destiny — **Destiny** is something that had to happen, especially related to the events in someone's life. *To die by dragon's breath was his destiny.*

providence — **Providence** is the care and protection of God, nature or some unknown power. *It must have been providence that the children survived overnight on the moors without any food.*

luck — **Luck** is something, either good or bad, which happens to a person without any apparent reason. *As luck would have it, the bus came just as it started to rain heavily.*

fortune — **Fortune** is so similar to **luck** that you can usually use either. *It was by good fortune that a doctor was close by when I broke my leg.*

chance — **Chance** can be fate or an accidental or unforeseen happening. *If by chance we find the treasure, we will be rich.*

fault *verb*

to find an error or mistake in something. *They couldn't **fault** his wonderful singing.*

criticise To **criticise** means to find fault with something or someone. *He criticised my table manners in front of my friends.*

condemn To **condemn** means to express strong disapproval of something or someone. *She condemned the fight in the playground.*

censure To **censure** means to **condemn** or to find fault with someone or something. This is rather a formal word. *The government censured its opponents for their policy concerning the nation's economy.*

damn To **damn** can mean to declare something to be bad, wrong or illegal. *He damned the activities of the hooligans in the district.*

pick to pieces To **pick to pieces** means to criticise something, especially in small details. *She picked my work to pieces and pointed out every little thing that was wrong with it.*

similar words: **scold, disapprove of**
contrasting words: **approve, praise**

fear *verb*

to feel concern or worry for something. *I always **fear** for your safety while you are away pot-holing.*

tremble To **tremble** can mean to feel so afraid that you can't help shaking. *She trembled when she saw the lightning.*

shudder To **shudder** can mean to feel so worried and afraid that you suddenly start to shake. *I shuddered at the thought of the exam.*

lose your nerve To **lose your nerve** means to be afraid to do what you set out to do. *The rider lost his nerve when he came to the high fence.*

panic To **panic** means to feel sudden great terror, sometimes without obvious reason. *He panicked when the fire spread to the fence.*

freak out To **freak out** means to be upset or angry. This is more suited to everyday language. *He freaked out when he found he had lost the money.*

similar words: **worry**

fearful *adjective*

feeling or showing fear. *When I first went to the farm I was **fearful** of the cows.*

timid — **Timid** can mean easily frightened. *The timid little girl wouldn't play tag with her new friends.*

cowardly — **Cowardly** means lacking courage in a way that disgraces you. *The cowardly bully only hit people smaller than himself.*

gutless — **Gutless** means having no courage. It is very similar to **cowardly**. *He showed he was gutless when he wouldn't even climb a tree.*

spineless — **Spineless** can mean having no strength of character or courage. *The parachutist wouldn't jump until the others said he was spineless.*

yellow — **Yellow** is so similar to **cowardly** that you can usually use either word. It is more suited to everyday language. *He said I was yellow because I let him take the blame for what I had done.*

contrasting words: **brave**

feeling *noun*

a particular physical experience, or mental state produced through one of your senses, such as touch or hearing. *There was a **feeling** of warmth in the air as summer approached.*

sensation — A **sensation** is a particular way you feel because of the working of one or more of your senses. *He had the sensation that someone was watching him.*

awareness — An **awareness** is a feeling or knowledge coming to you through your senses. *As she watched the waves beat against the rocks she felt an awareness of the power of the ocean.*

perception — **Perception** is **awareness** or the gaining of knowledge through your senses. *His perception of a movement in the darkness outside worried him.*

impression — An **impression** can be a vague feeling or indication of something. *She had the impression that nobody was very interested in her story.*

sense — A **sense** can be any physical or mental feeling. *A sense of sadness came over us as we heard the news on the radio.*

female *noun*

a woman or a girl. *At the camp, the **females** slept in one dormitory and the males in another.*

lady — **Lady** is a polite name for a woman. *Good morning ladies and gentlemen.*

maiden — A **maiden** is a young unmarried woman. This is a rather old-fashioned word. *The gallant knight saved the pretty maiden.*

lass — A **lass** is a girl or a young woman. *The butcher says 'Good morning, lass' every time Jennifer passes his shop on her way to school.*

tomboy — A **tomboy** is an adventurous high-spirited girl. *Everyone called her a tomboy because she loved playing football.*

crone — A **crone** is an old woman. *The children liked to pretend that the crone who lived in the village was really a witch.*

contrasting words: **male**

fickle *adjective*

likely to change your mind or behaviour. *She's such a **fickle** friend I never know when she is going to be pleasant to me.*

changeable — **Changeable** means likely to change or behave differently from one occasion to another. *He's so changeable that one day he'll smile at you and the next day he'll ignore you.*

flighty — **Flighty** means often changing your mind or feelings. *She's a flighty creature and can never decide what she's going to do.*

capricious — **Capricious** means likely to change your mind without any apparent good reason. *He's so capricious I can never be sure of him.*

mercurial — **Mercurial** means rapidly changing in mood. *Jan has such a mercurial nature she can be happy one moment then suddenly become very angry.*

temperamental — **Temperamental** means moody or **changeable** in your behaviour. *We had to wait while the temperamental star decided what to wear.*

similar words: **unfaithful**
contrasting words: **reliable**

fidget *verb*

to move about restlessly and not be able to keep still. *I **fidgeted** nervously as I waited for my turn.*

squirm	To **squirm** means to move around uncomfortably or uneasily. *She squirmed with embarrassment when everyone stared at her.*
wriggle	To **wriggle** means to move or twist about because you are feeling uneasy. *We wriggled in our chairs until we heard our names called.*
writhe	To **writhe** means to twist and **squirm** because you are embarrassed or uneasy. *His loud comments that everyone could hear made me writhe.*
toss and turn	To **toss and turn** means to move about restlessly, not able to feel comfortable. *My frightening dreams made me toss and turn all night.*

fight *noun*

a violent struggle or contest. *Adrian's arm was bruised in the **fight**.*

brawl	A **brawl** is a noisy struggle or fight. *The argument developed into a brawl.*
fray	A **fray** is a noisy fight or quarrel. *When we joined the fray the whole playground was in an uproar.*
battle	A **battle** is a large-scale or serious fight. *A battle was fought between the two armies.*
combat	A **combat** is a fight or struggle. *Soldiers are trained for combat.*
skirmish	A **skirmish** is a small **battle**. *The armies met but it was only a skirmish.*

similar words: **conflict**

fight *verb*

to take part in a violent contest. *They **fought** over who owned the ball.*

struggle	To **struggle** means to fight with an enemy, usually without weapons. *He struggled with the thief.*
grapple	To **grapple** means to **struggle** or fight with someone while gripping them firmly. *The angry men grappled with each other.*
tussle	To **tussle** means to fight roughly. *The children tussled on the grass.*
scuffle	To **scuffle** means to **struggle** or fight in a confused way. *A few people in the crowd began to scuffle when the referee sent a player off.*
come to blows	To **come to blows** means to start fighting with someone. *They came to blows over whose turn it was to use the computer.*

find *verb*

to come upon something by chance or after a search. *He **found** his glasses under a chair.*

discover	To **discover** means to find, especially for the first time. *I discovered a new way home.*
locate	To **locate** means to find the place where something is. *At last I located the fault in the engine.*
unearth	To **unearth** can mean to find or uncover something by chance or after a search. *Mum unearthed a lot of old clothes that she thought she had thrown out.*
detect	To **detect** means to notice or find, especially after looking carefully. *She detected some flecks of dust on his coat.*
trace	To **trace** can mean to find by looking in an orderly way. *I had to look through the index of the book to trace the passage I wanted.*

fine *adjective*

with the sun shining, or without rain. *I'm enjoying the **fine** weather that we are having at the moment.*

sunny — **Sunny** means having plenty of sunshine. *It was a lovely sunny day before the clouds came over.*

balmy — **Balmy** means fine or pleasant. *In the balmy spring weather they were often outdoors.*

mild — **Mild** can mean not cold, severe or extreme. *Why don't we go for a walk tonight since the temperature is so mild.*

fair — **Fair** can mean bright and free from clouds as the sky can be. *The forecast was for fair weather all weekend.*

temperate — **Temperate** can mean having a moderate temperature or climate. *We didn't use the heater as much this year because it was a temperate winter.*

contrasting words: **wintry, cloudy, dreary**

finish *verb*

to bring something to a satisfactory final point. *I am trying to think of an interesting way to **finish** my story.*

end — To **end** is so similar to **finish** that you can usually use either. *The referee ended the game when two players were injured.*

close — To **close** can mean to finish something or shut it down completely or only for a short time. *She closed the meeting by thanking everyone who came.*

conclude — To **conclude** can mean to finish something or bring it to an end. *We will conclude the lesson by reading the poem.*

complete — To **complete** can mean to bring something to an end after having done everything necessary. *We completed our plans for the surprise party just in time.*

terminate — To **terminate** means to bring something to an end, often something that could have gone on further. *The severe injury to his leg terminated the dancer's career.*

contrasting words: **begin, initiate**

flat *adjective*

having a fairly regular surface which is at right angles to something that is upright. *The long, **flat** road stretched out in front of us.*

level — **Level** means having no part higher than any other part. *We found a level area of ground where we could pitch our tents.*

smooth — **Smooth** means having no bumps or lumps. *The road had only recently been built and was smooth compared with the rough track we had just left.*

even — **Even** can mean flat, **smooth** or **level**. *At the start of the test, the cricket pitch had an even surface.*

horizontal — **Horizontal** means parallel or in line with the horizon. *When you are laying paving bricks, use a horizontal piece of string as a guide.*

---

flatter *verb*

to try to please someone by complimenting or praising them even if you don't mean it. *He **flattered** me so I would invite him to the party.*

sweet-talk — To **sweet-talk** means to persuade someone to do what you want by saying very nice things to them. It is more suited to everyday language. *If we sweet-talk her enough she might take us to the circus.*

soft-soap — To **soft-soap** means to use very smooth, pleasant or insincere words to persuade someone to do what you want. It is more suited to everyday language. *We soft-soaped her until she said yes.*

butter up — To **butter up** means to flatter someone in an open and obvious way. It is more suited to everyday language. *Let's butter Mum up so she'll give us money for ice-creams.*

make up to — To **make up to** can mean to speak or behave in a very flattering way to get what you want. It is more suited to everyday language. *If we make up to Dad we might be able to buy chocolates too.*

suck up to — To **suck up to** means to behave and speak in a very insincere way so as to get what you want. It is more suited to everyday language. *We thought if we sucked up to the teacher he would let us go early.*

---

similar words: **praise**

---

flee *verb*

to run away, especially from danger. *They **fled** from the burning house.*

escape — To **escape** means to get away, especially from somewhere unpleasant or dangerous. *He escaped from prison.*

abscond — To **abscond** means to run away secretly. *The treasurer absconded with the funds.*

elope — To **elope** means to run away secretly to be married. *They didn't want a big wedding so they eloped.*

take to your heels — To **take to your heels** means to run away quickly. It is more suited to everyday language. *They took to their heels when the rain started.*

scarper — To **scarper** means to run away from someone or from a situation, usually to avoid being caught. It is more suited to everyday language. *The burglar scarpered when he heard the police car's siren.*

similar words: **leave**

flexible *adjective*

easily bent into a different shape. *I need some **flexible** wire to tie around this gate.*

pliable — **Pliable** means easily bent. It is similar to **flexible**. *Bamboo is a kind of pliable grass used for weaving baskets.*

supple — **Supple** means able to bend easily without breaking or being harmed. *An athlete needs a strong, supple body.*

malleable — **Malleable** means easily worked or moulded into a different shape. *Clay is a malleable material used by potters.*

floppy — **Floppy** means bending in a droopy way, often out of its usual shape. *My beach hat has a big, floppy brim.*

contrasting words: **hard**

flood *verb*

to supply someone with a great amount of anything. *Our neighbours **flooded** us with gifts when our house was burned down.*

swamp To **swamp** can be so similar to **flood** you can usually choose either word. *Everyone swamped us with kindness and offers of help.*

overwhelm To **overwhelm** can mean to come upon you so that you feel crushed. *Our feeling of helplessness almost overwhelmed us.*

inundate To **inundate** can mean to load or heap someone with a very large amount of something. *Orders for the new dictionary inundated the publisher because it was so good.*

smother To **smother** can mean to surround someone with too much of something. *They smothered us with toys, books and every sort of knick-knack.*

engulf To **engulf** means to surround or swallow up someone with something. *Sorrow engulfed them after their tragedy.*

flourish *verb*

to grow strongly. *The lemon tree we planted began to **flourish** after we gave it some fertiliser.*

bloom To **bloom** can mean to flourish and produce flowers. *Our rose bush blooms in summer.*

flower To **flower** means to grow flowers. It is usually used about plants, often those whose flowers form and develop into fruit or vegetables. *Our tomato plant flowered early this year.*

blossom To **blossom** can mean to produce flowers. It is usually used about trees. *Many trees blossom in the spring.*

sprout To **sprout** means to send up shoots as a seed does. *I planted some carrot seeds last week and they sprouted.*

germinate To **germinate** means to begin to grow and send up shoots. *The seeds germinated and now we can see the little green shoots above the ground.*

flow *verb*

to move along in, or as if in a current. *The river **flows** out to the sea.*

stream To **stream** means to flow steadily or continuously. *Tears streamed from his eyes.*

surge To **surge** means to rush forwards or upwards in, or as if in waves. *The heavy rain caused the river to rise and surge over its banks.*

spurt To **spurt** means to flow suddenly. *Dirty water spurted out of the tap when we turned it on.*

wash To **wash** means to flow against or over something. *The waves washed against the sides of the boat.*

gush To **gush** means to flow suddenly in large amounts. *The sea gushed through the hole the torpedo had made in the side of the ship.*

similar words: **drip**

fluctuate *verb*

to change all the time. *He **fluctuated** between yes and no until I decided for him.*

waver To **waver** means to be unsure or show doubt. *Even after he said yes he began to waver.*

vacillate To **vacillate** means to be unsure or to put off making a decision. *He vacillated right up to the moment we got on the train.*

chop and change To **chop and change** means to keep on changing your mind. *The class chopped and changed as they tried to decide what to do for the concert.*

change your tune To **change your tune** means to change your attitude or way of looking at something. *We changed our tune about joining in when we saw how much fun everyone was having.*

fluent *adjective*

able to speak easily. *My cousin is a **fluent** Italian speaker.*

articulate — **Articulate** means able to say what you mean clearly. *Mary was chosen to explain the situation because she is very articulate.*

eloquent — **Eloquent** means able to speak in a flowing, expressive manner. *She was so eloquent that I was nearly crying by the time she finished.*

silver-tongued — **Silver-tongued** means able to speak so expressively that you can persuade people easily. *That politician is successful because he is silver-tongued.*

smooth — **Smooth** can mean having a pleasant speaking manner, especially when insincere. *He tricked her with his smooth talk.*

slick — **Slick** can mean having a pleasant and clever way of talking, although insincere. It is similar to **smooth**. *He is a slick salesman.*

contrasting words: **inarticulate**

fly *verb*

to move through the air with the help of wings, wind or some other force. *The emu is a bird which cannot **fly**.*

flap — To **flap** can mean to fly by moving the wings up and down. *The colony of bats suddenly took off and flapped across the darkening sky.*

flutter — To **flutter** can mean to fly by moving the wings quickly up and down. *Brightly-coloured butterflies fluttered amongst the flowers.*

flit — To **flit** means to move lightly and quickly. *Dragonflies flitted through the long grass.*

soar — To **soar** means to fly upwards. *The aeroplane soared through the clouds into the blue sky above.*

hover — To **hover** means to stay in one spot in the air as if hanging. *Bees hovered just above the flowers collecting nectar.*

follow *verb*

to come or go after someone or something. *You go ahead and I'll **follow** you.*

pursue To **pursue** means to follow someone or something so as to catch them. *The police pursued the youths who had stolen a car.*

chase To **chase** means to follow someone or something quickly in order to catch or overtake them. *The cat chased the mouse.*

shadow To **shadow** can mean to follow someone secretly. *The police officer shadowed the suspect to find out where he was going.*

tag along To **tag along** means to follow someone especially without having been invited. *Anne's little brother tagged along with her wherever she went.*

track To **track** can mean to follow, or hunt by following, the footprints or tracks of someone or something. *The hunters tracked the tiger through the jungle.*

similar words: **seek**

food *noun*

anything that can be eaten to keep your body alive and help it grow. *My favourite **food** is fruit.*

nosh **Nosh** means food. It is more suited to everyday language. *We went to the chippy for a good nosh.*

grub **Grub** can be food. It is more suited to everyday language. *This place serves good grub.*

chow **Chow** is food. It is more suited to everyday language. *Have you had enough chow?*

provisions **Provisions** are supplies of food. *They took provisions for ten days on their camping trip.*

victuals **Victuals** are food or **provisions**. It is an old-fashioned word. *The highwaymen asked for the travellers' money and victuals.*

similar words: **meal**

force *noun*

the ability to have a strong effect or influence on something, especially a physical one. *The **force** of the wind caused a lot of damage.*

power — **Power** can be so similar to **force** that you can usually use either. *The power of his punch knocked out his opponent.*

strength — **Strength** means the quality of being strong or having great **power** or effect. *The strength of the earthquake caused huge buildings to crumble.*

might — **Might** means force or **power**. *We felt the might of the tornado as it tore great trees out of the ground.*

muscle — **Muscle** can mean **strength** or force. It is usually used about people. *You need to put some muscle into chopping up that wood.*

vigour — **Vigour** means **strength** and energy, usually of a kind that helps you do something easily or happily. *We attacked the difficult job with vigour.*

---

force *verb*

to make someone do something, often by using threats or violence. *The thief **forced** them to hand over the money.*

compel — To **compel** means to make someone do something, usually because you are more powerful and they cannot disobey you. *They can compel us to go to school.*

coerce — To **coerce** means to force someone to do something, usually with arguments or threats. *The armed thief coerced the shopkeeper to open the till.*

drive — To **drive** can mean to use a lot of effort to make yourself or someone else do something. *He always drives himself hard to get his work finished on time.*

bully — To **bully** means to hurt, frighten or order about someone who is smaller and weaker than you. *She bullied us into agreeing with her.*

bulldoze — To **bulldoze** can mean to force someone to do something without caring whether they want to or not. It is more suited to everyday language. *You can't bulldoze us into going if we don't want to.*

similar words: **threaten**

forecast *noun*

an opinion about or warning of what is going to happen in the future. *The **forecast** for tomorrow is rainy weather.*

prediction A **prediction** is similar to a **forecast** and can often be used in the same way. *She made a prediction that the school team would win this year.*

prognosis A **prognosis** is a doctor's opinion of how an illness will affect a patient. *Dr Mack's prognosis was that my sister would recover.*

omen An **omen** is a sign of something that might happen in the future. *She thought that breaking the mirror was an omen of bad luck.*

tip A **tip** is a piece of useful information about something that might happen. *He gave us a tip that you might come.*

foreign *adjective*

from a country other than your own. *We learned a **foreign** language to help us when we travelled.*

migrant **Migrant** means leaving your own country to go and live in another one. *The migrant people settled happily in their new country.*

alien **Alien** means living in a country without being a citizen of it. *The alien residents decided to become citizens.*

ethnic **Ethnic** means having to do with the customs, history or language of a particular group of people. *We saw colourful costumes from all over the world during the display of ethnic dancing.*

imported **Imported** means brought in from another country. *A lot of people buy imported cars from Japan.*

exotic **Exotic** means foreign or not belonging naturally to your own country. *Many exotic plants were brought here from other countries.*

forgive *verb*

to give up bad feelings against someone or any wish to punish them. *I will **forgive** you if you say you are sorry.*

excuse To **excuse** can mean to overlook a wrongdoing or fault. *I'll excuse your bad behaviour this time, but don't do it again.*

let off To **let off** can mean to **excuse** someone and not punish them. *I'll let you off this time but never call him rude names again.*

pardon To **pardon** can mean to forgive and not punish someone. This can be a legal word. *The Queen pardoned the prisoner who was set free immediately.*

spare To **spare** means to forgive and not harm someone you have power over. *The king spared his treacherous cousin.*

clear To **clear** can mean to free someone from blame. *The jury's verdict cleared her of guilt.*

contrasting words: **accuse**

formal *adjective*

following the proper and usual procedure. *They decided to have a **formal** wedding.*

established **Established** means done in the customary or usual way. *This is the established method of applying for a passport.*

official **Official** means properly approved or arranged. *We made an official request for a pedestrian crossing outside our school.*

ceremonial **Ceremonial** means following the proper procedure used on an important occasion. *The Queen attended the ceremonial opening of parliament.*

ritual **Ritual** means following the set procedure used on religious occasions. *The tribe believed their ritual dancing would bring rain.*

similar words: **legal**
contrasting words: **informal**

fragile *adjective*

very easily broken or damaged. *I held the **fragile** china cup very carefully and admired its fineness.*

delicate — **Delicate** means easily damaged or weakened. *I dusted everything on the shelf except the delicate glass animals.*

frail — **Frail** can mean easily destroyed or broken. *The frail lace curtain tore as we pulled it.*

brittle — **Brittle** means likely to break very easily. *We packed the brittle seashells in cottonwool to keep them safe.*

breakable — **Breakable** means easily fractured or broken into pieces. *I wiped up the saucepans while Dad dried all the breakable plates and glasses.*

---

frank *adjective*

open or not pretending in what you say. *We had a **frank** discussion about our differences of opinion.*

direct — **Direct** can mean going straight to the point. *His direct question about the financial affairs of the committee embarrassed the treasurer.*

straightforward — **Straightforward** is so similar to **direct** that you can usually use either. *He approached the situation in a straightforward manner and asked Amy what was bothering her.*

candid — **Candid** means honest and sincere. *He gave a candid answer to the judge's question.*

forthright — **Forthright** means speaking your mind openly. *He is a very forthright person and sometimes hurts people's feelings without meaning to.*

genuine — **Genuine** can mean showing real, not pretended feelings. *She was genuine in her praise of my painting.*

---

similar words: **honest**
contrasting words: **dishonest**

---

free *adjective*

not confined, restricted or limited. *In a democracy people are* ***free*** *to express their opinions.*

uninhibited	**Uninhibited** means behaving just as you like without worrying about what people think. *He was quite uninhibited about doing somersaults across the ballroom floor.*
unconventional	**Unconventional** means not doing things according to the usual or accepted ways. *It used to be unconventional for young unmarried couples to go out alone, but customs have changed.*
spontaneous	**Spontaneous** means doing things in a natural and sometimes unexpected way. *Her spontaneous smile pleased me because I didn't think she liked me.*
open	**Open** can mean doing things in a way that shows you are not hiding anything. *He was quite open about trying to take my place in the team.*
wild	**Wild** can mean not restrained or controlled. *Our parents had to stop the wild party.*

free *verb*

to set something or someone at liberty or enable them to move or act as they wish. *I want to* ***free*** *my caged parrot but it may not survive in the wild.*

release	To **release** means to set someone or something free, especially from being locked up. *The government decided to release the convicted man when new evidence was brought forward.*
liberate	To **liberate** means to set someone or something free, especially from some kind of oppression. *The army liberated the enemy-occupied town.*
emancipate	To **emancipate** means to set someone free from any kind of restraint. *Abraham Lincoln wanted to emancipate the slaves in the southern states of America.*
rescue	To **rescue** means to free someone or something from a dangerous situation, being locked up, or evil. *We told the police our plan to rescue our kidnapped friend.*
deliver	To **deliver** can mean to save someone or set them free. *The rescuers delivered me from certain death as my raft neared the waterfall.*

contrasting words: **subdue, confine, capture**

friend *noun*

someone you like and who likes you. *My **friend** and I spend our spare time together.*

playmate A **playmate** is someone you play with. *The girl next door has been my playmate since we were little.*

pal A **pal** is a good friend. This is more suited to everyday language. *Good pals do things for each other.*

mate A **mate** is a good friend. *Tim is a real mate.*

companion A **companion** is someone you go out with or travel with. *I like to go fell-walking with a companion.*

acquaintance An **acquaintance** is someone you don't know very well. *He is only an acquaintance I talk to on the bus.*

similar words: **associate**
contrasting words: **enemy**

friendly *adjective*

showing friendship or acting like a friend. *Everyone at the party was **friendly**.*

warm **Warm** can mean kind and affectionate. *They gave us a warm welcome.*

neighbourly **Neighbourly** means kind and friendly. *Mrs Jones gave some neighbourly help when my mother was sick.*

outgoing **Outgoing** means able to mix with people easily. *Outgoing people usually make friends quickly.*

sociable **Sociable** means wanting to be with other people. *Sociable people are easy to talk to.*

genial **Genial** means having a warm and friendly manner. *His genial behaviour made us all feel relaxed.*

similar words: **agreeable**
contrasting words: **unfriendly**

frighten *verb*

to fill someone with fear. *The barking dog **frightened** the baby.*

scare To **scare** means to fill someone with sudden fear. *The loud clap of thunder scared us all.*

alarm To **alarm** means to frighten someone and make them feel they are in danger. *The smell of smoke in the house alarmed me.*

petrify To **petrify** can mean to make someone unable to move because they are stiff with fear. *The snarling dog petrified me.*

terrify To **terrify** means to frighten someone very, very much. *The sound of someone trying to open the back door terrified me.*

terrorise To **terrorise** can mean to frighten someone or cause them to feel very great fear. *The burglars terrorised the old lady so much that she gave them all her money.*

similar words: **shock, threaten**
contrasting words: **pacify**

frightened *adjective*

showing or feeling fear. *The **frightened** children huddled together during the storm.*

scared **Scared** means feeling sudden fear. *The scared boys ran away from the angry man.*

afraid **Afraid** means frightened or feeling great fear. It is never used before the noun it is describing. *They were afraid of being punished.*

panicky **Panicky** means feeling so frightened that you can't think clearly or act sensibly. *The teacher calmed the panicky boys who had seen the snake.*

trembly **Trembly** means shaky and quivery with fear. *I was trembly after the accident.*

petrified **Petrified** can mean feeling so frightened that you can hardly move or do anything sensible. *The petrified children wished they hadn't gone into the haunted house.*

similar words: **nervous, fearful**
contrasting words: **calm**

frightening *adjective*

causing you to feel afraid. *The car accident was a **frightening** experience.*

scary — **Scary** means causing fear or fright. It is more suited to everyday language. *Walking along the road at night is scary.*

creepy — **Creepy** means frightening or unpleasant. *We got a creepy feeling when we found the skull in the garden.*

hairy — **Hairy** can mean very frightening. It is more suited to everyday language. *It was a hairy drive down the mountain when the brakes failed.*

grim — **Grim** can mean having such a fierce or angry appearance that it makes you feel afraid. *When we saw his grim face we knew we could expect no mercy.*

forbidding — **Forbidding** means dangerous and frightening. *The forbidding appearance of the cliff made us decide not to climb to the top.*

similar words: **horrible**

frisk *verb*

to leap around playfully, as a lamb or kitten does. *They **frisked** around joyfully in the warm, spring sunshine.*

dance — To **dance** can mean to move about quickly and lightly, usually because you are excited or happy. *We danced for joy when we heard the good news.*

caper — To **caper** means to jump or **dance** about. *They were so excited that they capered about the room.*

gambol — To **gambol** means to jump around in play. *Jean and Robert gambolled along the water's edge.*

skip — To **skip** means to jump lightly from one foot to the other. *He skipped up the path and through the open door.*

prance — To **prance** means to leap about gracefully. *The crowd cheered as the horses pranced into the ring.*

similar words: **jump**
contrasting words: **walk, limp, trudge**

frown *verb*

to wrinkle your forehead to show you are annoyed. *They stopped talking when she **frowned** at them and shook her head.*

glare — To **glare** means to give a long fierce look to show that you are angry. *He glared at them when they rudely laughed at him.*

glower — To **glower** means to look or stare in a bad-tempered way. *Paul just sat and glowered when he didn't get his own way.*

scowl — To **scowl** means to have an angry look on your face. *I scowled when she said I couldn't go.*

pout — To **pout** means to push out your lips in a sulky way. *He pouted until we gave in and let him play with us.*

contrasting words: **smile**

full *adjective*

filled up. *The milk bottle was **full**.*

crowded — **Crowded** means filled with people or objects. *We couldn't see our friends on the crowded footpath.*

packed — **Packed** means so full that no more people or things can fit in. *The pianist played to a packed hall.*

bursting — **Bursting** means very full, as if ready to break open. *The bag of apples was filled to bursting point.*

laden — **Laden** means having a full load or holding a lot. *We climbed the laden apple tree to pick the fruit while it was ripe.*

crammed — **Crammed** means stuffed tight. *Nothing else would fit into my crammed suitcase.*

contrasting words: **empty**

funny *adjective*

causing you to laugh. *We all enjoyed his **funny** stories.*

amusing — **Amusing** means causing laughter or smiles. *We watched the clown's dogs perform many amusing tricks.*

comical — **Comical** means funny, often because it is odd or unusual. *The clown's dogs were comical walking on their hind legs and wearing clothes.*

humorous — **Humorous** means funny or full of humour. *His humorous comment about being able to run as fast as a snail made us laugh.*

hilarious — **Hilarious** means very, very funny. *We had a hilarious time playing charades.*

droll — **Droll** means amusingly odd. *His droll sense of humour made us realise how funny the situation was.*

further *verb*

to help, improve or develop something. *Regular training will **further** your chances of becoming a top swimmer.*

advance — To **advance** means to develop something and make it better. *Nuclear bombs do not advance the cause of world peace.*

promote — To **promote** means to further something so that it has a better rank or position. *They promoted the new drink by putting ads on television.*

facilitate — To **facilitate** means to help or further something by making things easier. *The open window facilitated the burglar's entry into the house.*

ease — To **ease** means to help something by taking away any problems or difficulties. *Talks between the United States and the Soviet Union eased the tension between the two nations.*

similar words: **help**
contrasting words: **hinder, block**

future *adjective*

having to do with, or happening in the time which has not yet come. *Our future plans are to hire a boat for the holidays.*

prospective **Prospective** means happening in, or of the future, especially something pleasant. *We are looking forward to our prospective holiday.*

next **Next** can mean immediately following in time. *At last we could say that the holidays would begin the next day.*

imminent **Imminent** means likely to happen at any moment. *We said goodbye and boarded the plane when we knew its departure was imminent.*

impending **Impending** means near at hand or **imminent**. *Our departure was delayed by the impending arrival of another plane.*

contrasting words: **past**

gasp *verb*

to struggle for breath with your mouth open. *The people who were trapped in the smoke-filled room were **gasping** for air.*

pant To **pant** means to breathe hard and quickly because of effort or emotion. *All the runners were panting after the relay.*

wheeze To **wheeze** means to breathe with difficulty, making a whistling sound. *My brother has to stay home from school when he wheezes with asthma.*

puff To **puff** means to breathe quickly, especially after vigorous exercise. *You shouldn't be puffing after such a short run.*

blow To **blow** can mean to produce a strong current of air with your mouth. *Take a long, deep breath then blow out slowly.*

heave To **heave** can mean to breathe heavily and noisily, with a great effort. *The exhausted swimmer dragged herself to shore and heaved and gasped until she got her breath.*

gather *verb*

to bring together. *I **gathered** my belongings and put them in a bag.*

collect To **collect** means to gather things together, usually in order to keep examples of them or for a particular reason. *She collects stamps.*

accumulate To **accumulate** means to bring something together or heap it up in a large quantity. *He has accumulated a great deal of money.*

amass To **amass** means to gather things together for yourself. *By the end of his life the successful businessman had amassed a large fortune.*

pile up To **pile up** means to bring things together into a pile. *We piled the junk up outside the house ready for the refuse collection.*

rake in To **rake in** means to gather or **collect** a lot of something. *They raked in donations during the sponsored walk for the new hospital.*

similar words: **store**
contrasting words: **scatter**

gaudy *adjective*

very bright or ornate in order to attract attention. *My **gaudy** towel is very easy to find on the crowded beach.*

showy **Showy** means attracting attention in a very obvious way. *The peacock's brightly-coloured tail is very showy.*

flashy **Flashy** means bright and **showy**. *We went for a ride in the flashy red sports car.*

loud **Loud** can mean very brightly coloured, usually in an unpleasant way. *I thought his new tie was too loud.*

tawdry **Tawdry** means cheap and gaudy. *She said the glass beads I bought at the fair were too tawdry to wear.*

kitsch **Kitsch** means **showy** or gaudy in a way that you think is in bad taste. It is more suited to everyday language. *I thought the pink and yellow plastic roses were kitsch.*

similar words: **colourful, spectacular**
contrasting words: **drab, simple**

generous *adjective*

unselfish or ready to give money or gifts. ***A generous** lady has given a lot of new books to our library.*

liberal — **Liberal** is very similar to **generous.** *We were glad to receive her liberal gift.*

lavish — **Lavish** means very generous in giving. *He is lavish with his money.*

hospitable — **Hospitable** means being very welcoming and generous to strangers or your guests. *Our hospitable neighbours invited us to dinner the day we moved to our new house.*

charitable — **Charitable** means giving money or help to people who need it. *Our school collects money for charitable organisations.*

magnanimous — **Magnanimous** means unselfish and generous in a noble way. *She is too magnanimous to hold a grudge.*

similar words: **kind**
contrasting words: **mean, selfish**

genuine *adjective*

true or real. *She has a **genuine** antique grandfather clock.*

authentic — **Authentic** means genuine or known to be what it claims to be. *We saw an authentic Egyptian mummy at the museum.*

legitimate — **Legitimate** can mean true or reasonable. *He had a legitimate excuse for being late.*

factual — **Factual** means based on facts. *This book gives a factual account of life in China.*

proven — **Proven** means shown to be true or right. *It is a proven fact that worn car tyres cause accidents.*

similar words: **actual, true**
contrasting words: **fake**

get *verb*

to obtain. *I **got** full marks in my maths exam.*

gain To **gain** means to get or obtain, usually something you desire. *You will gain more confidence if you practise making the speech.*

acquire To **acquire** can mean to get as your own, usually through your own actions or effort. It is a more formal word. *She acquired a wonderful collection of paintings during her lifetime.*

win To **win** can mean to get something by making a special effort. *She won fame as a result of her courageous behaviour during the marathon.*

receive To **receive** can mean to get something or have it given to you. *He received some good books for his birthday.*

procure To **procure** means to get or obtain, especially using a lot of care or effort. *The detective procured all the evidence he needed to arrest the thief.*

similar words: **grab**
contrasting words: **give**

ghost *noun*

the spirit of someone who has died, imagined as visiting living people. *I screamed because I thought the white shape in the corner was a **ghost**.*

spectre **Spectre** is so similar to **ghost** that you can usually use either. *Shakespeare's play 'Hamlet' is about a man who is visited by the spectre of his father.*

phantom A **phantom** is a ghost or a ghostly appearance. *She wrote a story about the phantom that haunted the old house.*

spook A **spook** is a ghost. It is more suited to everyday language. *The attic is supposed to be full of spooks.*

apparition An **apparition** is something, such as a ghost, that appears in an out-of-the-ordinary way. *He fainted because he said he saw an apparition of a very old man in the mirror.*

wraith A **wraith** is the ghostlike appearance of a living person, supposed to be seen just before that person's death. *Some people thought they saw the wraith of the dying king in the palace grounds.*

gift *noun*

something that is given to you. *Our **gifts** were under the Christmas tree.*

present — A **present** is so similar to **gift** that you can usually use either. *I always give birthday presents to my brothers and sisters.*

legacy — A **legacy** is a gift of money or property made after someone's death through their will. *He left her a legacy of £500 as well as his house.*

donation — A **donation** is a gift, usually of money. *We made a donation to the fund for freedom from hunger.*

contribution — A **contribution** is a **donation** or a gift of money. *Our family made a contribution to the appeal for aid to the cyclone victims.*

alms — **Alms** are money and other gifts given to poor people. *The church collected alms for the poor.*

---

give *verb*

to hand something over freely. *We like to **give** presents at Christmas time.*

donate — To **donate** means to give something as a gift. *We donated some money to the Red Cross.*

present — To **present** means to give, especially in a formal way. *The mayor presented the prizes.*

award — To **award** means to give somebody something for merit or achievement. *The school awards prizes for pupils who do very well in a subject.*

confer — To **confer** means to give something to somebody as a gift, favour or honour. *The queen conferred a medal for bravery on the boy.*

grant — To **grant** means to give something to somebody, usually when they have asked for it. *The head teacher granted the children's request to act a play.*

contrasting words: **take, get**

give in *verb*

to admit that you are defeated. *Do you **give in** now you know you can't win?*

yield — To **yield** means to give in because you are powerless to go on. *The country yielded to the invader.*

surrender — To **surrender** means to give yourself up into someone else's power. *They surrendered when they ran out of bullets.*

capitulate — To **capitulate** means to give in without making any terms or conditions. *They capitulated after only a short battle.*

submit — To **submit** means to give in in obedience. *He finally submitted to the orders.*

succumb — To **succumb** means to give in to a stronger force. *In the end she succumbed to temptation and bought a double ice-cream.*

contrasting words: **resist**

glad *adjective*

happy about something. *I am **glad** that you have arrived safely.*

pleased — **Pleased** means happy or satisfied with something. *We are pleased that you are working hard.*

delighted — **Delighted** means very glad. *We are delighted that the holidays are starting soon.*

thrilled — **Thrilled** means so glad that you feel excited. *Her face had a thrilled expression when she heard they were going to the circus.*

tickled pink — **Tickled pink** means greatly pleased or amused. It is more suited to everyday language. *She was tickled pink by his compliments.*

similar words: **happy, joyful**
contrasting words: **sad, miserable, glum, angry, annoyed, satisfied.**

glue *noun*

a substance used to stick things together. *Buy a special hobby **glue** to stick the pieces of your model plane together.*

gum — **Gum** is a liquid glue. *Squeeze out just a little bit of gum and spread it over the whole surface with a brush.*

paste — **Paste** is a mixture of flour and water used for sticking paper onto another surface. *Make up some paste so you can put these pictures in your scrap book.*

adhesive — An **adhesive** is any substance used for sticking things together. *What's the best adhesive for mending this broken chair leg?*

cement — **Cement** is a soft substance that hardens or sets to join or bind things together very strongly. *I'll need some special cement to stick these broken tiles back together.*

mortar — **Mortar** is the special mixture used for joining bricks together. *If you don't use enough mortar the bricks won't stick firmly and the wall will fall down.*

gluey *adjective*

sticky like glue. *I didn't cook the toffee properly and instead of being brittle, it was all **gluey.***

thick — **Thick** can mean not runny or pouring easily. *We whipped the cream until it was thick enough to pile onto the cake.*

gelatinous — **Gelatinous** means jelly-like. *The gelatinous mass on the beach was the body of a dead jellyfish.*

viscous — **Viscous** means sticky and **thick**. *I took the treacle from the refrigerator and tried to spread the viscous fluid on my bread.*

mucous — **Mucous** means consisting of the thick liquid which builds up in your nose and throat when you have a cold. *A mucous secretion clogged the asthmatic child's bronchial tubes.*

slimy — **Slimy** means unpleasantly wet and slippery. *There was slimy, green scum on top of the boggy ground.*

similar words: **liquid**

glum *adjective*

unhappy or depressed. *After trying so hard he was really **glum** when he failed.*

moody	**Moody** means angry or unhappy. *She was moody because her parents criticised her so much.*
sullen	**Sullen** means angry, silent and ill-mannered. *He is sullen because he was accused of cheating.*
surly	**Surly** means unfriendly and bad-tempered. *Nobody was friendly to him because of his surly manner.*
morose	**Morose** means bad-tempered or unfriendly because you are unhappy. *It was hard for him not to be morose when everything was going wrong.*
gloomy	**Gloomy** can mean feeling unhappy or depressed. *I'm gloomy today because I forgot my lunch.*

similar words: **sad, miserable**
contrasting words: **happy, joyful, glad**

good *adjective*

of a high standard or worthy of praise. *This is a **good** piece of work.*

satisfactory	**Satisfactory** means good enough to meet your requirements. *He gave a satisfactory answer.*
fine	**Fine** can mean very good or of a high quality. *He's a fine musician.*
first rate	**First rate** means very high standard. *We saw a first rate film at the cinema the other day.*
terrific	**Terrific** means very enjoyable. It is more suited to everyday language. *That was a terrific party last night!*

similar words: **great, excellent, nice, best**
contrasting words: **bad, nasty**

gossip *noun*

silly or unkind chatter about another person's business. *There was a lot of **gossip** going around the school about the new teacher.*

talk — **Talk** can be so similar to **gossip** that you can usually use either word. *The new girl's love-life was the talk of the school.*

rumour — A **rumour** is a story that is widely spread, without any proof as to the facts. *Are the rumours true about your leaving school next year?*

hearsay — **Hearsay** is so similar to **rumour** that you can usually use either word. *The story that the headmistress was leaving at the end of term was just hearsay.*

whisper — A **whisper** can mean a **rumour** or private information. *I heard a whisper that we might be having a spelling test next week.*

similar words: **information**

grab *verb*

to take something suddenly. *Don't **grab** the ball before it's your turn.*

seize — To **seize** means to take hold of something suddenly or by force. *She seized my pencils and wouldn't give them back.*

snatch — To **snatch** means to take hold of something suddenly or rudely. *The thief snatched my purse as I walked down the crowded street.*

snap up — To **snap up** means to grab something quickly. *The shoppers snapped up the bargains at department store sales.*

nab — To nab means to catch or **seize** someone suddenly. It is more suited to everyday language. *My father nabbed me as I was trying to sneak off to play.*

nail — To **nail** can mean to catch or seize someone, usually a criminal. It is more suited to everyday language. *'We've nailed you!' said the police as they burst into the criminals' hide-out.*

similar words: **take, capture**

grade *noun*

a particular position on a scale of standing, status, quality or value. *Her work is of the highest **grade**.*

step — A **step** can be a particular position or degree on a scale. *We must all understand the first step before we can learn anything new.*

stage — A **stage** is a single **step** on a scale or in a particular process. *Now we are ready to go on to the next stage.*

level — A **level** is one person's position on a scale compared with other people's positions. *She has a job at the top level of the company.*

rank — A **rank** can be an official position or grade. *He reached the rank of colonel before the war ended.*

class — **Class** can be someone's place in society, judged by their possessions or their family. *Since my grandfather started a factory our family has been part of the middle class.*

grand *adjective*

fine, splendid or important. *The royal wedding made a **grand** spectacle.*

lofty — **Lofty** can mean very noble or high in character. *I wish everyone had her lofty ideals.*

dignified — **Dignified** means showing nobleness of mind or character. *Her dignified conduct when she lost the race inspired us.*

lordly — **Lordly** means making a noble appearance or show. *The crowd cheered the king's lordly entrance into the room after his coronation.*

majestic — **Majestic** can mean great or impressive in appearance. *The majestic view left them speechless.*

stately — **Stately** means looking formal, grand or **majestic**. *We couldn't stop staring at the stately procession which moved majestically through the streets.*

similar words: **important, distinguished**
contrasting words: **humble**

grateful *adjective*

feeling or showing gratitude or thanks. *Mum said she was* ***grateful*** *that I cooked dinner when she was sick.*

thankful — **Thankful** means feeling or showing thanks to someone who has been kind. It is very similar to **grateful.** *I was thankful when David offered to drive me home when it was raining.*

appreciative — **Appreciative** means showing or feeling appreciation or gratitude. *Colin was most appreciative of Ian's offer to help him paint the house.*

obliged — **Obliged** means feeling under an obligation because of a kindness which has been shown. *I am obliged to you for lending me your car while mine is being repaired.*

indebted — **Indebted** means feeling that you owe a great debt of gratitude for help, a favour or the like. *I am indebted to you for looking after the baby when I had to go to work.*

beholden — **Beholden** means bound to feel grateful or **indebted**. It is a very old-fashioned word. *Pam never accepts help because she hates to be beholden to anybody.*

contrasting words: **ungrateful**

great *adjective*

very good or fine. When **great** is used this way it is more suited to everyday language. *We had a* ***great*** *time at the party.*

ace — **Ace** can mean first-rate or outstanding. *He's an ace racing driver.*

splendid — **Splendid** means extremely good. *The orchestra gave a splendid performance.*

superb — **Superb** is so similar to **splendid** that you can usually use either. *The meal was superb. She is a superb cook.*

super — **Super** means extremely good or pleasing. It is more suited to everyday language. *We had a super holiday at the beach.*

similar words: **good, excellent, best**
contrasting words: **bad, nasty**

greedy *adjective*

wanting an unreasonable amount of something, especially food or money. *Those **greedy** children ate all my chocolates.*

grasping — **Grasping** means wanting much more than you are entitled to. *The grasping landlord said he was going to raise the rent.*

avaricious — **Avaricious** means greedy for money. *The avaricious boss underpaid his workers.*

rapacious — **Rapacious** means taking things from other people in a greedy and violent way. *The rapacious outlaw robbed the villagers and burnt their houses.*

insatiable — **Insatiable** means never being satisfied with what you have. *The politician had an insatiable desire for power.*

voracious — **Voracious** means eager or greedy for something, especially food. *I have a voracious appetite when I come home from school.*

contrasting words: **satisfied**

green *adjective*

of the colour of growing leaves and grass. *Sheep and cattle grazed along the lush, **green** banks of the river.*

emerald — **Emerald** means having a clear, bright green colour. *The dewy emerald fields glistened in the sun.*

lime — **Lime** means having a greenish-yellow colour. *We mixed some yellow and green together to make a lime paint for the kitchen.*

hazel — **Hazel** means having a greenish-brown colour. *He stared at me through his large, hazel eyes.*

olive — **Olive** means having a dull brownish-green colour. *We recognised the army trucks by their olive colour.*

turquoise — **Turquoise** means having a bright greenish-blue colour. *The peacock displayed the beautiful turquoise feathers in his tail.*

grey *adjective*

of a colour between black and white. *We looked at the **grey** sky and knew there would be a storm.*

charcoal — **Charcoal** means of a very dark grey which is almost black. *After the bushfire the tree trunks had turned a charcoal colour.*

slate — **Slate** means of a dull, dark, bluish-grey. *The paint we chose was a slate colour to match the tiles on the roof.*

silver — **Silver** means of a shiny whitish-grey colour. *The snail left a silver trail on the grass.*

steel — **Steel** means of a dark bluish-grey colour with a metallic look. *Our new car is a shiny steel colour.*

grieve *verb*

to feel very sad because you have suffered some sorrow. *I **grieved** for our broken friendship.*

mourn — To **mourn** can mean to grieve or express sorrow because someone you love has died. *He mourned for a long time after his wife died.*

lament — To **lament** means to feel or express deep sorrow or grief. *She lamented over the disappearance of her new kitten.*

pine away — To **pine away** means to become sick from grief and longing. *She has been pining away since her pet dog died.*

brood — To **brood** can mean to worry or think moodily about something. *He brooded for a long time after they said such hurtful things to him.*

mope — To **mope** means to be sunk in an unhappy mood. *He has moped ever since he was dropped from the team.*

contrasting words: **rejoice**

groove *noun*

a long narrow cut or hollow, especially one made by a tool. *There is a **groove** in my desk for my pencils.*

rut A **rut** is a groove made in the ground. *The whirling wheels of the bogged down car made deep ruts.*

furrow A **furrow** is a groove, especially one made in the earth by a plough. *The farmer planted his wheat in the furrows.*

ditch A **ditch** is a long narrow hollow dug in the earth. *I fell off my bicycle into the muddy ditch by the side of the road.*

channel A **channel** can be a **ditch** dug for water to flow through. *Farmers pump water from irrigation channels to water their crops.*

trench A **trench** is a deep **ditch,** especially one dug by soldiers to protect themselves from the enemy. *The soldiers in the trenches fired at the approaching enemy.*

group *noun*

a number of people connected in some way and sometimes gathered together. *He has a large **group** of friends.*

bunch A **bunch** can be a group of people. It is more suited to everyday language. *She is one of our bunch.*

gang A **gang** is a group of people acting together. *They were robbed by a gang of outlaws.*

band A **band** is a group of people organised to act together. It is similar to **gang**. *Robin Hood had a band of merry men.*

troop A **troop** is an organised group of people. It is similar to both **gang** and **band**. *John went on a camp with his Scout troop.*

huddle A **huddle** is a small group of people crowded together to discuss something in private. *The huddle of friends whispered together in a corner.*

similar words: **crowd, club**

grumpy *adjective*

bad-tempered. *I'm always **grumpy** when I wake up in the mornings.*

cross — **Cross** means annoyed or slightly angry about something. *I'm cross if someone else is in the bathroom when I want to use it.*

irritable — **Irritable** means easily annoyed. *I'm irritable until I've eaten my breakfast.*

snappy — **Snappy** means speaking angrily or sharply. *The shopkeeper was snappy with the customer who was always complaining.*

crotchety — **Crotchety** means bad-tempered or **irritable.** *The crotchety old man next door wouldn't let me go in to get my ball when it went over his fence.*

petulant — **Petulant** means showing impatient annoyance, especially over something unimportant. *She gave a petulant toss of her head when her pencil broke.*

similar words: **annoyed, touchy, angry**
contrasting words: **happy**

halt *noun*

a stop, especially a temporary one. *The union leaders called a **halt** to the work.*

stoppage — A **stoppage** is a situation or time during which everything has stopped. *Cargo could not be unloaded from the ships because of the stoppage at the wharf.*

stalemate — A **stalemate** is a situation where no progress can be made. *The government and the unions have reached a stalemate in the dispute.*

deadlock — A **deadlock** is the point in an argument when neither side will give way. *Brian and Jenny have reached a deadlock over who is going to use the car tonight.*

standstill — A **standstill** is a stopping, especially of work or movement. *Work came to a standstill in the factory during the electricity workers' strike.*

happen *verb*

to take place. *The accident **happened** just as we were leaving home.*

occur — To **occur** is so similar to **happen** that you can usually use either word. *The incident occurred yesterday.*

arise — To **arise** means to happen or to come into being. *The problem arose when they couldn't find the map showing them how to get there.*

transpire — To **transpire** can mean to happen or take place. *It transpired that the goat had eaten the map.*

come about — To **come about** means to **occur** or to happen in the due course of time. *It came about that after a hundred years a prince kissed Sleeping Beauty and she awoke from her long sleep.*

fall — To **fall** can mean to happen or take place. *My birthday falls on a Monday this year.*

happiness *noun*

pleasure, contentment or gladness. *The children's **happiness** was complete when they were given a puppy.*

merriment — **Merriment** is happiness mixed with laughter. *The house was filled with sounds of merriment.*

mirth — **Mirth** is amusement and laughter, such as is caused by something silly. *The audience rocked with mirth at the clowns' tricks.*

high spirits — **High spirits** is a very happy mood. *We went to the party in high spirits.*

gaiety — **Gaiety** is cheerfulness or **high spirits**. *We enjoyed looking at the scenes of gaiety during the street carnival.*

glee — **Glee** is a feeling of joy. *We set out for the beach with glee.*

contrasting words: **misery**

happy *adjective*

delighted, pleased or glad about something. *I was very **happy** when he invited me to the disco.*

cheerful — **Cheerful** means happy and full of high spirits. *She is a cheerful person to be with.*

merry — **Merry** means happy and laughing. *We were a merry group as we hiked along.*

jolly — **Jolly** means good-humoured and full of fun. *The bus driver was a jolly man who made us laugh a lot.*

blithe — **Blithe** means happy or **cheerful**. *He was blithe and gay as he walked along in the sunshine.*

gleeful — **Gleeful** means very happy or full of joy. *They were gleeful at the thought of the long summer holidays.*

similar words: **joyful, glad**
contrasting words: **sad, miserable, glum, solemn**

hard *adjective*

solid and not able to be pushed out of shape. *Rocks and wood are **hard**.*

stiff — **Stiff** means hard or not easily bent. *The stiff cardboard armour of my fancy dress costume was uncomfortable.*

firm — **Firm** means solid, hard or **stiff**. *I like to sleep on a firm mattress.*

rigid — **Rigid** means not able to be bent or moved. *The tent pole was rigid and withstood the strong winds of the storm.*

tough — **Tough** means not easily broken or cut. *The vines growing in the forest were so tough that we couldn't hack our way through them.*

contrasting words: **soft, flexible**

harden *verb*

to become solid or firm to touch. *The icing on the cake had to **harden** before we could cut it.*

set — To **set** means to become hard or solid. *The jelly has set in time for dinner.*

stiffen — To **stiffen** means to become so hard and firm that it is not easily bent. *The napkins have stiffened with all that starch you used.*

solidify — To **solidify** means to become firm or solid right through. *The molten metal solidified as it cooled.*

petrify — To **petrify** can mean to become changed into stone or something like stone. *It took millions of years for the dinosaur's skeletons to petrify.*

freeze — To **freeze** can mean to become hard by being exposed to very low temperatures. *The iceblocks took a long time to freeze in the refrigerator.*

contrasting words: **soften**

hardy *adjective*

able to stand up to rough treatment or conditions. *A brick fence is more **hardy** than a wooden one.*

durable — **Durable** means lasting for a long time. *School clothes should be made of durable material.*

sturdy — **Sturdy** means strong and able to stand up to rough use. *Use this sturdy spade.*

tough — **Tough** can mean not easily broken or damaged by bad conditions. *They tied up the boat with a tough rope.*

heavy-duty — **Heavy-duty** means strong and designed for heavy use. *A heavy-duty battery will last you much longer than an ordinary one.*

rugged — **Rugged** can mean hardy and strong in your body. *We admired the rugged mountain climber.*

similar words: **strong**
contrasting words: **weak**

hate *verb*

to regard something or someone with strong dislike. *I **hate** washing the dishes.*

detest To **detest** means to dislike something or someone intensely. *I detest the smell of rotten egg gas.*

loathe To **loathe** means to feel strong opposition, hatred or distaste for something or someone. *I loathe having to tidy my room.*

despise To **despise** means to look down on someone or something, especially with hate or scorn. *They despised him for not daring to face the enemy.*

abhor To **abhor** means to think of something or someone with disgust and hatred. *I abhor cruelty to animals.*

abominate To **abominate** means to regard something or someone with great hate or disgust. It is very similar to **abhor**. *I abominate the way Adolf Hitler treated the Jews during World War II.*

contrasting words: **love, worship**

healthy *adjective*

free from disease or sickness. ***Healthy** children have lots of energy.*

well **Well** means in good health. *Now that I've had a holiday I'm well again.*

fine **Fine** is so similar to **well** that you can usually use either. *She was in hospital last week but is fine now.*

sound **Sound** means healthy or in good condition. *Even though Grandpa is 96 his heart is sound.*

fit **Fit** can mean strong and healthy. *He is very fit after the weekend training camp.*

robust **Robust** means strong, healthy and hardy. *They chose only the most robust mountaineers to climb Mount Everest.*

contrasting words: **sick**

heathen *noun*

someone who does not believe in the God of the Bible. *Christian missionaries went to the Pacific Islands to convert the* ***heathens****.*

atheist An **atheist** is someone who believes there is no God. *The atheists were married in a registry office.*

agnostic An **agnostic** is someone who believes that you can't know anything about God. *The minister tried to convince the agnostic that Jesus was the Son of God.*

pagan A **pagan** is someone who does not follow one of the main religions of the world. *The witchdoctor of the African pagans frightened them with stories of evil spirits.*

infidel An **infidel** is someone who doesn't accept a particular religious faith. *Some Muslims regard Christians as infidels.*

heavy *adjective*

hard to lift or carry. *The piano was so* ***heavy*** *that three men had to move it for us.*

weighty **Weighty** means heavy or having considerable weight. *Your suitcase is rather weighty — what have you got in it!*

hefty **Hefty** means big, strong and heavy. It is more suited to everyday language. *The football players were all hefty young men.*

solid **Solid** can mean heavy or not flimsy, slight or light. *She's a solid child and I can't carry her now.*

stodgy **Stodgy** means thick and heavy as food can be. *I'm afraid this cake is too stodgy to eat.*

ponderous **Ponderous** means large and heavy. *He's a ponderous dog and can't move quickly.*

similar words: **stocky**
contrasting words: **light**

help *noun*

support, or something that makes what you have to do easier. *Keep hanging on because **help** is on its way.*

assistance — **Assistance** is support or help. *The Royal National Institute for the Blind gives assistance to blind people.*

aid — **Aid** is so similar to **help** and **assistance** that you can usually use any one of these. *The government sends aid to the developing countries of the world.*

relief — **Relief** can be freedom or release from pain, unhappiness or worry. *The volunteers provided some relief for the overworked nurses.*

charity — **Charity** can be help or **aid** given to people who need it. *When the man offered the poor people some money, they said that they didn't need his charity.*

backing — **Backing** means support of any kind, such as money made available to help a project. *Is the sportwear company going to give you their backing?*

help *verb*

to do something with someone so that it is done more easily. *Will you **help** me with my homework please?*

assist — To **assist** means to help someone do something, often in a time of trouble. *She assisted me when I lost my job.*

aid — To **aid** means to help or to make something easier for someone. *Studying will aid you in your exams.*

oblige — To **oblige** means to help by doing someone a favour. *Please oblige me by giving me a lift home.*

support — To **support** means to give help, strength or courage to someone. *He supported her with kindness and advice when she failed the exam.*

nurse — To **nurse** can mean to help something or someone by looking after it carefully. *She nursed the seedlings until they were big enough to plant in the garden.*

similar words: **befriend, further**
contrasting words: **hinder**

helper *noun*

someone who does something with you so that it is done more easily. *I need three **helpers** to set out the paints.*

assistant An **assistant** is someone who helps another person, especially one in a more important position or job. *The scientist hired an assistant to do some of the experiments.*

aide An **aide** is a personal helper or **assistant**, especially to an important official such as an army officer or a governor. *The general's aide handed out the new orders.*

colleague A **colleague** is a fellow worker who is equal or almost equal in rank to you. *When I am very busy I ask my colleague to stand in for me.*

deputy A **deputy** is a person chosen to assist, or act for another person. *We elected a deputy to help the director and to take over when she is away.*

attendant An **attendant** is someone who helps or looks after someone else. *The attendant at the door will show you to your seats.*

similar words: **associate, friend**

helpful *adjective*

willing to help or support someone. *Thanks for being so **helpful** and clearing the table.*

useful **Useful** means of use or service to someone or something. *Tidying your bedroom would be a useful thing to do.*

cooperative **Cooperative** means showing a desire to be helpful. *He was always so cooperative at his grandparent's place but he never helps anyone at home.*

obliging **Obliging** means willing to do someone a favour or be of service. *The shop assistant was most obliging and showed us lots of shoes to choose from.*

accommodating **Accommodating** means easy to deal with. *The bank clerk was most accommodating when I opened my account.*

supportive **Supportive** means giving help, strength and encouragement to someone else. *My friends were very supportive when I was unhappy.*

hermit *noun*

someone who lives alone and keeps away from other people. *The **hermit** came out of the forest once a month for his supplies.*

recluse A **recluse** is someone who lives alone and doesn't mix with other people. *After her husband died she became a recluse and never left her house.*

loner A **loner** is someone who doesn't like being with other people. *He was such a loner that no-one remembered to invite him to their parties.*

introvert An **introvert** is someone who is mainly interested in their own thoughts and feelings. *She did not make many friends because she was an introvert.*

monk A **monk** is a member of a religious group of men living apart from the rest of the world. *The monks lived in the monastery and spent their days praying and working in the grounds.*

hide *verb*

to keep something from being seen or discovered. *He knew he had to **hide** the disaster from his parents.*

conceal To **conceal** means to hide something or keep it out of sight. *She concealed the present at the top of her cupboard.*

cover To **cover** can mean to put something on or over a thing in order to hide it. *She covered her face with her hands so we couldn't see her tears.*

disguise To **disguise** means to try to hide your true identity, or the way something really is by changing your appearance, or making it seem different. *I disguised myself by wearing a wig. She tried to disguise her anger by smiling sweetly.*

mask To **mask** means to hide or **disguise** something. *We laughed and joked to mask our annoyance at her rude comment.*

camouflage To **camouflage** can mean to do something that you hope will hide or **disguise** the way things really are. *He had left his radio on to camouflage his absence from the room.*

contrasting words: **show, reveal**

high-pitched *adjective*

played, sung or spoken at a high pitch of sound. *It annoys me when my brother's digital watch makes a **high-pitched** beep every hour.*

shrill — **Shrill** means loud and high-pitched. *We could hear her shrill voice as she played in the backyard with the puppy.*

high — **High** can mean sharp in sound. *I can't sing the very high notes in that song.*

treble — **Treble** means of the highest pitch or range when referring to a voice part, singer or instrument. *I'll play the treble recorder and you can play the alto one.*

soprano — **Soprano** means of the range of notes which can be sung by a woman or boy with a high voice. *She sang in the soprano section of the choir.*

falsetto — **Falsetto** means very high-pitched. *The man used a falsetto voice when he pretended to make the puppet speak.*

hinder *verb*

to slow down something or make it difficult. *My sore leg hindered my efforts to run.*

hamper — To **hamper** means to hold back or hinder something or someone. *The loose wheel hampered his progress in the bike race.*

frustrate — To **frustrate** means to hinder or stop someone or something by putting difficulties in their way. *We wanted to arrive early but the traffic jam frustrated us.*

retard — To **retard** means to hinder something or someone slowing it down. *The muddy road retarded our progress.*

impede — To **impede** means to slow down or block the way of something or someone. *The demonstration impeded the traffic.*

inhibit — To **inhibit** means to hold back or control something or someone. *Black plastic spread over your garden should inhibit the growth of weeds.*

similar words: **prevent, block, interrupt**
contrasting words: **further, help**

hint *verb*

to make a roundabout or indirect suggestion. *She **hinted** she'd like to come to my party.*

suggest — To **suggest** can mean to hint, or give the idea of something indirectly. *I think his appearance suggests a serious illness.*

insinuate — To **insinuate** means to **suggest** something unpleasant without saying so outright. *I was angry when he insinuated I had cheated.*

imply — To **imply** means to **suggest** something without actually stating it. *She didn't look friendly but the tone of her voice implied it.*

allude to — To **allude to** means to refer casually to something. *He alluded to the book he had just read.*

hit *verb*

to give a hard blow to someone or something. *He **hit** the nail with a hammer.*

strike — To **strike** means to hit or give a blow to something or someone. *Strike the ball with the middle of the bat.*

knock — To **knock** can mean to bump or **strike** something. *She knocked his hat off his head.*

bat — To **bat** means to hit something with, or as if with a bat. *She batted the ball over the fence.*

clip — To **clip** can mean to give someone a short sharp hit. *He clipped his attacker on the jaw.*

tap — To **tap** means to hit something or someone lightly. *We tapped the wall to find the secret cupboard.*

similar words: **beat**

hold *verb*

to have or keep something in your hands or arms. *I **held** the books while she put them on the shelf.*

grip — To **grip** means to hold something very firmly or strongly. *The abseilers gripped the rope tightly as they climbed down the cliff.*

grasp — To **grasp** means to **seize** something or hold it firmly in your hands. *I grasped the railing to stop myself falling.*

clutch — To **clutch** means to hold or grip something tightly in your hands. *She clutched her father's hand as they crossed the busy street.*

clasp — To **clasp** means to take a firm hold of something. *He clasped his teddy bear tightly and wouldn't let me hold it.*

cling to — To **cling to** means to hold tightly to something. *The frightened little boy clung to his father's hand.*

similar words: **hug, grab**

hole *noun*

an opening in or through something. *Do you think this **hole** in the cliff is an entrance to a cave?*

gap — A **gap** is a break or opening in something. *Here's a small gap in the fence that we can crawl through.*

slit — A **slit** can be a straight narrow opening. *There was a slit in the top of the money box to push the coins through.*

perforation — A **perforation** is a hole punched or pierced through something. *I made some perforations in the top of the box so the silkworms could breathe.*

chink — A **chink** can be a narrow opening in something. *I could just slip my fingers through the chink in the wall.*

aperture — An **aperture** can be any hole or opening.It is often used about the opening in a camera that limits the amount of light entering the lens. *We squeezed through the narrow aperture in the rocks.*

similar words: **break, cut**

holy *adjective*

set apart for, or dedicated to God. *Easter is a **holy** festival for Christians.*

sacred — **Sacred** means holy or worthy of religious respect. *The Koran is the sacred book of the Muslims.*

hallowed — **Hallowed** means regarded or honoured as holy. *Some religions don't allow suicide victims to be buried in hallowed ground.*

blessed — **Blessed** means set apart as holy. *Many Christian hymns refer to 'the blessed name of Jesus'.*

saintly — **Saintly** means like or suited to a saint. *The parson praised the woman for her saintly acts of compassion.*

similar words: **religious**
contrasting words: **sacrilegious**

homicide *noun*

the crime of killing someone on purpose. *All the members of the gang were charged with **homicide** when the guard was killed during the robbery.*

manslaughter — **Manslaughter** is the accidental killing of someone. *The car driver was convicted of manslaughter when he killed a pedestrian on a crossing.*

capital punishment — **Capital punishment** is punishment by death, usually of a criminal who has committed a very serious crime. *The sentence of capital punishment is not used in Great Britain today.*

euthanasia — **Euthanasia** is the act of helping someone to die, or letting them die when they want to, usually because their pain or suffering is too great to bear. *Euthanasia is not lawful in Great Britain.*

suicide — **Suicide** is the act of killing yourself deliberately. *She committed suicide in a state of depression after she was crippled.*

harakiri — **Harakiri** is the national form of honourable **suicide** in Japan, formerly used by the higher classes of Japanese people when they were disgraced or sentenced to death. *The general committed harakiri after being defeated in battle.*

honest *adjective*

truthful, fair and honourable. *If you are always **honest** people will know they can trust you.*

truthful	**Truthful** means showing you can be relied on to tell the truth. *I don't doubt his story as he is always truthful.*
honourable	**Honourable** means acting with high principles and honesty. *I believe what you say because you are an honourable person.*
upright	**Upright** means honest and just. *That policeman is an upright man whom we all respect.*
sincere	**Sincere** means expressing true and honest feelings. *Her sincere compliment pleased me.*
scrupulous	**Scrupulous** means being very strict about doing what is right. *He was scrupulous in his dealings with his customers.*

similar words: **frank, decent**
contrasting words: **dishonest, cunning**

horrible *adjective*

causing a strong feeling of fear and disgust. *We couldn't bear to look at the **horrible** accident.*

dreadful	**Dreadful** means causing great fear or terror. *They spent a dreadful night when the cyclone struck the town.*
horrendous	**Horrendous** means horrible and **dreadful.** *He never recovered from the horrendous sight of his house burning down.*
terrible	**Terrible** means causing great fear. *In my nightmare a terrible giant was chasing me.*
frightful	**Frightful** means alarming and unpleasant. *They had a frightful time trying to cross the flooded river.*

similar words: **nasty, frightening**
contrasting words: **nice**

hot *adjective*

having a high temperature or giving out heat. *Don't touch the stove because it's very **hot**.*

blazing — **Blazing** means very hot or burning fiercely. *The blazing fire soon warmed the whole room.*

sweltering — **Sweltering** can mean causing you to feel very hot and damp with perspiration. *We were glad of the air-conditioning on that sweltering day.*

fiery — **Fiery** can mean like fire. *A blast of fiery heat hit me as I opened the door.*

tepid — **Tepid** means lukewarm or slightly warm. *I can't drink that tea because it's tepid now.*

warm — **Warm** means having some heat that can be felt. *Are you warm enough or shall I put the heater on?*

similar words: **humid**
contrasting words: **cold, wintry**

hug *verb*

to put your arms tightly around someone in order to show your affection for them. *I **hugged** my father when I went home.*

cuddle — To **cuddle** means to hug someone gently. *My mother cuddles me if I am hurt or unhappy.*

embrace — To **embrace** means to hug someone or hold them in your arms. This is a more formal word. *The two sisters embraced each other after their long separation.*

nurse — To **nurse** can mean to hold someone lovingly and gently in your arms, especially a baby. *I nursed my baby sister before putting her in her pram.*

cradle — To **cradle** means to hold someone or something and rock them gently, especially a baby. *The mother cradled her sick baby in her arms.*

press — To **press** can mean to hug someone tightly or hold them close to you. *He pressed her to him and begged her never to leave him.*

similar words: **hold**

huge *adjective*

very, very large or immense. *We couldn't even see the top of the **huge** mountain.*

gigantic — **Gigantic** means extremely large or huge. *The gigantic man towered over everyone else.*

colossal — **Colossal** means huge or of extremely great size. *There was a colossal pile of dishes to wash up after my party.*

enormous — **Enormous** means much larger than usual. *It was an enormous house with more rooms than I had ever seen.*

massive — **Massive** means large, heavy and often quite bulky. *The huge tractor pulled a massive load of logs with ease.*

vast — **Vast** means huge or of very great area, bulk or size. *The Antarctic is a vast region of ice and snow.*

similar words: **big, heavy**
contrasting words: **small**

humble *adjective*

being aware of your weaknesses and having a low opinion of your own importance or abilities. *She was too **humble** to try out for a part in the class play.*

modest — **Modest** means having a moderate opinion of yourself and your abilities. *We were surprised at the modest behaviour of such a famous actress.*

meek — **Meek** means being obedient and patient in a humble way, even though you are treated badly. *The boy was so meek that he obeyed all the unfair orders we gave him.*

self-effacing — **Self-effacing** means keeping yourself in the background because you feel humble. *She was so self-effacing no-one even noticed she was there.*

lowly — **Lowly** means being humbly obedient and not having a high opinion of your abilities. *I can't give you any advice because I'm only a lowly servant.*

contrasting words: **proud, pompous, conceited, grand**

humid *adjective*

moist and damp, especially when it's also warm. *We perspired a lot in the **humid** weather.*

muggy	**Muggy** means unpleasantly warm and humid. *The air was very muggy as we walked through the rainforest.*
sultry	**Sultry** means unpleasantly hot and humid. *It was sultry before the thunderstorm.*
close	**Close** can mean lacking fresh air. *The room was close and someone fainted.*
oppressive	**Oppressive** can mean causing discomfort because it is so great. *The heat was so oppressive we couldn't do any work outside.*

similar words: **hot**

hurry *verb*

to act quickly to save time. ***Hurry** or you'll miss the bus.*

dash	To **dash** means to move very quickly and suddenly. *I dashed into the lift just before the doors closed.*
rush	To **rush** means to move very quickly or to do something in a great hurry. *Sally rushed to finish her dinner so she could go out to play.*
hasten	To **hasten** means to move or act quickly. *He hastened to catch her before she fell.*
shake a leg	To **shake a leg** means to hurry as fast as your legs will carry you. This is more suited to everyday language. *If you don't shake a leg Tessa will leave without you.*
get a move on	To **get a move on** means to hurry up. This is more suited to everyday language. *Get a move on or you won't finish in time!*

similar words: **speed, dart**
contrasting words: **dawdle, walk**

hurt *verb*

to cause pain or damage to someone or something. *He **hurt** his hand in the accident.*

harm To **harm** means to hurt or damage someone or something. It is mostly used when there has been a danger of some hurt or damage, but it hasn't happened. *The hijacker did not harm his hostages.*

injure To **injure** means to hurt a living thing, especially a person or animal. *The falling rocks injured the climbers.*

wound To **wound** means to hurt someone, using a weapon of some kind. *She fired at the escaping prisoner but only wounded him.*

maim To **maim** means to cause an injury to someone, especially to an arm or leg. *The accident maimed him for life.*

mutilate To **mutilate** means to injure someone or something or disfigure them very badly. *The accident mutilated her hand so badly she needed plastic surgery.*

similar words: **damage**

ignorant *adjective*

knowing little or nothing. *He was quite **ignorant** before I started teaching him.*

uneducated **Uneducated** means not having been taught or instructed. *He's completely uneducated and can't even write.*

illiterate **Illiterate** means unable to read or write. *The government runs classes to teach illiterate people the skills they lack.*

innumerate **Innumerate** means not knowing the basic rules of maths. *People who are innumerate find it hard to understand calculators.*

backward **Backward** can mean behind the others in the ability to learn. *Pupils who are backward often just need a little extra help.*

similar words: **stupid**
contrasting words: **educated**

illegal *adjective*

not allowed by law. *Smoking in theatres is **illegal**.*

illicit — **Illicit** means unlawful or not having permission to operate. *The police raided the illicit gambling house.*

criminal — **Criminal** means having to do with crime. *His criminal activities soon became known to the police.*

felonious — **Felonious** means having to do with a serious crime, such as murder or burglary. *He was jailed for his felonious assault on the security guard.*

fraudulent — **Fraudulent** means having to do with deliberate trickery or cheating. *The manager discovered his bookkeeper's fraudulent attempt to fake the accounts.*

contraband — **Contraband** means having to do with goods that have been imported or exported illegally. *The woman was fined for trying to smuggle contraband radios into Britain.*

similar words: **dishonest**
contrasting words: **legal**

imaginary *adjective*

existing only in your mind. *When everyone else is busy I play with my **imaginary** friend.*

made-up — **Made-up** means invented or worked out in your mind. *It was only a made-up story about a unicorn.*

fanciful — **Fanciful** means unreal or imaginary. *She has many fanciful notions about her dolls coming alive at night.*

fictitious — **Fictitious** means not real or genuine, coming instead from your own imagination. *We didn't believe her fictitious story about meeting a goblin at the bottom of the garden.*

fantastic — **Fantastic** can mean imaginary or without basis or reason. *Don't let such fantastic fears worry you!*

mythical — **Mythical** can mean imaginary or invented. *The centaur is a mythical creature from Greek legend.*

contrasting words: **actual**

imagine *verb*

to form a picture of something in your mind. ***Imagine** you are exploring a new continent.*

dream — To **dream** means to imagine something that is usually pleasant or enjoyable. *I dreamed about becoming a famous actor.*

pretend — To **pretend** means to imagine something to be true, usually as a game. *The children pretended they were on a desert island.*

make believe — To **make believe** is so similar to pretend that you can usually use either. *Let's make believe we are pirates.*

feign — To **feign** means to pretend or to appear to have something, usually in order to deceive someone. *She feigned illness so that she could stay home.*

---

important *adjective*

having great influence or power. *We planned a special welcome for the **important** visitor.*

great — **Great** can mean notable or important. *We went to a concert of the great composer's works. The great occasion was celebrated with fireworks and parades.*

eminent — **Eminent** means well-known or high in rank. *The eminent scientist talked to us about his nuclear experiments.*

prominent — **Prominent** means very important or standing out ahead of others. *Because she was a prominent member of the council everyone listened to her.*

pre-eminent — **Pre-eminent** means most important or much better than others. *He is the pre-eminent scientist in his field.*

prestigious — **Prestigious** means having a high reputation or standing. *The famous singer earned his prestigious position by practising for hours every day.*

similar words: **grand, famous**
contrasting words: **insignificant**

impossible *adjective*

not able to be done or used. *It is **impossible** for my son to carry me.*

impracticable — **Impracticable** means not being able to be done using what you have. *She had an impracticable plan for keeping a horse in the backyard.*

unattainable — **Unattainable** means not able to be achieved even with great effort. *I have an unattainable ambition to be able to fly like Superman.*

unthinkable — **Unthinkable** can mean not able to be done or imagined. *A hundred years ago it was unthinkable that people would ever walk on the moon.*

hopeless — **Hopeless** means not likely to be carried out. *Escape from the maximum security prison was hopeless.*

contrasting words: **possible, likely**

improve *verb*

to make something of higher quality or bring it into a better condition. *I want to **improve** my handwriting.*

better — To **better** means to improve something or to increase its good qualities. *He bettered his last score by ten runs.*

enrich — To **enrich** means to improve the quality of something. *Farmers enrich the soil with fertiliser.*

upgrade — To **upgrade** can mean to improve the standard of something. *The farmer upgraded his farm by buying a new milking machine.*

enhance — To **enhance** means to increase or improve something. *A coat of paint should enhance the value of the house.*

perfect — To **perfect** can mean to improve something or bring it nearer to perfection. *The inventor perfected his invention before selling it.*

similar words: **correct, repair**

inarticulate *adjective*

not able to use clear speech that every one can understand. *His rage made him **inarticulate** and we didn't know what he was trying to say.*

hesitant — **Hesitant** can mean pausing while or before speaking, usually because you are unsure of yourself or of what you are saying. *We became bored with trying to understand her hesitant lecture.*

faltering — **Faltering** can mean **hesitant** or often stopping and starting again when speaking. *His faltering speech showed us how nervous he was.*

tongue-tied — **Tongue-tied** means not able to speak, usually because you are too shy or nervous. *She was so tongue-tied when she went on stage that we had to remind her what to say.*

disjointed — **Disjointed** means not fitting together properly. *His story was so disjointed we couldn't work out who had really hidden the chocolate biscuits.*

quavery — **Quavery** means shaking or trembling as your voice does sometimes. *It was hard to understand the frail old man's quavery voice.*

contrasting words: **fluent**

include *verb*

to consist of or contain as a part. *Education **includes** what we learn both at home and at school.*

comprise — To **comprise** means to include or be composed of something. *This school comprises an infants department and a junior department.*

involve — To **involve** means to include as a necessary part of something. *The job of an art gallery guide involves a knowledge of art history.*

incorporate — To **incorporate** means to include something and make it part of something else. *We incorporated several ideas into the design of the house.*

embrace — To **embrace** can mean to include or contain something. *The committee's decision embraced all the points raised in the meeting.*

cover — To **cover** can mean to provide for something or take it in. *This book covers the whole French course.*

contrasting words: **exclude**

incompetent *adjective*

lacking the skill or ability you should have. *The **incompetent** plumber couldn't fix the leaking tap.*

unskilful — **Unskilful** means showing or having very little skill. *He made an unskilful attempt to fix it.*

amateurish — **Amateurish** means having very little skill or knowledge of a job. *Dad did an amateurish job of painting the house.*

fumbling — **Fumbling** means handling something clumsily. *His fumbling fingers tore open the parcel.*

inept — **Inept** means awkward or lacking in skill. *She made an inept attempt to sew on the button.*

similar words: **experienced, clumsy**
contrasting words: **competent**

incomplete *adjective*

not being whole or having some parts missing. *This jigsaw is **incomplete**.*

partial — **Partial** can mean not total or complete. *There will be a partial eclipse of the sun today.*

fragmentary — **Fragmentary** means broken or not whole. *The news from the war zone was fragmentary because the walkie-talkies picked up so much static.*

scrappy — **Scrappy** means made up of small pieces. *We could only have a scrappy conversation because of so many interruptions.*

piecemeal — **Piecemeal** means done piece by piece. *She is very disorganised and has a piecemeal approach to her work.*

deficient — **Deficient** means incomplete or lacking something. *The crops died because of the deficient water supply.*

similar words: **insufficient**
contrasting words: **whole, thorough**

incorrect *adjective*

wrong or having mistakes. *Your answer is **incorrect**.*

inaccurate — **Inaccurate** means not right or exact. *This copy is inaccurate.*

untrue — **Untrue** means not true or right. *He knew his statement was untrue.*

false — **False** means incorrect or not true. *He made a false accusation about me to get me into trouble.*

erroneous — **Erroneous** means incorrect or containing a mistake. *Your theory about the crime is erroneous.*

off beam — **Off beam** means wrong or incorrect. This is more suited to everyday language. *That answer is way off beam.*

contrasting words: **true**

increase *verb*

to become more or bigger. *The population of Australia **increases** every year.*

expand — To **expand** can mean to increase in size, especially by spreading out. *The more he blew into the balloon, the more it expanded.*

grow — To **grow** means to become bigger. *The town began to grow when gold was discovered nearby.*

multiply — To **multiply** can mean to increase in amount or number. *Every time you put some money in the bank your savings multiply.*

mount — To **mount** can mean to increase in amount. It is similar to **multiply**. *Our costs are mounting every day.*

accumulate — To **accumulate** can mean to increase by growing into a heap. *Don't let too much junk accumulate on your desk.*

contrasting words: **decrease**

indecent *adjective*

not proper or in good taste. *We were shocked by his **indecent** language.*

immoral — **Immoral** means wicked or wrong. *Their immoral behaviour caused gossip in the small town.*

corrupt — **Corrupt** means dishonest or able to be bribed. *The corrupt magistrate had been in the pay of criminals for years before he was found out.*

depraved — **Depraved** means evil or morally bad. *He was as depraved as the cruel, wicked thieves he mixed with.*

degenerate — **Degenerate** means becoming bad or worse than before. *She began to take drugs and now her lifestyle is completely degenerate.*

perverted — **Perverted** means turned from what is right or proper in your behaviour or beliefs. *His perverted sense of humour gets him into a lot of trouble.*

similar words: **evil, dishonest**
contrasting words: **decent**

independent *adjective*

not needing or relying on the help of others. *As children get older they are more **independent** and want to move away from home.*

self-sufficient — **Self-sufficient** means able to supply your own needs. *They led a self-sufficient life because they grew all their own food.*

separate — **Separate** means not connected to anything or anyone else. *After they were divorced, they led completely separate lives.*

unattached — **Unattached** can mean not connected with any particular person or group. *I asked you to dance because you are the only unattached girl at the party.*

autonomous — **Autonomous** means self-governing or able to govern or rule on your own. *Kenya was once a British Colony. It is now an autonomous nation.*

freelance — **Freelance** means not working for a wage but selling work to more than one employer, especially as a writer does. *The freelance journalist sold his stories to several magazines and newspapers.*

indicator *noun*

something that points to or shows something. *The **indicator** on the petrol gauge showed that the car was nearly out of petrol.*

sign A **sign** can be anything that shows something exists or is likely to happen. *Dark clouds are a sign of rain.*

marker A **marker** is something used to mark or indicate something. *We used a pile of stones as a marker to show the others which way we had gone.*

pointer A **pointer** is anything that draws your attention to something of interest. *The blackened trees are a pointer to recent forest fires.*

guide A **guide** is something or someone who shows you the way. *The reflectors on the posts by the side of the road are a guide to drivers at night.*

clue A **clue** is something that guides or directs you to the solution of a puzzle or mystery. *The fingerprints on the window were the best clue to the identity of the burglar.*

inedible *adjective*

not able or fit to be eaten. *Those biscuits are so hard they're **inedible**.*

unpalatable **Unpalatable** means tasting so unpleasant it is difficult to eat. *The dinner was so unpalatable even the dog wouldn't eat it.*

stale **Stale** means so old it is no longer pleasant to eat. *Give the stale bread to the chickens and we will eat the fresh loaf.*

rank **Rank** can mean having a strong unpleasant taste or smell. *Some people like seaweed but I think it is too rank to eat.*

rancid **Rancid** means having a stale sour smell or taste. *Don't use that butter — it is rancid and will make the sandwiches taste awful.*

off **Off** can mean not fit for eating, usually because it is too old or overripe. It is more suited to everyday language. *The milk was off and made my cornflakes taste terrible.*

contrasting words: **delicious**

inexperienced *adjective*

lacking the knowledge or skill you gain from doing, seeing or living through something yourself. *An **inexperienced** driver has to be particularly careful in wet weather.*

raw — **Raw** can mean inexperienced or not trained. *Daily drills and training turned the raw recruits into fine soldiers.*

amateur — **Amateur** can mean not skilled, or having only slight knowledge of a job. *He is an amateur bricklayer and his wall is very uneven.*

untrained — **Untrained** means having had no training for a particular activity. *She is an untrained singer but has a lovely voice.*

callow — **Callow** means young and inexperienced. *He was a callow youth but has grown into a self-confident young man.*

green — **Green** can mean **untrained** or inexperienced. It is usually used after a verb. *As we set up camp we discovered he was green when we saw him trying to pitch his tent.*

similar words: **incompetent, naive**
contrasting words: **experienced, competent**

inferior *adjective*

of low quality or value. *I'm afraid that I think your work is **inferior**.*

poor — **Poor** can be so similar to **inferior** that you can usually use either. *That is a very poor novel.*

shoddy — **Shoddy** means badly made. *This cupboard is so shoddy the doors won't close properly.*

crummy — **Crummy** means of low quality. It is more suited to everyday language. *I want a new bike because my old one is crummy.*

worthless — **Worthless** means of such low quality as to have no value. *This worthless toy broke two days after I bought it.*

dud — **Dud** means useless or **worthless**. This is more suited to everyday language. *The enemy dropped a dud bomb so no damage was done.*

similar words: **defective, mediocre**
contrasting words: **superior, distinguished**

influence *noun*

some force that affects or produces a change in someone or something else. *He is a good **influence** on his brother.*

power — **Power** can mean strength or force, especially in controlling others. *The new government will have the power to change many things.*

hold — **Hold** can mean a controlling force or influence. *The politician had a hold on his leader because he knew about his dishonesty.*

clout — **Clout** can mean influence or effectiveness. *You need some clout to get a good job like that.*

sway — **Sway** can mean control or rule. *The Prime Minister has held sway for many years.*

charisma — **Charisma** is the power to attract and influence people. *A successful leader should have charisma.*

---

influence *verb*

to have an effect on someone or something. *Try to make up your own mind without letting your friends **influence** you too much.*

manipulate — To **manipulate** can mean to influence someone cleverly or unfairly. *She always gets her own way because she manipulates people.*

prejudice — To **prejudice** means to influence someone without sensible reason. *His colour prejudiced the manager against him when he applied for the job.*

bias — To **bias** means to influence someone, usually unfairly. *He tried to bias my opinion about the film by telling me what he didn't like about it.*

condition — To **condition** means to influence or affect someone by training them in a particular way. *What we are taught by our parents and teachers conditions the way we live.*

brainwash — To **brainwash** means to influence someone's way of thinking so much that they change their beliefs, especially their political beliefs. *The guards tried to brainwash the prisoner so that he would speak out against the leader of his country.*

---

similar words: **persuade**

inform *verb*

to give news or knowledge to someone. ***I informed** him of your success.*

instruct To **instruct** can mean to inform or give information to someone. *The man instructed me to go straight ahead and then turn left.*

notify To **notify** means to inform someone of something or tell it to them, especially in an official way. *The Headmistress notified the parents that the meeting time had changed.*

advise To **advise** can mean to give someone information about something important. *We advised the bank that we were moving to the country.*

put in the picture To **put in the picture** means to inform someone about a particular situation. *When the babysitter arrived my mother put her in the picture as to when we go to bed.*

announce To **announce** means to tell something to someone or make it known in public. *Felicity announced her intention to leave school in front of the class.*

similar words: **tell, reveal, publish**

informal *adjective*

without ceremony or formality. *The Prime Minister had an **informal** chat with the visiting cricket team.*

unofficial **Unofficial** can mean not done formally or with official approval. *According to an unofficial report 10 000 people were killed in the earthquake.*

casual **Casual** can mean informal or not having to do with special occasions. *We wore casual clothes to the pool party.*

relaxed **Relaxed** can mean informal and at ease. *Once the ceremony was over the wedding guests were more relaxed.*

easygoing **Easygoing** means not being strict about the way things are done. *Our school has an easygoing attitude towards children who don't wear school uniform.*

contrasting words: **formal**

information *noun*

knowledge given or received about some fact or happening. *It is always a good idea to get some **information** about a country if you plan to visit it.*

news — **News** can be information considered suitable for reporting or not known before. *Have you heard any news about the lost children?*

dope — **Dope** means the actual facts or information about something. It is more suited to everyday language. *Give me the dope on that new computer.*

intelligence — **Intelligence** can be information or knowledge of an event or happening given to, or received from someone. *Have you heard the latest intelligence from the Far East.*

low-down — **Low-down** means information or advice. It is more suited to everyday language. *I'm new here, so you'd better give me the low-down on the place.*

propaganda — **Propaganda** is information which is used to try to convince you of a certain point of view. *The magazine was full of political propaganda.*

similar words: **gossip**

inhabit *verb*

to live or dwell in a place, as people or animals do. *Before the Battle of Hastings, the Normans inhabited France.*

populate — To **populate** can mean to inhabit or live in a place, as a group of people do. *In those days many tribes populated the great land.*

occupy — To **occupy** can mean to **settle** or take possession of a place. *When explorers crossed the Atlantic Ocean farmers soon followed to occupy the new land.*

settle — To **settle** means to go to live in a new, undeveloped place. *The pioneers took many risks so that they could settle the new land.*

colonise — To **colonise** means to start a settlement in a new land ruled by the parent country. *England colonised Australia and added it to her Empire.*

initiate *verb*

to begin something or to set it going. *Let's **initiate** an annual fun run at school.*

establish To **establish** means to set something up. *There were so many children they had to establish a new school.*

found To **found** means to set something up or **establish** it. *The early settlers founded towns wherever gold was discovered.*

institute To **institute** means to set something up or set it going. *Our sports club instituted a new course in judo.*

launch To **launch** means to set something going. *We launched our attack on the other team as soon as the whistle blew.*

pioneer To **pioneer** means to begin something or to be one of the first to do it. *British scientists pioneered research into microcomputers.*

similar words: **begin, invent**
contrasting words: **finish, cancel**

inquiry *noun*

a search or probe into a matter. *The police **inquiry** into the robbery took several weeks.*

investigation An **investigation** is a close look at something. *The investigation into the cause of the fire showed that there had been an electrical fault.*

examination An **examination** means the act of careful looking and testing. *The dentist's examination of her teeth revealed a broken filling.*

analysis An **analysis** means the separation of something into its basic parts to discover something about it. *Current affairs programmes give an analysis of the most important issues in the news.*

survey A **survey** is the act of asking the views of people in order to write a report about what people think or do. *They did a survey to see what people thought about daylight saving.*

poll A **poll** means a counting of people, votes or opinions. *The TV station did a telephone poll on the government's plans to change the tax system.*

inquisitive *adjective*

wanting to find out all about something. *Our new cat was very **inquisitive** and looked all around our house.*

questioning — **Questioning** can mean so inquisitive about the world around you that you can't help asking questions. *He has such a questioning mind that he spends a lot of time looking things up in the library.*

enquiring — **Enquiring** means seeking information or knowledge. *The child had an enquiring mind and was eager to learn.*

curious — **Curious** can mean wanting to learn, especially about things that are strange or new. *We were curious about the new person in our class.*

nosy — **Nosy** means interested in things that aren't your business. *Our next-door neighbour was nosy and always wanted to know what we were doing.*

snoopy — **Snoopy** means prying into things in a mean or sly way. *My snoopy sister was always trying to discover here I hid my diary.*

similar words: **alert**

insert *verb*

to put or set in something. ***Insert** the key in the lock.*

enclose — To **enclose** can mean to put something in. *I enclose a photograph with this letter.*

slip — To **slip** can mean to put or pass something into anything else with a smooth, sliding movement. *I slipped her note into my desk so the teacher wouldn't see it.*

introduce — To **introduce** can mean to bring or put something new into a place, surroundings, and so on. *I tried to introduce some new curtains into my grandmother's old home.*

ease — To **ease** can mean to move something or someone slowly and carefully into anything. *I eased the logs onto the fireplace.*

insinuate — To **insinuate** can mean to get yourself gradually and slyly into a certain position. *Brian insinuated himself into the boss's favour.*

similar words: **add**
contrasting words: **remove**

inside *noun*

the inner part or side of something. *The **inside** of their house is always gloomy.*

interior The **interior** is the internal or inside part of something. *The interior of the shop was decorated with striped wallpaper.*

contents The **contents** are whatever is inside or contained in something. This is a plural noun. *We were keen to discover the contents of the old box we found in the storeroom.*

guts **Guts** can be the essential or inner parts of something. This is a plural noun. It is more suited to everyday language. *I have to get to the guts of the matter to see what the problem is.*

belly A **belly** can be the inside of anything. *The sailor crawled right into the belly of the ship to look for the leak.*

similar words: **centre**
contrasting words: **outside**

insignificant *adjective*

not having much power or not worth consideration. *He is an **insignificant** member of the club and won't take on any responsibilities.*

unimportant **Unimportant** means not powerful or worthy of notice. *She is an unimportant member of the staff.*

dispensable **Dispensable** means able to be done without. *Our new house is much smaller and we had to decide which furniture was dispensable.*

expendable **Expendable** means able to be sacrificed or used up for a purpose. *The general had to decide which soldiers were most expendable in the task of recapturing the town.*

peripheral **Peripheral** means not essential or important. *The work of the social committee was peripheral to the club's main purpose of raising money for the hospital.*

small-time **Small-time** means of little importance. This is more suited to everyday language. *The police kept a watch on the small-time criminal and hoped he would lead them to the mastermind of the bank robberies.*

similar words: **minor, subordinate**
contrasting words: **significant, main, important**

inspect *verb*

to look carefully at something. *The general **inspected** his troops.*

look over — To **look over** means to view or examine something carefully. *We looked over several houses before we decided which one we would buy.*

search — To **search** means to look at or through something very carefully, hoping to find something. *The tracker searched the ground for footprints.*

survey — To **survey** means to take a general view of something. *We surveyed the beautiful valley from the top of a hill.*

scan — To **scan** means to look at something closely. *The doctor scanned the blood sample for any evidence of disease.*

reconnoitre — To **reconnoitre** means to look carefully at a place in order to gain useful information. *The scouts reconnoitred the village before the soldiers marched in.*

similar words: **examine, see**

insufficient *adjective*

not enough or not having as much as is wanted or needed. *There is **insufficient** paint to give the room a second coat.*

inadequate — **Inadequate** means not enough to fill a need. *The dam was half empty because of inadequate rain.*

lacking — **Lacking** means showing the lack or absence of some important part. *This soup is lacking in flavour.*

deficient — **Deficient** means incomplete or **lacking**. *Eat plenty of fresh fruit and vegetables or you will be deficient in vitamins.*

wanting — **Wanting** can mean having a part or parts missing. *Nobody would buy this machine because the most important parts are wanting.*

short — **Short** can mean not having or being enough. *Please lend me £2 because I'm short of money. Don't use the photocopier because paper is rather short at the moment.*

similar words: **scant, incomplete**
contrasting words: **enough, abundant, extra**

insult *verb*

to act or speak rudely to someone. *I was hurt when she* ***insulted*** *me in front of everyone.*

slight To **slight** means to treat someone rudely. *She slighted me by not replying to my invitation.*

snub To **snub** means to insult someone by ignoring them. *He snubbed me when I met him in the street.*

humiliate To **humiliate** means to make someone feel ashamed or foolish. *His rude remarks humiliated me.*

belittle To **belittle** means to make someone or something feel unimportant. *She belittled their efforts to help even though they had done their best.*

affront To **affront** means to hurt someone's feelings or pride. *She affronted her visitors by making rude comments about their appearance.*

similar words: **tease**
contrasting words: **worship**

intend *verb*

to have as an idea you are going to carry out. ***I intend*** *to make a model aeroplane this weekend.*

mean To **mean** is to intend or have a particular purpose. *Rita means to learn to sew during the holidays.*

plan To **plan** is to form a purpose or scheme. *We plan to build a tree-house next week.*

vow To **vow** is to declare solemnly as your intention. *He vowed to be very careful if he ever went hiking by himself.*

have in mind To **have in mind** is to be thinking about or to intend. *I have in mind to buy Mum a new scarf for her birthday.*

choose To **choose** can mean to decide or prefer to do something. *Justine chose to go to the pictures instead of the zoo.*

intense *adjective*

very great or strong. *I couldn't walk when I sprained my ankle because of the **intense** pain.*

severe — **Severe** can mean harsh or extreme. *A hundred years ago punishments were severe; a man could be imprisoned for stealing bread.*

profound — **Profound** means very deep, not superficial. *We thought for a long time about the minister's profound words.*

vivid — **Vivid** means strong and clear. *She is always telling unbelievable stories based on her vivid imagination.*

passionate — **Passionate** means showing a strong feeling or emotion. *She had a passionate belief in her plan to encourage the council to stop the new development.*

violent — **Violent** can mean forceful or intense in a rough way. *His violent temper scared us.*

contrasting words: **moderate**

interrupt *verb*

to stop someone or something, or break into the middle of what they are doing. *She **interrupted** me many times with her questions.*

disturb — To **disturb** means to interrupt someone or something in a way that hinders or interferes with what they are doing. *Your constant chatting is disturbing me and I am taking longer to finish.*

punctuate — To **punctuate** can mean to interrupt quite often. *They punctuated his speech with cheers.*

cut off — To **cut off** means to break in in the middle of something. *I cut his speech off before he finished.*

disconnect — To **disconnect** means to break a connection or link between two things. *The telephonist disconnected us in the middle of our conversation.*

similar words: **hinder**

intrude *verb*

to enter or force yourself in where you are not wanted or invited. *We were having fun playing together until he **intruded**.*

interfere To **interfere** means to take part in someone else's affairs without being asked. *She always interferes by trying to tell us what to do.*

meddle To **meddle** means to **interfere** with something that doesn't concern you. *He finished his own work early and then started to meddle in ours.*

chip in To **chip in** can mean to interrupt a conversation without being asked. This is more suited to everyday language. *Don't chip in while we're busy talking.*

interject To **interject** means to make a remark that interrupts a conversation or speech. *I interjected loudly because I didn't agree with what he said.*

butt in To **butt in** means to interrupt or **interfere**. This is more suited to everyday language. *We were having a private talk when John butted in.*

---

invent *verb*

to think up something new. *Do you know who **invented** the motor car?*

originate To **originate** means to invent or start something. *Bill originated the idea of walking home by the back lane.*

devise To **devise** means to think out, plan or invent something. *I have devised a way for us all to fit in the car.*

conceive To **conceive** means to think of or form something. *We have conceived a new plan.*

innovate To **innovate** means to bring in something new. *He innovated a lot of rules when he first came to our school.*

coin To **coin** means to make or invent something. *She coined a word that no one had heard before.*

---

similar words: **create, concoct**

---

investigate *verb*

to look into or examine something closely. *The police are **investigating** the murder at the moment.*

probe — To **probe** means to examine or search something thoroughly. *The police have to probe the whole area in order to solve the murder.*

scrutinise — To **scrutinise** means to examine something closely and carefully. *The art dealer scrutinised the painting to see whether it was genuine.*

explore — To **explore** means to examine or go over something very carefully. *They explored every inch of the cave to see if there was another way out.*

research — To **research** means to study something closely or scientifically in order to understand or learn more about a subject. *The students researched the topic thoroughly for their geography assignment.*

delve into — To **delve into** means to search or look into something thoroughly or in great depth. *He delved into all the encyclopaedias he could find for information for his project.*

similar words: **examine, test**

invisible *adjective*

unable to be seen. *We could all hear the aeroplane even though it was **invisible** in the sky.*

unseen — **Unseen** means invisible or not seen. *The unseen enemy fired on the soldiers as they advanced.*

hidden — **Hidden** means kept from sight. *The entrance to the rabbit's burrow was hidden in the long grass.*

concealed — **Concealed** means placed out of sight. *Dad had a concealed safe installed in his study after we were burgled.*

inconspicuous — **Inconspicuous** means not standing out or not noticeable. *The Prime Minister's bodyguard was inconspicuous in the crowd around him.*

imperceptible — **Imperceptible** means not easily seen or noticed. *The slope in the ground was imperceptible so that I did not notice I was climbing a small hill.*

contrasting words: **visible**

irrational *adjective*

absurd or not based on sound judgment. *Jan had an **irrational** fear of water.*

illogical — **Illogical** means not based on sensible or correct thinking. *Wearing an overcoat on a hot day is illogical.*

unreasonable — **Unreasonable** means not based on good sense. *It's an unreasonable demand to insist on going skiing when there's no snow.*

groundless — **Groundless** means without any reason or basis. *I know you are frightened that there is a ghost in the cellar but your fears are groundless.*

inconsistent — **Inconsistent** means having no order or agreement between the parts of something. *Your inconsistent behaviour is very confusing and we never know if you'll be cross or not.*

arbitrary — **Arbitrary** means based on your own feelings and ideas rather than on rules or reasons. *The teacher made an arbitrary decision as to who was going to be the first on the stage.*

similar words: **silly, fickle**
contrasting words: **sensible, sane**

irritate *verb*

to annoy someone or make them angry. *The audience's chatter **irritated** the speaker.*

vex — To **vex** means to annoy or worry someone. *Her laziness vexed her parents.*

pique — To **pique** means to annoy and upset someone. *Mary's refusal to help Craig piqued him.*

provoke — To **provoke** means to make someone or something angry or annoyed. *He provoked me by telling me I was useless.*

goad — To **goad** can mean to tease someone until you make them angry. *She goaded me until I lost my temper.*

bug — To **bug** means to annoy or irritate someone. It is more suited to everyday language. *Her silly questions bugged me.*

similar words: **annoy**
contrasting words: **please**

isolate *verb*

to set or place someone or something apart from everything else so that they are alone. *The guards **isolated** the most dangerous prisoners.*

ostracise To **ostracise** means to keep someone away from others or send them away from everyone else, especially as a punishment. *The other children ostracised the boy who sneaked on his friends.*

quarantine To **quarantine** means to isolate people or animals for a certain period of time to make sure they don't spread a disease to others. *The officials quarantined the animals that had been in contact with the sick cow.*

cold-shoulder To **cold-shoulder** means to act coldly towards someone to keep them away from you. *The rest of the class cold-shouldered the spiteful girl.*

shut away To **shut away** means to hide or confine someone or something. *The evil magician shut away the enchanted prince so that no-one would find him.*

similar words: **expel, exclude**

jealous *adjective*

wanting very much to have what other people have. *Peter is **jealous** of his brother's good looks.*

envious **Envious** means feeling or showing discontent and ill will, at seeing what someone else has. It is very similar to **jealous**. *I am envious of your good luck in winning the prize.*

covetous **Covetous** means wanting what someone else has very much. *She was so covetous of David's new book that she took it when he wasn't looking.*

possessive **Possessive** means wanting to control or possess someone or something all by yourself. *My little brother is very possessive of his remote control car.*

green **Green** can mean extremely jealous. It is more suited to everyday language. *I was green when I saw his new bike.*

job *noun*

employment for which you are paid. *I have a **job** selling newspapers after school.*

work Your **work** can be the job by which you earn money. *His work is teaching.*

occupation Your **occupation** is your usual job or employment. *What is your father's occupation?*

business A **business** is the job or trade you have in order to earn a living. *We have a business building swimming pools.*

career A **career** is the job or profession you hope to have for the rest of your life. *She wants to make acting her career.*

vocation A **vocation** is a particular job or profession which you believe to be very important. *I want to make nursing my vocation.*

similar words: **profession, position**

join *verb*

to put two or more things together. *I have **joined** the broken pieces with glue.*

connect To **connect** means to join or unite something. *Carl connected the ends of the toy railway track.*

link To **link** is so similar to **join** and **connect** that you can usually use either. *You can link these rings together to make a chain.*

couple To **couple** means to join one thing to another. *The men had to couple the carriages together before the train could leave.*

unite To **unite** means to join two or more people or things together as one. *The minister united the man and woman in marriage.*

knit To **knit** means to join people or things closely and firmly together. *The coach knitted the players into an unbeatable team.*

similar words: **combine**
contrasting words: **separate**

joke *noun*

something that is said or done to make people laugh. *She told us a **joke** about a man who took a refrigerator to the South Pole.*

jest — A **jest** is a joke which is sometimes a mocking one. *He made a jest about his clumsiness to hide his embarrassment.*

laugh — A **laugh** is something that makes you laugh. It can be used to mean the opposite of what is being said. *Walking through the Hall of Mirrors was a laugh. 'That's a laugh', he said when I asked if he had any money.*

gag — A **gag** is a joke or funny trick. *The comedian's gag kept the audience laughing.*

crack — A **crack** can be a joke, often an unkind one. It is more suited to everyday language. *He made a crack about my red hair.*

similar words: **wisecrack**

journey *noun*

a course you take when travelling from one place to another, especially by land. *Our **journey** took us out into the southernmost tip of England.*

trip — A **trip** is a journey, usually taken for pleasure. *We'll plan a trip to the city next holidays.*

tour — A **tour** is an organised journey through a place or from one place to another. *We went on a bus tour to the main historical sites.*

expedition — An **expedition** is a journey made for a special reason. *Many explorers made expeditions to see what lay beyond the Atlantic Ocean.*

excursion — An **excursion** is a short journey or **trip**, usually taken for a special reason. *Our class is going on an excursion to the zoo.*

jaunt — A **jaunt** is a short **trip** made for fun. *Let's go on a jaunt to the beach.*

joyful *adjective*

full of great happiness and delight. *The family had a **joyful** reunion when their grandparents came from Poland.*

jubilant — **Jubilant** means joyful because you have been successful. *The family were jubilant when they got permission for the grandparents to come.*

elated — **Elated** means in very high spirits. *The children were elated when they were allowed to stay home from school that day.*

ecstatic — **Ecstatic** means having a sudden feeling of great joy. *They were ecstatic when they saw each other at the airport.*

rapturous — **Rapturous** means filled with great joy and happiness. *It was a rapturous moment for the grandparents when they saw their grandchildren for the first time.*

blissful — **Blissful** means extraordinarily happy. *They had a blissful time together after so many years apart.*

similar words: **happy, glad**
contrasting words: **glum, miserable, sad**

judge *verb*

to form an opinion about something. *I didn't **judge** the width of the car properly so I scratched the car door on the wall of the garage.*

adjudicate — To **adjudicate** means to make a judgment about something. *The headmaster adjudicated the speeches in our debate.*

evaluate — To **evaluate** means to test and find the value or quality of something. *Our essay topic was to evaluate the statement: 'Smoking is bad for you'.*

appraise — To **appraise** means to judge the value of something. *The judges appraised the paintings in the competition.*

value — To **value** means to form an opinion about how much something is worth. *The jeweller valued Mum's ring at £1000.*

size up — To **size up** something means to form an idea about it. *The policeman walked around the smashed cars and sized up the situation.*

similar words: **measure**

jump *verb*

to move yourself suddenly from the ground or some other support, using your leg muscles. *She was so happy she **jumped** up and down.*

leap To **leap** means to jump lightly and quickly. *I leaped over the puddle in the middle of the track.*

spring To **spring** means to **leap** or move upwards with sudden energy. *She sprang out of her seat when the bell went. The dog sprang into the air.*

bound To **bound** means to move with jumps or big steps. *He bounded right over the fence and ran up the path.*

lollop To **lollop** means to move with awkward jumps. *The big, friendly dog lolloped down the road after the children.*

vault To **vault** means to jump, often with your hands on something to support you. *She vaulted on to her horse. When she couldn't open the gate she vaulted over it.*

similar words: **frisk**

justify *verb*

to show an act, or something similar, to be right or reasonable. *The policeman had to **justify** the shot he fired at the suspect as he ran away.*

warrant To **warrant** can mean to show there is a good reason or need for something. *The urgency of the situation warranted her hasty action.*

explain To **explain** can mean to account for something or make the reason for it clear. *Please explain your absence.*

excuse To **excuse** can mean to justify or serve as a reason for a fault or wrongdoing. *Your tiredness does not excuse your rudeness.*

vindicate To **vindicate** means to show someone or something to be innocent or right. This is rather a formal word. *The evidence of the witnesses vindicated the man who had always claimed he was innocent.*

keep *verb*

to make something continue in the same way or state. *We must **keep** our room as clean as we can.*

maintain To **maintain** means to keep something up or keep it in good condition. *The labourer's job was to maintain the roads.*

preserve To **preserve** means to keep something from going bad. *We picked so much fruit from our tree that we had to preserve some of it.*

retain To **retain** means to keep or keep on using something. *She is managing to retain the old family home.*

sustain To **sustain** means to keep something up. *It's hard to sustain a conversation with him because he gives such short answers to my questions.*

prolong To **prolong** means to make something last longer. *We should prolong our holiday because we're having such a good time.*

contrasting words: **change**

kill *verb*

to cause the death of something or someone. *We **killed** the rats with poison.*

murder To **murder** means to kill someone deliberately. *The detective overheard the plan to murder the nightwatchman.*

assassinate To **assassinate** means to **murder** a well-known person, such as a politician. *The man who assassinated the president was arrested with the gun in his hand.*

execute To **execute** can mean to put someone to death in a way allowed by the law. *The hangman executed the murderer.*

put down To **put down** can mean to kill an animal to stop it suffering any longer. *The dog was so badly injured that the vet had to put it down.*

slay To **slay** means to kill someone or something using violence. *David, the shepherd, slew the giant Goliath with a sling and a stone.*

kind *adjective*

warm-hearted, friendly and wishing good things for other people. *It was **kind** of him to show the new boy around the school.*

nice — **Nice** can mean kind or pleasant. *They were nice people to play with.*

thoughtful — **Thoughtful** means thinking of other people and considering their needs. *It was thoughtful of you to give me some flowers when I was feeling sad.*

considerate — **Considerate** means kind or thinking of other people's needs and feelings. *Although he could hardly keep his eyes open the considerate boy read his sister her favourite story.*

unselfish — **Unselfish** means thinking about other people and not just yourself. *It was very unselfish of you to share your last piece of cake with her.*

well-meaning — **Well-meaning** means having good intentions in the way you act or treat people. *She is very well-meaning but when she attempted to help she managed to flood the kitchen.*

contrasting words: **unkind, selfish**

label *noun*

a piece of paper put on something to show what it is, who owns it or where it is going. *I put a **label** showing my name and address on my holiday suitcase.*

tag — A **tag** is a piece of cardboard or strong paper attached to something as a label. *I took the price tag off the shirt before I gave it to Dad.*

tab — A **tab** is a small label. *A tab with the manufacturer's name was sewn on the inside of the collar of the shirt.*

ticket — A **ticket** is a label or **tag** showing how much something costs. *The clothes in the sale all have red tickets.*

sticker — A **sticker** is an adhesive or gummed label, usually with an advertisement or other information printed on it. *Her suitcase was covered with stickers from the different cities she had visited overseas.*

label *verb*

to describe something with a label. *We always **label** our suitcases when we travel on trains or planes.*

mark To **mark** means to put a sign or label on something to give some information about it. *When I go to camps, Mum marks my clothes with my name.*

brand To **brand** means to **mark** something with the name of the owner or maker. *The farmer brands his new calves every year.*

tag To **tag** can mean to put a tag or label on something giving information about it. *The shopkeeper tagged every item of new stock when it came into the store.*

identify To **identify** means to establish or prove as being a particular thing or person. *As soon as he comes on the air, the disc jockey plays this song to identify his programme.*

lack *noun*

absence of something you want or need. *The refugees became ill due to the **lack** of good food.*

shortage A **shortage** is a lack in the supply of something. *There was a serious shortage of water during the long drought.*

insufficiency An **insufficiency** can be an amount which is less than you need for something. *The club had an insufficiency of funds to pay for the new sports equipment.*

deficiency A **deficiency** can be an inadequate amount of something. *We made up for our deficiency in numbers by working extra hard to finish on time.*

dearth A **dearth** is a lack or very small supply of something. *The dearth of medical supplies made the situation even more serious.*

deficit A **deficit** is an amount lacked, especially money. *Dad promised that if I saved up half the money he would make up the deficit.*

contrasting words: **excess**

lake *noun*

a large area of water surrounded by land. *Lake Windermere is the largest expanse of water in England.*

lagoon A **lagoon** is a pond of shallow water which is often separated from the sea by low banks of sand. *The children played safely in the lagoon only a hundred metres from the crashing surf.*

basin A **basin** is an area of water in a hollow surrounded by higher land. *The river basin lies between the two mountain ranges.*

dam A **dam** is a lot of water held back by a wall built across a river. *The farmers use water from the dam to irrigate their crops.*

reservoir A **reservoir** is a place where water is stored. *Pipes carry water from the dam to the town reservoir.*

similar words: **bay, swamp**

land *verb*

to come to rest by the shore or on the ground. *The ship will **land** late this afternoon.*

touch down To **touch down** is similar to land but is only used about aircraft. *The plane will touch down at Manchester and then Heathrow.*

alight To **alight** means to get down out of a vehicle after a journey. *The passengers alighted from the bus.*

dismount To **dismount** means to get off a horse or a bike after a ride. *He pulled up outside the gate and dismounted hurriedly.*

disembark To **disembark** means to get off a ship or out of a plane after a journey. *Passengers should check their luggage before they disembark.*

language *noun*

the arrangement of words we use when we speak or write. *English is the most widely spoken **language** in the world.*

dialect A **dialect** is a variety of a language spoken in a particular area or by a particular group of people. *Some people from Scotland speak a dialect which Americans find hard to understand.*

tongue **Tongue** can be another word for a language or a **dialect**. *The stranger spoke in a foreign tongue.*

pidgin **Pidgin** is a language based on a mixture of languages. It is used by people who have no other language in common. *In Papua New Guinea, pidgin developed as a result of English people trading with the native people.*

jargon **Jargon** is the language made up of special words and phrases used only by people in a particular job or occupation. *Most people find it hard to understand the legal jargon of documents.*

slang **Slang** is everyday language which is not suitable for formal speech or writing. *Try not to use slang in your essays.*

---

laugh *verb*

to make sounds that show amusement, happiness or scorn. *The children **laughed** as the waves wet their feet.*

chuckle To **chuckle** is to laugh softly with amusement. *I chuckled as I read Justine's funny letter.*

chortle To **chortle** means to laugh loudly. *We chortled with glee when they invited us to the circus.*

cackle To **cackle** means to laugh with the harsh noisy sound a hen makes after laying an egg. *The witch cackled as she stirred her magic brew.*

guffaw To **guffaw** means to laugh loudly and noisily. *The workmen guffawed when they saw their mate stuck in the mud.*

crack up To **crack up** can mean to explode into, or collapse with laughter. It is more suited to everyday language. *We cracked up when she came in wearing the funny mask.*

---

similar words: **smile**
contrasting words: **cry**

---

lawyer *noun*

someone whose work is to give advice about the law and to argue on behalf of people in law courts. *A **lawyer** has to know all about new laws so that he can advise his clients.*

solicitor A **solicitor** is a lawyer who advises clients and prepares cases for a **barrister** to present in court. *The solicitor recommended a barrister to Mrs Brown and then researched similar cases for him.*

barrister A **barrister** is a lawyer whose main work is in the higher courts where important cases are heard. *The barrister defended the man accused of murder in the High Court.*

counsel A **counsel** is a lawyer who is paid to give someone advice in a court case. *The barrister took his counsel to court with him to help him argue the difficult case.*

advocate An **advocate** is someone who speaks on behalf of other people or of causes. *The lawyer devoted himself to being an advocate for conservationists who are arrested.*

attorney An **attorney** is someone, usually a **solicitor,** whom you appoint to do business for you. *Our attorney will sign our business papers while we are overseas.*

layer *noun*

a single thickness. *The wedding cake had three **layers.***

stratum A **stratum** is a horizontal layer of any material. *We could see a stratum of lignite in the cliff face.*

seam A **seam** can be a thin layer of a different kind of rock or mineral in the ground. *The new seam of coal discovered yesterday will keep the miners working for another year.*

vein A **vein** can be a layer of coal or gold in the middle of rock. *The miners were excited when they found the rich vein of gold.*

band A **band** can be a layer of stone containing valuable ores or gemstones. *There were rich bands of gold in the Welsh mountains.*

deposit A **deposit** can be a layer which collects on a surface. *As the flooding river went down it left a deposit of rich soil on the farmer's land.*

laze *verb*

to be lazy or spend your time doing very little. *It was so hot that I just **lazed** around all weekend.*

idle — To **idle** can mean to spend your time doing nothing. *Instead of doing her homework she just idled at the table.*

loaf — To **loaf** means to do nothing. It is similar to **laze** and to **idle**. *You can loaf all through your holidays.*

skive — To **skive** means to avoid doing what you should. It is more suited to everyday language. *While the others worked, he skived.*

not pull your weight — To **not pull your weight** means to avoid doing your fair share of something. *When we do anything together she doesn't pull her weight.*

loll — To **loll** means to lean or lie around in a lazy way. *She said she just wanted to loll on the bed all day.*

similar words: **rest**
contrasting words: **work**

lazy *adjective*

not liking work or effort. *A **lazy** sheepdog is of no use to a farmer.*

idle — **Idle** means not doing or wanting to do anything. *The idle workmen grabbed their tools when they saw the foreman.*

indolent — **Indolent** means lazy or tending to avoid work. *He is so indolent that he spends the weekends lying in front of the television.*

slack — **Slack** can mean lazy, careless and neglectful. *She is slack about doing her homework.*

slothful — **Slothful** means extremely lazy. It is often used in an insulting way. *My slothful sister never plays any sport.*

similar words: **lethargic**
contrasting words: **busy, energetic**

learn *verb*

to come to have knowledge about or skill in something. *She **learns** the piano and can play very difficult pieces.*

memorise To **memorise** means to put something into your memory or learn it by heart. *She memorised the poem 'Meg Merrilies' by John Keats.*

absorb To **absorb** can mean to take something into your mind. *The student absorbed all the facts.*

assimilate To **assimilate** means to learn or **absorb** something so completely that it becomes part of you. *I assimilated all the information I could find about horses until I could give the talk without using any notes.*

take in To **take in** can mean to understand and remember something. *Did you take in what she was telling you?*

digest To **digest** can mean to think something over and take it into your mind. *Make sure you have time to digest all the information before the exam.*

contrasting words: **teach**

leave *verb*

to go away from somewhere. *We will **leave** when our taxi comes.*

depart To **depart** means to leave. It is a more formal word. *The train departs at 10 a.m.*

withdraw To **withdraw** means to take yourself away from a place, especially a room. *She withdrew to her study.*

retreat To **retreat** means to go back. *The soldiers retreated to a safer position.*

retire To **retire** can mean to go away from other people or leave what you are doing for a particular reason. *The cricketer had to retire after he injured his knee.*

emigrate To **emigrate** means to **leave** your own country to go to live in another one. *Many people have emigrated from Europe to Australia.*

similar words: **flee**
contrasting words: **come**

legal *adjective*

allowed or decided by law. *She took **legal** action to stop people walking through her land to the beach.*

lawful — **Lawful** means allowed by law. *There are some beaches where it is lawful to swim and sunbathe without a swimming costume.*

legitimate — **Legitimate** means in accordance with the law or established rules. *She runs a legitimate business importing drugs for hospitals and doctors.*

permitted — **Permitted** means allowed. *Meat is not a permitted import if you are a traveller from overseas.*

authorised — **Authorised** means having been given the legal power to do something. *The police were authorised to search the suspect's house.*

proper — **Proper** means right or approved. *If you see someone breaking into a house, the proper thing to do is to call the police.*

similar words: **formal**
contrasting words: **illegal, dishonest**

lengthy *adjective*

long or using many words. *He gave us a **lengthy** explanation.*

rambling — **Rambling** can mean lengthy and not keeping to one train of thought. *Her rambling account of what happened puzzled us.*

wordy — **Wordy** means using more words than are needed. *We didn't listen to her wordy explanation.*

tedious — **Tedious** means too long and boring. *We didn't listen to the politician's tedious speech.*

long-drawn-out — **Long-drawn-out** means stretched out by using too many words. *The story would have been funny if it hadn't been such a long-drawn-out one.*

longwinded — **Longwinded** means talking for too long. *He is so longwinded that he talks for half an hour if you ask him the simplest question.*

contrasting words: **brief**

lenient *adjective*

not harsh or severe in treatment. *The judge was **lenient** because it was Alice's first offence.*

merciful — **Merciful** means showing kindness by not punishing someone, or not being cruel. *Christians believe God is merciful and forgiving.*

compassionate — **Compassionate** means showing pity and kindness to someone. *The compassionate employer did not call the police when his employee confessed to stealing from him.*

humane — **Humane** means showing feelings of pity or tenderness in the way that kind and decent human beings should. *The governor of the jail was well-known for his humane treatment of prisoners.*

mild — **Mild** means not severe or harsh. *His mild manner made me feel less worried about the scolding.*

gentle — **Gentle** can mean not rough or violent. *Her gentle rebuke showed how kind and understanding she is.*

contrasting words: **strict**

lesson *noun*

a time during which a pupil or a class is taught one subject. *I have seven **lessons** today and the first one is English.*

lecture — A **lecture** is a long speech made in front of an audience or class and meant to teach or inform them. *We had a very interesting lecture on road safety today.*

seminar — A **seminar** is a meeting of students to discuss a particular subject. *I enjoyed the discussion in our English seminar and I asked lots of questions.*

sermon — A **sermon** is a serious talk, usually one preached in a church and meant to teach the congregation about their religion. *The minister's sermon was about loving your neighbour.*

course — A **course** is a series of lessons. *I'm doing an art course once a week for the next ten weeks.*

lethargic *adjective*

being in a state of sleepy laziness. *I feel so* ***lethargic*** *today that I don't want to do anything energetic.*

listless **Listless** means having no energy or interest in anything. *It was such a hot day that we were all very listless.*

sluggish **Sluggish** means moving slowly with no energy. *The car was very sluggish going up the hill.*

languid **Languid** means weak, tired or slow-moving. *She was languid for days after she had the flu.*

inert **Inert** means slow or not active. *The teacher faced an inert class on the hot summer day.*

similar words: **apathetic, lazy, tired**
contrasting words: **energetic, lively**

lift *verb*

to move or bring something upwards or to a higher position. *Please* ***lift*** *this heavy box for me.*

raise To **raise** is so similar to **lift** that you can usually use either. *She was so tired that she couldn't raise her head from the pillow.*

elevate To **elevate** can mean to lift or **raise** something. This meaning is usually used in more formal language. *The priest elevated the holy cup so that everyone in the church could see it.*

hoist To **hoist** means to lift something up, often with an effort. *Santa Claus hoisted the sack onto his shoulders.*

lever To **lever** means to lift and move something by putting a bar under it and pushing down on the other end of the bar. *The workman levered the boulder out of the way.*

jack up To **jack up** means to lift something very heavy with a special tool called a jack. *We had to jack up the car so that we could change the tyre.*

contrasting words: **drop**

light *adjective*

of little or less than usual weight. *I'm glad to be wearing **light** clothing in this heat.*

delicate — **Delicate** can mean easily damaged or weakened. *The butterfly unfolded its delicate wings after it came out of its cocoon.*

fine — **Fine** can mean very thin or slender. *I don't think this thread will be strong enough because it's too fine.*

flimsy — **Flimsy** means not strongly made. *This flimsy fence will probably blow down in the wind.*

gauzy — **Gauzy** means as thin and light as a particular transparent cloth called gauze. *Why don't we use gauzy material to make the curtains so that the sunshine can still come through.*

feathery — **Feathery** means light and airy like feathers. *The ballet dress was soft and feathery.*

contrasting words: **heavy**

like *verb*

to find someone or something pleasant. *I **like** everyone in my class.*

fancy — To **fancy** can mean to take a liking to someone or something. *I fancied your brother as soon as I saw him.*

enjoy — To **enjoy** means to take pleasure in something. *I enjoy barbecues.*

relish — To **relish** means to **enjoy** something to the full. *My grandmother relishes a hot cup of tea.*

appreciate — To **appreciate** means to value or be aware of the good things about something or someone. *He appreciates my cooking.*

welcome — To **welcome** can mean to receive or regard something or someone with pleasure. *I welcome the cooler weather after all this heat.*

similar words: **love**
contrasting words: **hate**

likely *adjective*

reasonably or apparently going to happen. *It is **likely** that it will rain tomorrow.*

probable — **Probable** is so similar to **likely** that you can usually use either. *Do you think it is probable that she will be better by this afternoon?*

expected — **Expected** can mean likely to happen or come about. *The expected result in the election is for the government to be returned with an increased majority.*

liable — **Liable** can mean **likely**. It is so similar that you can usually use either. *Problems are liable to come up.*

apt — **Apt** means likely or inclined to do something. *He is apt to lose his temper at any moment.*

odds-on — **Odds-on** means more likely to win or succeed when you take a chance. *It's odds-on that this record will go to the top of the charts.*

similar words: **possible, believable**
contrasting words: **unbelievable, impossible**

limit *verb*

to keep something within a certain amount or space. *I limit **myself** to one soft drink a week.*

restrict — To **restrict** is so similar to **limit** you can usually choose either word. *We had to restrict the time we spent watching TV so that we could finish our homework.*

control — To **control** can mean to keep something in check. *We had to control our spending so that our pocket money would last all week.*

curb — To **curb** means to **control** or hold back something. *I tried to curb my anger when she said such nasty things to me.*

inhibit — To **inhibit** means to hold back or hinder something. *No-one supported Melanie's idea and this inhibited her enthusiasm.*

stifle — To **stifle** can mean to keep back or stop. *His parents did not encourage him and this stifled John's ambition to be a pianist.*

limp *verb*

to walk unevenly and with difficulty, because one leg or foot is injured or lame. *My foot ached as I **limped** along on my sprained ankle.*

hobble To **hobble** means to walk unevenly and with difficulty. *Jillian hobbled around with a walking stick after her accident.*

shuffle To **shuffle** means to walk slowly, dragging your feet along the ground. *Bruce was so tired after the long walk that he shuffled straight off to bed.*

stagger To **stagger** means to walk or move along very unsteadily, looking as though you might fall over. *He staggered during the last few metres of the marathon to cross the finishing line in third place.*

totter To **totter** means to sway or to walk unsteadily. *Angela tottered around the room in high-heeled shoes from the fancy-dress box.*

toddle To **toddle** means to walk with short unsteady steps. *The baby toddled along on his chubby little legs.*

similar words: **walk, march, trudge**
contrasting words: **frisk**

line *noun*

something arranged like a thin mark or stroke made on a surface. *A **line** of trees grew on either side of the street.*

row A **row** is a line of people or things. *Some pupils still sit in rows in the classroom.*

queue A **queue** is a single line of people, cars or animals waiting in turn for something. *We waited in a queue to buy tickets for the movie.*

string A **string** is a **row** or line of things. *There is a string of islands off the coast of Japan.*

file A **file** is a line of people or things one behind the other. *The teacher told us to walk in single file.*

rank A **rank** is a row or line, especially of soldiers. *The soldiers stood in their ranks waiting to be inspected.*

liquid *adjective*

flowing like water. *Oil is sometimes referred to as* ***liquid*** *gold because it is so valuable.*

runny **Runny** means pouring out liquid, or flowing. *The little boy had a runny nose because he had a cold. I couldn't eat the runny custard.*

sloppy **Sloppy** means wet and slushy. *The baby could only eat sloppy food.*

fluid **Fluid** means liquid or able to flow. *Lava is the fluid rock that comes out of a volcano.*

molten **Molten** means made liquid by heat. *The fire had to be very, very hot to make the molten metal.*

contrasting words: **gluey**

list *verb*

to make a set of the names of things written down one under the other, so that you'll remember them. ***List*** *all the books you need from the library and I'll try to get them for you.*

index To **index** means to make an alphabetical list of names, places or subjects in a book, showing their page numbers. *If you write a thesaurus, it is a good idea to index all the words you have included and put it at the back.*

tabulate To **tabulate** means to make a plan or chart listing things that are related to one another. *We tabulated the scores of all our cricketers to see who made the most runs.*

itemise To **itemise** means to give details about each part of an overall group. *We itemise our accounts so that our customers know exactly what they are paying for.*

enumerate To **enumerate** means to name things one by one or make them clear in a list. *Let's enumerate the arguments for and against buying it before you decide.*

similar words: **arrange, record**

live *verb*

to be alive. *I will never forgive you as long as I* ***live****.*

be — To **be** can mean to live or have reality. *I'm afraid he is no more.*

exist — To **exist** can mean to have life or be real. *Do ghosts exist?*

breathe — To **breathe** can mean to **exist** or have life. *Everything that breathed was destroyed in the flood.*

survive — To **survive** means to stay alive or in existence, especially after someone's death or the end of something. *Three people were killed in the accident and one survived.*

remain — To **remain** can mean to stay alive. *Of my grandmother's ten brothers and sisters, now only two remain.*

contrasting words: **become extinct, die**

lively *adjective*

full of energy or spirit. *We need a* ***lively*** *person to be the school captain.*

frisky — **Frisky** means jumping around in a lively way. *The horses were very frisky after their long rest in the paddocks.*

vivacious — **Vivacious** means lively and energetic. *The vivacious girl attracted a lot of admirers.*

playful — **Playful** means full of fun. *The playful puppy loved to run after the ball.*

frolicsome — **Frolicsome** means enjoying happy or energetic play. *The adventure playground was full of frolicsome children.*

jaunty — **Jaunty** means lively and confident. *He walked into the room with a jaunty step.*

similar words: **energetic**
contrasting words: **lethargic**

lonely *adjective*

without friendly company. *He was **lonely** when his best friend was away.*

alone — **Alone** means by yourself. *She was alone in the house.*

lone — **Lone** means unaccompanied or not with anyone. *They could see a lone traveller coming towards them.*

solitary — **Solitary** means quite **alone** or without any companions. *She is a solitary sort of person.*

reclusive — **Reclusive** means wanting to live by yourself and not see other people. *He is reclusive by nature but his family try to visit him often.*

---

loot *noun*

anything that has been obtained by stealing. *The burglars became frightened and ran away without any **loot**.*

booty — **Booty** is something stolen, especially by violence or in war. *The pirates shared their booty of gold.*

plunder — **Plunder** is something stolen by open force, as in a war. It is similar to **booty.** *The soldiers came home with a lot of plunder.*

spoils — **Spoils** are all sorts of loot taken by violence. It is similar to **booty** and **plunder.** *The highwayman held up three coaches but the spoils were not worth much.*

pickings — **Pickings** can be things obtained easily or in a way that is not strictly honest. *There were plenty of pickings for the cleaners when the crowd had left the sports ground.*

---

loud *adjective*

producing a lot of sound so that you can hear it easily. *The* ***loud*** *noise startled me.*

blaring — **Blaring** means producing a loud harsh sound. *It was hard to relax at the beach because there were so many blaring radios.*

deafening — **Deafening** means so loud that it could make someone deaf. *The pneumatic drills were deafening so the workmen had to wear earmuffs.*

raucous — **Raucous** means harsh-sounding. *We heard raucous laughter coming from the party.*

shrill — **Shrill** means loud and piercing. *The canary's shrill whistle woke us up every morning.*

resonant — **Resonant** means deep and booming. *He has a resonant baritone voice that can be heard all through the auditorium.*

contrasting words: **quiet**

love *verb*

to feel strong affection for another person. ***I love*** *my parents and my brothers and sisters.*

adore — To **adore** means to feel very strong love for something or someone. *The children adored their puppy.*

dote on — To **dote on** means to love someone or something so much that you appear to be silly. *She dotes on horses and talks about them all the time.*

cherish — To **cherish** can mean to feel love for someone or hold them dear. *He cherishes his grandfather and enjoys making him presents.*

care for — To **care for** means to have a fondness for someone or something. *I don't care for spinach.*

court — To **court** means to try to get someone's love. *Your father courted me for two years before I decided to marry him.*

similar words: **like, worship**
contrasting words: **hate**

loving *adjective*

feeling or showing love. *Her **loving** parents always tried to do the best for her.*

affectionate	**Affectionate** means having and showing feelings of love towards someone. *The affectionate puppy kept licking my hand.*
fond	**Fond** means having warm feelings towards someone. *I have fond memories of the people we met during our holidays.*
tender	**Tender** can mean loving in a romantic way. *The film ended with the two lovers in a tender embrace.*
devoted	**Devoted** means showing a very strong attachment to something or someone. *He is devoted to his pets and spends hours caring for them.*

lucky *adjective*

having good luck or good fortune. *We were **lucky** to find a park so close to the picture theatre.*

fortunate	**Fortunate** means being lucky or having good fortune. *You were fortunate to find the money you lost.*
happy	**Happy** can mean **fortunate** or lucky for everyone concerned. *It was a happy coincidence to meet you at the movies.*
promising	**Promising** means likely to turn out well. *The weather looks promising, so perhaps we could have a picnic.*
auspicious	**Auspicious** means favourable or showing signs of success. *All the signs were auspicious so our parents decided to set up their own business.*

contrasting words: **unlucky**

mad *adjective*

mentally ill or unbalanced. *She went **mad** in her old age.*

crazy — **Crazy** is so similar to **mad** that you can usually use either. *He has lived alone for so long that he has become crazy.*

insane — **Insane** means mentally ill. It is similar to **mad** and **crazy** but is often used in a more serious way. *She lives in a home for insane people.*

maniacal — **Maniacal** means violently or dangerously mad. *I was scared because his face had a maniacal look.*

dotty — **Dotty** means mad. It is used in a less serious way and is more suited to everyday language. *I think she is a bit dotty.*

nutty — **Nutty** can mean mad. It is so similar to **loony** that you can usually use either. *I'm going to visit my nutty old aunt.*

similar words: **silly**

main *adjective*

most important or biggest. *My **main** reason for training so hard is to get into the swimming team for the Olympics.*

major — **Major** means greater in importance or size. *His major interest in life seems to be surfing.*

chief — **Chief** means most important or main. *My chief problem is with spelling.*

key — **Key** means main or important. *The goal-keeper is a key member of the team.*

fundamental — **Fundamental** means most important or basic. *You have to learn the fundamental rules of the road before you can get a licence to drive a car.*

primary — **Primary** means first in order of importance. *Your primary need when you grow up is to earn enough money for food and clothes.*

similar words: **significant**
contrasting words: **minor**

make *verb*

to bring something into being. *Grandma is **making** a new jumper for me.*

produce To **produce** means to bring something forth or into existence. *My favourite author produces a new book every year.*

manufacture To **manufacture** means to make or **produce** something by hand or machine, especially in large numbers. *Dad works for a company that manufactures furniture.*

form To **form** means to make or **produce** something. *The children piled up sand to form a sandcastle.*

prepare To **prepare** means to make something ready. *Mum took the whole afternoon to prepare a special birthday dinner.*

whip up To **whip up** means to make something quickly. *Mum whipped up a meal when the visitors came.*

similar words: **create, build**
contrasting words: **destroy**

male *noun*

a man or boy. *At the camp, there was one block of toilets for the **males** and one for the females.*

gentleman **Gentleman** is a polite name for a man. *Good morning ladies and gentlemen.*

youth A **youth** is a young man. *A youth was arrested for stealing the motor car.*

lad A **lad** is a boy or young man. *The lad always liked to go sailing with his father.*

bloke A **bloke** is a man. It is more suited to everyday language. *My dad says the man next door is a good bloke because he never complains about our dogs.*

guy A **guy** is a man or boy. It is more suited to everyday language. *I went to the beach with the guys from school.*

contrasting words: **female**

maltreat *verb*

to treat someone roughly or cruelly. *The dog bit him when he **maltreated** it.*

abuse To **abuse** means to speak to someone in a nasty way. *Don't abuse me again in front of my friends.*

victimise To **victimise** means to punish or harm someone unfairly. *The school bullies always victimise the new children.*

torment To **torment** means to cause someone a lot of pain or suffering. *Please don't torment me any more with your teasing.*

hound To **hound** means to worry or pursue someone unkindly and continually. *The detective hounded the ex-prisoner even though he had reformed.*

torture To **torture** means to cause someone severe pain, usually to make them tell you something they know. *They tortured the spies to learn the enemy's plans.*

similar words: **subdue**

manage *verb*

to be in charge of something or someone. *The young stockman cannot **manage** the cattle on his own.*

run To **run** can mean to conduct or administer something, such as a business or an experiment. *My parents run a small printing business.*

direct To **direct** can mean to guide something or someone by giving instructions. *Our class teacher will direct the school play this year.*

govern To **govern** can mean to guide and have a controlling influence over something or someone. *Public opinion governed the committee's decision to stop the project.*

control To **control** means to be in charge of or **direct** someone or something. *The teacher had to control a large group of children on the excursion to the zoo.*

supervise To **supervise** means to manage or keep an eye on someone or something and be responsible for them. *The head teacher supervised my class during the French exam.*

similar words: **rule**

manager *noun*

someone who runs a business. *The bank **manager** has been transferred to Perth.*

director A **director** can be one of a group of people who control the affairs of a company or a government department. *The board of directors meets once a month to make sure the manager is following their orders.*

superintendent A **superintendent** is someone who is in charge of work being done, a business, or a building. *He is the superintendent of all the road work carried out in our suburb.*

administrator An **administrator** is someone who directs or manages something according to set rules or ways. *The lawyers appointed an administrator who looked after the business.*

commissioner A **commissioner** can be someone in charge of a public department. In such cases it is spelt with a capital 'C'. *The EEC has a Commissioner for Agriculture.*

official An **official** is someone who has the authority to do a particular job, usually in connection with government. *The council official said he would tell the garbage collectors not to be so noisy.*

similar words: **boss**

manner *noun*

a way of behaving or of doing things. *The doctor has a good bedside **manner**.*

attitude An **attitude** can be the way you hold your body or behave. *His threatening attitude frightens me.*

bearing Your **bearing** is the way you behave or stand. *Even without his crown and robes the king had a very noble bearing.*

carriage Your **carriage** is the way you hold your head and body when you walk or stand. *He has the tall, straight carriage of a soldier.*

stance Your **stance** is the position of your body when you are standing. *He took up a boxer's stance, ready to fight off the blow.*

posture Your **posture** is the particular position of your body at any time. *He photographed them in a kneeling posture.*

similar words: **appearance**

march *verb*

to walk like a soldier, with swinging arms and even steps. *We **marched** in time to the drum beat.*

parade To **parade** means to march, often in a procession or for display. *Scottish pipers paraded down the main street.*

stride To **stride** means to walk with long bold steps. *He strode quickly along the street without looking to the left or right.*

strut To **strut** means to walk in a proud or pompous way, with your back straight and your head held high. *She strutted across the stage to collect her prize.*

swagger To **swagger** means to walk in a pompous way, hoping to draw attention to yourself. *He was so proud of his new clothes that he swaggered along when he wore them.*

similar words: **walk, limp, trudge**

meal *noun*

food eaten at more or less fixed times each day. *Breakfast is my favourite **meal**.*

snack A **snack** is a small quick meal. *I have a snack every afternoon after school.*

feast A **feast** is a large meal set out for many guests. *They held a feast after the wedding.*

spread A **spread** can be a large meal for many people. It is similar to **feast** but is more suited to everyday language. *They put on a wonderful spread to welcome their friends from overseas.*

feed A **feed** is a meal or something to eat. It is more suited to everyday language. *I need a good feed after all that exercise.*

repast A **repast** is a meal. It is a slightly old-fashioned or formal word. *Let us sit down to our evening repast.*

similar words: **food**

mean *adjective*

not willing to give anything away or spend money unnecessarily. *She is too **mean** to share her lollies.*

stingy — **Stingy** means not wanting to spend money, especially on other people. *The stingy man would not buy his children ice-creams.*

tight — **Tight** is so similar to **stingy** that you can usually use either. *He's so tight with his money that he won't give anyone birthday presents.*

miserly — **Miserly** means trying to keep as much of your money as you can. *He is so miserly he won't buy things he really needs.*

penny-pinching — **Penny-pinching** means being **stingy** for no good reason. *She is too penny-pinching to buy a raffle ticket.*

mingy — **Mingy** means mean or **miserly**. It is more suited to everyday language. *You're mingy to give me such a small piece of cake.*

contrasting words: **generous**

meaning *noun*

something which is intended to be said or shown. *The teacher explained the **meaning** of the poem.*

gist — **Gist** is the most important part of something. *I understood the gist of the French comprehension passage.*

drift — **Drift** can be the general meaning of something. *Did you get the drift of his argument.*

significance — **Significance** can be so similar to **meaning** that you can usually use either. *The guide explained the significance of the war memorial.*

sense — **Sense** can be the particular meaning of a word, statement or a passage in a book. *In what sense is the poet using that word?*

essence — **Essence** is the basic nature or character of someone or something. *The artist has caught the essence of the Prime Minister in that portrait.*

measure *verb*

to decide the size or quantity of something by using a special instrument such as a ruler or scales. *We **measured** the length of rope we would need.*

gauge — **Gauge** means to measure the size, capacity, amount or force of certain things. *Airports have instruments to gauge the rate at which the wind is blowing.*

estimate — To **estimate** means to measure or work out roughly the quantity, size or amount of something. *We estimated how much food we would need for our camping trip.*

survey — To **survey** can mean to find out the form and boundaries of land by measuring it. *He surveyed the new area and pegged out the allotment.*

sound — To **sound** can mean to measure how far below the surface of the water something is. *The trawler sounded the channel to locate the school of fish.*

similar words: **judge, calculate**

mediocre *adjective*

neither good nor bad. *It was a **mediocre** film but we watched it to the end.*

indifferent — **Indifferent** can mean neither good nor bad in quality or character. *I am a very indifferent chess player.*

second-rate — **Second-rate** can mean mediocre, or not very good. *He's a second-rate actor and is often out of work.*

middling — **Middling** can mean mediocre or **second-rate**. It is more suited to everyday language. *She's only middling at tennis.*

banal — **Banal** means unoriginal or dull because it has been used too much. *The plot of the TV soap opera was so banal we didn't watch it.*

mundane — **Mundane** means ordinary, dull or boring. *We rejected his mundane suggestion when Sarah made a better one.*

similar words: **ordinary, inferior**
contrasting words: **superior**

meet *verb*

to come face to face with someone. *I **meet** my friend on the way to school each morning.*

encounter To **encounter** means to meet someone, especially unexpectedly. *I encountered an old friend in town yesterday.*

come across To **come across** means to meet someone by chance. *Whom do you think I came across yesterday?*

run into To **run into** can be so similar to **come across** that you can usually use either. *She ran into her uncle on the train.*

bump into To **bump into** means to meet someone by chance. *I bumped into him at the supermarket.*

join up with To **join up with** means to meet someone by arrangement. *I will join up with you at your place after dinner.*

meeting *noun*

an arrangement to come together for a purpose. *Next week's **meeting** of the chess club will be on Wednesday.*

appointment An **appointment** can be an arrangment made between people to meet to do somethig. *Daniel has an appointment to have his hair cut this afternoon.*

date A **date** is an **appointment**, usually made with a friend to do something enjoyable. *Clare and Tessa have a date to go to the movies.*

rendezvous A **rendezvous** is a meeting arranged beforehand. *The whole world waited eagerly for the rendezvous between the Giotto spacecraft and Halley's comet.*

assignation An **assignation** is a secret or forbidden meeting. *The ship's captain sent word to the smugglers to come to an assignation at midnight.*

tryst A **tryst** is a **rendezvous**, especially between lovers. *Romeo and Juliet arranged a secret tryst in the garden.*

mess *noun*

a dirty or untidy state. *Mum says the house is always in a* ***mess*** *when it rains.*

muddle A **muddle** is a confused mess. *I left my room in a muddle this morning because I slept in.*

jumble A **jumble** is a confused and disorderly mixture. *The clothes were in a jumble on the bed.*

clutter A **clutter** is an untidy group or pile of things. *There was a clutter of paper on the floor after we had opened our presents.*

shambles **Shambles** means any place or thing that is in confusion or disorder. *The classroom was a shambles after the vandals had broken into it.*

litter **Litter** is rubbish scattered about. *The park attendant was angry when he saw the litter the picnickers had left.*

message *noun*

information sent to one person from another. *Evan took a* ***message*** *about the picnic from Dorothy to Charles.*

note A **note** is a short letter. *My mother sent a note to my teacher when I stayed home sick.*

epistle An **epistle** is a letter. This is a rather formal or old-fashioned word but it is sometimes used in fun. *We received a long epistle from Susan when she went to Paris.*

word **Word** can mean a message or news. *Len had to go but he left word that I was to follow immediately.*

dispatch A **dispatch** is an official message sent by a messenger. *Captain Collins sent a dispatch to the general asking for reinforcements.*

communiqué A **communiqué** is an official news report. *After the meeting the premiers issued a communiqué to the public.*

similar words: **report**

messenger *noun*

someone who carries a message. *Large companies often employ **messengers** to take letters to their customers or to branch offices.*

courier A **courier** is someone who carries messages, letters or parcels for other people. *The courier took the important package from the country branch to the head office.*

postman A **postman** is someone who takes letters and packages from post offices to the people to whom they are addressed. *The postmen are always extra busy at Christmas time.*

envoy An **envoy** is someone who is sent to represent another person or a country. *The general sent an envoy to the besieged town demanding that its troops surrender.*

herald A **herald** is someone who carries messages or announces coming events. *The herald told the parliament that the Queen was on her way.*

method *noun*

a way of going about something, especially in an orderly way. *If you follow this **method** when you do the sum, you will find it easy.*

approach An **approach** is a particular way of going about something. *The new approach to reading has been accepted at our school.*

procedure A **procedure** is a way of doing something. *She followed the usual procedure for applying for a job and was offered an interview.*

technique A **technique** is a particular way of doing or performing something. *His serving technique is influenced by his tennis instructor.*

means **Means** can be a method or way used to reach an end or a goal. *Cars, buses and trains are the common means of transport in cities.*

mimic *verb*

to copy someone's voice or movements. *Some birds can **mimic** human voices.*

imitate To **imitate** means to copy someone or to use them as a model. *She often imitates her mother talking on the phone.*

ape To **ape** means to copy or mimic someone, sometimes without thinking about or realising what you are doing. *He is only four but he apes his big brother.*

send up To **send up** means to mimic someone in an exaggerated way in order to mock them. *They sent up the teacher's accent.*

caricature To **caricature** can mean to mimic someone by exaggerating or making fun of their unusual features. *The actor caricatured the Prime Minister.*

impersonate To **impersonate** means to pretent to be someone else. *The thief impersonated a policeman to persuade the old lady to open the door.*

minimise *verb*

to make something seem as small or unimportant as possible. *We must not **minimise** the risks we are taking.*

lessen To **lessen** can be so similar to **minimise** that you can usually use either. *In his description he deliberately lessened the dangers of the trip so we would not be scared.*

trivialise To **trivialise** means to make something important seem unimportant. *That book trivialises the subject of war.*

play down To **play down** means to treat something as unimportant in order to keep attention away from it. *She played down the amount of help she had given.*

make light of To **make light of** means to treat something as unimportant or amusing. *She made light of her injuries.*

laugh off To **laugh off** means to treat something lightly, even though you may not really feel that way. *He laughed off the pain he was feeling.*

contrasting words: **emphasise**

minor *adjective*

lesser in importance or size. *His plan had only a few **minor** faults.*

secondary — **Secondary** means next after the first in order of importance. *Moving the damaged cars was secondary to attending to the injured people.*

trivial — **Trivial** means of very little importance. *Trivial everyday chores seem to take up more time than they are worth.*

trifling — **Trifling** is so similar to **trivial** you can usually use either word. *I interrupted her work but she said it was a trifling matter that could wait.*

petty — **Petty** means of little importance. *Dad said I could attend to the petty details like working out which of our rugs to take on the picnic.*

slight — **Slight** can mean minor or small. *There is a slight change in our plans to go away next week.*

similar words: **insignificant, subordinate**
contrasting words: **main, significant**

misbehave *verb*

to behave badly. *He was punished because he **misbehaved**.*

make mischief — To **make mischief** means to behave in an annoying or teasing way. *Alice is always making mischief by playing tricks on her mother.*

act up — To **act up** means to cause trouble. It is more suited to everyday language. *She acted up in the restaurant so we all had to go home.*

be foolish — To **be foolish** means to misbehave in a silly way. *The class was kept in because one child was foolish.*

mess around — To **mess around** means to waste time doing useless things. It is more suited to everyday language. *Stop messing around and do your work.*

lapse — To **lapse** means to return to or fall into a bad habit or way of life. *She was good for a week but then she lapsed back into her silly ways.*

contrasting words: **behave**

miserable *adjective*

very unhappy. *We were* ***miserable*** *because we couldn't go away for a holiday.*

depressed — **Depressed** means feeling dejected or miserable. *She was depressed when her friends wouldn't let her play with them.*

despondent — **Despondent** means feeling down-hearted or in low spirits. *He was despondent when he realised that he had no chance of winning the race.*

forlorn — **Forlorn** means miserable because you are left all alone. *The sick boy was forlorn when his friends went camping without him.*

heart-broken — **Heart-broken** means completely overcome with sadness or grief. *She was heart-broken when her best friend died.*

cut up — **Cut up** means sad or depressed. It is more suited to everyday language. *He was cut up when they went to the party without him.*

similar words: **sad, glum**
contrasting words: **happy, joyful, glad**

misery *noun*

great unhappiness. *He caused* ***misery*** *to his parents when he was arrested for car-stealing.*

sorrow — **Sorrow** means grief or sadness. *My friend told me of her sorrow when her grandfather died.*

anguish — **Anguish** is very great **sorrow** or worry. *The parents of the lost child suffered terrible anguish.*

depression — **Depression** is the state of your mind when you feel worried, miserable and hopeless. *He suffered from depression when he was told he would never walk again.*

melancholy — **Melancholy** is a feeling of sadness or **depression**. *Her melancholy was so deep none of us could cheer her up.*

gloom — **Gloom** can be a feeling of unhappiness or **depression**. *Gloom fell on us all when we heard about our classmate's accident.*

contrasting words: **happiness**

misfortune *noun*

bad luck. *Losing your house in the fire was a terrible* ***misfortune.***

accident An **accident** is an unwanted or unlucky happening. *Our car accident stopped us from going on our holiday.*

mishap A **mishap** is an unfortunate accident. *I had a mishap on my way to school — I fell over and hurt my knee.*

hardship **Hardship** means bad luck or suffering in the way you live. *Many families endured great hardship during the great Depression.*

blow A **blow** is a sudden shock or misfortune. *It was a blow when they found their house wasn't insured when it burnt down.*

evil An **evil** is something that can cause suffering or misfortune or disaster. *The selling of drugs in our schools is an evil we will fight against.*

similar words: **disaster**

misrepresent *verb*

to describe or show something in an incorrect or false way. *He* ***misrepresented*** *our feelings towards her when he told her we thought she was stupid.*

twist To **twist** can mean to change the meaning of something on purpose. *You twisted what I said to make it sound as though I agreed with you.*

distort To **distort** can mean to misrepresent or **twist** something. *She distorted the facts so that it looked as though I was to blame.*

slant To **slant** can mean to present or tell something in a way that makes one particular thing seem more important. *They slanted the report to make their own ideas seem more sensible.*

exaggerate To **exaggerate** means to say more than is true about something to make it sound better. *He exaggerated the story until it sounded as though he alone had saved the whole town.*

falsify To **falsify** means to represent something in a false or incorrect way. *The accountant falsified the records to cover up his stealing.*

mistake *noun*

something someone has done wrongly without realising it. *I made three **mistakes** in my spelling.*

error — An **error** is so similar to **mistake** you can usually use either word. *I saw my error and corrected it.*

slip — A **slip** is so similar to **mistake** and **error** that you can usually choose any of them. *I made a slip in adding up the bill.*

blunder — A **blunder** is a silly mistake. *What a blunder to tell you the wrong day!*

boo-boo — A **boo-boo** is a mistake, especially in making a judgment about doing something. It is more suited to everyday language. *He made a boo-boo when he decided to try to trick her.*

gaffe — A **gaffe** is a social blunder. *She made a gaffe when she called the Queen Mrs. Windsor.*

mix *verb*

to combine or blend things together. *I **mixed** the eggs, sugar, milk and flour together and made some pancakes.*

mash — To **mash** means to mix something by pounding or crushing. *I mashed the potatoes until they were soft and creamy.*

emulsify — To **emulsify** means mix things together so that they form a liquid that looks like milk and is often rather oily. *The chemist emulsified a number of ingredients to make up the nasty medicine I had to take.*

stir — To **stir** means to mix something by moving a spoon or something similar around in it. *When you make a sauce you have to stir it all the time it is cooking.*

fold — To **fold** can mean to mix something in gently by turning one part over another with a spoon or something similar. *The cook folded the flour into the mixture to make a sponge cake.*

similar words: **combine**

mixture *noun*

any combination of different kinds, parts, qualities, and so on. *We need a **mixture** of food in our diet to keep healthy.*

assortment An **assortment** is a collection of things of various kinds. *We have a wide assortment of travel books in our library.*

jumble A **jumble** is a confused or disorderly group of things. *Her clothes were in a jumble on the floor.*

hotchpotch A **hotchpotch** is an unordered mixture. It is so similar to **jumble** you can often use either word. *Her bookshelves were a hotchpotch of books, magazines and photo albums.*

medley A **medley** is mixture of different kinds of things, especially a piece of music combining passages from other musical compositions. *The band played a medley of jazz music.*

miscellany A **miscellany** is a collection in one book of a variety of writings by different authors. *School magazines are a miscellany of stories and poems of interest to children.*

---

moderate *adjective*

keeping within proper bounds, or not extreme. *We put a **moderate** price on the goods at our school fete and sold everything.*

reasonable **Reasonable** means fair or moderate. *We made a reasonable profit at the garage sale.*

modest **Modest** can mean of medium value, quality or amount. *Our parents bought a modest home for us to live in.*

restrained **Restrained** means controlled or kept in check. *There was polite, but restrained applause for the amateur singer.*

middle-of-the-road **Middle-of-the-road** means moderate or not going to extremes in thought or behaviour. *Her opinions in politics are middle-of-the-road.*

temperate **Temperate** means moderate or controlled. *He is temperate in his use of alcohol.*

contrasting words: **intense**

modern *adjective*

belonging to or used in the present time. ***Modern** aeroplanes are much bigger and faster that the early ones.*

contemporary — **Contemporary** can mean modern or existing now. *The house was decorated in a contemporary style.*

current — **Current** means belonging to the present time. *We read about many of the current problems of the world in the newspaper.*

up-to-date — **Up-to-date** can mean modern or to do with the newest ideas and styles. *He only used the most up-to-date books to teach us science.*

recent — **Recent** can mean made or done not long ago. *Recent fashions have featured knee-length skirts.*

late — **Late** can mean new or **recent.** *At the car show we saw both early and late models of the Ford.*

similar words: **new**
contrasting words: **old-fashioned, old**

momentary *adjective*

lasting for a very short space of time. *There was a **momentary** flash of light before we heard the explosion.*

brief — **Brief** can mean short in time. *We are having a brief rest before finishing our work.*

fleeting — **Fleeting** means passing swiftly away. *We had a fleeting view of the racing cars as they went round the bend.*

passing — **Passing** can mean **brief** or going by quickly. *They hope my passion for very loud music is only a passing phase.*

ephemeral — **Ephemeral** means not lasting for very long. *The beauty of a rose is ephemeral as it fades and dies within a day or two.*

spasmodic — **Spasmodic** means happening suddenly, briefly and only from time to time. *Her illness causes her hands to make spasmodic jerking movements.*

contrasting words: **permanent**

move *verb*

to change from one place or position to another. *David was so comfortable in his hammock he didn't want to **move**.*

shift — To **shift** means to move from one place or position to another. This is a more informal word than **move**. *We tried to shift the crate but it wouldn't budge.*

stir — To **stir** can mean to move gently or in a slight way. *The leaves of the tree stirred in the gentle breeze.*

budge — To **budge** means to move away. This is usually used with the word 'not' or 'can't'. *She would not budge from the desk until the teacher made her.*

give way — To **give way** can mean to move or yield. *We all tried to push the heavy rock and it finally gave way.*

---

moving *adjective*

changing from place to place. *The **moving** shadows on my bedroom wall frightened me.*

mobile — **Mobile** means able to move or be moved. *After two weeks in bed with a broken leg Timothy is mobile again.*

manoeuvrable — **Manoeuvrable** means easy to move about. *The small car was very manoeuvrable in busy traffic.*

dynamic — **Dynamic** means having to do with the power that causes movement. *A battery is the dynamic force in some children's toys.*

kinetic — **Kinetic** means having to do with movement. *A mobile is an example of kinetic art.*

---

contrasting words: **steady, still**

---

mumble *verb*

to speak softly and not clearly. *If you **mumble** no-one will know what you are saying.*

mutter To **mutter** means to speak or grumble in a low voice that is hard to understand. *He muttered angrily to himself.*

lisp To **lisp** means to speak in such a way that you pronounce 's' and 'z' like the 'th' sound of *thin. She tries to speak clearly but she has always lisped.*

stammer To **stammer** means to speak with breaks and pauses that you can't control or with repetitions of some words or sounds. *He was so surprised and pleased he could only stammer out his thanks.*

stutter To **stutter** means to speak with a broken halting rhythm, repeating many sounds. *She was so nervous that she stuttered and stumbled as she spoke before the huge crowd.*

splutter To **splutter** means to talk quickly and in a confused way, making it difficult to pronounce the words. *He spluttered with rage when he heard the news.*

contrasting words: **pronounce**

musical *adjective*

pleasing to your ears like music. *The **musical** tones of the bellbirds drifted through the valley.*

tuneful **Tuneful** means full of or producing pleasant and agreeable sounds. *We enjoyed the tuneful singing of the children.*

melodious **Melodious** means having an attractive sound like a melody or tune. *We were wakened by the melodious ringing of nearby church bells.*

lyrical **Lyrical** means having the form and musical quality of a song. *He recited the lyrical poem in his light singsong voice.*

mellow **Mellow** can mean having a very deep and rich sound. *The last mellow notes of the organ echoed around the concert hall.*

sweet **Sweet** can mean light and pleasant to your ears. *She fell asleep to the sweet sounds of the lullaby.*

contrasting words: **discordant**

musician *noun*

someone who plays or composes music. *She wants to be a **musician** in an orchestra when she leaves school.*

virtuoso — A **virtuoso** is a highly skilled musician. *He is a virtuoso on the violin.*

instrumentalist — An **instrumentalist** is someone who plays a musical instrument. *There were six instrumentalists at the chamber concert.*

soloist — A **soloist** is someone who performs a piece of music for one singer or player, with or without an accompaniment. *The soloist at the concert was a violinist.*

accompanist — An **accompanist** is someone who provides a musical backing for a melody. *I played the piano as the accompanist for my sister who played a violin solo.*

naive *adjective*

ingorant, or understanding little about the affairs of the world. *His **naive** comment showed us that he had no idea how serious the situation was.*

simple — **Simple** can mean lacking knowledge, ignorant or unaware. *She was a simple soul and only really enjoyed knitting.*

unworldly — **Unworldly** means having little or no knowledge of the ways of the world. *The monk lived an unworldly life and spent most of his time meditating alone in his cell.*

unsophisticated — **Unsophisticated** means not changed by or experienced in the interests and pleasures of the world. *She is very unsophisticated in the way she dresses.*

gullible — **Gullible** means easily deceived or cheated. *People always played practical jokes on her because she was so gullible.*

innocent — **Innocent** can mean having the simplicity of a person who isn't experienced in the ways of the world. *She's so innocent that she was shocked to hear them swearing in the playground.*

name *noun*

what something or someone is called. *Have you thought of a **name** for your new kitten?*

title — A **title** is a name given to someone to show their occupation or rank in society. *She earned the title 'Doctor' by studying hard for her medical degree.*

pseudonym — A **pseudonym** is a made-up name used instead of a writer's real name. *He decided to use a pseudonym so nobody would know he had written the book.*

pen-name — A **pen-name** is the same as a **pseudonym**. *Some authors use pen-names so they can remain anonymous.*

alias — An **alias** is a false name someone uses to try to hide who they really are. *The criminal gave an alias to get a new passport and flee the country.*

nickname — A **nickname** is a name people call you, usually in a friendly way, instead of your real name. *We gave her the nickname 'Bubbles' because she was always so happy.*

---

name *verb*

to give a name to someone or something. *They **named** the baby Emma.*

call — To **call** can be so similar to **name** that you can usually use either word. *They called the kitten Garfield.*

christen — To **christen** means to give a name to someone or something in a special ceremony. *The minister christened the baby Peter William.*

title — To **title** means to **call** or name something. *What have you titled your new book?*

dub — To **dub** can mean to make up a name or title for someone to use instead of their real name. *We dubbed him 'The Rat'.*

tag — To **tag** can mean to use a special word or phrase to describe someone. *They tagged him a coward.*

---

narrow *adjective*

not wide. *The path through the garden was very **narrow**.*

tight — **Tight** can mean fitting closely, especially too closely. *We all got into the bus but it was a tight squeeze.*

close — **Close** can mean narrow or **tight**. *Your jeans are a very close fit.*

small — **Small** can mean narrow or not great in extent. *The dog squeezed through a small hole in the fence.*

confined — **Confined** means restricted to a very small space. *The children had only a very confined area to play in.*

cramped — **Cramped** can mean narrow or not having enough space. *The room was cramped with three desks in it.*

contrasting words: **wide, spacious**

narrow-minded *adjective*

lacking in understanding of other people's ideas. *He's so **narrow-minded** he doesn't understand that migrants can still love the countries they were born in.*

intolerant — **Intolerant** means not allowing other people to have or express opinions different from your own. *She is very intolerant of people who like to go to the pictures instead of playing sport at the weekend.*

bigoted — **Bigoted** means being convinced that your opinion, especially about religion, is right and everyone else's is wrong. *The bigoted Christian was very rude to my Jewish friend.*

biased — **Biased** can mean having a strong opinion which stops you from seeing the other side of an argument. *The soccer player was too biased in favour of his sport to see any good in cricket.*

prejudiced — **Prejudiced** means influenced without a sensible or balanced reason. *The dog-show judge was prejudiced in favour of the poodle because he has one himself.*

conservative — **Conservative** means opposed to new ideas and sudden changes of any kind. *She is so conservative in her dress that she never wears jeans.*

contrasting words: **broad-minded**

nasty *adjective*

unpleasant or disgusting. *We saw a* ***nasty*** *accident on our way to the city.*

awful — **Awful** means very bad or unpleasant. *The children made an awful mess with the paints.*

repulsive — **Repulsive** means dreadful or disgusting. *The food was so repulsive it made her feel quite ill.*

revolting — **Revolting** means disgusting or **repulsive.** *The milk tasted revolting because it had turned sour.*

vile — **Vile** means disgustingly bad. *He used vile language when he shouted at us.*

ugly — **Ugly** can mean unpleasant to see or hear. *The boys' language was as ugly as their behaviour.*

similar words: **bad, horrible**
contrasting words: **nice, agreeable, good**

naughty *adjective*

behaving in an annoying or irritating way. *He is the* ***naughtiest*** *boy in the class because he is always bullying other children.*

badly-behaved — **Badly-behaved** means not behaving properly. *I was badly-behaved because I didn't like my baby-sitter.*

mischievous — **Mischievous** means behaving in a way that is naughty without meaning serious harm. *The mischievous toddler threw his daddy's shoes in the bath.*

incorrigible — **Incorrigible** means showing that you intend to do what you like even though it's naughty. *The incorrigible child had every intention of pouring water all over the kitchen floor.*

uncooperative — **Uncooperative** means not helpful or unwilling to work together. *The work will take longer if you are uncooperative.*

perverse — **Perverse** means deliberately going against what is expected or wanted. *She is in a perverse mood and won't go to bed.*

similar words: **disobedient**
contrasting words: **well-behaved, obedient**

nautical *adjective*

having to do with ships, sailors or sailing. *If you want to learn to sail you will have to learn the proper **nautical** terms.*

seafaring — **Seafaring** means travelling on the sea. *It has been a seafaring nation for generations.*

seagoing — **Seagoing** means designed for or able to sail on the open sea. *They have bought a seagoing launch and are going to sail around the world.*

maritime — **Maritime** means having to do with ships or the sea. *International maritime law states that any ship must go to the aid of another ship in trouble.*

seaworthy — **Seaworthy** means in a fit condition to sail at sea. *The inspector said the boat was seaworthy and they could start as soon as they wished.*

naval — **Naval** can mean having to do with ships, nowadays only war ships. *They fought a naval battle not far from the islands.*

---

near *adjective*

being at a short distance from something. *We will walk to the **near** paddock today and go to the far one tomorrow.*

close — **Close** can have almost the same meaning as **near**. *My house is close so we'll go there now.*

next — **Next** means nearest in place or position. *I'll just be in the next room.*

adjacent — **Adjacent** means lying near or alongside something. *The school bought the adjacent block of land to give us a bigger playground.*

neighbouring — **Neighbouring** means living or placed near something or someone. *We went to play in the neighbouring park.*

warm — **Warm** sometimes means being quite near to something you're looking for, usually in a game. This is usually used in everyday language. *Keep looking, you're very warm now.*

contrasting words: **distant**

necessary *adjective*

unable to be done without. *Water is **necessary** for life.*

essential — **Essential** means absolutely necessary. *Flour is an essential ingredient in bread.*

vital — **Vital** can be so similar to **essential** that you can usually use either. *Careful preparations are vital if this project is to be a success.*

crucial — **Crucial** means of the greatest importance. *Checking the air tanks before you go scuba diving is crucial.*

imperative — **Imperative** means necessary or not to be avoided. *It was imperative that our boat reach the shore before the storm came.*

obligatory — **Obligatory** means necessary, required or considered as binding. *Typing will be an obligatory part of this job.*

contrasting words: **extra**

neglect *verb*

to pay no attention to something, usually by ignoring it. *He **neglected** his appearance when he grew old.*

overlook — To **overlook** means to miss or ignore something. *The burglars overlooked the ring because it was in a cheap box.*

leave out — To **leave out** someone or something means to forget about or ignore them. *He did badly in the exam because he left out one question.*

omit — To **omit** means to **leave out** or fail to do something. *He is so bad-mannered he omitted knocking before he came it.*

disregard — To **disregard** means to fail to pay any attention or thought to something or somone. *She disregarded my wishes.*

forget — To **forget** can mean to fail to remember someone or something, sometimes on purpose. *Some people forget their parents when they are old.*

contrasting words: **remember**

negotiate *verb*

to deal with someone in order to prepare some kind of agreement, such as between countries or in business. *The two countries **negotiated** to write a peace treaty to end the fighting.*

decide To **decide** can mean to settle something in doubt. *Let's ask the teacher to decide for us.*

arbitrate To **arbitrate** means to judge or settle a disagreement between other people. *Will you arbitrate for us because we can't agree?*

mediate To **mediate** means to come between people who are arguing to try to help them to agree. *The consumer affairs officer mediated between the shop and the customer until they reached an agreement over the damaged goods.*

intervene To **intervene** means to step in, in order to solve a problem. *When the unions still couldn't agree the government finally intervened.*

intercede To **intercede** means to speak or act on behalf of someone in trouble. *He interceded for the school thief with the head teacher.*

---

nervous *adjective*

worried or frightened, especially about something that might happen in the future. *I am **nervous** about going to my new school.*

anxious **Anxious** means very worried or uneasy. *We were anxious when the hikers didn't get back on time.*

apprehensive **Apprehensive** means afraid of what might happen. *She was apprehensive about going to London by herself.*

edgy **Edgy** means nervous and irritable. *Dad's been edgy ever since he gave up smoking.*

jumpy **Jumpy** means so nervous that you are likely to make sudden uncontrolled movements. *I'm jumpy if I'm alone in the house at night.*

jittery **Jittery** means nervous or **jumpy**. *We were jittery before the race started.*

similar words: **frightened, upset**
contrasting words: **calm**

neutral *adjective*

not taking one side or the other. *Sweden was a **neutral** country in the war.*

even-handed **Even-handed** means not favouring or preferring one side to the other. *The referee was known for his even-handed treatment of players.*

disinterested **Disinterested** means not directly involved in something. *They called for a disinterested outsider to settle the dispute.*

non-committal **Non-committal** means not giving your decision or opinion so you can't be held to it. *His non-committal answer could have meant anything.*

detached **Detached** means remaining apart or not being concerned with or involved in something. *She maintained a detached attitude throughout the whole dispute.*

similar words: **fair**
contrasting words: **unfair**

new *adjective*

recently arrived, obtained or come into being. *I really like the **new** books about Halley's Comet.*

novel **Novel** means new or different, usually in an unusual way. *He had a novel excuse each day for not doing his homework.*

original **Original** can mean newly thought up or invented, and not like anything else. *The car shaped like a rocket won a prize for the most original design.*

innovative **Innovative** means completely new in a clever or creative way. *We admired the innovative projects they displayed in the classroom on Open Day.*

fresh **Fresh** can mean new or different. *That is a very fresh approach to our problem.*

avant-garde **Avant-garde** means modern and usually produced as an experiment, especially drawing, painting, architecture, or something similar. *Not everyone admired the avant-garde sculpture.*

similar words: **modern**
contrasting words: **old-fashioned, old**

nice *adjective*

pleasing or delightful. *She was wearing a **nice** dress.*

pleasant — **Pleasant** means agreeable or pleasing. *We all had a pleasant day at the zoo.*

enjoyable — **Enjoyable** means pleasing or to your liking. *The party was enjoyable because everyone chatted happily together.*

lovely — **Lovely** can mean very pleasant or good. *The weather was lovely while we were away.*

acceptable — **Acceptable** means pleasing to the person receiving it. *The meal was quite acceptable even though it was not really hot enough.*

welcome — **Welcome** can mean pleasing and wanted. *Her letter was especially welcome as I hadn't heard from her for a long time.*

similar words: **agreeable, good**
contrasting words: **nasty, pathetic, annoying, horrible**

noise *noun*

any kind of sound, especially a sound which is too loud or which you don't like. *Stop making that **noise,** I can't hear the TV!*

din — A **din** is a loud noise that goes on and on. *The children made a terrible din as they set the table.*

hubbub — A **hubbub** is a loud confused noise, like that made by many voices. *There was a hubbub in the room as everyone talked at once.*

racket — A **racket** can be a loud confused noise. *The carpenter building our deck made a racket as he moved the wood and hammered in the nails.*

uproar — An **uproar** is a noisy disturbance. *The audience was in an uproar when the rock concert was cancelled at the last minute.*

pandemonium — **Pandemonium** means wild and noisy confusion. *There was pandemonium when the people in the shopping centre heard about the bomb scare.*

similar words: **commotion**
contrasting words: **whisper**

nonsense *noun*

words that are silly or without meaning. *His **explanation** sounded like nonsense to me.*

rot — **Rot** can be so similar to **nonsense** that you can usually use either. It is more suited to everyday language. *He talks a lot of rot.*

rubbish — **Rubbish** can be so similar to **nonsense** that you can usually use either. *That advertisement sounds like rubbish.*

mumbo jumbo — **Mumbo jumbo** is meaningless words, especially when thought to have a magical effect. *The magician said some mumbo jumbo as he did his trick.*

piffle — **Piffle** means nonsense or idle talk. It is more suited to everyday language. *We were unconvinced by his argument because we thought it was utter piffle.*

bunkum — **Bunkum** means insincere or foolish talk. *When he was drunk he always spoke a lot of bunkum.*

number *noun*

a word or symbol you use to indicate an amount or the position of something. *Everyone in the game was given a **number** so they would know when it was their turn.*

figure — A **figure** is a symbol that stands for a number. *Write the figure 3 next to the circle with three crosses in it.*

numeral — A **numeral** is a symbol or group of symbols which express a number. *The Roman numeral for nine is IX.*

digit — A **digit** is any of the **numerals** from 0 to 9. *There are only ten digits.*

integer — An **integer** is any whole number. *We made a list of all the integers up to a hundred that could be divided evenly by three.*

fraction — A **fraction** is a part of a whole number or **integer**. *I know that ¾ is a fraction.*

numerous *adjective*

very many. *The doctors and nurses looked after **numerous** casualties after the motorway pile-up.*

multiple — **Multiple** means having or involving many parts. *The man who fell over the cliff had multiple injuries.*

multitudinous — **Multitudinous** means forming a great number or crowd. This is an old-fashioned word. *The multitudinous waves swamped the buccaneer's boat.*

innumerable — **Innumerable** means more than can be counted. *As soon as we started our picnic, innumerable flies descended on us.*

legion — **Legion** means great in number. *She is such a lovely person her friends are legion.*

similar words: **countless**
contrasting words: **scarce, single**

obedient *adjective*

following someone else's wishes or orders. *The **obedient** puppy is being trained as a guide dog.*

docile — **Docile** means quiet and easy to manage. *The children learned to ride on the docile horse.*

tractable — **Tractable** means easily managed. *Her tractable nature made her an ideal pupil.*

law-abiding — **Law-abiding** means obeying the laws. *The law-abiding citizens helped the police in their search.*

compliant — **Compliant** means agreeing with someone else readily or willingly. *He was so compliant that he seemed to have no mind of his own.*

dutiful — **Dutiful** means doing what you should do. *The dutiful daughter helped her parents when they were old and sick.*

similar words: **well-behaved, submissive**
contrasting words: **disobedient, naughty**

obey *verb*

to carry out the commands of someone. *The children **obeyed** their parents.*

heed To **heed** means to pay attention to someone or something. *We decided to heed the 'No Swimming' notice at the lake.*

observe To **observe** can mean to obey or **follow** rules or laws. *You should observe the traffic rules when riding a bicycle on the road.*

follow To **follow** can mean to accept someone or something as a guide. *I'll follow your instructions.*

comply with To **comply with** means to act in accordance with rules, laws or requests. *The audience complied with the request to remain in their seats.*

contrasting words: **disobey**

obsession *noun*

a strong idea or feeling which controls someone's behaviour. *She has an **obsession** about horses and goes riding every weekend.*

hang-up A **hang-up** is something which worries you and which you can't get off your mind. This is more suited to everyday language. *He had a hang-up about being too short.*

complex A **complex** is so similar to **hang-up** that you can usually use either. This is more suited to everyday language. *He had a complex about speaking in public.*

phobia A **phobia** is an overpowering fear. *She has a phobia about spiders.*

fetish A **fetish** is an obsession which is usually expressed by ritualistic behaviour. *He had a fetish about cleanliness and washed his hands everytime he touched something.*

obstacle *noun*

something which is in your way or which holds you up. *We could see that the **obstacle** holding up the traffic was a fallen tree.*

hindrance — A **hindrance** is something that slows you down or hinders your progress. *Lack of money has been a real hindrance to our school's plans to buy a computer.*

hitch — A **hitch** is something that obstructs or makes things difficult. *The total fire ban was a hitch in our camping plans.*

handicap — A **handicap** is any disadvantage that makes success harder. *Wearing uncomfortable shoes turned out to be a handicap for him in the cross-country.*

drawback — A **drawback** is a disadvantage or an inconvenience. *The plan is great except for one drawback — we haven't got enough money.*

barrier — A **barrier** is anything which bars or blocks the way. *Not being able to speak the same language can often be a barrier between people.*

obvious *adjective*

easily seen. *It was **obvious** from his red eyes that he had been crying.*

clear — **Clear** can mean obvious or without any doubt. *It was very clear to us that we would miss the bus if we didn't run.*

evident — **Evident** can mean obvious or easily understood. *It's evident from your red face that you are embarrassed.*

plain — **Plain** can mean clearly seen. It can be very similar to **clear** and **evident**. *The tangle in your knitting is a plain case of what happens if you start before you know what you are doing.*

apparent — **Apparent** can mean able to be seen. *My failure to follow the recipe was apparent because the cake was as flat as a pancake.*

distinct — **Distinct** can mean obvious and unmistakable. *Don't worry, you will see a distinct difference between the twins.*

similar words: **visible**

offer *noun*

something that is presented to someone for them to consider or accept. *We made him an **offer** of help but he refused.*

proposal A **proposal** is a plan or scheme offered to someone for approval. *We presented our proposal for the new swimming pool to the committee.*

proposition A **proposition** is a plan or subject suggested as something to be acted upon or discussed. *Our neighbours suggested that we should have a picnic, but I had a better proposition.*

bid A **bid** is an offer of money for something, especially one made at an auction. *She made a bid of £200 for the table.*

tender A **tender** is an offer to do a job for a certain price. *They will accept the lowest tender to build the house.*

similar words: **suggestion**

offspring *noun*

the baby animal or child of a particular parent. *A lion's **offspring** is called a cub.*

young **Young** can be offspring, usually of animals. *The female kangaroo carries its young in a pouch.*

issue **Issue** can be offspring, usually of people. *The king's first male issue was the heir to the throne.*

descendant A **descendant** is an offspring or a person who has descended from a particular ancestor. *I'm a descendant of William the Conqueror.*

progeny **Progeny** means the offspring or **descendants** of people or animals. *Before long I didn't have any more room for my pet rabbits' progeny.*

contrasting words: **ancestor**

old *adjective*

of or from an earlier time. *In the **old** days there were hardly any cars on the roads.*

ancient — **Ancient** means of, happening or living a very long time ago. *We read stories about the gladiators in ancient Rome.*

antique — **Antique** means dating from earlier times. *They found some antique statues in the pyramid.*

prehistoric — **Prehistoric** means belonging to the time before history was written or records were kept. *We saw the bones of a prehistoric dinosaur in the museum.*

vintage — **Vintage** can mean from a time in the past. *We saw some vintage aeroplanes at the air show.*

similar words: **old-fashioned**
contrasting words: **modern, new**

old-fashioned *adjective*

belonging to a time in or style of the past. *We dressed up in **old-fashioned** clothes and pretended we were our grandparents.*

out-of-date — **Out-of-date** means not in fashion or no longer used. *You need a modern computer to replace that out-of-date one.*

obsolete — **Obsolete** means no longer used because something newer and more fashionable has replaced it. *My computer is so obsolete that it only belongs in a museum.*

antiquated — **Antiquated** means old-fashioned or **out-of-date**. *That antiquated textbook has some interesting diagrams in it that show how people thought the human body worked in those days.*

archaic — **Archaic** means very old-fashioned or belonging to the very distant past. *'Thee' and 'thou' are archaic words that are not used very often today.*

square — **Square** can mean dressing or behaving in an old-fashioned way. *Dad's so square he won't even let me wear jeans.*

similar words: **old**
contrasting words: **chic, new, modern**

opaque *adjective*

not able to be seen through. *I couldn't see who was there because the glass in the door was **opaque**.*

dense — **Dense** can mean too thick to see through. *The airport was closed due to the dense fog.*

thick — **Thick** can often be used instead of **dense**. *The smoke was so thick we couldn't see where we were going.*

turbid — **Turbid** means not clear or **dense**. This is a rather formal word. *I could only see white through the window as the plane flew through the turbid clouds.*

cloudy — **Cloudy** can mean not clear. *We added ammonia and now the water is cloudy.*

muddy — **Muddy** can mean not clear or **turbid**. *The water was too muddy for us to see the bottom of the creek.*

contrasting words: **transparent**

opinion *noun*

what you think or decide. *What is your **opinion** about the suggestion of a new law against smoking?*

attitude — An **attitude** can be the way you behave towards or feel about something. *The market researcher at the shopping centre asked me what was my attitude towards battery eggs compared with free-range ones.*

outlook — An **outlook** is an **attitude** or point of view. *Diana has a friendly nature and an optimistic outlook on life.*

viewpoint — A **viewpoint** is a way of considering or thinking about something or someone. *He asked me my viewpoint about having three terms or four in the school year.*

stand — A **stand** can be a definite opinion that you declare openly. *The Prime Minister took a strong stand on defence.*

conviction — A **conviction** can be an opinion or belief that you hold strongly. *It is my conviction that we would all be safer if nuclear weapons had never been invented.*

opposite *adjective*

completely different in every way. *His behaviour was* ***opposite*** *to what I had expected.*

converse — **Converse** means turned about or opposite in direction, action or meaning. *If we go around in converse directions we should meet in the middle.*

antithetical — **Antithetical** means in direct or complete opposition or contrast. *Which of these two antithetical statements will you believe?*

contradictory — **Contradictory** means in exact or direct opposition. It is very similar to **antithetical**. *The results of your experiments are contradictory.*

contrary — **Contrary** means opposed or different to something else, but it may not be exactly opposite. *My opinion is contrary to yours.*

conflicting — **Conflicting** means clashing, disagreeing or in opposition. *We were surprised at our conflicting ideas about religion.*

contrasting words: **similar**

optimistic *adjective*

expecting that things will turn out well. *Her* ***optimistic*** *outlook helped us all believe we would be rescued.*

positive — **Positive** can mean tending to see what is good or gives hope. *His positive approach helped him to find a solution to the problem.*

confident — **Confident** means having a strong belief, or feeling quite certain about something, usually something that is good or desirable. *I am confident that they will find us soon.*

hopeful — **Hopeful** means looking forward to or expecting something, especially something good. *We were hopeful of finding the lost climbers before nightfall.*

buoyant — **Buoyant** means light-hearted and cheerful. *They expressed the buoyant feelings they had by laughing and joking as they set out.*

happy-go-lucky — **Happy-go-lucky** means trusting cheerfully to luck. *They're so happy-go-lucky that their preparations were not adequate and they lost their way.*

contrasting words: **pessimistic**

orange *adjective*

having a reddish-gold or yellow colour. *We planted some seeds and weeks later dug up huge, **orange** carrots.*

amber — **Amber** means having a yellowish-brown colour. *Dad slowed the car, ready to stop, when he saw the amber light.*

terracotta — **Terracotta** means having a brownish-red colour. *We chose terracotta tiles, instead of a brighter red, for the roof of our new house.*

ginger — **Ginger** means having a reddish-brown colour. *I named my cat Ginger after her ginger fur.*

peach — **Peach** means having a light pinkish-orange colour. *Their cheeks were a healthy, peach colour after their swim.*

gilt — **Gilt** means having a golden-orange colour. *I bought a frame with a gilt edge to put my favourite photograph in.*

---

order *noun*

an instruction that you must obey. *The general gave the **order** to march.*

command — A **command** is so similar to an **order** that you can usually use either word. *At last he gave the command to stop.*

decree — A **decree** is an official order, usually made by a government or someone in a position of power. *The new government decree stated that no-one could go out at night during the state of emergency.*

writ — A **writ** is an official order telling a person or group something that they must or must not do. *We obtained a writ from the council ordering our neighbours not to cut down more trees.*

summons — A **summons** is an order to appear in a certain place, often a law court. *I received a summons to appear as a witness at his trial.*

warrant — A **warrant** is a paper given by a magistrate to the police allowing them to arrest someone or search a building. *We have a warrant for your arrest.*

similar words: **demand**

ordinary *adjective*

usual or normal, and as such, rather boring. *It was just another **ordinary** working day.*

average — **Average** can mean usual or ordinary. *An average Monday consists of sport, maths, drama and spelling.*

standard — **Standard** can mean normal or ordinary. *I wish we didn't have to wear standard school uniform.*

fair — **Fair** can mean of an ordinary or moderately good standard. *His marks in the exam were fair.*

nondescript — **Nondescript** means very ordinary-looking without any easily recognisable qualities. *It's hard to describe the house because it's quite nondescript.*

similar words: **mediocre**
contrasting words: **excellent, unusual**

organisation *noun*

a group of people which runs or manages something. *We need to set up a money-raising **organisation**.*

company — A **company** can be a group of people brought together to run a business. *This book is produced by a publishing company.*

firm — A **firm** is a business organisation. It is very similar **company**. *She went to work for the family firm.*

corporation — A **corporation** is a business **company** especially one established by law. *The government set up a broadcasting corporation.*

syndicate — A **syndicate** is a group of business people or business organisations, especially one formed to carry out a particular project. *The engineering firms formed a syndicate to build the big new hotel.*

outfit — An **outfit** can be a business organisation or group of people working together. *He belongs to a military outfit.*

outside *noun*

the outer part or side of something. *We covered the **outside** of the box with coloured paper.*

exterior — **Exterior** means the outer part of something. *The exterior of the building was in bad shape and needed painting.*

surface — **Surface** can mean the top or outer side of something. *The workmen were repairing the surface of the road because it was full of potholes.*

face — **Face** can mean the main side or front of something. *The face of the cliff was too steep to climb.*

facade — A **facade** is the front of something as seen from the outside, especially of a building. *The historic building had a very attractive facade although the inside was quite plain.*

contrasting words: **inside**

outskirts *noun*

the outer areas. This is a plural noun. *There are small farms on the **outskirts** of the city.*

periphery — The **periphery** is the outside edge of an area or thing. *The chairs were arranged around the periphery of the room.*

perimeter — The **perimeter** is the outside edge of a shape or area. *The spectators sat around the perimeter of the oval.*

boundary — The **boundary** is the outside edge which separates one area from another. *The foreman drove around the boundary of the farm checking that there were no broken fences.*

limit — The **limit** is the outermost or furthest point of an area. *The king sent messengers out to the limits of his kingdom to find someone who could slay the dragon.*

frontier — A **frontier** is the outer area or end of known territory. *The early settlers explored the frontier.*

similar words: **edge**
contrasting words: **centre**

overbalance *verb*

to fall or trip over. *People learning to skate usually **overbalance** a lot.*

tumble To **tumble** can mean to roll or fall over. *I tumbled on the slippery grass.*

somersault To **somersault** can mean to perform a gymnastic movement, or something similar, in which you roll completely heels over head. *The car somersaulted a couple of times after hitting the rail.*

capsize To **capsize** means to turn over. *The boat capsized and we had to swim to shore.*

keel over To **keel over** means to turn over or turn upside down. *The yacht keeled over in the strong wind.*

similar words: **fall**

overturn *verb*

to turn something over on its side, back or face. ***I overturned** the wheelbarrow to tip the grass onto the compost.*

invert To **invert** means to turn something upside down, inside out or inwards. *The magician inverted the glass of water without spilling any.*

upset To **upset** can mean to knock or turn something over. *When the cat jumped on my lap, it upset my cup of tea.*

skittle To **skittle** means to knock someone or something over or send them flying like ninepins. *The car skittled the garbage tins as it ran up onto the footpath.*

bowl over To **bowl over** can mean to knock someone or something over forcefully. *The dog bowled the old woman over as it ran past her.*

tip over To **tip over** means to topple something over. *The cat tipped the milk bottles over as it ran out the door.*

contrasting words: **steady**

own *verb*

to have something which belongs to you. *My parents **own** the house we live in.*

possess To **possess** means to own or have something. *The art gallery possesses several valuable paintings.*

hold To **hold** means to have in your possession. *He holds a large number of shares in BP.*

have all to yourself To **have all to yourself** means to have something completely for your own use. *You will have the house all to yourself this weekend because we are going away.*

monopolise To **monopolise** means to get or have complete control of something. *The new children found it hard to join in because the others had monopolised all the toys.*

occupy To **occupy** can mean to own or live in a building or house. *The new owners moved in to occupy our house as soon as we sold it.*

pacify *verb*

to make something or someone quiet or peaceful. *She quickly **pacified** the frightened horse.*

mollify To **mollify** means to make someone calmer or less angry. *The shop owner mollified the angry customer by replacing the faulty iron.*

appease To **appease** means to make someone peaceful, quiet or happy. *The factory manager appeased the angry workers by promising them a pay rise.*

calm To **calm** means to make someone or something less excited or emotional. *The teacher calmed the hysterical children and told them the vicious dog had been caught.*

quieten To **quieten** can mean to make someone or something more calm or peaceful. *The speaker came back on stage to quieten the jeering crowd.*

defuse To **defuse** can mean to **calm** a tense situation. *When the argument started to get nasty, Leah defused the situation by cracking a joke.*

similar words: **comfort**
contrasting words: **anger, frighten**

pain *noun*

a feeling of hurt or soreness in a particular part of your body. *My brother had a lot of **pain** in his leg after he broke it.*

ache An **ache** is a dull continuous pain. *I had a stomach ache after eating so much food.*

twinge A **twinge** is a pain that lasts only a moment. *My grandmother gets twinges of rheumatism in her hands.*

stitch A **stitch** can be a sudden sharp pain, especially between your ribs. *I had a stitch after my aerobics class.*

cramp A **cramp** is a sudden tightening of a muscle in your body. *My mother suggested that I pull my foot forward when I had a cramp in my leg.*

spasm A **spasm** is an uncontrolled movement of your muscles. *I had a spasm in my leg after the cross-country run.*

pardon *noun*

a formal declaration of forgiveness for a crime. *The governor gave the prisoner a **pardon** because he was too old and sick to be in jail.*

release A **release** can be the act of setting someone free from imprisonment, arrest or other confinement. *The newspaper report about the prisoner's release said that the police didn't have enough evidence to convict him.*

reprieve A **reprieve** means a delay, especially in carrying out a punishment. *The judge granted the prisoner a reprieve from execution.*

amnesty An **amnesty** is a pardon given to everyone, especially for crimes against the government. *The government declared an amnesty for all petty criminals, to mark the nation's bicentenary.*

acquittal An **acquittal** is a declaration of innocence. *The man's acquittal by the jury was announced on the news.*

part *noun*

a piece or fragment of something. *Daniel cut **part** of the shelf off to make it fit.*

portion A **portion** is a part or share of something. *I left my lunch at home so Jasper gave me a portion of his.*

section A **section** is a part or division of something. *The boys played in one section of the playground and the girls played in another.*

segment A **segment** is a piece or a **section**. *Alexandra divided her orange into segments and gave each of her friends one.*

proportion A **proportion** is a part of something compared to the whole of it. *Linsay did a larger proportion of the work than anyone else.*

fraction A **fraction** can be a small amount or piece. *Dominic did his composition in a fraction of the time the rest of the class took.*

similar words: **share, piece**

pass *verb*

to go by or move past something. *We **passed** the station on our way to the shops.*

overtake To **overtake** means to catch up with someone or something and pass them. *The police overtook the speeding driver and made her stop.*

outstrip To **outstrip** can mean to pass someone or something when running or travelling quickly and to leave them behind. *I outstripped my nearest rival in the 100 metres sprint.*

beat To **beat** can mean to defeat someone or do better than them. *She beat him in the race.*

lose To **lose** can mean to leave someone or something far behind in a race or a chase. *The winner of the marathon lost the other runners towards the end of the race and won by nearly half a kilometre.*

lap To **lap** can mean to get ahead of other competitors by a complete round of a racing track or length of a swimming pool in a race. *The winning car lapped the others early in the race and never gave up its lead.*

past *adjective*

gone by in time. *My past hobby was pot-holing but now I prefer mountain climbing.*

former — **Former** means coming before someone or something else in time, or from an earlier or past time. *The former headteacher of our school came back to visit us.*

bygone — **Bygone** means past or gone by. *We read stories about bygone days when highwaymen roamed the countryside.*

sometime — **Sometime** means having been formerly or in the past. *He is a sometime champion and now coaches younger athletes.*

late — **Late** can mean having recently died. *The young prince took over the throne of his father, the late king.*

contrasting words: **future**

pathetic *adjective*

causing feelings of pity or sadness. *The picture of the starving children on TV was a* ***pathetic*** *sight.*

pitiful — **Pitiful** means causing or deserving pity. *The mouse made a pitiful attempt to escape as the cat pounced on it.*

wretched — **Wretched** means **pitiful** and causing misery. *The homeless people were living in wretched conditions after the cyclone.*

Miserable can mean causing unhappiness or distress. *It's cruel to keep birds in such a miserable little cage.*

dismal — **Dismal** means feeling or causing deep sadness. *Our plan to raise a lot of money was a dismal failure.*

woeful — **Woeful** means **miserable** and deserving pity. *He has been so woeful since his best friend moved.*

similar words: **bad**
contrasting words: **nice**

patient *adjective*

waiting quietly and calmly. *The **patient** customer let the elderly lady be served first.*

tolerant — **Tolerant** means putting up with or allowing things that you may not like or feel happy about. *She was very tolerant of the noise we made playing with our new toys.*

long-suffering — **Long-suffering** means continually putting up with something that annoys or hurts you. *My long-suffering friend puts up with my moodiness.*

persevering — **Persevering** means continuing to do something even though it is very difficult. *His persevering work brought him success in the exams.*

persistent — **Persistent** means keeping on doing something until you have finished, no matter how hard it is. *We were persistent and at last completed the job.*

stoical — **Stoical** means behaving in a patient and calm way that shows you have courage. *We were impressed by your stoical behaviour while you were waiting to be rescued.*

---

pay *noun*

the money you are paid for the work you do. *Most people try to save some of their **pay**.*

salary — A **salary** is the money you earn, especially for office work. *The bank manager earns a bigger salary at his new branch.*

wage — A **wage** is the money you are paid for working, especially in a factory or as a labourer. *The mechanic earned a good wage.*

commission — **Commission** is the extra money paid to someone who sells things for his employer. *The car salesman earned 10% commission on each car he sold.*

fee — A **fee** is the money you pay to a doctor, lawyer or a private school. *Our school fees are for tuition and the use of sporting equipment.*

income — **Income** is all the money you get from your work or investments. *You have to pay tax on your income.*

---

similar words: **profit**

---

pay *verb*

to give money, or something similar in return for goods or services. *I **paid** £2.50 for the new tyre for my bike.*

spend — To **spend** means to pay out money, wealth, or something similar. *I spent of lot of my savings at the show.*

expend — To **expend** can mean to pay out or **spend** money, usually large amounts. *We expended nearly all our capital on the new farm machinery.*

invest — To **invest** means to pay out a large sum of money for something, hoping that you will make more money from the deal. *She invested her inheritance in real estate and before long became a millionaire.*

similar words: **buy, repay**

peaceful *adjective*

calm and free from strife or trouble. *We enjoyed living in the **peaceful** country town where people were so friendly.*

serene — **Serene** means peaceful or showing no signs of stress or strife. *The nun's faith in God showed in her serene face.*

tranquil — **Tranquil** means peaceful, calm or free from disturbance. *We found a tranquil spot on the bank of a river to have a rest.*

quiet — **Quiet** can mean calm and peaceful. *We enjoyed a quiet evening at home after a hard day at school.*

gentle — **Gentle** can mean not rough or violent. *The gentle little boy loved to cuddle his baby brother.*

harmonious — **Harmonious** means showing agreement in feeling or action. *The harmonious atmosphere in the club returned when the president told the trouble-makers to go.*

similar words: **calm**
contrasting words: **violent**

perfect *adjective*

with nothing missing and no faults. *It was a **perfect** day to go on a picnic.*

faultless — **Faultless** means without any mistakes or blemishes. *They gave a faultless performance at the concert.*

impeccable — **Impeccable** means completely free from any faults. It is very similar to **faultless**. *His manners were impeccable during his visit.*

immaculate — **Immaculate** means free from any fault, blemishes or errors. *Their work was immaculate.*

ideal — **Ideal** means being a perfect example of something. *She will make an ideal captain for the team.*

complete — **Complete** can mean perfect in every way. *Our happiness was complete as we rode beside the river.*

similar words: **excellent**
contrasting words: **defective**

permanent *adjective*

lasting forever or for a very long time. *There is **permanent** snow on the top of the highest mountains.*

everlasting — **Everlasting** means lasting or continuing for a long time or forever. *I'm sick of your everlasting complaints.*

eternal — **Eternal** means lasting forever or not having any end. *Some people believe that if you have eternal life your soul will never die.*

immortal — **Immortal** means lasting or living forever. *The immortal works of William Shakespeare will be learned and loved by every generation to come.*

perpetual — **Perpetual** means without a fixed end or lasting forever. *I don't think we'll ever have rain to break this perpetual drought.*

perennial — **Perennial** means continually coming back or lasting for a long time. *Jill is a perennial trouble-maker and is always being punished.*

contrasting words: **temporary, momentary**

permission *noun*

formal allowance given to do something. *I have **permission** to go.*

leave — **Leave** is so similar to **permission** that you can usually use either. *I need my parents' leave before I can go.*

approval — **Approval** can mean permission or **consent**. *We had to get the headmaster's approval before we could change the school uniform.*

clearance — A **clearance** can be official permission to go ahead with something. *They needed a clearance from the council to add an extra storey to their house.*

consent — **Consent** means permission or agreement to do something. *We are waiting to get the council's consent before we start altering our house.*

dispensation — **Dispensation** can be special permission given to break a rule for a particular occasion. *He was given a dispensation to miss cricket practice because he had a sore ankle.*

---

persist *verb*

to continue or keep on with something, even when people oppose you. *He **persisted** with his questions even though his teacher wanted him to stop.*

persevere — To **persevere** means to continue with something you have started, even though it may be difficult. You can often use it instead of **persist**. *Although I am tired I will persevere with my work.*

last the distance — To **last the distance** means to keep on with a difficult task or some physical activity until you have finished. *He knew he couldn't win the race but he was determined to last the distance.*

press on — To **press on** means to keep on trying and is often used when talking of physical activities that you might want to give up. *Although the children were tired of walking, the teacher urged them to press on.*

stick to your guns — To **stick to your guns** means to keep your position in an argument and so on, when people oppose you. *My friends tried to talk me out of going to the concert but I stuck to my guns.*

---

persistence *noun*

the fact or action of continuing to do something in spite of opposition from someone. *Because of his **persistence** in asking for a bike his parents finally gave in.*

perseverance **Perseverance** is the determination to continue to do something in spite of difficulty. *We admired her perseverance in doing the painful exercises after her accident.*

tenacity **Tenacity** means the stubborn determination to continue to do something. *The ant's tenacity in dragging the huge crumb to its nest amazed us.*

stamina **Stamina** is physical strength or power, especially to fight off sickness or tiredness. *The cross-country race will test your stamina.*

endurance **Endurance** is the ability to bear or hold out against some difficulty or problem. *The early settlers in Australia showed their endurance by not giving in to the hardship they had to face.*

grit **Grit** can mean courage or strength of character. *He showed a lot of grit in overcoming the difficulties of life in a wheelchair.*

persistent *adjective*

continuing in spite of opposition. *We watched with interest the spider's **persistent** attempts to put its web across the path we use every day.*

tenacious **Tenacious** means stubbornly persistent. *The detective's tenacious questioning of the witness finally got him the evidence he needed.*

determined **Determined** means firm in purpose. *We are determined to win the championship again this year.*

dogged **Dogged** means unflinching, or resolved not to give in. *Anthony's parents rewarded his dogged attempts to learn to swim.*

single-minded **Single-minded** means showing you have decided or resolved to succeed in a particular thing. *Amanda is single-minded about saving her pocket money to buy a bicycle.*

unflagging **Unflagging** means not weakening or giving up. *They were unflagging in their efforts to raise money for the school swimming pool.*

similar words: **stubborn**

persuade *verb*

to cause someone to do or believe something by advising, arguing with or influencing them. *We **persuaded** her to come with us.*

convince To **convince** means to make someone believe or feel sure about something. *His test results convinced him that he had to work harder at school.*

talk into To **talk into** means to persuade someone to do something by talking to them. *We finally talked them into having a holiday this year.*

induce To **induce** can mean to cause someone to decide something. *I will induce him to join the school committee.*

coax To **coax** means to persuade someone gently and patiently. *She coaxed the sick child to eat.*

lobby To **lobby** means to try to get political support for a particular issue or cause. *The environmental group lobbied various politicians on the issue of saving the rainforest.*

similar words: **influence, encourage**
contrasting words: **discourage**

pessimistic *adjective*

expecting that things will turn out badly. *He was **pessimistic** about our chances of being rescued.*

discouraging **Discouraging** means making things appear in the worst possible way. *His discouraging talk began to make us lose hope.*

off-putting **Off-putting** means **discouraging** or upsetting. *It was off-putting to listen to his stories about people lost in the bush.*

gloomy **Gloomy** means causing great unhappiness or depression. *Our gloomy situation looked even worse as it grew dark.*

depressing **Depressing** means causing gloom or misery. *We finally told him to keep his depressing comments to himself.*

contrasting words: **optimisitc**

piece *noun*

a bit or part of something. *I cut off a **piece** of my new dress material to show Pat.*

scrap A **scrap** is a small piece. *Hamish made a toy car out of a scrap of wood.*

fragment A **fragment** is a part that has been broken off. *He cut his foot on a fragment of the broken bottle lying in the grass.*

morsel A **morsel** is a very small piece or amount. *She was too tired to eat more than a morsel of food before she fell asleep.*

particle A **particle** is a very small bit. *A particle of dust got in her eye and made it very sore.*

sliver A **sliver** is a small thin piece. *We used a sliver of wood as a wedge to stop the window rattling.*

similar words: **trace, part**

pity *noun*

a feeling of sorrow for the suffering of others. *We looked at the poor trapped animal with **pity**.*

sympathy **Sympathy** is a feeling of sorrow you share with someone else who is sad or in trouble. *We felt great sympathy for our neighbours when their house burnt down.*

compassion **Compassion** means pity together with a feeling that you want to help. *The Red Cross asked us to show compassion for the victims of the earthquake by sending money.*

tenderness **Tenderness** is a gentle loving feeling of pity. *The mother cared for her sick baby with tenderness.*

mercy **Mercy** is the pity or kindness you show someone when you don't punish them for doing something wrong. *The lawyer asked the jury to show mercy on the young man because it was his first offence.*

similar words: **comfort**

place *noun*

a particular area or part of space. *We're going to a new **place** for our holidays.*

position A **position** is a particular place. *I chose a position near the window.*

spot A **spot** can be a less formal word for a **place**. *Pick a good spot for the barbecue.*

location A **location** can be a particular place or area. *The post office has been moved to a new location nearer the shops.*

site A **site** is a particular place where something has happened or is going to happen, or the place on which something is or will be built. *Many people gathered at the site of the rocket launch. We want a house on a site overlooking the lake.*

venue A **venue** is a place where a particular event is held. *The venue for the school play will be the village hall.*

place *verb*

to put something in a particular position. *When he finished drinking he **placed** his cup back on its saucer.*

set To **set** can be so similar to **place** that you can usually use either word. *He set the vase on the table.*

rest To **rest** can mean to lie or lean one thing against another. *She rested the ladder against the wall.*

deposit To **deposit** can mean to put something down. *She deposited her bag on the bed.*

lodge To **lodge** means to put something somewhere for safekeeping. *Before we went on holidays we lodged our valuables with the bank.*

park To **park** means to place something in a particular position. It is more suited to everyday language. *He parked himself right in the middle of the doorway.*

similar words: **position**

plan *verb*

to make careful preparations for something. *We **planned** the picnic so that we wouldn't forget anything.*

arrange To **arrange** can mean to prepare or plan something. *We arranged a party for the last day of school.*

organise To **organise** can mean to **arrange** something or make plans for it. *We organised a holiday at the beach.*

engineer To **engineer** means to plan or **arrange** something in a clever way. *Everyone was surprised when she engineered a friendly meeting between the two rivals.*

mastermind To **mastermind** means to plan and direct something in a skilful clever way. *Not a thing went wrong when she masterminded the concert.*

set up To **set up** means to organise or arrange something. *We have set up a meeting for you in the morning.*

similar words: **plot**

please *verb*

to make someone happy or satisfied. *The gift **pleased** them very much.*

delight To **delight** means to give someone great pleasure. *Being invited to the party delighted me.*

charm To **charm** can mean to please very much. *Her personality charmed me.*

attract To **attract** means to draw or win someone by your appearance, behaviour and so on. *His smile attracts me.*

appeal to To **appeal to** means to have the ability to attract or interest someone. *This perfume appeals to me.*

satisfy To **satisfy** means to please someone or make them happy. *My test results satisfied my parents.*

contrasting words: **disgust, irritate, annoy**

plot *noun*

a secret plan or idea, usually to harm someone. *I discovered his **plot** to tear up my project.*

conspiracy A **conspiracy** is similar to a **plot**. It always involves more than one person. *The rebels entered into a conspiracy to assassinate the president.*

scheme A **scheme** can be a secret plan. *They worked out a scheme to kidnap the millionaire's son.*

intrigue An **intrigue** can be a secret plan made by dishonest or sly people. *Political intrigue caused the downfall of the government.*

ruse A **ruse** is a dishonest trick or plan. *His mother saw through his ruse to avoid mowing the lawn.*

stratagem A **stratagem** is a plan or trick for deceiving an emeny. *The Greeks' stratagem for conquering the city of Troy was to hide inside a wooden horse.*

similar words: **trick**

plot *verb*

to plan secretly, especially something harmful or evil. *They **plotted** to overthrow the government.*

scheme To **scheme** can mean to plot or make up a secret plan. *He schemed for the downfall of all those who disagreed with him.*

conspire To **conspire** means to plan secretly with another person or group of people. *The terrorists conspired to hijack a plane.*

collude To **collude** means to **conspire** to cheat people. *The ship's captain colluded with the smugglers to escape the customs officers.*

intrigue To **intrigue** means to plot in a crafty way. This is a rather old-fashioned way to use this word. *He knew they were intriguing against him behind the locked door.*

connive To **connive** can mean to work together secretly. *The spy connived with the government scientist to steal the secret plans for the new rocket.*

similar words: **plan**

poisonous *adjective*

containing poison which may kill you or make you very sick if you swallow it or it pierces your skin. *Drinking the **poisonous** concoction was the cause of his death.*

venomous **Venomous** means producing a poisonous substance that can kill you or make you very sick. It is used about some snakes and spiders. *The adder is the only venomous snake found in the British Isles.*

toxic **Toxic** can mean poisonous, or acting as a poison. *The toxic waste from the mill was killing the fish in the river.*

noxious **Noxious** means harmful to your health. *Many people were taken to hospital when the noxious gas escaped from the factory.*

carcinogenic **Carcinogenic** means able to cause cancer in your body. *Any known carcinogenic chemicals and food additives are banned by law.*

polish *verb*

to make something smooth and bright by rubbing. *He **polished** his shoes until they glistened.*

shine To **shine** can mean to polish or make something sparkle or glisten. *Mum decided to shine all the silver cutlery in the drawer.*

buff To **buff** means to polish metal or give a smooth bright glow to other surfaces. *She buffed the brass knocker on our door.*

burnish To **burnish** means to make something glistening and bright by rubbing. It is similar to **buff**. *She burnished the copper kettle, too.*

furbish To **furbish** can mean to polish or **burnish** armour or weapons. It is a rather old-fashioned word. *The knight furbished his sword and put it carefully into its sheath.*

wax To **wax** means to polish something by rubbing it with wax. *We asked the garage to wax our car.*

similar words: **smooth**
contrasting words: **roughen**

polite *adjective*

having good manners. *What a **polite** girl you are to offer me your seat in the bus.*

courteous — **Courteous** is so similar to **polite** you can usually use either word. *He asked in such a courteous way that we all agreed to do what he said.*

gracious — **Gracious** means very kind and **courteous**. *Alison was a gracious hostess and thanked everyone for coming to her party.*

gallant — **Gallant** means very polite and helpful. *It was a gallant act to carry my heavy suitcase for me.*

chivalrous — **Chivalrous** means very polite and attentive. It is usually only used about men's behaviour towards women. *Have you read the story of the chivalrous knights of King Arthur and the Round Table?*

similar words: **well-behaved**
contrasting words: **rude, bold, vulgar**

pompous *adjective*

showing too much sense of your own importance. *Nobody really liked John because he was rather **pompous**.*

pretentious — **Pretentious** means having an exaggerated outward show of importance, wealth and so on. *The pretentious woman always talked about the important people she knew and the expensive clothes she bought.*

uppity — **Uppity** means behaving in a bold or forward way, or acting as if you are superior. It is more suited to everyday language. *The people who lived in the big house next door were rather uppity.*

affected — **Affected** can mean behaving in an artificial way to impress people. *That actor is very affected, especially in the way he speaks.*

snooty — **Snooty** means snobbish, proud or arrogant. It is more suited to everyday language. *We thought the boys from the other school were snooty.*

la-di-da — **La-di-da** means **pretentious**, especially in your manners or speech.This is more suited to everyday language. *She's so la-di-da since her father was elected mayor.*

similar words: **proud**
contrasting words: **humble**

ponder *verb*

to consider or think deeply or carefully about something. *We **pondered** the question of whether we would let him join our secret club.*

contemplate — To **contemplate** means to consider something thoughtfully. *He contemplated the letter for several minutes.*

weigh — To **weigh** can mean to consider carefully by thinking about all apsects of something. *Give me some time to weigh your suggestion in my mind.*

meditate on — To **meditate on** means to think long and deeply about something. *If you meditate on a problem you can often find a solution to it.*

reflect on — To **reflect on** means to think carefully about something. *Mum told me I should reflect on my unkindness to Cathy and then apologise to her.*

pore over — To **pore over** means to read or study something very carefully. *The students pored over their books.*

similar words: **concentrate on**

poor *adjective*

having little money, property or means of producing wealth. *The **poor** family barely made enough money to live on.*

needy — **Needy** means very poor or not having enough money or belongings. *There are many organisations which help needy people by giving them food, clothes and furniture.*

impoverished — **Impoverished** means having been made very poor. *The farmers were impoverished after the many years of drought.*

disadvantaged — **Disadvantaged** can mean not having a reasonable standard of living because you don't have enough money or the means of making it. *Many disadvantaged people receive a pension to help them buy some of the things they need.*

hard up — **Hard up** means very poor or urgently in need of money.It is more suited to everyday language. *I was so hard up I had to borrow some money for lunch today.*

similar words: **broke**
contrasting words: **wealthy**

position *noun*

a job or duty for which you are employed. *She began her career in the bank with a **position** as a teller.*

post A **post** is a job or duty. *She has a teaching post.*

situation A **situation** is a position in which you are employed. *I've been looking for a new situation ever since I lost my last job.*

station A **station** can be a place or position of duty. *The soldier went to his station by the gates.*

office An **office** is a position of trust or power, usually in the government or a business. *He has the office of press secretary to the Prime Minister.*

appointment An **appointment** is a job or special position someone is given. *We were pleased at his appointment as general manager of the company.*

similar words: **job, profession**

position *verb*

to put in a particular place. *He **positioned** his chair right in front of the television.*

locate To **locate** means to put something in a particular position or area. *The council located the new car park near the railway station.*

site To **site** means to place something in a certain position. It is very similar to **locate**. *They sited the new hospital on the other side of town.*

station To **station** means to place something in a position for a particular reason. *The police stationed guards at every exit.*

install To **install** means to put something into place so it can be used. *Dad installed the new stove just in time for us to cook lunch.*

establish To **establish** means to set up. *They established the new school exactly where the old one had been.*

similar words: **place**

possible *adjective*

able to be done or be used. *It is **possible** to drive there in one day.*

feasible — **Feasible** means likely to work. *I think your plan is feasible.*

viable — **Viable** means possible or able to succeed in operation. *I don't think it is viable for us all to go in your car.*

workable — **Workable** means able to be put into operation. *I have thought of a workable plan.*

practicable — **Practicable** means able to be done or put into practice because it is sensible or uses what you have. *It will be more practicable for us to go there by bus.*

similar words: **likely, useful**
contrasting words: **impossible, useless**

poverty *noun*

the condition of having little money, few possessions or means of producing wealth. *They lived in **poverty** because they could not get jobs.*

want — **Want** is the condition of not having the necessities of life. It is very similar to **poverty**. *There are people living in want in all our big cities.*

need — **Need** can mean a situation or time when you want the things necessary to live. *They were in great need when they lost all their belongings in the fire.*

distress — **Distress** can mean the state of suffering or hardship caused by poverty. *Try to imagine a whole African nation in distress.*

destitution — **Destitution** means the state of having no money or the means of getting any. *Their church sent them gifts of food and clothing to relieve their destitution.*

deprivation — **Deprivation** can mean the state of being without the things you need because you have no money. *Both their parents were invalids so they suffered from great deprivation.*

contrasting words: **wealth**

powerful *adjective*

having great force, authority or influence. *The American President is one of the most **powerful** men in the world.*

mighty — **Mighty** means having or showing power, force or ability. It is rather an old-fashioned word. *Some of the ancient kings were mighty rulers.*

forceful — **Forceful** means strong, powerful and able to influence people. *The politician was a forceful speaker.*

potent — **Potent** can mean strong or having great power. *There are potent arguments against building the new airport so close to the city.*

dominant — **Dominant** means most important or powerful. *The dominant group at the meeting was the one that supported the mayor.*

strong — **Strong** can mean having great power or effect. *She is such a strong headteacher that all the children respect her.*

contrasting words: **powerless**

powerless *adjective*

not having the power or ability to do things. *With my hands and feet tied up I was **powerless** to escape.*

impotent — **Impotent** is very similar to **powerless**. *When his soldiers deserted him the old leader was impotent.*

incapacitated — **Incapacitated** means having been made powerless or unable to do something. *The ambulance carried the incapacitated victims of the road accident to hospital.*

feeble — **Feeble** means lacking in force, strength or effectiveness. *The tired survivors could only make feeble attempts to yell for help.*

pathetic — **Pathetic** can mean showing a great lack of ability. *I made such a pathetic attempt at writing my essay that I decided to try again.*

gutless — **Gutless** can mean lacking in power, especially when it describes a car or motor. *Our gutless car struggled up even the smallest hill.*

similar words: **useless**
contrasting words: **powerful**

practical *adjective*

sensible and facing things as they really are. ***Practical** people do not keep wanting things they cannot have.*

realistic — **Realistic** means facing life as it really is. *I won't keep on discussing this unless you are realistic.*

down-to-earth — **Down-to-earth** means practical and sensible. *He's always down-to-earth in the way he solves his problems.*

matter-of-fact — **Matter-of-fact** means so sensible that it is rather uninteresting. *He gave a matter-of-fact speech rather than an imaginative one.*

pragmatic — **Pragmatic** means thinking about the results or usefulness of your actions. *She is too pragmatic to sulk for long.*

similar words: **sensible**

practice *noun*

a performance or action that is repeated regularly to improve skill. *I have to do my piano **practice** every afternoon this week.*

drill — A **drill** can be an exercise or a strict way of training that is repeated regularly. *We must do fire drill once a month.*

training — **Training** can be a session to develop fitness or a time to practise certain physical skills. *We go to football training twice a week.*

run-through — A **run-through** is a quick trial or practice, usually before the official performance. *We had a run-through of what we were going to say before we went in to see the mayor.*

warm-up — A **warm-up** is a short period of preparation for a sporting event, musical or theatrical performance. *The orchestra had a warm-up before the performance.*

rehearsal — A **rehearsal** is a private practice of something before giving a public performance. *We had several rehearsals before the opening night of our school play.*

praise *verb*

to say that you admire or approve of someone or something. *Although we didn't win the game the coach **praised** our efforts.*

compliment To **compliment** means to praise or say that you admire someone or something. *She complimented me on my new pink jumper.*

commend To **commend** means to say that you admire and approve of someone or something. *I commend you for your hard work this year.*

speak well of To **speak well of** means to say very good or complimentary things about someone or something. *I heard your teacher speak well of your friend.*

sing someone's praises To **sing someone's praises** means to praise someone very highly. *The people sang the king's praises when he returned victorious from battle.*

similar words: **acclaim, approve**
contrasting words: **disapprove of, fault, slander**

precise *adjective*

absolutely right in every detail. *Do you know the **precise** time?*

exact **Exact** can mean completely right. It is very similar to **precise**. *Please tell me the exact date.*

accurate **Accurate** can mean careful and **exact**. *Is that an accurate copy of the original?*

spot-on **Spot-on** means absolutely right or **accurate**. This is more suited to everyday language. *Your cartoon of the Prime Minister is spot-on.*

definite **Definite** means precise and clearly stated. *I found the definite instructions you gave me very helpful.*

pat **Pat** can mean exactly to the point. *I approve of your pat reply to my query.*

contrasting words: **vague**

predict *verb*

to tell what is going to happen in the future. *The journalists tried to **predict** which party would win the election.*

divine To **divine** means to use magic to guess what will happen in the future. *The gypsy looked into her crystal ball to divine my future.*

foresee To **foresee** means to see what is going to happen before it does. *I foresaw trouble when the puppy got into the sheep paddock.*

forecast To **forecast** is so similar to **predict** that you can often use either word. **Forecast** is mostly used to tell about the weather. *The weather man has forecast rain for next weekend.*

prophesy To **prophesy** means to tell what you believe is going to happen. *He prophesied a huge flood after the cyclone.*

warn To **warn** means to tell someone that something dangerous may happen. *The weather report warned the sailors that a heavy storm was expected.*

prefer *verb*

to regard one thing or person as better than another. *I **prefer** caramel topping to chocolate on my ice-cream.*

favour To **favour** can mean to prefer someone unfairly. *Everyone favours Maria because she is pretty.*

single out To **single out** means to pick or choose someone or something ahead of others. *They singled her out for a special award because of her kindness.*

opt for To **opt for** means to choose one thing instead of another or other things. *I opt for the train because it's faster.*

elect To **elect** can mean to pick out or choose something. *I elected art as my extra subject at school.*

similar words: **choose**

press *verb*

to act upon something with weight or force. *We **pressed** the button at the pedestrian crossing and waited for the 'walk' sign.*

compress To **compress** means to press things together, or force something into less space. *The workers compressed the wool into bales ready for transportation.*

jam To **jam** can mean to push or force something into a space tightly. *I jammed the books into the small bookcase.*

squeeze To **squeeze** means to press hard, so as to remove something. *Let's squeeze some oranges so that we can have a drink of fresh orange juice.*

squash To **squash** means to flatten or crush something or someone. *The wheel squashed my hat.*

trample To **trample** means to crush or tread heavily on something or someone. *The neighbour's dog trampled the flowers in our garden.*

pretty *adjective*

pleasant or pleasing to look at, especially in a dainty or graceful way. *The **pretty** girl was admired by everyone. I bought a **pretty** vase.*

fair **Fair** can mean very pretty or beautiful. This is a rather an old-fashioned way of using the word. *The prince fell in love with the fair maiden.*

good-looking **Good-looking** means pleasant to look at. *Everyone in my family is good-looking.*

handsome **Handsome** means having a fine or pleasant appearance. *Her brother is very handsome.*

attractive **Attractive** means quite pleasing to look at. *It's an attractive colour scheme. He's an attractive man.*

similar words: **beautiful**
contrasting words: **ugly**

prevent *verb*

to keep or hinder something or someone from doing something. *We'll build a high fence to **prevent** the dog from getting out.*

stop To **stop** can mean to prevent, restrain or hinder someone or something from doing something. *I'm going to stop you from going to the dance.*

prohibit To **prohibit** can mean to prevent or hinder. *I'm afraid your bad leg prohibits your jumping all the hurdles.*

oppose To **oppose** can mean to hinder or stand in the way of something. *They did everything they could to oppose her marriage.*

suppress To **suppress** can mean to keep something hidden or from being known or published. *They will try to suppress the news of his death.*

forbid To **forbid** can mean to prevent or make it impossible for someone to do something. *The train strike forbids his return home.*

similar words: **hinder, block, ban**
contrasting words: **allow**

price *noun*

the amount of money for which something is bought or sold. *I'll buy it if the **price** is right.*

cost The **cost** is the price to be paid for something. *What's the cost of the bike with the red handlebars?*

charge The **charge** is the price or **cost** of something. *The entry charge for the show is £2.*

expense The **expense** is the amount of money to be paid for something. *We couldn't go by plane because the expense was too great.*

rate The **rate** is a specially worked out **charge** or payment for something. *Mum borrowed money for a new car and has to pay the bank's interest rate of 10% a year.*

outlay An **outlay** can be the amount of money spent in getting something. *We hired two videos for the party for a very small outlay.*

prison *noun*

a place where criminals are kept locked up. *The bank robber was sent to **prison** for ten years.*

jail A **jail** is so similar to a prison you can usually use either word. *He spent ten years in jail.*

penitentiary A **penitentiary** is a prison for people who have committed serious crimes, where the punishment is designed to change criminal behaviour. It is often used in America. *The death sentence is still carried out in some American penitentiaries.*

compound A **compound** can be a closed-off area with buildings where people can be kept. *The soldiers guarded the captured airmen in a compound for prisoners-of-war.*

lockup A **lockup** is a small prison often attached to a police station, where offenders are kept until they appear in court. *The constable took the drunken driver to the lockup.*

clink A **clink** is a prison. It is more suited to everyday language. *He's in the clink.*

---

prisoner *noun*

someone who is kept somewhere against their will. *The **prisoners** were locked in their cells after tea.*

captive A **captive** is someone who has been taken prisoner. *The terrorists kept the captives locked up for almost a year.*

convict A **convict** is someone who has been found guilty of a crime and is serving a prison sentence. In former times, it referred to a person sent to a British colony, like Australia, to serve their sentence. *Police are searching for the escaped convict.*

inmate An **inmate** is someone who has to stay in a prison, hospital or other institution. *She is an inmate of a girls' reformatory.*

internee An **internee** is someone who is held as a prisoner in a guarded area during wartime. *The German internees in England tried to escape from their compound and return to Germany.*

similar words: **criminal**
contrasting words: **escapee**

prize *noun*

a reward for winning something such as a race or competition. *The winner's **prize** was a free trip to the zoo.*

trophy A **trophy** is a prize won in a contest, usually a silver cup or something similar. *My trophy for winning the race was a cup with my name on it.*

award An **award** is a prize won for good work or achievement. *He was given an award for his brave action.*

medal A **medal** is a metal disc or cross given as a prize or an **award** for bravery. *The soldier received a medal for his bravery under fire.*

pennant A **pennant** is a triangular flag, usually flown on the rigging of a ship or yacht to identify the owner or captain. *We could see the Admiral's pennant flying from the masthead.*

produce *verb*

to bring something or someone into being. *This soil **produces** good crops.*

bear To **bear** can mean to produce by natural growth or to give birth to a child. *This tree bears oranges. The queen bore a son who would one day be the king.*

yield To **yield** can mean to produce or **bear** something.It is not used to refer to animals or people. *The crops will yield a good harvest this year.*

breed To **breed** can mean to raise, or produce young by encouraging the parents to mate. *He breeds prize bulls.*

grow To **grow** means to develop or cause to come into being. *We grew these plants from seeds.*

contrasting words: **destroy**

profession *noun*

an occupation in which special knowledge is needed. *She is a doctor by **profession**.*

craft — A **craft** is an occupation for which you need special skill with your hands. *His craft is watchmaking.*

trade — A **trade** is a particular kind of work using your hands, for which you need special training. *He decided that carpentry was the best trade to learn.*

gig — A **gig** is a job for a musician, usually a booking for one show. It is more suited to everyday language. *Our band has a gig at the rock concert next Friday night.*

racket — A **racket** can be an illegal business or way of making money. It is more suited to everyday language. *The police arrested the leaders of the drug racket.*

similar words: **job, position**

profit *noun*

money made by selling something for more than it cost to produce or buy. *The lawn-mower factory made a big **profit** this year.*

proceeds — **Proceeds** means the money you get when you sell something. *The proceeds of the sales were higher than the costs of running the factory.*

return — A **return** can be the extra money you receive as a profit from an investment and so on. *The owners were pleased with the return on the money and work they had put in to the factory.*

dividend — A **dividend** is your share in the profit made by a business. *They paid a good dividend to the investors in the business.*

bonus — A **bonus** is extra money paid to a worker as a reward for good work. *Each worker received a bonus.*

royalty — A **royalty** is money paid to a writer, composer or inventor as a share of the profits made from their work. *The inventor of the lawn-mower received a royalty each year.*

similar words: **pay**

promise *noun*

a statement telling someone that you will be sure to do or stop doing something. *I made a **promise** to be good.*

pledge A **pledge** is a promise made very seriously. *She made a pledge that she would not steal again.*

vow A **vow** is a solemn promise. It is very similar to a **pledge**. *The secret agent took a vow not to reveal any secret information.*

oath An **oath** is a promise you make that what you say will be true. *When you give evidence in court, you take an oath that you will tell the truth.*

word of honour Your **word of honour** is a serious promise you make to someone that what you say can be trusted. *I give you my word of honour that I won't do it again.*

pact A **pact** is a solemn promise or agreement. *We made a pact that we would always be friends.*

---

pronounce *verb*

to make the sound of a word or letter. *We had an argument about how to **pronounce*** the word 'neither'.

enunciate To **enunciate** means to pronounce words or sounds in a particular manner, usually clearly. *He enunciates his words very well although he is only three.*

articulate To **articulate** means to speak words or sounds clearly. *He articulated every word so that everyone could hear.*

sound To **sound** can mean to speak, pronounce, or express words or sounds clearly. *He sounded each letter as he went.*

voice To **voice** means to express a thought or feeling with your voice. *She voiced her opinion.*

utter To **utter** means to speak or pronounce. *The judge uttered those terrible words so that we could all hear.*

---

contrasting words: **mumble**

property *noun*

something that is owned by a person or group of people. *Everything with my name on it is my **property**.*

possessions — **Possessions** are the things someone owns. *We hired a van to move all our possessions to our new house.*

belongings — **Belongings** are things that you own. It is very similar to **possessions.** *I had to decide where to put my belongings in my new bedroom.*

gear — **Gear** can be very similar to **possessions** and **belongings**. It is usually used in less formal language. *The new house was so small that we had to give away some of our gear.*

paraphernalia — **Paraphernalia** means things you own, especially things you don't really need. *We didn't realise how much paraphernalia we had collected until we had to pack and move it all.*

assets — **Assets** are things you own, especially things that are valuable. *Our house and car are our most important assets.*

---

protect *verb*

to keep something or someone from injury, danger or annoyance. *The building workers wore helmets to **protect** their heads.*

guard — To **guard** means to protect something or someone or keep them safe from harm. *Our Alsatian dog guards our house and barks if strangers come.*

defend — To **defend** means to protect something or someone or keep them safe, especially from attack. *The soldiers defended the town from the enemy.*

shield — To **shield** can mean to protect someone or something with anything that acts as a shield. *I shielded my small brother with my body.*

screen — To **screen** can mean to protect or shelter someone or something with anything that acts as a screen. *The gigantic beach umbrella screened him from the sun.*

secure — To **secure** means to make something safe from harm or danger. *A burglar alarm will secure the house against intruders.*

---

contrasting words: **endanger**

---

protrude *verb*

to stick out or stretch out more than is usual. *I need a brace on my teeth because the bottom row **protrudes**.*

jut To **jut** means to stick out sharply. *Watch out for the shelf that juts from the wall.*

project To **project** means to stand out or stick out beyond the surface. *Frogs' eyes project noticeably.*

bulge To **bulge** means to stick out as a rounded mass or hump. *The squirrel's cheeks were bulging with nuts.*

swell To **swell** means to **bulge** out. *After I sprained my ankle I put ice on it so that it wouldn't swell so much.*

billow To **billow** means to **bulge** out because of being filled with air. *The clothes on the line flapped and billowed in the strong breeze.*

---

proud *adjective*

having too high an opinion of your own importance or ability. *I'm so **proud** of the way I read that I don't bother to listen to anyone else.*

arrogant **Arrogant** means showing that you think you are very important. *Her arrogant reply was that she knew she was very clever.*

supercilious **Supercilious** means proud and scornful. *I was upset when she sneered at my new jeans in that supercilious way.*

smug **Smug** means showing or feeling that you are very pleased with yourself. *I gave a smug smile when I won first prize.*

haughty **Haughty** means feeling too proud of yourself and scornful of others. *The haughty film star looked down on the other actors.*

snobbish **Snobbish** means looking down on people who are not as wealthy, important or clever as you. *We think that she is snobbish because she only plays with rich kids.*

similar words: **pompous, conceited**
contrasting words: **humble**

prove *verb*

to show something to be true or genuine. *The jeweller's valuation of my gold necklace **proves** its worth.*

confirm To **confirm** means to strengthen or make more certain someone's belief in something. *Nicola's news confirmed my suspicions about how ill he really was.*

corroborate To **corroborate** means to make something more certain by giving additional, similar information about it. *The information I gave the policeman corroborated Geoffrey's report of what had happened.*

substantiate To **substantiate** means to prove something by producing evidence. *You will have to substantiate your accusation that she stole your book.*

verify To **verify** means to prove something is true or correct. *You can verify the spelling of a word by looking it up in a dictionary.*

bear out To **bear out** means to prove someone or something is right. *The facts you have given him bear me out.*

contrasting words: **disprove**

public *adjective*

used by or having to do with the people of a community or the people as a whole. *Many people use **public** transport to go the the city so that they don't have to worry about finding a car park.*

general **General** means concerning all or most people. *The general feeling at the meeting was that the school fete should be postponed.*

popular **Popular** means widely liked by a particular group or people in general. *Lots of people listen to this radio station because it plays popular music.*

collective **Collective** means having to do with a group of people taken as a whole. *The job will be done more quickly if we make a collective effort.*

communal **Communal** means shared by several people. *The flats have their own bathrooms and a communal laundry.*

common **Common** means shared by two or more people. *The two friends shared a common interest in stamp collecting.*

publication *noun*

something that has been printed for sale to the public. *This library contains mainly Australian **publications**.*

newspaper A **newspaper** is a publication which is produced daily or weekly and contains news reports and advertisements. *We read the newspaper every day so that we know what's happening in Britain and the rest of the world.*

magazine A **magazine** is a paper or a booklet containing stories, articles and advertisements, usually issued once a week or once a month. *We enjoy reading the weekly sports magazine.*

journal A **journal** is a **magazine** that is issued regularly by a professional or learned group to inform or educate the readers. *The doctor always reads the monthly medical journals.*

pamphlet A **pamphlet** is a very small paper-covered book or a single sheet of paper with advertisements printed on it. *We found a pamphlet on the department store sale in our letterbox.*

similar words: **book**

publish *verb*

to make something known to the public. *The newspaper **published** the story about the hijack.*

report To **report** means to describe or give an account of something. *At the meeting, he reported that his latest overseas trip had been successful.*

declare To **declare** means to announce something or make something known officially. *The government declared war.*

proclaim To **proclaim** means to announce something publicly. *The young prince was proclaimed king in the market place.*

advertise To **advertise** means to draw attention to something or someone, especially in order to sell it or their services. *We advertised our car in the newspaper because we wanted to sell it.*

broadcast To **broadcast** means to spread information, especially by radio. *The radio station broadcast the latest news on the disaster.*

similar words: **inform, reveal**

pull *verb*

to move something by tugging it towards you. ***I pulled*** *my fishing line into the boat but the bait was gone.*

haul To **haul** means to pull something hard. *We hauled the anchor into the boat.*

drag To **drag** means to pull something slowly or heavily along. *We dragged the cupboard across the floor.*

draw To **draw** means to pull, move or take something in a particular direction. *I quickly drew my hand away from the hot stove.*

tow To **tow** means to **drag** or pull something behind you using a rope or chain. *The tractor towed our car out of the flooded river.*

lug To **lug** means to pull or carry something along with a great deal of effort. *We lugged our heavy suitcases from the taxi into the railway station.*

contrasting words: **push**

punish *verb*

to make someone suffer in some way because they have done something wrong. *He* ***punished*** *the bullies by making them stay in at lunch time.*

discipline To **discipline** means to punish someone in a way that will teach them not to do the same thing again. *He disciplined us for being careless by making us pay for the new window.*

chastise To **chastise** means to punish or scold someone. *Their mother chastised them for being late for dinner.*

penalise To **penalise** means to punish someone by taking something away from them, or not letting them do somethingthey like. *She penalised them for being late by not letting them have any dessert.*

correct To **correct** can mean to scold someone, especially a child, or tell them what they are doing wrong so they won't do it again. *She corrected him when he snatched the ball without asking for it.*

similar words: **scold**

purple *adjective*

coloured dark reddish-blue. *The plums are **purple**.*

magenta — **Magenta** means coloured reddish-purple. *The blood in your veins is a magenta colour.*

mauve — **Mauve** means coloured light purple. *If you mix purple and white paint you get a mauve colour.*

lilac — **Lilac** means coloured pale reddish-purple. *The flowers on a lavender bush are a lilac colour.*

indigo — **Indigo** means coloured a deep violet blue. *One of the bands of the rainbow is an indigo colour.*

cerise — **Cerise** means having a clear red or bright pinkish-red colour. *Some cherries are cerise.*

---

push *verb*

to move something by pressing or leaning against it. *Julian likes to **push** the pram with his baby brother in it.*

shove — To **shove** means to push something roughly. *Someone shoved me from behind and I fell over.*

thrust — To **thrust** means to force or push something hard. *James Bond thrust his knife into his enemy's heart.*

drive — To **drive** means to make someone or something go forward. *The sheepdog drove the sheep into the pen.*

ram — To **ram** can mean to push or **drive** something with great force. *Tom rammed the earth down around the fence posts.*

propel — To **propel** means to push or **drive** something forward energetically. *The rowers propelled their boat across the finishing line.*

contrasting words: **pull**

puzzle *verb*

to make someone uncertain or unable to understand. *The signpost **puzzled** me because the name of the street was spelt differently from that on the map.*

perplex To **perplex** means to make someone confused and uncertain. It is very similar to **puzzle**. *That exam question perplexed me because we haven't had any lessons about how bees find their way home.*

baffle To **baffle** means to puzzle or confuse someone. *The disappearance of the suspect baffled the police.*

bewilder To **bewilder** means to confuse someone hopelessly. *The maze completely bewildered him and he couldn't see how to lead the rabbit to the carrot.*

mystify To **mystify** means to confuse someone completely with something that seems strange or unusual. *The mark on the wall mystified her until she realised there was a secret sliding door there.*

confound To **confound** means to puzzle and surprise someone. *She confounded the experts by solving the mystery.*

similar words: **confuse**
contrasting words: **explain**

question *verb*

to ask someone for information about something. *The doctor **questioned** the patient about her symptoms.*

interrogate To **interrogate** means to question someone closely in order to find out something. *The police interrogated the suspect for several days.*

grill To **grill** can mean to question someone harshly and closely. It is more suited to everyday language. *Our teacher grilled us in order to find out who had stolen the money.*

interview To **interview** means to meet with someone formally in order to ask them particular questions, often related to getting a job or as part of a radio or television programme. *The hospital superintendent interviewed all the doctors who applied for the job.*

quiz To **quiz** means to ask someone many questions. *My mother quizzed me on all the work I had studied for my exam.*

contrasting words: **answer**

quiet *adjective*

free from or making little noise or sound, especially an annoying sound. *This is a **quiet** street because there is no through traffic.*

soft — **Soft** can mean making little sound. *We could hardly hear her soft voice.*

faint — **Faint** can mean lacking loudness or strength. *We could hear the faint sound of singing in the distance.*

low — **Low** can mean not loud. *The owl gave a low hoot.*

indistinct — **Indistinct** can mean not sounding clear. *On the long distance phone call, my mother's voice was indistinct and I had trouble understanding her.*

muffled — **Muffled** means deadened or made less in sound, usually because of being covered by or wrapped in something. *When we were playing hide-and-seek, I heard a muffled voice coming from behind the clothes in the wardrobe.*

contrasting words: **loud**

quit *verb*

to give up or leave something. *He **quit** his job.*

evacuate — To **evacuate** means to leave a place in order to escape danger. *We evacuated the building when the fire started.*

vacate — To **vacate** means to leave a house or building, usually because someone else wants it. *We had to vacate our holiday flat before lunch.*

abandon — To **abandon** means to leave a place and intend to stay away. *We had to abandon the sinking ship.*

desert — To **desert** means to leave a place where you are on duty and not come back. *The sentry deserted his post.*

forsake — To **forsake** means to give up someone or something. *She decided to forsake the world and enter a convent.*

rain *verb*

to come down from the sky in drops of water. *We won't have to water the garden because it **rained** all night.*

spit To **spit** can mean to fall in light scattered drops or flakes, usually of rain or snow. *We'd better take the washing off the line because it has started to spit.*

drizzle To **drizzle** means to rain gently and steadily in fine drops. *I wish the sun would come out because it has been drizzling for days.*

pour To **pour** means to rain heavily. *It started to pour and we were soaked coming home from school.*

teem To **teem** means to rain very hard. *It has been teeming all day and the roads are very slippery.*

---

ramble *verb*

to talk or write without keeping to the subject. *He **rambled** on and on about things that I didn't understand.*

wander To **wander** can mean to move or turn idly towards another thing. *Her mind wandered off the subject and she started to talk about her youth.*

stray To **stray** can mean to turn aside from the subject you were talking or writing about. *She strayed from the topic of her essay and wrote about horses instead.*

digress To **digress** means to **wander** away from the main subject when writing or speaking. *I started to lecture on the effects of smoking but I'm afraid I have digresssed.*

diverge To **diverge** can mean to **wander** off or turn aside from a plan, discussion and so on. *We have diverged from the points on the agenda and I'd like to return to them.*

---

rash *adjective*

acting too quickly and without thought of possible danger or trouble. *Diving into the shallow creek was a **rash** act.*

reckless — **Reckless** means not caring about danger, often in a foolish way. *Riding a bike without lights at night is a reckless thing to do.*

foolhardy — **Foolhardy** means foolishly adventurous or not thinking about danger. It is quite similar to **reckless**. *You were foolhardy to explore the cave by yourself.*

impetuous — **Impetuous** means acting quickly and thoughtlessly, but not necessarily in a dangerous way. *The impetuous boy rushed off without hearing the end of what his mother was saying.*

hasty — **Hasty** means acting in a hurry and without thinking. *He was sorry later for his hasty decision.*

harebrained — **Harebrained** means **reckless** or not sensible. *It was his harebrained idea to go surfing at midnight.*

contrasting words: **wary**

rave *verb*

to talk wildly making little sense, especially when you are very ill. *The delirious patient was **raving** so the nurse gave him a sedative to put him to sleep.*

babble — To **babble** means to speak words quickly and unclearly. *The shy boy babbled in reply to her question.*

jabber — To **jabber** means to speak words quickly, unclearly or foolishly. *The teacher looked annoyed as the silly girl jabbered on and on about why she hadn't done her homework.*

waffle — To **waffle** means to speak or write vaguely and for a long time. *His speech was boring because he just waffled on.*

talk rubbish — To **talk rubbish** means to say something that has no meaning. *Don't talk rubbish.*

similar words: **yak, talk**

reaction *noun*

something done as a result of an action by someone else. *Her* ***reaction*** *to my rudeness was to walk away.*

response A **response** is a reaction caused by something which provokes it. *The sunflower turns in response to light.*

reply A **reply** can be so similar to **response** that you can usually use either. *She made a face at me in reply to the one I made her.*

answer An **answer** can be an action done in **response** to another. *His answer to my teasing was to step on my toe.*

feedback **Feedback** can be information passed back about something that has been done or said. *I've had a lot of feedback about my new book.*

acknowledgment An **acknowledgment** can be a thing done or given to show that you are grateful or think highly of something. *My friends bought me some flowers in acknowledgment of the help I had given them.*

read *verb*

to look at and understand writing or printing. *My father* ***reads*** *a story to my little sister every night.*

browse through To **browse through** means to glance through a book in a casual and leisurely way. *I browsed through a magazine while I was waiting to see the dentist.*

leaf through To **leaf through** means to turn the pages of a book, or something similar, quickly. *I leafed through the book to make sure it was the one I needed to borrow from the library.*

skim To **skim** can mean to glance over something without taking everything in. *I skimmed the headlines of the newspaper while I was having my breakfast this morning.*

study To **study** can mean to look at something closely. *The lawyer studied all the documents for the case.*

wade through To **wade through** can mean to make your way through something with difficulty or with a lot of effort. *We waded through all our receipts and papers so that we could fill out our tax return.*

ready *adjective*

in the right condition for immediate action or use. *I'm always **ready** to leave for school at 8 o'clock.*

prepared — **Prepared** means made ready for something. *When you go camping you should be prepared for any emergency.*

equipped — **Equipped** means provided with whatever is needed to do something. *The plumber was equipped for a very dirty and difficult job.*

rigged out — **Rigged out** means provided with equipment. *The soldiers were rigged out for a day's march.*

fitted — **Fitted out** means provided or supplied with all the clothing, equipment, furniture or other things you need. *Mrs Brown's children were fitted out for school by the middle of January.*

---

realise *verb*

to find out or come to understand clearly. *At last I **realised** the truth.*

discover — To **discover** can mean to find out something you didn't know before. *They soon discovered the truth about the smashed windows.*

learn — To **learn** can mean to find out or come to know something. *She was surprised when she learnt what a good swimmer he was.*

ascertain — To **ascertain** means to find out or make sure of something. *I am trying to ascertain the facts.*

glean — To **glean** can mean to gather something slowly and with difficulty, one bit at a time. *It took them many weeks to glean all the information they needed.*

tumble to — To **tumble to** means to become suddenly aware of something you didn't know before. This is more suited to everyday language. *It did not take him long to tumble to the fact that she tells lies.*

similar words: **sense, understand**

rebel *verb*

to fight against the government or resist those who rule or have power. *The people **rebelled** against the president and exiled him.*

disobey To **disobey** means to refuse to do as you are told. *If you disobey again I will have to punish you.*

mutiny To **mutiny** means to rebel against someone in authority. It is usually used about sailors or soldiers. *The crew mutinied because of their captain's unfair treatment.*

rise up To **rise up** is so similar to **rebel** that you can usually choose either. *The people rose up against the cruel king.*

revolt To **revolt** means to rebel against those who have power over you. *The prisoners revolted against their jailers.*

run riot To **run riot** means to behave without control and ignore those in authority. *The spectators ran riot at the football match and smashed the seats.*

contrasting words: **give in**

rebellion *noun*

a refusal to obey someone who is in charge or who has power over you. *There was a **rebellion** against the king's harsh new laws.*

revolt A **revolt** is so similar to **rebellion** that you can usually choose either word. *Several prison officers were injured in the revolt at the prison.*

revolution A **revolution** is the complete overthrow of a government or a complete change in the form of government. *After the revolution in 1917, Russia no longer had a Czar.*

uprising An **uprising** is a violent rebellion against the government or other authority by a large number of people. *In the uprising of the French peasants in 1789, many members of the ruling class lost their lives.*

coup A **coup** is a sudden successful move, especially against a government. *The generals have been in power since the army coup.*

mutiny A **mutiny** is a rebellion against authority, especially by sailors or soldiers against their officers. *The captain was killed in the mutiny.*

record *verb*

to write down information so that it can be kept. *Myles **recorded** all his team's cricket scores for the season.*

note — To **note** means to write something down, usually so you can remember it. *I noted the time of my dentist's appointment on the calendar.*

register — To **register** means to write down, or have written down in a list of names, acts, or events that are to be kept as a record. *Dad registered the birth of my sister at the Registry Office.*

enter — To **enter** can mean to write something on a list. *Luke entered his name on the list of volunteers.*

log — To **log** can mean to write down important details of a voyage or flight, such as the weather, speed and so on. This is usually done by the captain of the ship or plane. *The captain logged the weather information as soon as he received it.*

similar words: **list**

recover *verb*

to get well again after being sick. *He has now **recovered** from his accident.*

recuperate — To **recuperate** is so similar to **recover** that you can usually use either word. *She is recuperating from measles.*

pick up — To **pick up** can mean to recover or regain your health. This is rather an informal word. *He picked up well after the doctor treated him with antibiotics.*

convalesce — To **convalesce** means to grow stronger after an illness. *He is convalescing at home after his operation.*

rally — To **rally** can mean to begin to recover or gain fresh strength, often after an illness. *We were relieved when she rallied after fainting.*

brighten — To **brighten** can mean to become more lively or cheerful, especially if you haven't been feeling well. *She gradually brightened as her fever went down.*

contrasting words: **deteriorate**

red *adjective*

coloured like a ripe tomato. *The **red** peppers looked lovely in the green lettuce salad.*

crimson — **Crimson** means coloured a deep, purplish-red. *Crimson blood gushed from the cut artery in my leg.*

scarlet — **Scarlet** means coloured a bright red. *The guards at Buckingham Palace wear scarlet coats.*

ruby — **Ruby** means rich red-coloured, like the precious stone called a ruby. *The guests drank the sparkling ruby wine from crystal glasses.*

maroon — **Maroon** means having a dark brownish-red colour. *A Victoria plum has a maroon skin.*

pink — **Pink** means having a pale red colour. *The baby had healthy, pink cheeks.*

similar words: **rosy**

reduce *verb*

to make something less. ***Reduce** your speed when you drive through a town.*

lessen — To **lessen** is so similar to **reduce** that you can usually use either. *Rubbing in this ointment will lessen the pain of your sunburn.*

decrease — To **decrease** means gradually to make less. *I am decreasing the amount of sugar I take in my tea.*

lower — To **lower** means to make something less, especially something that you can count or measure on a scale. *People will buy more of these books if you lower the price.*

cut back — To **cut back** means to reduce something, often to an earlier rate or amount. *The company decided to cut back the number of its workers.*

minimise — To **minimise** means to reduce something to the smallest possible amount. *We must minimise our expenses.*

contrasting words: **enlarge, add**

refuge *noun*

a place giving shelter or protection from danger or trouble. *The cave was a perfect **refuge** during the storm.*

shelter — A **shelter** is a place that provides protection or safety when there is danger or trouble. *Many people built lead-lined shelters in case there was a nuclear war.*

haven — A **haven** can be a place of safety and protection. *The fishermen used the sheltered bay as a haven whenever the sea became too rough.*

asylum — An **asylum** can be any refuge offering safety or care. *My grandmother's quiet house is my asylum in time of trouble.*

retreat — A **retreat** is a sheltered remote place where people go to find peace and quiet. *We go to our retreat in the country nearly every weekend.*

sanctuary — A **sanctuary** can be a place protected by law where plants and animals cannot be harmed. *The wildife sanctuary was a perfect place to see animals living in their natural state.*

refuse *verb*

to say you will not accept something offered to you. *He **refused** my help and said he could manage by himself.*

decline — To **decline** means to refuse to accept something in a polite way. *He declined my invitation to the party.*

reject — To **reject** means to refuse to accept or use something, usually because it isn't satisfactory. *They rejected her story because they said they couldn't read her writing.*

renounce — To **renounce** means to refuse to accept something which you are entitled to. *The man renounced his legal right to the money.*

turn down — To **turn down** means to refuse an offer or a proposal. *The local council turned down the plan for the new motorway.*

rebuff — To **rebuff** means to refuse to accept something in a definite and strong way. *She rebuffed all his attempts to be friendly.*

similar words: **prevent, ban**
contrasting words: **allow**

rejoice *verb*

to be glad or delighted. *The whole family **rejoiced** when the baby was born.*

celebrate To **celebrate** means to have a party for a special reason. *When the exams are over we are going to celebrate.*

revel To **revel** means to have a wild party. *Our neighbours revelled all night and kept us awake.*

live it up To **live it up** means to have a very energetic celebration. *After we won the match we decided to live it up at the captain's house.*

whoop it up To **whoop it up** means to have a party or celebration. It is more suited to everyday language. *He really whooped it up on his birthday.*

contrasting words: **grieve**

related *adjective*

of a similar kind or having something in common. *Geography and geology are **related** subjects of study.*

connected **Connected** can mean thought of as related. *The detective gathered a connected set of clues which solved the crime.*

associated **Associated** means related to or **connected** with something in your mind or thoughts. *Holidays and their associated pleasures are memories you have all your life.*

allied **Allied** means joined together in reality or in your thoughts. *Running and its allied sport, hurdling, interests me a lot.*

relevant **Relevant** means related to what is being discussed. *Her remark about men landing on the moon was very relevant to the topic of space travel.*

similar words: **similar**
contrasting words: **unrelated**

reliable *adjective*

trusted or able to be relied on. *He is such a **reliable** friend I know he will keep his promise.*

responsible	**Responsible** means reliable, or able to accept and be trusted with special responsibilities or duties. *We need a responsible person to be in charge of the sports equipment.*
dependable	**Dependable** is so similar to **reliable** that you can usually use either word. *We let Alison do the shopping because we knew she was dependable.*
conscientious	**Conscientious** means reliable because you are very careful and particular in what you do. *We gave the most important jobs to Scott because he was such a conscientious worker.*
dutiful	**Dutiful** means always doing what you think is right. *We elected her again because she had been a very dutiful prefect.*

similar words: **faithful, steadfast**
contrasting words: **fickle**

religion *noun*

any particular system of worship that usually involves confidence and trust in a supernatural power that made and controls the world and that you should worship and obey. *All the main **religions** in the world teach that you should treat other people the way you would like them to treat you.*

faith	**Faith** can mean a particular religion with its collection of principles and teachings. *He was brought up in the Jewish faith.*
belief	**Belief** can be very similar to **faith**. *Their family is of the Hindu belief.*
denomination	**Denomination** means a large, organised religious group, especially in the Christian church. *She belongs to the Baptist denomination.*
theology	**Theology** means the collection of beliefs held by a particular religion. *Christian theology teaches that Jesus is the Son of God.*

religious *adjective*

believing in your religion. *The **religious** man went to church every week.*

pious — **Pious** means showing religious devotion and respect. *They are so pious they will not do any work on the Sabbath.*

devout — **Devout** means sincerely believing in and praising your God. *The devout Muslim prayed to Allah every day.*

reverent — **Reverent** means showing deep respect for the goodness and greatness of God. *The little girl's reverent behaviour in church was surprising in one so young.*

god-fearing — **God-fearing** means respecting God and his laws. *The god-fearing Jewish family praised God for the commandments He gave to Moses.*

similar words: **holy**
contrasting words: **sacrilegious**

remains *noun*

what is left. This is a plural noun. *The police inspected the **remains** of the building after the fire.*

remnants — **Remnants** are parts or amounts that are left. This is a plural noun. *I made a patchwork cushion from remnants of material.*

odds and ends — **Odds and ends** are scraps or **remnants.** This is a plural noun. *We made toys out of odds and ends from our parents' workshops.*

residue — **Residue** is something that is left. This is a singular noun. *Most of the grass cuttings went into the catcher of the lawnmower and I raked up the residue.*

leftovers — **Leftovers** are things that remain or were not used, especially from a meal. This is a plural noun. *We gave the leftovers to the dog.*

surplus — **Surplus** means what is left over after what is needed has been used up. *We filled the tank with petrol and stored the surplus in fire-proof containers.*

remember *verb*

to bring something back to, or to keep it in your mind. ***I remember*** *the way to do that puzzle.*

recollect To **recollect** is very similar to **remember** and you can often choose either word. *I recollect the fun we had at the beach last summer.*

recall To **recall** means to remember or **recollect** something. These three words are so similar you can usually use any of them. *He does well in exams because he can recall facts very easily.*

place To **place** can mean to remember someone or something by connecting them in your mind with certain places, events or other things. *I could only place her when I heard her sing the same song she sang at our last concert.*

recognise To **recognise** means to know someone or something again when you see or hear them at a later time. *I recognised him even though I met him over a year ago.*

remove *verb*

to take something off or away. *Please* ***remove*** *your shoes before coming inside the house.*

withdraw To **withdraw** means to take something out. *I withdrew some money from the bank.*

extract To **extract** means to pull or take something out. *The dentist extracted my tooth.*

excise To **excise** means to cut something out. *The doctor excised the wart from my finger.*

dislodge To **dislodge** means to remove something from its existing position. *When the men were lopping the tree, they dislodged a bird's nest.*

erase To **erase** means to remove something by rubbing. *We erased the writing from the blackboard.*

contrasting words: **insert, add**

repair *verb*

to bring something back into a good condition. *I have to **repair** my old bike.*

mend — To **mend** means to put something into working order. *Dad is going to help me mend the brakes.*

fix — To **fix** means to repair or **mend** something. These three verbs are so similar you can usually choose any one of them. *I will have to fix the broken headlight.*

restore — To **restore** means to bring something back to its original condition. *The Historical Society wants to restore the first house built in our town.*

renovate — To **renovate** means to repair something so that it is like new. *We are going to renovate our house.*

patch up — To **patch up** means to repair something, especially in a makeshift way. *When the car broke down we patched it up until we could find a garage.*

similar words: **improve, correct**
contrasting words: **damage**

repay *verb*

to pay back or return something. *I want to **repay** the money you lent me.*

reimburse — To **reimburse** means to pay back to someone money they have spent on behalf of someone else. *I bought new tennis balls and the treasurer reimbursed me.*

recompense — To **recompense** means to make a repayment to someone, especially for time or trouble they have had in doing something. *I recompensed the dressmaker for the extra time she spent looking for matching buttons.*

compensate — To **compensate** means to make something up to someone. *We will compensate you for the cost of repairing your car.*

refund — To **refund** means to give or pay back money you have already spent. *The theatre refunded the cost of our tickets when the show was cancelled.*

reward — To **reward** means to give something to someone in return for their work or help. *The neighbours rewarded me for feeding their dog while they were on holidays.*

similar words: **pay**

repeated *adjective*

done again and again. *They were exhausted after making **repeated** attempts to pull the boat up onto the beach.*

regular — **Regular** means following a rule or pattern, especially having to do with fixed times. *Regular eating and sleeping habits help keep you healthy.*

periodic — **Periodic** means happening or appearing at regular intervals. *It is a good idea to pay periodic visits to your dentist.*

recurrent — **Recurrent** means happening or appearing again and again. *She has recurrent attacks of asthma throughout spring.*

rhythmical — **Rhythmical** means happening in a regular pattern of timing. *The rhythmical beat of the music set our feet tapping.*

frequent — **Frequent** means happening often. *We make frequent visits to the beach during summer.*

contrasting words: **erratic**

repel *verb*

to drive someone or something away or force them back. *Her dog **repelled** the man who tried to attack her.*

repulse — To **repulse** is so similar to **repel** that you can usually use either. *The soldiers repulsed the enemy's attack.*

scare off — To **scare off** means to drive someone or something away by frightening them. *We made loud noises to scare off the lion.*

dispel — To **dispel** means to drive or send something away in all directions. *His explanation of what the noise really was dispelled all my fears.*

rebuff — To **rebuff** means to drive someone away who is offering you something, or trying to be pleasant. *I went to put my arms around him but he rebuffed me.*

spurn — To **spurn** means to refuse to have anything to do with someone or something because you are scornful of them. *At the ball the prince spurned Cinderella's ugly sisters.*

contrasting words: **attract**

report *noun*

an account of the important facts, especially of a meeting, an event, or someone's progress at work or school. *Could you write me a **report** on the committee meeting?*

document A **document** is a paper giving information or evidence. *Keep an important document like your birth certificate in a safe place.*

statement A **statement** is something spoken or written that presents facts or details about something or someone. *The policeman told us that we'd have to make a statement at the police station after the accident.*

dossier A **dossier** is a bundle of documents containing information about a person or subject. *The police kept a dossier on the bank robber.*

brief A **brief** is an outline of information or instructions on a subject, especially for use by a barrister conducting a legal case. *The barrister went over the brief with the solicitor and his client.*

bulletin A **bulletin** is a short written or spoken report or account, especially of news or events. *Did you see the latest bulletin on the floods on TV?*

similar words: **summary, message**

resentful *adjective*

having a feeling of jealousy, hurt or anger about someone or something. *They were **resentful** of his rapid success.*

bitter **Bitter** can mean filled with sour feelings. *She is bitter towards her friend because he would not help her.*

spiteful **Spiteful** means full of a bad-tempered wish to annoy or hurt someone else. *The spiteful child hit the little girl for no reason.*

malicious **Malicious** means having the desire to harm or hurt someone. *She was just being malicious when she broke his pencil.*

vindictive **Vindictive** means paying someone back for something they have done to you. *She could be a vindictive person when things didn't go her way.*

vengeful **Vengeful** means wanting to take revenge. *The vengeful boy pushed me over when I accidentally bumped into him.*

similar words: **angry**

reside *verb*

to have your home in a particular place. It is a fairly formal word. *We **reside** in Manchester now.*

live To **live** means the same as **reside**. It is a much less formal word. *He lives in a friendly country town.*

dwell To **dwell** means to **live** in a particular place or condition. It sounds rather old-fashioned and isn't used as much as **live**. *They dwell in peace and harmony.*

board To **board** means to pay for the use of a room and for meals. *He has to board at school because his parents live in the country.*

lodge To **lodge** can mean to reside or **board** for a while in someone else's house. *I lodge at Mrs Smith's house.*

squat To **squat** can mean to **live** without permission on land or in a property you don't own. *The poor students squatted in the derelict houses until they were evicted.*

resist *verb*

to stand up to or fight against someone. *The army **resisted** the invaders until they retreated.*

defy To **defy** can mean to resist someone or something boldly. *The patriots defied the invading army's savage attack.*

oppose To **oppose** means to disagree with and resist someone or something. *The protestors opposed the government's new law.*

withstand To **withstand** means not to give way to something or someone. *She tried hard to withstand their pleas but eventually gave in.*

obstruct To **obstruct** means to **oppose** someone by making things difficult for them. *The captured spy obstructed the enemy's efforts to get information by refusing to talk.*

counter To **counter** means to act against someone or something. *The manager countered the workers demands by closing the factory.*

contrasting words: **give in**

respect *noun*

feelings of admiration. *I have the greatest **respect** for our early explorers.*

regard — **Regard** can be respect for, or a favourable opinion of someone or something. *I have a very high regard for her knowledge of these matters.*

esteem — **Esteem** is the good opinion you have of someone. *His courage earned him the esteem of the whole team.*

honour — **Honour** can mean respect or **esteem**. *The scientist was treated with honour when he visited his old school.*

veneration — **Veneration** means a feeling of deep respect and love. *We were filled with veneration for our grandfather who had saved the little boy from drowning.*

devotion — **Devotion** can be loyalty or great affection. *The general won the devotion of his men.*

contrasting words: **scorn**

rest *noun*

a time of sleep or recovery. *I think I'll have a **rest** after I finish my homework.*

break — A **break** is a short rest. *They took a break from work.*

leisure — **Leisure** is time that is free from work. *I like to go to the beach when I have the leisure.*

contrasting words: **work**

rest *verb*

to take time off from working. *Little children often **rest** in the afternoon.*

relax	To **relax** means to rest and feel at ease. *You can sit down and relax for an hour.*
wind down	To **wind down** means to rest after working very hard. *Watching TV helps me wind down after a busy day.*
put your feet up	To **put your feet up** means to lie down and have a rest. It is more suited to everyday language. *What a busy day! Let's put our feet up before the children come home from school.*
take it easy	To **take it easy** means to have a restful time. It is more suited to everyday language. *You should take it easy after running such a long cross-country race.*

similar words: **laze**
contrasting words: **work**

restaurant *noun*

a place where you can buy and eat a meal. *That **restaurant** serves both English and Chinese food.*

cafe	A **cafe** is a restaurant that serves coffee, tea, and small meals. *We had lunch in a cafe.*
bistro	A **bistro** is a small restaurant or wine bar. *Let's meet in the French bistro on the corner.*
cafeteria	A **cafeteria** is a cheap self-service restaurant. *Is there a cafeteria in this store?*
canteen	A **canteen** is a self-service restaurant or counter where food is sold in a factory, office or school. *Mum works in the school canteen on Thursdays.*

result *noun*

something that springs or proceeds from an action or event. *The success of the play was the* ***result*** *of our group's terrific effort.*

outcome	An **outcome** is something that results from what has happened previously. *My book was so exciting, I couldn't wait to discover the outcome.*
effect	An **effect** is a result, or something which is produced by some cause. *Wrinkles are an effect of old age.*
consequence	A **consequence** is the inevitable or expected result of something. *This mess is the consequence of your foolishness.*
conclusion	**Conclusion** can mean a final result. *The signing of an agreement was the conclusion of the peace talks.*
sequel	A **sequel** can be anything which follows or results from something. *The author wrote a sequel to her popular novel.*

retaliate *verb*

to strike back. *If you tease him he will* ***retaliate****.*

reciprocate	To **reciprocate** means to act in a similar way in return. *If you are spiteful to me, I will reciprocate.*
get even	To **get even** means to **retaliate** or strike back. *I hid his books and now I'm afraid he'll try to get even.*
take revenge	To **take revenge** means to cause hurt or damage because of something someone has done to you. *When they spoilt our game, we took revenge by hiding their bikes.*
settle a score	To **settle a score** means to avenge a wrong done to you. *I settled a score with him by breaking his calculator.*

reticent *adjective*

not inclined to talk a lot or openly. *She is a **reticent** person and doesn't talk about her problems.*

reserved — **Reserved** means inclined to keep your feelings or thoughts to yourself. It is similar to **reticent**. *He seems unfriendly but he is really only reserved.*

quiet — **Quiet** can mean shy and not inclined to talk. *The new girl in the class is rather quiet.*

taciturn — **Taciturn** means not inclined to communicate by talking. *He is rather taciturn when he is in a bad mood.*

laconic — **Laconic** means using few words when talking. *She is always laconic in her replies.*

secretive — **Secretive** means liking to keep things to yourself. *A lot of people don't like her because she is secretive.*

similar words: **shy**
contrasting words: **talkative**

reveal *verb*

to uncover something or make it known. *He **revealed** the secret of the door to the hidden room.*

disclose — To **disclose** can mean to tell something or allow it to be known. *He then disclosed the history of the castle.*

show — To **show** can mean to explain something or make it clear. *He showed the special technique to me so I could open the door too.*

expose — To **expose** can mean to reveal something that has been hidden from most people. *The story he told me exposed many family secrets.*

unfold — To **unfold** can mean to reveal or explain something little by little. *As he unfolded the whole saga I began to understand his pride in his family's history.*

similar words: **admit, publish, inform, blab**
contrasting words: **hide**

reverse *verb*

to turn back or go backwards. *The road was so narrow we had to* ***reverse*** *onto the footpath to let the truck pass.*

back To **back** can be so similar to **reverse** that you can usually use either. *Dad backed into the garage.*

recede To **recede** means to move back and become more distant. *As we drove away, the hills receded into the distance.*

ebb To **ebb** means to flow back or away. *We waited until the tide ebbed before we walked around the rocks.*

rebound To **rebound** means to bounce or spring back. *The ball rebounded off the wall.*

contrasting words: **advance**

rhythm *noun*

the pattern of regularly repeated groups of strong and weak pulses, stresses or accents in music or speech. *They clapped to the* ***rhythm*** *of the music.*

beat **Beat** can be the units of time in a piece of music, or the rate at which accents or stresses follow one another, giving a feeling of pattern or regularity. *Pop music usually has a strong, regular beat.*

time **Time** can be the speed of movement of a piece of music. *This music is marked to be played in waltz time.*

tempo **Tempo** is the speed at which you perform a piece of music, and is usually indicated for you. It is very similar to **time**. *This song has a fast, lively tempo.*

swing **Swing** can be a steady marked rhythm or movement in music or speech. *Everything the band played had a swing to it.*

ridiculous *adjective*

so silly or funny that people feel like laughing, often with contempt. *Why are you wearing that **ridiculous** hat?*

absurd — **Absurd** can mean ridiculous or foolish. *She gave an absurd explanation as to why her hair was pink.*

nonsensical — **Nonsensical** means foolish or making no sense. *We found ourselves in a nonsensical situation that no-one could explain.*

ludicrous — **Ludicrous** means so ridiculous that no-one could take it seriously. *Your suggestion that we walk from Land's End to John O'Groats is ludicrous.*

preposterous — **Preposterous** means annoyingly ridiculous. *Don't come to me with any more of your preposterous suggestions.*

farcical — **Farcical** means so ridiculous that it doesn't seem like a real situation. *It was farcical the way we kept on not recognising each other.*

similar words: **silly**
contrasting words: **sane**

ring *verb*

to make or give out a clear musical sound. *The bells are **ringing**.*

peal — To **peal** means to ring loudly and for a long time. *The bells pealed in celebration of the prince's wedding.*

chime — To **chime** can mean to make the sound of a bell that has been struck. *This clock chimes on every hour.*

knell — To **knell** means to ring slowly and with a sad sound. *The church bells knelled for her funeral.*

toll — To **toll** means to ring with single, slow, sad sounds, usually at a funeral. It is similar to **knell**. *Do you know for whom the bell is tolling?*

room *noun*

a part of a building separated by walls from other parts. *Our house has eight **rooms**.*

chamber A **chamber** is a private room, usually a bedroom. It is an old-fashioned word. *The sick woman received visitors in her chamber.*

den A **den** can be a quiet, cosy, private room. *My father likes to read in his den.*

compartment A **compartment** is a room or separate section in a railway carriage, ship or aircraft. *We shared our compartment with two other passengers.*

cubicle A **cubicle** is a very small, partly enclosed room. *We left our clothes in the changing cubicle.*

cell A **cell** can be a small room in a prison, a convent or monastery. *The prisoners were locked in their cells each night.*

rosy *adjective*

pink and healthy-looking. *She had lovely **rosy** cheeks and a clear skin.*

flushed **Flushed** means having skin that has gone red. *His face was flushed from running in the heat.*

ruddy **Ruddy** means having a healthy red colour. *They came home from their camping holiday with ruddy faces and strong muscles.*

florid **Florid** means red-coloured. *That fat person's florid complexion does not look healthy.*

bloodshot **Bloodshot** means having eyes with red streaks from enlarged blood vessels. *Her eyes were bloodshot from staying up late for too many nights.*

inflamed **Inflamed** means made red by emotion or an infection. *Her inflamed eyes showed she had been crying.*

similar words: **red**

rot *verb*

to go bad. *The refuse is **rotting**.*

decay To **decay** can be so similar to **rot** that you can usually use either. *The apples fell from the tree and decayed on the ground.*

decompose To **decompose** means to break up as it rots. *The leaves decomposed on the forest floor.*

putrefy To **putrefy** can mean to rot with a very unpleasant smell. *The lost hiker's badly broken leg putrefied and it had to be amputated when he was rescued.*

fester To **fester** means to go bad and form pus. This is mostly used about a wound or a sore. *Put some ointment on that cut before it festers.*

perish To **perish** can mean to rot or **decay**. This is mostly used about things made of rubber. *The elastic band perished and snapped when I stretched it.*

similar words: **deteriorate**

rough *adjective*

feeling uneven or not smooth. *I touched the **rough** skin of the pineapple.*

bumpy **Bumpy** means having a lumpy or uneven surface. *That toad has bumpy skin.*

gnarled **Gnarled** can mean rough and worn by old age or the weather. *He stroked his dog with his gnarled, old hand.*

coarse **Coarse** means thick or not having a fine smooth feel. *This dog has coarse hair.*

shaggy **Shaggy** can mean rough and matted. *The pony's coat was so shaggy that I couldn't brush it easily.*

bristly **Bristly** means rough because of having short stiff hairs. *I don't like kissing Dad's bristly face before he's had a shave.*

contrasting words: **smooth**

roughen *verb*

to make something feel worn or not smooth. *Hard work has **roughened** his hands.*

coarsen To **coarsen** can mean to make something feel rough or no longer fine. *Too much sun has coarsened her skin.*

chap To **chap** means to make your skin cracked, red and rough. *The cold wind chapped her hands.*

chafe To **chafe** means to wear down or make something sore by rubbing it roughly. *The saddle chafed the horse's back.*

rasp To **rasp** means to scrape something with a rough tool. *The carpenter rasped the piece of wood with a file.*

ruffle To **ruffle** means to spoil the smoothness of something. *Birds ruffle their feathers when they are cleaning themselves.*

contrasting words: **smooth**

rubbish *noun*

useless leftover material or matter. *We put our **rubbish** in the litter bin.*

garbage **Garbage** is an American word meaning **rubbish** or **refuse**. *Our household garbage is collected every week by the council.*

refuse **Refuse** is rubbish or waste material. *Rain washed refuse off the footpaths into the gutters.*

debris **Debris** is the rubbish left when something is broken or destroyed. *The rescuers had to clear away piles of debris to get to the victims of the earthquake.*

junk **Junk** means old or unwanted things. *We are going to clean out all the junk from our garage tomorrow.*

trash **Trash** is rubbish or anything that you think is worthless or useless. *We put our pile of trash outside the house for the council to collect but we saw some people take things they could use from it.*

rude *adjective*

bad-mannered or not behaving politely. *The **rude** woman did not thank the boy who opened the door for her.*

impolite — **Impolite** is so similar to **rude** that you can usually choose either word. *It's impolite to talk when someone else is speaking.*

cheeky — **Cheeky** means not showing respect. *Mum was annoyed when the cheeky boy pushed in front of her at the shop.*

impudent — **Impudent** means rude and disrespectful. *The teacher was cross with her impudent answer.*

insolent — **Insolent** means boldly and openly rude and disrespectful. *We were surprised by their insolent behaviour towards their parents.*

insulting — **Insulting** means showing rudeness by saying hurtful things. *I ignored his insulting remark about my shabby clothes.*

similar words: **bold, vulgar, abrupt**
contrasting words: **polite**

rule *noun*

an instruction telling you what to do. *I'll read out the **rules** of the game.*

law — A **law** is a rule made by a government or ruler for all the people to follow. *There is a law which says you must wear your seat belt in a car.*

regulation — A **regulation** is a rule made by an authority such as a school or a local council. *Local regulations forbid you to walk on the grass in the park.*

convention — A **convention** is a rule, often not written down, that everyone understands and follows. *It is a convention to eat a hot roast dinner on Christmas Day.*

precept — A **precept** is a general rule or saying about behaviour. *'Look before you leap' is a wise precept.*

formula — A **formula** is a rule or recipe which you should follow. *Helping others is a formula which brings happiness.*

rule *verb*

to have or exercise power over something or someone. *The king **ruled** over his subjects wisely.*

reign To **reign** means to rule or use authority as a king or queen does. *Queen Victoria reigned over her people for many years.*

preside To **preside** means to have control over something. *The chairperson's job is to preside over the meeting.*

officiate To **officiate** means to perform the duties that accompany a particular position. *My father was the umpire who officiated at our cricket match last week.*

dominate To **dominate** can mean to rule or control because you have the most power. *When she's playing with us, she always dominates because she's the oldest.*

command To **command** can mean to give orders or be in charge. *He commanded and we obeyed immediately.*

similar words: **manage**

sacrilegious *adjective*

showing disrespect to something sacred. *The church members were saddened by the **sacrilegious** destruction of the altar.*

profane **Profane** means showing a deep lack of respect for religion. *Drawing cartoons in a hymn book would be a profane act.*

irreverent **Irreverent** means not showing respect for sacred things. *The priest asked the boys not to be irreverent in their behaviour in church.*

blasphemous **Blasphemous** means speaking disrespectfully about God or sacred things. *My Muslim friend was angry when he heard the blasphemous joke about Allah.*

impious **Impious** means lacking reverence for God or the gods of a particular religion. *The Roman slave was punished for his impious remarks about Jupiter.*

contrasting words: **holy, religious**

sad *adjective*

sorrowful or miserable. *I was **sad** when my best friend left our school.*

unhappy — **Unhappy** means not cheerful or happy. *He was unhappy when he couldn't go to the picnic.*

homesick — **Homesick** means unhappy because you are not living at home. *Children are often homesick when they go to boarding school.*

low — **Low** can mean **unhappy** or sad. *He was in low spirits when he didn't pass the examination.*

hurt — **Hurt** can mean sad because someone has been unkind to you. *I was hurt when she didn't invite me to her house to play.*

upset — **Upset** means feeling sad or **hurt**. *She was upset when she wasn't picked for the team.*

similar words: **miserable, glum**
contrasting words: **happy, joyful, glad**

safe *adjective*

free from danger or risk. *We knew we were **safe** when the wind and waves died down.*

protected — **Protected** means guarded or shielded from danger or harm. *I was protected as I huddled in the tiny cave away from the storm.*

sheltered — **Sheltered** means **protected** from bad weather, danger and so on. *We planted the seedlings in a sheltered corner of the garden.*

secure — **Secure** means safe or free from danger. *We were secure knowing we had a map and compass in case we lost our way.*

immune — **Immune** means free or **protected** from danger, harm or disease. *We knew the desert so well we were immune from most of its dangers.*

right as rain — **Right as rain** means safe or free from any problems or difficulties. This is more suited to everyday language. *As long as we kept to the track we knew we would be as right as rain.*

contrasting words: **vulnerable, dangerous**

sag *verb*

to hang loosely. *His trousers **sagged** over his hips.*

droop	To **droop** means to bend or hang down. *Her head drooped with tiredness.*
collapse	To **collapse** can mean to fall down suddenly, often from weakness. *The sick man collapsed onto the bed.*
loll	To **loll** can mean to hang loosely, or sink down. *The dog's tongue lolled from its mouth as it panted.*
slump	To **slump** means to drop heavily and loosely. *He slumped into the chair.*
slouch	To **slouch** means to sit or walk not holding yourself up straight. *He slouched along the street.*

sail *verb*

to travel in a ship or boat. *During our holidays we **sailed** down the Thames in a converted barge.*

cruise	To **cruise** means to sail from place to place, especially for pleasure. *We cruised among the islands looking at the lovely scenery.*
glide	To **glide** can mean to move slowly and easily through the water. *The sailing boat glided across the calm lake.*
skim	To **skim** can mean to move lightly across the surface of the water. *The canoe skimmed across the finishing line to the cheers of the watching crowd.*
float	To **float** means to move gently on top of the water. *We floated on our raft for a couple of hours after our launch sank.*

sailor *noun*

a member of a ship or boat's crew. *Every* ***sailor*** *had a special job to do to make sure the ship travelled safely across the sea.*

seafarer A **seafarer** is someone who travels on the sea, especially someone who does it for a living. *The Vikings of long ago were brave and war-like seafarers.*

mariner A **mariner** is someone who makes a living as a sailor. *Because he loved boats and travelling to new places he decided to be a mariner.*

seaman A **seaman** is someone who can sail or handle a boat skilfully. *The captain was looking for experienced seamen to help sail his ocean-going yacht.*

marine A **marine** is someone who belongs to a branch of the forces which serves both on ships and on land. *The marines left their ship and fought the enemy on the nearby island.*

tar A **tar** is someone who makes a living as a sailor. It is more suited to everyday language. *When he retired, the old tar bought a small boat and spent his days fishing.*

sane *adjective*

sensible or based on common sense. *When we realised that we were lost, we knew the only* ***sane*** *thing do was to find shelter for the night.*

sound **Sound** can mean sure or reliable. *He always gives me sound advice when I'm in trouble.*

well-balanced **Well-balanced** can mean sane or sensible. *This is a well-balanced approach to the problem.*

coherent **Coherent** means consistent or thought of in the same way throughout. *Her essay had a coherent argument.*

logical **Logical** can mean based on sensible or correct reasoning. *The logical course of action, now that it's pouring, is to go inside.*

similar words: **sensible**
contrasting words: **irrational**

satisfied *adjective*

pleased and happy because your wishes or needs are fulfilled. *She looked at her exam results with a **satisfied** smile.*

content — **Content** means satisfied with what you have. *We are very content with our new house.*

complacent — **Complacent** means satisfied or quietly pleased, especially with yourself. *She is too complacent to realise she has to work harder.*

comfortable — **Comfortable** can mean having enough to be satisfied. *They live a comfortable life.*

satiated — **Satiated** means satisfied to a very great extent. *We were satiated with pleasure after our day at the circus.*

contrasting words: **dissatisfied, greedy**

save *verb*

to keep, free or deliver someone or something from danger or harm. *Their life jackets **saved** them from drowning.*

rescue — To **rescue** means to save someone or something from danger. *Anita climbed up the tree and rescued the terrified kitten.*

preserve — To **preserve** can mean to keep something or someone safe. *Our fear of small, dark places preserved us from the dangers of the cave.*

safeguard — To **safeguard** means to protect something or someone or to keep it from harm. *We all took turns watching the bird's nest to safeguard it from wild animals.*

salvage — To **salvage** means to save or recover something, especially from a shipwreck or fire, or something similar. *We salvaged most of the cargo before the ship sank.*

similar words: **protect**
contrasting words: **endanger**

saying *noun*

something that is often said. *My mother has a funny **saying** for every situation.*

adage An **adage** is a wise saying. *'More haste less speed' is a common adage.*

proverb A **proverb** is a short, popular, usually wise saying that has been used by people for a long time. *'A stitch in time saves nine' is an old proverb.*

epigram An **epigram** is a short witty saying which goes straight to the point of a matter. *'Speech is silver, but silence is golden' is a well-known epigram.*

maxim A **maxim** is a saying containing a general truth or rule. *'Look before you leap' is a wise maxim.*

motto A **motto** is a short saying, often taken as summing up the aims or beliefs of a particular organisation or group. *The motto of the Scouts is 'Be prepared'.*

---

scant *adjective*

barely enough of something. *There was only enough water for a **scant** mouthful each.*

sparse **Sparse** can mean of small amount, especially when what exists is thinly spread out or scattered. *Shady trees were sparse after the long drought.*

skimpy **Skimpy** can mean having less thickness, size or amount than you would like. *My skimpy jumper didn't stop me getting cold.*

meagre **Meagre** means of a small amount or of poor quality. *We gulped down a meagre breakfast of bread and butter before we raced for the bus.*

paltry **Paltry** means having such a small amount of something that it is not of much use or value. *I couldn't even go to the pictures with my paltry pocket money.*

measly **Measly** means having an annoyingly small amount of something. It is more suited to everyday language. *There was only a measly two pence left in my purse.*

similar words: **insufficient**
contrasting words: **extra, abundant, sufficient**

scarce *adjective*

not often seen or found. *Jacob's sheep are **scarce** nowadays.*

rare — **Rare** means unusual or uncommon. *Scurvy is a rare disease in Britain.*

infrequent — **Infrequent** means not happening very often. *Our grandparents' visits to us have been very infrequent since they sold their car.*

sporadic — **Sporadic** means irregular and not very frequent. *He made sporadic attempts to go to soccer training and was soon dropped from the team.*

occasional — **Occasional** means happening or appearing sometimes. *I've only received an occasional letter from Sally since she went to Australia.*

similar words: **unusual**
contrasting words: **numerous, countless**

scatter *verb*

to throw something loosely about. *I **scattered** crumbs for the birds to eat.*

strew — To **strew** means to scatter or throw things everywhere. *He strews his clothes all over the floor.*

distribute — To **distribute** can mean to put or scatter something around. *She distributed the fertiliser over the lawn.*

disperse — To **disperse** can mean to scatter something around. *The wind dispersed my pile of leaves and blew them into the air.*

spread — To **spread** can mean to scatter something or send it around. *Cover your mouth when you cough or you will spread your germs to everyone else.*

dissipate — To **dissipate** means to scatter something or use it wastefully. *He dissipated his money by gambling.*

contrasting words: **gather, store**

scholar *noun*

a learned person. *A rabbi is a* ***scholar*** *and teacher of the Jewish religion.*

intellectual — An **intellectual** is someone who shows great mental ability. *Peter Mark Roget was an intellectual who devised the first English thesaurus.*

philosopher — A **philosopher** is someone who searches for truth and wisdom. *The philosopher has written many books containing her thoughts on the meaning of life.*

sage — A **sage** is a very wise person. *People come from far and near to consult the sage about their problems.*

genius — A **genius** is an unusually talented or clever person. *Everyone regards Leonardo da Vinci as a genius.*

mastermind — A **mastermind** can be a very clever or knowledgeable person. *She scored so well in the general knowledge quiz she must be a mastermind.*

---

scold *verb*

to find fault with someone. *She* ***scolded*** *me for being careless.*

rebuke — To **rebuke** means to scold someone or show them you disapprove of their behaviour. *She rebuked us for splashing in the bath.*

reprimand — To **reprimand** means to scold or **rebuke** someone, especially in a formal way. *The bus driver reprimanded them for standing on the seats.*

tick off — To **tick off** means to scold or speak crossly to someone. *Our mother ticked us off for getting so dirty.*

admonish — To **admonish** means to warn or caution someone not to do something. *We admonished the boys not to be noisy.*

---

similar words: **fault**
contrasting words: **praise, acclaim**

scorn *noun*

a complete and obvious lack of respect. *She showed her **scorn** for his remark by turning her back on him.*

contempt	**Contempt** is the feeling you have for someone or something that is mean and disgraceful. *I have nothing but contempt for anyone who is cruel to animals.*
disrespect	**Disrespect** is rudeness and lack of respect. *The demonstrators showed their disrespect for the new law by heckling the Prime Minister.*
disdain	**Disdain** is a feeling of dislike for something or someone you think is unworthy. *She gave the rude young man a look of disdain.*
ridicule	**Ridicule** is words or actions meant to cause scornful laughter at a person or thing. *Her ridicule of his shyness made him blush with embarrassment.*
derision	**Derision** is the act of laughing or making fun of someone. *The children treated the crybaby with derision.*

contrasting words: **respect**

scratch *verb*

to mark or cut something roughly. *The knife **scratched** the polished table.*

nick	To **nick** means to cut something slightly. *She nicked her hand with the scissors.*
lance	To **lance** means to cut something open with a sharp instrument. *The doctor lanced my boil.*
score	To **score** means to make a deep scratch, especially in wood or metal. *The screwdriver slipped and scored the wood.*
graze	To **graze** means to scratch the skin of part of your body. *He grazed his hand against the wall.*

similar words: **cut, tear**

scruffy *adjective*

dirty, shabby and uncared-for. *The **scruffy** little boy looked as though his clothes had never been washed or ironed.*

unkempt — **Unkempt** means in an uncared-for or untidy condition. *He did not get the job because of his unkempt appearance.*

dishevelled — **Dishevelled** means untidy and disordered. *Her dishevelled appearance was surprising as she was usually very neat.*

bedraggled — **Bedraggled** means wet, dirty and hanging limply. *Their clothes were bedraggled when they came out of the storm.*

sleazy — **Sleazy** means untidy and dirty. *Everyone avoided the sleazy old drunk lying on the grass in the park.*

sloppy — **Sloppy** means loose and untidy. *She wears sloppy clothes that never seem to fit her.*

similar words: **untidy**
contrasting words: **tidy**

secret *adjective*

done or made without others knowing. *This is a **secret** plan to spy on the children in the flat below.*

confidential — **Confidential** means secret or not public. *Don't let anyone else read this confidential letter.*

classified — **Classified** can mean known or used by only a few people, and not made public, especially top-secret military or government information. *Lock the classified files away where no-one else can read them.*

private — **Private** can mean secret or not public. *I won't let anyone read my private diary.*

hush-hush — **Hush-hush** means extremely secret. It is more suited to everyday language. *Their meeting was so hush-hush they wouldn't even tell us what it was about.*

similar words: **secretive**

secretive *adjective*

liking to keep things secret or to yourself. *She is very* ***secretive*** *about what she did in the holidays.*

stealthy — **Stealthy** means done or made in a hidden or sly, secretive way in the hope that it won't be discovered. *We knew something was wrong when we heard a faint, stealthy movement in the next room.*

furtive — **Furtive** means done or acting in a **stealthy** or secretive way. *She gave us a quick, furtive look and then disappeared through the hole in the fence.*

surreptitious — **Surreptitious** means made, done or behaving in a secret or **stealthy** way. *He didn't notice the surreptitious glance we gave him as we walked past.*

underhand — **Underhand** means secret and sly, usually in regard to things that are not very honest or honourable. *They met in the middle of the night to carry out their underhand dealings in stolen goods.*

cagey — **Cagey** means secretive or careful not to reveal much. *She was very cagey when I asked her where she went yesterday afternoon.*

similar words: **secret**
contrasting words: **frank**

see *verb*

to take things in with your eyes. *I* ***see*** *the cows coming across the paddock.*

observe — To **observe** means to see or look at something. *Douglas observed the hooded men go into the bank and immediately rang up the police.*

view — To **view** means to look at or see something. *We went to the Art Gallery to view the collection of Constable paintings.*

notice — To **notice** means to see or take note of something. *I noticed she was wearing a new dress.*

watch — To **watch** means to look at something attentively. *The pupils watched a film on goldmining.*

witness — To **witness** means to be present at and see something. *We witnessed the breaking of the European High Jump record.*

similar words: **inspect**

seek *verb*

to try to find or get something. *Dick Whittington set out for London to **seek** his fortune.*

hunt for — To **hunt for** means to look for something. *I hunted for my pencil everywhere but I couldn't find it.*

search for — To **search for** means to look for something thoroughly. *I searched for a four-leafed clover all summer but I didn't find one.*

pursue — To **pursue** can mean to try hard to find something. *In the 'Wizard of Oz', Dorothy helped the tin man pursue his goal of getting a heart.*

strive for — To **strive for** means to struggle to find or get something. *Paul is striving for top marks in the final exam.*

similar words: **follow**
contrasting words: **avoid**

selfish *adjective*

thinking only of your own interests. *The **selfish** boy never shared his toys with the other children.*

self-centred — **Self-centred** means being interested only in yourself. *She didn't know that she had hurt my feelings because she was too self-centred.*

inconsiderate — **Inconsiderate** means not caring about other people's rights or feelings. *It was inconsiderate of him to slam the door when the baby was asleep.*

spoilt — **Spoilt** means selfish because you are used to getting your own way. *Spoilt children aren't usually popular.*

possessive — **Possessive** means wanting to have or control something all by yourself. *Don't be so possessive! Let the others play with the kitten too.*

similar words: **ungrateful**
contrasting words: **kind, generous**

sell *verb*

to give up something in exchange for money. *I **sold** my skates for £20.*

auction To **auction** means to sell something by holding a public sale where people offer higher and higher amounts of money. *We auctioned our house.*

wholesale To **wholesale** means to sell large quantities of goods to shop owners rather than directly to the public. *Tim's father manufactures and wholesales furniture.*

peddle To **peddle** means to take things around from place to place in order to sell them. *A man was peddling brooms from house to house.*

hawk To **hawk** means to offer things for sale in the street or by calling at people's homes. It is similar to **peddle.** *The student needed money so he tried to hawk his paintings.*

flog To **flog** means to sell or try to sell something.It is more suited to everyday language. *My brother flogs used cars.*

contrasting words: **buy**

seller *noun*

someone who sells something or gives up goods in exchange for money. *The **seller** of the second-hand surfboard I bought was moving to the country.*

vendor A **vendor** is someone who sells things, especially small articles. *Everyone crowded around the ice-cream vendor on the beach.*

retailer A **retailer** is someone, such as a shopkeeper, who sells things directly to the public. *My uncle is a furniture retailer.*

merchant A **merchant** is someone who buys and sells goods to make a profit, usually not dealing directly with the public. *The timber merchant was busy all the time.*

dealer A **dealer** is someone who buys and sells things. *That dealer only sells second-hand cars.*

broker A **broker** is someone who buys or sells things for someone else. *They asked the share broker to invest their money for them.*

contrasting words: **buyer**

send *verb*

to cause something to go somewhere. *I'll **send** a postcard as soon as I get there.*

dispatch To **dispatch** means to send something off. *I dispatched an urgent message asking Dad to come home at once.*

forward To **forward** means to send something on. *Will you forward my mail to me while I'm away?*

pass on To **pass on** means to send something or give it to someone. *Would you like me to pass on your message when she gets home?*

relay To **relay** means to pass or send something on. *They relayed the cyclone warning to the ship by radio.*

transmit To **transmit** means to send something over, or along to a person or place. *My grandparents transmitted a telegram to me for my birthday.*

similar words: **carry**

sense *verb*

to notice or feel something with your senses. *You could **sense** the excitement at the Cup Final.*

experience To **experience** means to meet with, or have something happen to you that you can sense. *She experienced a lot of friendliness from other people during her visit.*

feel To **feel** can mean to sense or **experience** something. *She doesn't like winter because she feels the cold. He felt sad when he heard the news.*

perceive To **perceive** means to come to know or realise something through one of your senses, such as sight, hearing and so on. *He perceived a faint smell of roast chicken wafting out of the house.*

recognise To **recognise** can mean to realise or understand something clearly. *I recognised my mistake almost immediately but it was too late to do anything about it.*

similar words: **realise, understand**

sensible *adjective*

able to act with good judgment. *The **sensible** boy made sure the cars had stopped before he stepped onto the crossing.*

wise — **Wise** can mean showing good judgment. *He made a wise decision to take no notice of that stupid dare.*

level-headed — **Level-headed** means being calm and sensible, with good judgment. *The level-headed girl quickly got the class out of the room when the fire started.*

sage — **Sage** means sensible or **wise,** especially as a result of learning or experience. *The sage old lady advised the young couple to forgive each other after their quarrel.*

prudent — **Prudent** means showing you are careful and sensible in a practical way. *Prudent people always lock up their houses when they go out.*

reasonable — **Reasonable** means showing good sense or sound judgment. *Reasonable people don't leave their keys in their cars.*

similar words: **shrewd, sane, practical**
contrasting words: **stupid, silly**

separate *verb*

to put things apart. *Rebecca **separated** her pencils from her crayons.*

divide — To **divide** means to split up or separate into parts. *A river divides the two parts of the city.*

disconnect — To **disconnect** means to separate two things which are usually connected to each other. *Dennis disconnected the antenna of the television.*

detach — To **detach** means to separate or unfasten one thing from another. *Please detach the top piece of paper and keep it.*

break off — To **break off** means to separate one thing from another using force. *The storm broke off a large branch of the tree.*

free — To **free** means to separate one thing from another with difficulty. *His grip was so strong that I couldn't free my hand.*

contrasting words: **join, combine**

series *noun*

a number of things or events arranged or happening in a certain order. *A **series** of unusual events led to the conviction of the suspect.*

sequence A **sequence** is a series of things following each other. *His work involved the same sequence of tasks every day.*

chain A **chain** can be a series of connected things. *A strange chain of events led me to the conclusion that she was the murderer.*

succession A **succession** can be a number of people or things following one another in order. *Dad had a succession of people coming to see him today at the office.*

course A **course** is a set series of things. *I'm having a course of injections for my illness.*

cycle A **cycle** is a series of events happening in a regular repeating order. *The seasons come and go in a cycle.*

sew *verb*

to join with loops of yarn, using a needle and thread. *I am going to **sew** a pocket on my shirt.*

stitch To **stitch** is very similar to **sew** and you can often use either word. *She stitched some braid around the hem of her skirt.*

embroider To **embroider** means to sew decorative patterns on something. *I embroidered a tray cloth for my mother.*

work To **work** can mean to sew or **embroider** something. *I worked a design of roses on the handkerchief.*

darn To **darn** means to mend something with crossing rows of stitches. *I darned the hole in my sock.*

tack To **tack** means to sew loosely with large stitches. *Linsay tacked the hem before she tried on the dress.*

shadowy *adjective*

seeming faint and unreal. *Our early history seems rather* ***shadowy*** *but it becomes more real if you read about the settlers.*

nebulous — **Nebulous** means cloudy or vague. *His ideas of how he should be doing the job were very nebulous.*

ghostly — **Ghostly** means looking or appearing like a ghost. *The trees were ghostly shapes in the fog.*

ethereal — **Ethereal** means light, airy or not solid. *The clouds made ethereal shapes in the sky.*

intangible — **Intangible** means not able to be touched or seen. *Courage is an intangible but valuable asset.*

contrasting words: **actual**

shake *verb*

to move backwards and forwards with short quick movements. *The branches of the trees* ***shook*** *as the wind blew.*

vibrate — To **vibrate** means to keep on moving quickly up and down or to and fro. *The hummingbird's wings vibrated as it drank the flower's nectar.*

tremble — To **tremble** means to shake or quiver, especially from cold, weakness or fear. *Trevor's hands trembled as he tried to take off his snow-covered boots.*

shudder — To **shudder** means to shake suddenly from horror, cold or fear. *Kate shuddered when she saw that the cars couldn't avoid a collision.*

quake — To **quake** means to shake or **tremble.** *Louise quaked with fear when she saw the robbers come into the bank.*

rock — To **rock** means to move from side to side or to and fro. *The boat was rocking on the waves.*

similar words: **sway**

shape *noun*

the way something looks or appears from its outline. *The children made animal **shapes** out of the pastry.*

form	A **form** is the shape or appearance of something. *The little boy had a birthday cake in the form of a '6'.*
design	**Design** can mean the shape or outline of something. *I like the streamlined design of our new car.*
structure	**Structure** can be the way something is put together and gets its shape. *Look at this model which shows the structure of an atom.*
build	Your **build** is the way your body is shaped or structured. *The weight-lifter had a heavy build.*
figure	Your **figure** is the shape of your body. *The dancer has a graceful figure.*

share *noun*

the part given to or owned by someone. *We each received a **share** of the cake made for the school's Christmas party.*

quota	A **quota** is the share that you are entitled to. *Each boy had a quota of work to do before he could go home.*
allocation	An **allocation** is a part of something set apart for a special purpose. *The Education Department made an allocation of funds for school libraries.*
allotment	An **allotment** is something handed out or distributed. *We each received our allotment of pocket money on Saturday.*
cut	A **cut** can be a share of profits made. It is more suited to everyday language. *My cut from the sale of the home-made toys was £10.*
helping	A **helping** is a share of food. *May I have a second helping of dessert, please?*

similar words: **part**

share *verb*

to distribute parts of something with each person receiving a part. *The children **shared** the sultanas.*

divide To **divide** means to separate anything into parts. *I divided the books among the children.*

split To **split** can mean to separate something into parts in any way. *After our lunch at the restaurant, we split the bill between the four of us.*

dole out To **dole out** means to give something out in small quantities. *She doled out the pieces of fruit until we all had some.*

allot To **allot** is very similar to share. *Each child was allotted a part in the play.*

similar words: **distribute**

shine *verb*

to give out light. *The sun **shone** all day.*

beam To **beam** means to send out rays of light. *The searchlight beamed over the ocean.*

glow To **glow** can mean to shine like something very hot. *The forest was full of insects that glowed in the dark.*

burn To **burn** can mean to shine brightly. *The lights in the house burned all night.*

blaze To **blaze** can mean to shine brightly like a flame or fire. *The headlights of the car blazed into my eyes and I couldn't see anything.*

flare To **flare** can mean to shine brightly and suddenly. *All was dark and then the lights flared.*

similar words: **sparkle**

shining *adjective*

giving out or reflecting bright light. *She looked at me with **shining** eyes when I told her the good news.*

gleaming — **Gleaming** means giving out flashes or beams of light. *The rooms of the castle were lit up by gleaming torches held by the soldiers.*

flaming — **Flaming** can mean shining very brightly. *I could pick her out in the crowd by her flaming hair.*

luminous — **Luminous** means giving off or reflecting light. *I am able to tell the time in the dark because the hands of my watch are luminous.*

incandescent — **Incandescent** means shining or white with heat. *The bar of iron was heated until it was incandescent and then began to melt.*

phosphorescent — **Phosphorescent** means giving out light with little or no heat. *A special substance called phosphorus is used to make a phosphorescent light.*

similar words: **shiny, bright**
contrasting words: **dull**

shiny *adjective*

having a bright shining surface. *She polished the table until it was **shiny**.*

glossy — **Glossy** is so similar to **shiny** that you can usually use either. *I like a book to have a glossy cover.*

lustrous — **Lustrous** can mean shiny or with a glistening sheen like silk. *She chose a lustrous material for her wedding dress.*

sleek — **Sleek** means shiny and smooth. *That dog has a very sleek coat of hair.*

satin — **Satin** means shiny and very smooth like the cloth called satin. *This paint has a satin finish.*

silky — **Silky** means shiny and soft like silk. *The manufacturer says you will have silky hair if you use this shampoo.*

similar words: **shining**
contrasting words: **dull**

shock *verb*

to strike someone with very great surprise, mixed with horror or disgust. *The number of burglaries these days **shocks** me.*

appal To **appal** can mean to shock, displease or dismay someone. *The fact that one of our teachers had to be sacked appalled all our parents.*

startle To **startle** can mean to disturb or surprise someone suddenly. *The news flash startled us and we ran to tell Mum about the train crash.*

take aback To **take aback** means to cause someone great surprise and confusion. *My best friend's cold attitude towards me certainly took me aback.*

bowl over To **bowl over** means to surprise, upset and confuse someone. *The news that I had failed the test really bowled me over.*

similar words: **frighten**

shop *noun*

a building where goods are sold. *You buy meat at a butcher's **shop**.*

store A **store** is a large shop with many departments or branches. *We do most of our shopping at the large store in town.*

outlet An **outlet** is a shop selling a wholesaler's or manufacturer's goods. *This pharmacy is an outlet for the new brand of suntan cream.*

supermarket A **supermarket** is a large self-service shop selling food and other household goods. *We buy our food at the supermarket each week.*

market A **market** is a place where things are bought and sold, often at many different **stalls**. *We always buy our fruit and vegetables at the big market in the city.*

stall A **stall** is a stand, tent or table where goods are sold, such as at a fete. *I'm helping on the cake stall at the school fete.*

shorten *verb*

to make something short or shorter. *Can't you **shorten** the discussion because I'm getting bored.*

condense To **condense** can mean to say or write something in fewer words. *He condensed his story into just a few pages.*

abbreviate To **abbreviate** means to make a word, phrase or story shorter by leaving out some letters or words. *We abbreviate 'Mister' to 'Mr' to save space.*

abridge To **abridge** means to shorten a book, interview and so on, by leaving out some parts. *Sometimes a writer abridges a famous novel to make it easier for children to read.*

summarise To **summarise** means to say or write something in a short clear way, giving the main points only. *The prefect summarised the school rules for the new pupils.*

sum up To **sum up** means to give only the main points of something that has already been said or done. *I will sum up all I have just said so that everyone understands our plan.*

contrasting words: **expand**

shout *verb*

to call or cry out loudly. *He **shouted** at me when I broke a string on his tennis racquet.*

yell To **yell** is so similar to **shout** that you can usually use either. *The man yelled to the boy crossing the road to watch out for the car.*

bellow To **bellow** means to shout out angrily. *The sergeant bellowed at the troops when they disobeyed his order.*

roar To **roar** means to make a loud deep sound such as a lion makes. *The man roared with rage.*

bawl To **bawl** means to cry noisily. *He bawled when he fell over.*

belt out To **belt out** means to sing very loudly. *The team supporters belted out the club song when their side won the football match.*

similar words: **shriek**

show *verb*

to cause or allow something to be seen. *He **showed** his drawing to his mother.*

display To **display** means to show something so that it can be clearly seen. *He displayed his prize roses in a beautiful vase.*

exhibit To **exhibit** means to show something in a place where the public can go to see it. *The young artist is going to exhibit her paintings in the church hall.*

demonstrate To **demonstrate** means to show something clearly and plainly. *He demonstrated his skill at gymnastics before an astonished crowd.*

parade To **parade** means to show by making something move or march in an orderly way. *The farmer paraded his cattle round the ring.*

flaunt To **flaunt** means to show something off boldly. *He flaunted his medals until we were sick of him.*

contrasting words: **hide**

show-off *noun*

someone who says or does things to make people pay them attention or praise them. *She's such a **show-off** she wants everyone to watch her do her handstands.*

exhibitionist An **exhibitionist** is someone who tries to attract other people's attention in an annoyingly showy way. It is more formal than **show-off**. *The exhibitionist practised his dancing in the middle of the playground where everyone could see him.*

boaster A **boaster** is someone who talks too much about how good or clever they are. *The boaster kept telling us that she would win the prize.*

know-all A **know-all** is someone who thinks they know everything. *I grew tired of the know-all correcting me whenever I started to say something.*

smart alec A **smart alec** is someone who likes to show everyone how much they know or how clever they are. It is more suited to everyday language. *Stop being such a smart alec and let me have a go!*

shrewd *adjective*

clever at making good judgments. *The **shrewd** antique dealer realised the chair was a fake.*

astute — **Astute** means able to understand things clearly and quickly. *The astute manufacturer saw how good my invention was.*

sharp — **Sharp** can mean mentally quick and alert. *The sharp young lad saw the hold-up and took the number of the get-away car.*

canny — **Canny** can mean shrewd or wise. *The canny businessman always bought his supplies from people he trusted.*

knowing — **Knowing** means having a good, and sometimes unexpected, understanding of something. *My brother is a knowing little fellow when he wants his own way.*

similar words: **clever, sensible**
contrasting words: **stupid, silly**

shriek *verb*

to make a loud, sharp, high-pitched cry or noise. *The fans **shrieked** with delight when the pop-star appeared on the stage.*

screech — To **screech** means to make a harsh high-pitched cry or noise. *The tyres screeched on the wet road when the car stopped suddenly.*

squeal — To **squeal** means to make a sudden high-pitched cry, as if in pain or fear. *The little girl squealed when she saw the spider.*

yelp — To **yelp** means to give a quick sharp cry. *The dog yelped when the boy hit him.*

scream — To **scream** means to make a loud piercing cry or sound. *The sirens screamed as the fire-engines raced to the fire.*

squawk — To **squawk** means to make a loud unpleasant cry. *The chickens squawked when the fox chased them.*

similar words: **shout**

shrink *verb*

to become smaller. *Oh dear! Your woollen clothes have* ***shrunk*** *in the hot water.*

shrivel To **shrivel** can mean to shrink and wrinkle. *The plant shrivelled and died when it wasn't watered.*

wither To **wither** can mean to dry up. It is very similar to **shrivel**. *You'd better water the ferns or they'll wither.*

atrophy To **atrophy** means to lose size or strength. *Muscles atrophy if they aren't used.*

dwindle To **dwindle** means to become smaller or fewer in number. *Enrolments in our local school dwindled last year.*

contract To **contract** can mean to become smaller in size. *Metal contracts as it cools.*

similar words: **decrease**
contrasting words: **increase**

shy *adjective*

not feeling relaxed with other people. *The* ***shy*** *boy found it hard to talk to people at parties.*

bashful **Bashful** means easily embarrassed. *She was bashful and knew people would look at her if she answered.*

modest **Modest** means having a moderate opinion of yourself and your abilities. *She was modest about her success in the art competition.*

demure **Demure** means shyly well-behaved. *In the olden days women were expected to be demure.*

diffident **Diffident** means not confident or sure of yourself. *He is diffident about being in the school play.*

coy **Coy** means pretending to be shy so that you can attract attention. *She gave him a coy look as she brushed past him on the bus.*

similar words: **reticent**
contrasting words: **bold**

sick *adjective*

having a disease or being unwell. *I was so* ***sick*** *Mum called the doctor.*

ill	**Ill** is so similar to **sick** that you can usually use either word. *'You are too ill to get out of bed', he said.*
ailing	**Ailing** means not being very well even though you may not have anything particularly wrong with you. *I told him I had been ailing for a long time.*
indisposed	**Indisposed** means just slightly sick. *Jenny was allowed out of bed because she was only indisposed with a cold.*
off-colour	**Off-colour** means not feeling very well. It is more suited to everyday language. *She was too off-colour to go to school.*
groggy	**Groggy** can mean sick. It is more suited to everyday language. *I was groggy for two weeks.*

contrasting words: **healthy**

side *noun*

one of the outer parts, edges or lines of something, usually not the top, bottom, front or back. *You run past the* ***side*** *of the house to get around to the back.*

flank	The **flank** can mean the side of anything. *The general made plans to defend the army's flank.*
wing	A **wing** can be a side part, especially when joined to a central building, or of a sports field, or of the stage of a theatre. *The governors decided to add a new wing to the school.*
jamb	A **jamb** is the side part of a doorway, window, or other such opening. *I will paint the door jambs white.*
profile	A **profile** is the outline of someone's face as seen from the side. *I'd rather be looking straight ahead for this photo because I hate my profile.*
sidepiece	A **sidepiece** is a part forming a side or some of the side of something. *Do up the sidepieces of your hood to keep your neck warm.*

sign *noun*

a mark, figure or other indicator used to stand for a word, idea or mathematical value. *We looked for a railway carriage with a 'No Smoking'* ***sign****.*

symbol A **symbol** is something that stands for or represents something else. *The dove is a symbol of peace.*

emblem An **emblem** is a badge or something that serves as a sign or **symbol**. *A picture of a boxing kangaroo is now quite popular as an emblem of Australia in international sporting events.*

token A **token** is a sign or **symbol** of something, usually given to someone. *A wedding ring is a token of love.*

totem A **totem** is something, often an animal, used as a **token** or **emblem** of a family or group. *Each North American Indian tribe had a different totem.*

significant *adjective*

important and likely to have great effect on something. *Your eighteenth birthday will be a* ***significant*** *event in your life.*

momentous **Momentous** means of great importance. *The formation of the United Nations was a momentous event in world history.*

memorable **Memorable** means worth remembering. *A Royal Wedding is a memorable occasion.*

critical **Critical** can mean having to do with an important or dangerous time. *He had to make a critical decision.*

fateful **Fateful** means important because of the seriousness of the things that happened. *The world will always remember the fateful day when the atomic bomb was first dropped.*

serious **Serious** can mean important, weighty or needing a lot of care. *I have brought you here to discuss a very serious matter.*

similar words: **main**
contrasting words: **insignificant, minor**

silly *adjective*

stupid or without sense. *He gave a **silly** answer.*

foolish — **Foolish** is so similar to **silly** that you can usually use either. *That was a foolish thing to do.*

senseless — **Senseless** means without good sense. It is similar to **silly** and **foolish**. *The plan she suggested was senseless.*

idiotic — **Idiotic** means extremely silly. *I won't listen to any more of your idiotic ideas.*

inane — **Inane** means silly or not intelligent. *I'm sick of your inane chatter.*

fatuous — **Fatuous** means silly without realising it. *He made a fatuous remark about animals not feeling pain.*

similar words: **ridiculous, stupid, mad, irrational**
contrasting words: **sensible**

similar *adjective*

having a likeness, especially in a general or not specific way. *Tom and Edward drew **similar** pictures.*

alike — **Alike** means the same as **similar** but is used at the end of a sentence, rather than before the noun. *The sisters' faces are very alike.*

comparable — **Comparable** means similar enough for it to be sensible to compare them. *If Katharine can beat Clare, she can probably beat Jane, because Clare and Jane are comparable runners.*

akin — **Akin** means related or **alike**. *Emus are akin to ostriches.*

corresponding — **Corresponding** means similar or matching. *She told a corresponding story to that of her friend.*

synonymous — **Synonymous** means very similar or the same in meaning. *This thesaurus groups together synonymous words.*

similar words: **equal, related**
contrasting words: **various**

simple *adjective*

not having complicated or unnecessary, added parts. *We like **simple** home cooking best.*

plain	**Plain** can mean simple and not fussily decorated. *I bought some plain, blue material to make a dress.*
natural	**Natural** can mean real and without pretence. *I don't know why she wants to dye her hair — I think it looks better if it's natural.*
unadorned	**Unadorned** means not having been made more attractive by adding decorations or ornaments. *How bare the unadorned room looked after the Christmas decorations had been taken down.*
unobtrusive	**Unobtrusive** means not making an effort to be noticed. *She looked very elegant in her simple black dress and unobtrusive gold jewellery.*
quiet	**Quiet** can mean toned down and not done up for show. *The mourners all wore quiet clothes to Grandpa's funeral.*

contrasting words: **gaudy, spectacular**

simplify *verb*

to make something easier to understand, do or use. *I will **simplify** the instructions for this test.*

streamline	To **streamline** means to simplify something so as to make it more efficient. *We will get the work done more quickly if we streamline the way we do it.*
sort out	To **sort out** can mean to simplify and understand something by separating it into parts and solving each one. *We'll soon sort out your problems.*
unravel	To **unravel** can mean to make something less complicated and easier to understand. *I eventually unravelled his explanation and understood what he was saying.*
disentangle	To **disentangle** can mean to work something out by simplifying it. It is very similar to **unravel**. *I think I've disentangled the mystery by talking to each person involved.*

singer *noun*

someone who can make musical sounds with their voice, often someone who has been specially trained. *We have thirty **singers** in our choir.*

vocalist — A **vocalist** is a singer. You can usually choose either word. *The vocalist who sings with that pop group is in our church choir.*

chorister — A **chorister** is someone who sings in a choir. *All the choristers on the stage were dressed in blue and white.*

crooner — A **crooner** is someone who sings in a soft and sentimental way. *The famous crooner, Frank Sinatra, toured Australia a few years ago.*

minstrel — A **minstrel** was a musician in the Middle Ages who sang or said poetry while playing a musical instrument. *The lord's minstrel entertained the feasters in the castle.*

troubadour — A **troubadour** was a singer or song-writer, especially in medieval France. *The troubadour sang for the king in his castle.*

single *adjective*

one alone. *My **single** reason for going is to see the new calves.*

only — **Only** means single or just one. *The only thing I haven't finished is my maths homework.*

sole — **Sole** means single or **only**. *Peter is the sole member of the team who hasn't been injured.*

exclusive — **Exclusive** can mean single or **sole**. *The school bus was his exclusive means of getting to school.*

unique — **Unique** means different from all others or having no equal. *Each person's fingerprints are unique.*

contrasting words: **numerous, double**

slander *verb*

to make a false statement about someone which harms their good name. This is often a legal word. *The reporter **slandered** the company director when she spoke about him on the radio.*

defame — To **defame** means to damage someone's good name, especially when they are well known. *The newspaper story defamed the politician.*

libel — To **libel** means to write or print a statement which damages someone's reputation. This is often a legal word. *The politician sued the newspaper that libelled him.*

malign — To **malign** means to speak unfavourably or badly of someone. *She maligned me when she said I lied.*

smear — To **smear** can mean to damage someone's good name, usually without any proof. *Your nasty stories smeared my reputation and I had to resign as leader.*

similar words: **insult**
contrasting words: **worship, praise**

slave *noun*

someone who is the prisoner of someone else and has to work without pay. *The **slave** escaped from his cruel owner and managed to stay free until the civil war began.*

serf — A **serf** was someone who, in feudal times, was not free but was thought of as belonging to the land that a lord owned. *When the lord sold his land, the serfs wondered if the new owner would let them keep more of their produce.*

vassal — A **vassal** was someone who, in feudal times, lived on a nobleman's land and had to fight and work for him in return. *The vassal's family had to work hard on the land when he went away to war.*

servant — A **servant** is someone who works for, or is in the service of, someone else. *She is a public servant working in the Taxation Department.*

subject — A **subject** can be someone who is under the rule of a monarch or a state. *We are British subjects.*

puppet — A **puppet** can be someone who is controlled by someone else. *The president was the puppet of his party and couldn't make any decisions.*

sleep *verb*

to rest with your eyes closed and your mind unconscious. *How long did you **sleep** last night?*

slumber To **slumber** means to sleep deeply. *Please be quiet because the baby is slumbering.*

doze To **doze** means to sleep lightly or off and on. *The cat is dozing in front of the fire.*

nap To **nap** means to sleep for a short time. *I think I will nap for half an hour or so.*

snooze To **snooze** means to sleep lightly for a short time. It is similar to **doze** and **nap**. *My grandmother likes to snooze on the lounge after lunch.*

drowse To **drowse** means to feel like sleeping. *I drowsed all the way through the film.*

slight *adjective*

small and thin. *If you want to be a jockey, you must have a **slight** build.*

petite **Petite** means very small and slim. It is usually used to describe a woman or girl. *Mum is so petite she sometimes has to buy children's clothes.*

dainty **Dainty** can mean small and fine in appearance or movement. *We saw a collection of dainty china dolls.*

delicate **Delicate** can mean so small and fragile as to seem likely to be easily hurt or broken. *He was very delicate after his long illness.*

elfin **Elfin** means being so small and **dainty**, or having such a mischievous appearance that you are reminded of an elf. *Annie's elfin looks matched her cheeky behaviour.*

puny **Puny** can mean small and weak. *Tom did weight lifting to improve his puny build.*

similar words: **thin**
contrasting words: **fat, heavy, stocky**

slope *noun*

a direction or line which leans to one side rather than being flat or completely upright. *Roofs are usually built with a **slope** to let the rainwater run off.*

slant — **Slant** is so similar to **slope** that you can usually use either. *Fix these awnings so that they have a slight slant.*

tilt — A **tilt** is a slope or a leaning to one side. *That post has such a tilt that it will probably fall over.*

incline — An **incline** is a surface that has a slope. *We walked down the incline of the hill.*

gradient — The **gradient** is the amount of slope of something. *What is the gradient of this road?*

pitch — The **pitch** is the degree of slope. It is similar to **gradient**. *This roof has a steep pitch.*

slope *verb*

to have a direction or line that is neither flat nor upright. *Our garden **slopes** down to a creek.*

slant — To **slant** is so similar to **slope** that you can usually use either. *Draw a line that slants to the left.*

lean — To **lean** means to be in a sloping position. *In the Italian town of Pisa, there is a famous tower that leans to one side.*

tilt — To **tilt** means to move into a sloping position. *The fence began to tilt as the boys climbed over it.*

tip — To **tip** means to fall to one side. *Be careful that your cup doesn't tip.*

list — To **list** means to lean to one side. It is usually used about ships. *The huge wave made the ship list to starboard.*

slow *adjective*

taking a long time or not moving or acting quickly. *It was such a **slow** trip we didn't arrive till after dark.*

leisurely — **Leisurely** means slow or without haste. *After lunch we went for a leisurely stroll by the river.*

unhurried — **Unhurried** means slow or without any rush. *We packed a picnic and had an unhurried meal by the river.*

plodding — **Plodding** means moving in a slow and heavy way. *I could tell that she was tired by her plodding steps.*

lazy — **Lazy** can mean slow-moving. *Even the smallest children could swim in the lazy stream.*

contrasting words: **fast**

small *adjective*

not very big or great. *The car was too **small** for everyone to fit into.*

little — **Little** means small in size. *These little puppies are only two weeks old.*

tiny — **Tiny** means very small or **little**. *The puppies were tiny when they were born.*

minute — **Minute** means extremely small. *The insect was so minute we could hardly see it.*

miniature — **Miniature** means being a very small copy of something. *There were miniature spacemen in the toy rocket.*

short — **Short** can mean not very tall. *He was too short to see over the top of the fence.*

contrasting words: **big, huge**

smell *noun*

the quality of something that you sense through your nose. *I like the **smell** of newly cut grass.*

odour — **Odour** is so similar to **smell** that you can usually use either. *There is a strange odour in this room.*

scent — A **scent** is a pleasant smell. *These flowers have a strong scent.*

fragrance — **Fragrance** is a sweet smell. It is similar to **scent**. *He could smell the fragrance of her perfume.*

aroma — An **aroma** is a special, usually pleasant, smell of something. *The kitchen was filled with the aroma of coffee.*

bouquet — A **bouquet** is the special smell of a wine or other drink such as brandy. It is similar to **aroma**. *A good wine can be judged by its bouquet.*

smelly *adjective*

giving out a strong or unpleasant smell. *Skunks are **smelly** animals.*

stinking — **Stinking** means very unpleasantly smelly. *There is a stinking mess on the floor.*

rank — **Rank** can mean having a strong unpleasant smell. *He was smoking a rank cigar.*

putrid — **Putrid** means having the smell of something rotting or going bad. *A bad egg has a putrid smell.*

high — **High** can mean bad-smelling and is similar to **putrid**. *This meat is high.*

fetid — **Fetid** means having a stale smell that makes you feel sick, like something rotting. *The room was filled with hot, fetid air.*

smile *verb*

to show you are happy or amused by widening your mouth and turning it up at the corners. *I **smiled** when I thought about my birthday party.*

grin To **grin** means to smile broadly. *I grinned at my friend across the classroom.*

smirk To **smirk** means to smile in a smug way that annoys people. *She smirked when the teacher praised her.*

giggle To **giggle** means to laugh in a silly way. *We giggled when he pulled a funny face.*

snigger To **snigger** means to **giggle** in a rather rude way and try to hide it. *They sniggered at their teacher's mistake.*

titter To **titter** means to **giggle** in a foolish or nervous way. *They tittered nervously when their teacher caught them talking about their boyfriends.*

similar words: **laugh**
contrasting words: **frown**

smooth *adjective*

feeling even and without bumps or lumps. *This pear has such a **smooth** skin.*

polished **Polished** means made smooth and shiny by rubbing. *She slipped on the polished floor.*

slippery **Slippery** means too smooth to get a hold on. *The slippery material slid through her fingers.*

silken **Silken** means smooth and soft like silk. *She has silken hair.*

glassy **Glassy** means feeling or looking smooth and transparent like glass. *We rowed across the glassy lake.*

creamy **Creamy** can mean feeling rich and smooth like cream. *I spread the creamy lotion all over my sunburnt skin.*

similar words: **shiny**
contrasting words: **rough**

smooth *verb*

to make something even or level. *She **smoothed** her hair with her hand.*

iron — To **iron** means to press the creases out of clothes with a heated iron. *I must iron your school uniform before tomorrow.*

rub down — To **rub down** means to make something smooth and clean by rubbing. *Dad rubbed down the walls before painting them.*

sand — To **sand** means to smooth something by rubbing it with sandpaper. *The workmen sanded our floor before polishing it.*

grind — To **grind** means to make something smooth by rubbing it with something rough. *The glassmaker ground the lens.*

plane — To **plane** means to smooth wood using a special tool called a plane. *The carpenter planed the pieces of wood before fitting them together.*

similar words: **polish**
contrasting words: **roughen**

soak *verb*

to wet something thoroughly, especially by leaving it in a liquid for a long time. *She **soaked** the clothes in the tub to loosen the dirt.*

drench — To **drench** means to make something very wet. *The rain drenched our hair and clothes.*

flood — To **flood** can mean to cover something with water as happens in a flood. *The river rose and flooded many houses along its banks.*

inundate — To **inundate** can be so similar to **flood** that you can usually use either word. *The tidal wave inundated the village on the island.*

swamp — To **swamp** can mean to cover something with water. It is similar to **flood**. *A wave swamped the boat and it nearly sank.*

similar words: **wet**

soft *adjective*

easily cut or pressed out of shape and usually pleasant to touch. *I kneaded the dough until it was **soft.** My woollen jumper is very **soft.***

downy — **Downy** means fluffy and soft as fine hair or feathers are. *I let my head sink into the downy pillow.*

silky — **Silky** means smooth and shiny like silk. *She brushed her dog's silky hair.*

velvet — **Velvet** can mean soft and smooth like fur. *The kitten padded through the house on her velvet paws.*

spongy — **Spongy** means soft and squashy like a sponge. *We walked carefully over the spongy ground.*

tender — **Tender** means not tough or hard. *She made a salad from tender young lettuce leaves.*

contrasting words: **hard**

soften *verb*

to make something easy to cut or press out of shape. *I **softened** the toffee in my mouth as I sucked it.*

thaw — To **thaw** means to make something that is frozen melt and become softer. *You should thaw frozen fish before you cook it.*

mash — To **mash** means to crush or beat something until it is softer. *Please mash the potatoes.*

squash — To **squash** means to crush something into a soft mass. *I squashed the grape when I trod on it.*

pulp — To **pulp** means to make into a soft wet mass. *Paper mills pulp wood, cloth and other materials to make paper.*

tenderise — To **tenderise** means to make something less tough or hard. *We tenderised the meat with lemon before we cooked it.*

contrasting words: **harden**

solemn *adjective*

sincere or earnest. *I made a **solemn** promise.*

serious — **Serious** means solemn and really meaning what you say. *I will give you some serious advice.*

grave — **Grave** means solemn and without humour. *She listened to his story with a grave expression.*

sober — **Sober** can mean solemn and quiet. *The sad news put us in a sober mood.*

stern — **Stern** can mean solemn and severe. *He gave them a stern warning.*

dour — **Dour** can mean gloomily solemn, **stern** or hard. *His dour manner was rather discouraging.*

contrasting words: **happy**

solve *verb*

to explain or find the answer to something. *He **solved** the mystery.*

work out — To **work out** can mean to solve something, using a great deal of effort. *It took me ages to work this maths problem out.*

crack — To **crack** can mean to find the answer to something. *They cracked the spy's code.*

puzzle out — To **puzzle out** means to untangle or solve something by careful study or effort. *We finally puzzled out the clue for the cryptic crossword.*

figure out — To **figure out** means to solve or understand something. *I can't figure out the inscription on this monument.*

resolve — To **resolve** means to solve or settle something. *We resolved the problem by taking both cars.*

song *noun*

a short musical composition with words. *Craig wrote the music and I made up the words for our new **song**.*

hymn — A **hymn** is a song praising God. *We began the service by singing our favourite hymn.*

anthem — An **anthem** is a song written for a country or organisation and sung on special occasions. *'God Save the Queen' is Britain's national anthem.*

ballad — A **ballad** is a simple poem that tells a story and is often set to music and sung. *We sat around the campfire singing ballads about gypsies and pirates.*

carol — A **carol** is a joyful song, especially one about Christmas. *We all gathered in the park with candles and sang Christmas carols.*

lullaby — A **lullaby** is a soft gentle song, sung to put a baby to sleep. *He finally fell asleep as his mother rocked him in her arms and sang a lullaby.*

sorry *adjective*

feeling sad because you have done something wrong. *I'm **sorry** I yelled at you.*

ashamed — **Ashamed** means feeling sorry or guilty for what you have done. *I was ashamed after I had hit her.*

remorseful — **Remorseful** means feeling deeply sorry for your wrongdoing. *He was so remorseful that he couldn't sleep all night.*

repentant — **Repentant** means feeling sorrow and regret for what you have done. *She was repentant for all the ways she had hurt him.*

contrite — **Contrite** means feeling or showing that you are sorry or sad, especially from guilt. *We knew he was contrite when he let us join his secret club.*

penitent — **Penitent** means sorry for something you have done wrong and willing to put it right. *I will clean up the mess to show you that I really am penitent.*

contrasting words: **unashamed**

sour *adjective*

having a sharp taste such as that of lemons. *These grapes are **sour** because they are not ripe.*

acid — **Acid** means having a very sharp taste. It is similar to **sour**. *Vinegar has an acid taste.*

bitter — **Bitter** means having an unpleasantly sharp taste. *This coffee is very bitter.*

tart — **Tart** means sour or sharp in taste. *This apple sauce is too tart.*

dry — **Dry** can mean not sweet. *I prefer a dry wine.*

green — **Green** can mean not ripe and therefore tasting sour. *I didn't buy any plums because they were green.*

contrasting words: **sweet**

souvenir *noun*

something you keep as a memory of a place or event. *I kept the concert programme as a **souvenir** of Sarah's first piano recital.*

memento — A **memento** is something that acts as a reminder of the past. *She gave them a book as a memento of her visit.*

keepsake — A **keepsake** is something you keep in order to remember a person or event. *Glen gave Ingrid a beautiful shell as a keepsake of their picnic at the beach.*

trophy — A **trophy** can be a souvenir kept from a war or hunting expedition. *My grandfather has a stuffed swordfish as a trophy from his fishing trip.*

token — A **token** is a sign or symbol of something you want to remember. *The bride and groom exchanged wedding rings as tokens of the vows they had made.*

spacious *adjective*

ample or having a lot of space. *We will use this room for assembly because it is **spacious**.*

roomy	**Roomy** is so similar to **spacious** that you can usually use either. *They live in a big roomy house.*
commodious	**Commodious** means conveniently spacious. *I need a more commodious office.*
wide	**Wide** can mean having plenty of space from side to side. *The kindergarten room is big and wide.*
open	**Open** can mean not limited or blocked. *We had a lovely open view from the veranda.*
expansive	**Expansive** means **open** and widespread. *Their house has an expansive garden.*

contrasting words: **narrow**

sparkle *verb*

to give out little flashes of light. *The raindrops **sparkled** in the sunshine.*

glitter	To **glitter** means to sparkle brightly, as gold or silver does. *Her dress glittered with jewels.*
shimmer	To **shimmer** means to give out a soft light that comes and goes. *The surface of the lake shimmered in the moonlight.*
glimmer	To **glimmer** means to give out a faint light that comes and goes. *The lamp glimmered in the distance.*
twinkle	To **twinkle** means to sparkle softly, as something a long way away does. *Twinkle, twinkle little star.*
flicker	To **flicker** means to give out an unsteady light. *The candle flickered and then went out.*

similar words: **shine**

spectacular *adjective*

excitingly or impressively unusual and attracting people's notice. *The audience clapped and cheered the **spectacular** display of ice-skating.*

eye-catching — **Eye-catching** means noticeable or attracting attention because of an unusual or attractive appearance. *The shopkeeper put the most eye-catching clothes in the shop window.*

resplendent — **Resplendent** means splendidly bright and noticeable. *The mounted soldiers were resplendent in their white and gold uniforms as they paraded down the street.*

opulent — **Opulent** means spectacular and richly decorated with gold, jewels and finery. *The opulent castle of King Ludwig is a great tourist attraction.*

ostentatious — **Ostentatious** means noticeable in an overdone and showy way. *I don't like Barbara's ostentatious diamond-studded glasses.*

flamboyant — **Flamboyant** means dazzlingly bright and noticeable. *Rock stars often set new fashion trends with their flamboyant style of dress.*

similar words: **gaudy**
contrasting words: **simple, drab**

speed *verb*

to move very quickly. *She **sped** away on her bike as fast as she could go.*

race — To **race** can mean to run or move very quickly. *I raced to the station only to see the train pull out.*

hurtle — To **hurtle** means to rush noisily. *The rickety old train hurtled straight through the quiet stations.*

tear — To **tear** can mean to move with a great rush. *We tore out of the door to see what the noise was.*

pelt — To **pelt** means to move with great speed and energy. *We pelted down the slope on our toboggan.*

streak — To **streak** can mean to move extremely quickly and suddenly. *Before I could stop him, the dog streaked across the road.*

similar words: **hurry, dart**
contrasting words: **dawdle, walk**

spin *verb*

to turn around and around. *Look how the top is* ***spinning****.*

gyrate	To **gyrate** means to move around in a circle. *The sails of the windmill gyrated slowly on their axle in the light breeze.*
whirl	To **whirl** means to turn around or spin rapidly. *We whirled faster and faster in time to the music.*
whirr	To **whirr** can mean to spin around quickly with a low buzzing noise. *The wheels whirred along the road as we pedalled harder.*
twirl	To **twirl** means to spin rapidly. *We twirled and twirled until we were so giddy we fell over.*
swirl	To **swirl** means to move or turn around in a whirling way. *The water swirled around the rocks in the middle of the river.*

similar words: **turn**

spoil *verb*

to ruin something or make it go bad. *Leaving the milk out overnight has* ***spoiled*** *it.*

taint	To **taint** means to spoil something slightly. *The bad smell in the refrigerator tainted the cheese.*
contaminate	To **contaminate** means to make something dirty or impure. *Flies crawling over the meat contaminated it.*
pollute	To **pollute** means to spoil something by adding dirty or damaging things to it. *Smoke from the factories polluted the air over most of the city.*
foul	To **foul** means to make something dirty and unpleasant. *Stray dogs have fouled our footpath.*
corrupt	To **corrupt** means to change something or someone from good to bad. *Using those disgusting words is really corrupting your language.*

similar words: **damage**

star *noun*

someone who is excellent in something or who is famous in an art or profession. *The **star** of a television show signed autographs at our school fete.*

celebrity	A **celebrity** is a famous or well-known person. *The audience clapped and cheered when the celebrity finished her violin recital.*
idol	An **idol** is someone who is adored or admired excessively. *The football captain became the idol of the school when the team won for the third time in a row.*
hero	A **hero** is someone who has done something brave or outstanding. *He was the hero of the hour when he saved the little boy from drowning.*
household name	A **household name** is someone almost everybody has heard about. *Terry Wogan was a household name in England for many years.*
leading light	A **leading light** is someone who is well-known or outstanding in a particular area. This is more suited to everyday language. *The Mayor of our town is also one of the leading lights of the musical society.*

similar words: **VIP**

stare *verb*

to look at directly for a long time, usually with your eyes wide open. *I **stared** at the zebra the first time I saw one at the zoo.*

gaze	To **gaze** means to look long and steadily. *The artist gazed at the scene he was about to paint.*
gape	To **gape** means to stare with your mouth wide open. *They all gaped at her green hair.*
goggle	To **goggle** means to stare with your eyes opened wide. *We goggled at the magician's amazing tricks.*
gawk	To **gawk** means to stare stupidly. It is more suited to everyday language. *We all gawked at the burning fence until someone shouted for a hose.*

start *noun*

the first part of something. *Everyone was lined up for the **start** of the race.*

beginning — **Beginning** is so similar to **start** that you can usually use either word. *We arrived just in time to see the beginning of the match.*

commencement — **Commencement** is very similar to **start** and **beginning**. It is usually used in more formal language, such as in written reports. *The commencement of the festival was marked by a display of fireworks.*

outset — **Outset** means the very start of something. *From the outset of the match we knew our team would win.*

onset — **Onset** means the start of a particular thing. *The onset of the disease was sudden and violent.*

origin — An **origin** is the place where something starts or comes from. *The origin of the Olympic Games was in Ancient Greece.*

contrasting words: **end**

start *verb*

to begin or set moving. *I **started** as soon as it was light enough to see.*

begin — To **begin** is so similar to **start** that you can usually use either word. *The rain began just as we reached home.*

get going — To **get going** means to start or make haste. *Get going — you're holding everyone up!*

set out — To **set out** means to start on a journey. *He set out before the sun rose and the day became too hot.*

get off — To **get off** is very similar to **set out**. This is more suited to everyday language. *We'll get off straight after breakfast.*

fire away — To **fire away** means to start speaking, usuallywhen someone tells you to. This is more suited to everyday language. *I'm listening, so fire away.*

contrasting words: **end**

steadfast *adjective*

constant and unchanging. *The two sisters have a **steadfast** love for each other.*

staunch — **Staunch** means loyal and steadfast. *Ian and Stephen are staunch friends who have had many adventures together.*

firm — **Firm** can mean strong, definite and unchanging. *They have been firm friends for many years.*

enduring — **Enduring** means lasting or permanent. *Their enduring friendship has not been spoiled by their occasional arguments.*

stout-hearted — **Stout-hearted** means brave and determined. *Our stout-hearted footballers didn't stop trying to win until the final whistle blew.*

sturdy — **Sturdy** can mean firm or unbeatable. *Our team this year will be sturdy defenders of the cup we won last year.*

similar words: **faithful, reliable**

steady *adjective*

firmly placed so that it won't move. *Make sure the ladder is **steady** before you climb it.*

stable — **Stable** means not likely to fall or move. *You need a stable foundation to build a house on.*

firm — **Firm** means **steady** or not likely to move or shake. *We made sure the rock was firm before we climbed onto it.*

secure — **Secure** means firmly fastened in place. *We checked that the boat's mooring was secure before we went ashore.*

well-balanced — **Well-balanced** means placed in a **steady** position or not likely to fall over. *Not even the strongest wind could blow down the well-balanced tree-house.*

fixed — **Fixed** means so firmly or securely placed that it cannot move. *We set the ladder in a fixed position so we could always reach our attic.*

similar words: **still**
contrasting words: **moving**

steady *verb*

to make something firm so that it won't move. ***Steady** the boat so it doesn't tip over while I'm getting in.*

secure To **secure** means to make something firm, usually by tying or fastening it in some way. *We secured our bikes to the fence so they would be there when we got back.*

fix To **fix** can mean to make something firm or to put it securely in place. *Fix the poles into the ground before you put up the tent.*

support To **support** means to hold or steady someone or something so that they won't fall. *Get ready to support me when I do my handstand.*

stabilise To **stabilise** means to make something firm or steady. *We stabilised the boat by changing the position of the sails.*

balance To **balance** means to make something steady. *He balanced the angel carefully on the top of the Christmas tree.*

similar words: **strengthen**
contrasting words: **overturn**

steal *verb*

to take something that does not belong to you. *I left my bike outside and someone **stole** it.*

thieve To **thieve** can mean to steal something. This way of using it is rather unusual. *Who thieved my bike?*

pilfer To **pilfer** means to steal things that are small or not worth much. *Stop pilfering biscuits from the tin.*

pinch To **pinch** means to steal or take something without asking. It is more suited to everyday language. *I bet you pinched that money.*

nick To **nick** means to steal something. It is similar to **pinch**. It is more suited to everyday language. *Someone nicked my pen.*

knock off To **knock off** can mean to steal something. This is more suited to everyday language. *Our neighbours are always knocking off things from the corner shop.*

similar words: **abduct, take**

still *adjective*

free from movement. *The mountains were reflected in the **still** waters of the lake.*

motionless — **Motionless** means not showing any movement. *The antelope was unaware of the motionless lioness as she crouched waiting to pounce.*

stationary — **Stationary** means standing still. *The car was stationary at the red light.*

immobile — **Immobile** means not moving or able to be moved. *This plaster cast will make sure the broken bones in your arm are immobile while they heal.*

sedentary — **Sedentary** can mean not often moving about, or joined to an object that cannot move. This is a scientific word used to describe some animals. *This sea anemone is sedentary and traps food with its sticky tentacles.*

stagnant — **Stagnant** means not running or flowing. It is used about water and air. *Mosquitoes breed in stagnant water.*

similar words: **steady**
contrasting words: **moving**

stocky *adjective*

short, solid and strong in the way you are built. *The **stocky** footballer was placed in the front row.*

thickset — **Thickset** means having a very thick and solid build. *He was too thickset to be a very fast runner.*

stumpy — **Stumpy** can mean short and **thickset**. It usually describes people. *He's a stumpy little fellow but he's really quite strong.*

squat — **Squat** means short and **thick**. It can describe things as well as people. *The squat old buildings were left standing next to the new skycraper.*

beefy — **Beefy** means solid and having plenty of muscles. *No-one could tackle the team's beefy forward.*

burly — **Burly** means big and solidly built. *His burly figure was just right for a wrestler.*

similar words: **fat, heavy**
contrasting words: **thin, slight**

stone *noun*

a piece of the hard substance that makes up part of the earth. *Please don't throw **stones**.*

rock A **rock** is a large mass of stone. *We explored the rocks at the end of the beach.*

boulder A **boulder** is a very large rounded **rock**. *We tried to move the boulder that was blocking the entrance to the cave.*

pebble A **pebble** is a small rounded stone. *Our garden path is made of pebbles.*

cobble A **cobble** is a specially shaped stone used in paving streets. *The horse's hooves clattered on the cobbles in the old town.*

stop *verb*

to end or finish. *Work **stopped** when the bell went.*

quit To **quit** means to finish or give up. *I'm sick of playing this game — let's quit.*

halt To **halt** means to stop for a while, especially when you are marching. *The soldiers halted when they reached the camp.*

pause To **pause** means to stop or rest for a short time. *He paused to look out the window before he sat down to do his homework.*

stall To **stall** means to stop, especially when you don't want to. *The car stalled at the lights.*

hesitate To **hesitate** means to wait or **pause** as if you are not sure if you should go on. *She hesitated before she came into the room.*

similar words: **end**
contrasting words: **start**

store *verb*

to put something aside or away so it will be ready when you need it. *We **stored** our winter clothes and blankets during summer.*

save To **save** can mean to keep something or to put it aside for when you need it. *I saved my money so I could buy a camera.*

stockpile To **stockpile** means to save up large amounts of something for when you need it. *We stockpiled wood so we could burn it in winter.*

stow To **stow** means to put something somewhere or to pack it away. *Stow your bags under your seats where no-one can trip over them.*

hoard To **hoard** means to save something up and hide it away where no-one else can find it. *We hoarded biscuits so we could have a midnight feast.*

bank To **bank** can mean to put or deposit something in a bank where it will be kept safe until you need it. *I banked some money every week because I was saving up for a bike.*

similar words: **gather**
contrasting words: **scatter**

strange *adjective*

unusual, extraordinary or queer. *We did not enjoy the movie because the story was rather **strange**.*

odd **Odd** is so similar to **strange** that you can usually use either. *Everyone wondered if he was feeling alright because his behaviour was so odd.*

peculiar **Peculiar** is so similar to **strange** and **odd** that you can usually use any of them. *We noticed a peculiar smell as we walked past the factory.*

abnormal **Abnormal** means different from usual, often not in a desirable way. *The heat is abnormal for this time of the year.*

bizarre **Bizarre** means very strange. *His multi-coloured car is bizarre.*

weird **Weird** means surprisingly and alarmingly strange. *She wore weird clothes to the party.*

similar words: **unconventional, unusual**
contrasting words: **usual**

strengthen *verb*

to make something or someone stronger. *He used examples to **strengthen** his argument.*

reinforce To **reinforce** means to strengthen something by adding to it. *Extra soldiers were sent to reinforce the army.*

brace To **brace** can mean to make something stronger and firmly fixed in place. *He braced the ceiling with long pieces of wood.*

prop up To **prop up** can mean to strengthen something by giving support to it. *They worked harder in order to prop up the failing business.*

shore up To **shore up** means to strengthen something by supporting it with a post or beam. *The builder shored up the cracked wall.*

fortify To **fortify** means to strengthen something against attack or damage. *They fortified the castle with a moat.*

---

similar words: **steady**
contrasting words: **weaken**

---

strict *adjective*

demanding that you behave well and obey the rules. *My parents are very **strict**.*

rigid **Rigid** can mean strict and not changing from what you have decided is right. *They are rigid disciplinarians.*

firm **Firm** can mean strong, definite and unchanging in what you have decided, have agreed to, or believe. *Once they have made a rule they are quite firm about it.*

straitlaced **Straitlaced** means too strict and proper in the way you behave. *Sometimes we think they are too straitlaced and old-fashioned.*

austere **Austere** can mean strict or severely simple, especially in the way you live or discipline yourself. *The Mother Superior was an austere person but seemed very serene.*

harsh **Harsh** means strict in a cruel way. *The harsh governor ordered the soldiers to flog the prisoner.*

---

contrasting words: **broad-minded, lenient**

---

strong *adjective*

having great bodily power or energy. *You are **strong** because you have had so much exercise.*

robust — **Robust** means strongly or solidly built. *He is a robust little baby.*

muscly — **Muscly** means having strong muscles. *Running has made his legs muscly.*

brawny — **Brawny** means having well-developed muscles. It is similar to **muscly**. *She liked the brawny lifesaver.*

husky — **Husky** can mean big and strong. *The husky axeman soon chopped down the tree.*

wiry — **Wiry** can mean thin and strong. *She looks weak but she is very wiry.*

similar words: **hardy**
contrasting words: **weak**

stubborn *adjective*

determined not to give way or change your mind. *We tried to talk her into wearing another dress but she was **stubborn** and wore the luminous pink one.*

obstinate — **Obstinate** means stubborn, even though you know you may be wrong. *She annoys everyone because she is obstinate and insists on doing everything her way.*

pig-headed — **Pig-headed** means stupidly stubborn. *It is no use trying to talk sense to a pig-headed person.*

adamant — **Adamant** means staying firm in what you decide. *He was adamant that he would not go.*

inflexible — **Inflexible** means not changing your mind under any circumstances. *We begged him not to punish us but he was inflexible.*

uncompromising — **Uncompromising** means having your mind made up without taking notice of other people's opinions or trying to fit in with them. *'No' was his uncompromising answer.*

similar words: **persistent**

stupid *adjective*

not clever or quick to understand. *What a **stupid** dog you are!*

dense — **Dense** can mean foolish or stupid. *I'm rather dense when it comes to following road maps.*

slow — **Slow** can mean not mentally quick. *Some slow learners are very good at making things.*

dull — **Dull** can mean stupid or not intelligent. *He seems to be a dull child but you should see his wonderful paintings.*

dumb — **Dumb** can mean stupid or silly. *That was a dumb thing to say.*

thick — **Thick** can mean stupid or unintelligent. *Don't worry about trying to explain to him because he's really thick.*

similar words: **silly**
contrasting words: **clever, shrewd, sensible**

subdue *verb*

to overcome someone or something, usually by force. *The invading army **subdued** the civilians who tried to resist them.*

overpower — To **overpower** means to subdue someone using your greater strength. *The ex-boxer overpowered the thug who attacked him on the street.*

repress — To **repress** means to keep something or someone under control by effort or force. *She repressed her anger with difficulty.*

dominate — To **dominate** means to control or rule someone or something. *Richard dominated his younger brother and led him into a life of crime.*

oppress — To **oppress** can mean to be cruel to someone in your power. *The soldiers oppressed their prisoners.*

persecute — To **persecute** means to constantly treat someone unfairly or cruelly, usually someone less powerful than you. *In some countries the governments persecute people because of their religious beliefs.*

similar words: **force**
contrasting words: **free**

submissive *adjective*

giving in obediently, without questioning. *The frightened girl was **submissive** when the bully threatened her.*

subservient — **Subservient** means very submissive. *She was so subservient she even gave the bully her lunch.*

weak-willed — **Weak-willed** means giving in to others because you have a weak character. *He was so weak-willed he obeyed every unfair order.*

servile — **Servile** means weakly allowing others to control you. *Everyone ordered around the servile boy.*

downtrodden — **Downtrodden** means governed or ruled so harshly that you are frightened not to obey. *The downtrodden people finally fought back.*

similar words: **obedient**
contrasting words: **defiant, argumentative, aggressive**

subordinate *adjective*

placed in or belonging to a lower order or rank. *He handed on his work to a **subordinate** employee.*

junior — **Junior** can mean of a low rank. *His brother is a junior officer in the navy.*

subsidiary — **Subsidiary** means of a secondary order or rank. *The manager's daughter was given a subsidiary position in the company.*

common — **Common** can mean of the ordinary rank. *Politicians should look after the interests of the common people.*

lowly — **Lowly** means of very low or humble position or rank. *He was given the most lowly job in the factory.*

similar words: **insignificant, minor**

subtract *verb*

to take away a part from a whole, or one number or quantity from another. *If you **subtract** 2 from 7, you get 5.*

deduct To **deduct** means to take away or subtract one quantity from another. *My father deducted £2 from my pocket money because I broke a window.*

remove To **remove** means to take something off or away. *Please remove your shoes before you walk on the new carpet.*

dock To **dock** means to cut off or take away a part from something. *The boss docked Dad's wages when he was late for work.*

diminish To **diminish** means to make something smaller. *The fact that I had read the book didn't diminish my enjoyment of the film.*

curtail To **curtail** means to cut something short. *We curtailed our trip and came home two weeks early.*

similar words: **reduce, remove**
contrasting words: **add**

succeed *verb*

to do or accomplish what you have attempted. *Anne **succeeded** in learning to play the violin.*

shine To **shine** can mean to be very good at something. *Kris shines at spelling.*

steal the show To **steal the show** means to achieve great success. *Maureen stole the show with her lovely singing.*

make the grade To **make the grade** means to reach the standard that has been set. *Jenny made the grade after very little practice.*

triumph To **triumph** means to have a victory or success. *Richard triumphed as usual in his tennis match.*

win To **win** means to gain a victory. *The competition was a hard one but Bill won.*

contrasting words: **fail**

sudden *adjective*

happening quickly and without warning. *We all jumped at the **sudden** noise.*

abrupt — **Abrupt** means sudden and unexpected. *His abrupt departure made us wonder what had happened.*

impulsive — **Impulsive** means acting on a sudden desire. *She reached out her hand in an impulsive gesture of friendship.*

snap — **Snap** means done quickly or suddenly. *She made a snap decision to go to town.*

impromptu — **Impromptu** means made up or done on the spur of the moment. *We surprised him with a farewell gift and he made an impromptu speech of thanks.*

meteoric — **Meteoric** can mean swift or happening quickly, like a meteor. *She is a brilliant architect and her progress in this career has been meteoric.*

sufficient *adjective*

having as much as is needed or wanted. *Julie bought **sufficient** material to make curtains for the living room and dining room.*

enough — **Enough** means the same as **sufficient**. You can usually use either. *There is only enough cake for one slice each.*

adequate — **Adequate** means **enough** or sufficient for the purpose. *I hope our clothes are adequate for the cold weather.*

satisfactory — **Satisfactory** means fulfilling all the requirements or demands. *Mum wouldn't pay for the car repairs until she was sure they were satisfactory.*

decent — **Decent** can mean sufficiently big to fulfil a particular need. *Robert won't give me a decent go on his skateboard.*

contrasting words: **abundant, extra**

suffocate *verb*

to kill by stopping someone from breathing. *Don't ever put a plastic bag over your face because it could **suffocate** you.*

choke To **choke** means to stop someone breathing. *This collar is so tight it is practically choking me.*

strangle To **strangle** can mean to kill someone by holding something tight around their neck. *The murderer strangled her with his bare hands.*

smother To **smother** means to suffocate someone by blocking the supply of air to their nose and mouth. *He tried to smother her with a pillow but she struggled free.*

asphyxiate To **asphyxiate** means to suffocate. It is a more formal, medical word. *We heard on the news that the gas had asphyxiated ten people.*

stifle To **stifle** means to **smother** or prevent someone from breathing. *The atmosphere at the heated swimming pool is so full of chlorine it almost stifles me.*

---

suggestion *noun*

an idea brought to someone for them to consider and possibly do something about. *My **suggestion** to dress up made all the children happy.*

recommendation A **recommendation** can be a suggestion about what to do, or how to do something. *The council made several recommendations on how the shopping centre should be designed.*

piece of advice A **piece of advice** is an opinion suggested, or offered, by someone who thinks it is worth following. *Let me give you a piece of advice — don't play at work and don't work at play.*

pointer A **pointer** can be a helpful suggestion. *The tennis coach gave me a few pointers on how to improve my backhand.*

tip A **tip** can be a piece of useful information. *My brother gave me a tip on how to solve a maths problem.*

similar words: **offer**

suit *verb*

to be satisfactory or convenient. *Will tomorrow **suit** for our meeting?*

serve To **serve** can mean to be fit to be used for a particular purpose. *There is no shelter at this bus stop but that tree will serve.*

suffice To **suffice** means to be enough to be satisfactory. *I think twenty sausage rolls will suffice for the party.*

qualify To **qualify** means to make or show yourself fit for something. *She qualified for the finals by winning the heat.*

fill the bill To **fill the bill** means to be entirely suitable for a particular purpose. It is more suited to everyday language. *I think Susie will fill the bill as form prefect.*

summary *noun*

a short statement in speech or writing giving the main points of something. *I gave the class a **summary** of the headmaster's speech.*

résumé A **résumé** is a summing up or a summary. It is so similar to **summary** you can usually use either. *The headmaster gave us a résumé of progress on the new tennis courts.*

precis A **precis** is a brief piece of writing containing the main points of a longer piece. *He wrote a precis of the article on grass snakes.*

synopsis A **synopsis** is a written outline or summary of a longer piece of writing. *She wrote a synopsis of the novel to persuade us to read it.*

outline An **outline** is a short description of something giving only its most important points. *We were all given an outline of what had to be done.*

plan A **plan** can be a scheme for something that is to be done. *I jotted down a plan for my story before I began to write it.*

similar words: **report**

superior *adjective*

of higher grade than usual. *I am only interested in buying **superior** goods.*

high class — **High class** is so similar to **superior** that you can usually use either. *I only stay at high class hotels.*

quality — **Quality** can mean excellent or of superior grade. *The stall had a sign saying 'Quality produce sold here'.*

deluxe — **Deluxe** means of expensive and luxurious quality. *I would expect a deluxe hotel to have a restaurant service all through the night.*

prize — **Prize** means so high in quality as to be greatly valued. *That gold pencil is his prize possession.*

similar words: **excellent, best**
contrasting words: **inferior**

support *noun*

someone or something that holds anything up. *This pole is one of the **supports** for the tent.*

base — A **base** is the bottom part of anything, which gives support. *The statue stood on a strong base.*

foundation — A **foundation** is the prepared or natural **base** on which something rests or stands. *The stone foundations of the old building had to be repaired.*

framework — A **framework** is a structure designed to support or enclose something. *The framework of the ship was made of steel.*

skeleton — A **skeleton** can mean a bare **framework** of something. *After the hurricane, only the skeleton of the house remained.*

sure *adjective*

having no doubt about something. *I am **sure** of what I am saying.*

certain — **Certain** is so similar to **sure** that you can usually use either. *I am certain my answer is correct.*

positive — **Positive** can mean absolutely sure. *I am positive you are lying.*

confident — **Confident** means having a strong belief about something. *She was confident that she had passed the exam.*

clear — **Clear** can mean not able to be doubted. *She achieved a clear win in the 100 metre race.*

definite — **Definite** means **clear** and **certain**. *It is a definite advantage to be able to run fast.*

contrasting words: **confused, uncertain**

surroundings *noun*

everything that is around or near someone or something. *We are all affected by our **surroundings**.*

environment — Your **environment** is the whole surroundings of your life. *He grew up in a city environment.*

habitat — A **habitat** is the surroundings in which a particular plant or animal naturally grows or lives. *These plants need a very warm habitat.*

environs — **Environs** are the surrounding districts of a place. *This is a map of Perth and its environs.*

setting — A **setting** is the surroundings in which something is placed or set. *The house had a pretty country setting.*

scene — **Scene** can be the place or surroundings in which an event happens. *We need to look at the scene of the crime.*

swamp *noun*

an area of soft wet ground. *Many water birds lived in the* ***swamp****.*

bog A **bog** is an area of muddy ground. It is similar to **swamp**. *Be careful you don't wander into the bog.*

marsh A **marsh** is an area of low-lying wet land. It is similar to both **swamp** and **bog**. *The marsh was full of reeds.*

mire A **mire** is an area of deep mud. *The car sank in the mire.*

quagmire A **quagmire** is a muddy patch of ground. *The rain has turned the backyard into a quagmire.*

similar words: **lake**

sway *verb*

to move or swing from side to side. *She* ***swayed*** *in time with the music.*

wave To **wave** means to move loosely to and fro or up and down. *The pennants waved in the strong wind.*

wobble To **wobble** means to move unsteadily from side to side. *When I first got on a bike I wobbled all over the road.*

waddle To **waddle** means to walk with short steps, swaying from side to side. *The duck waddled across to the pond followed by her ducklings.*

reel To **reel** means to stagger or sway, especially from giddiness or a blow. *She reeled across to us when she got off the merry-go-round.*

lurch To **lurch** means to move suddenly and unsteadily. *The drunken man lurched out of his chair towards the bar.*

similar words: **shake**

sweet *adjective*

having a pleasant taste like that of sugar or honey. *Do you like **sweet** biscuits or savoury biscuits best?*

sugary	**Sugary** means tasting too sweet because of having too much sugar. *I don't like this sugary drink.*
sickly	**Sickly** can mean so sweet that it makes you feel sick. *Don't eat any more of those sickly lollies.*
candied	**Candied** means cooked in sugar or having a crust of sugar. *The cake was decorated with pieces of candied orange peel.*
glacé	**Glacé** means cooked in or covered with sugar. It is similar to **candied**. *I gave her a box of glacé fruit.*

contrasting words: **sour**

swelter *verb*

to feel very hot and sweaty. *We **sweltered** all summer.*

boil	To **boil** can means to feel very hot. *We boiled in the hall because the air-conditioner had broken down.*
roast	To **roast** can mean to be or become very hot, like food cooked in an oven or over a fire. *We roasted sitting in the hot car.*
burn	To **burn** can mean to feel very hot and as if on fire. *His forehead burned with the fever.*
glow	To **glow** can mean to be or feel extremely hot. *The jogger's face glowed after her morning run.*

take *verb*

to get or receive something. *Will you **take** a cheque instead of cash?*

confiscate To **confiscate** means to take something and keep it. *The teacher confiscated my comic book.*

appropriate To **appropriate** means to take something because you want to use it yourself. *She appropriated Tom's desk while he was away.*

annex To **annex** means to obtain something and join it to what you already own. *The farmer annexed the neighbouring land.*

borrow To **borrow** means to take or get something on the understanding that you have to return it. *I borrowed three books from the library this week.*

adopt To **adopt** means to take something or someone as your own. *They adopted the baby.*

similar words: **grab, steal, abduct**
contrasting words: **give**

talk *noun*

an exchange of thoughts using spoken words, especially in a friendly or informal way. *We had a good **talk** after dinner.*

conversation **Conversation** is so similar to **talk** that you can usually use either. *Don't interrupt our conversation.*

discussion A **discussion** is a talk in which you consider something from all sides. *Our family had a discussion about where to go for our holidays.*

debate A **debate** is an organised talk in which the things for and against something are considered. It is similar to **discussion**. *The debate in parliament went on all through the night.*

interview An **interview** is a talk in which someone is asked questions about something. *The actor gave an interview about his latest film.*

dialogue **Dialogue** means a talk between two or more people, especially in a play or story. *The dialogue in the first part of the play was not very interesting.*

talk *verb*

to speak together. *The girls **talked** all the way to school.*

converse To **converse** means to talk with someone else. It is used in rather formal language. *We conversed about music.*

confer To **confer** means to have a discussion about something. *I will have to confer with the other teachers about that.*

chat To **chat** means to talk in a friendly way, not about a serious subject. *The children chatted about their holidays.*

gossip To **gossip** means to talk in a silly way about other people's business. *All the neighbours gossiped about her boyfriend.*

yarn To **yarn** means to talk for a long time, telling stories. *The old men sat outside the shop and yarned.*

similar words: **yak, rave**

talkative *adjective*

liking to talk a lot. *Susan finds it hard to keep quiet in class because she is very **talkative**.*

loquacious **Loquacious** is similar to **talkative**. It is a rather formal word. *My mother is loquacious when she talks on the phone.*

voluble **Voluble** means talking with a ready and continuous flow of words. *He is voluble if you get him talking about his favourite sport.*

communicative **Communicative** means liking to share or pass on thoughts, opinions, or information by talking. *Bill is a friendly, communicative person.*

chatty **Chatty** means liking to chat. *You can hear all the neighbourhood gossip from the chatty lady at the corner shop.*

garrulous **Garrulous** means very talkative, often in a silly way. *I think she is so garrulous because she is lonely.*

contrasting words: **reticent, abrupt**

tall *adjective*

of more than average height. *He can reach the box on top of the cupboard because he is so **tall**.*

high	**High** can mean stretching a long way upwards. *We have a high fence around our backyard to keep the dog in.*
lofty	**Lofty** means reaching high into the air. *The lofty mountains seemed to touch the clouds.*
towering	**Towering** means very tall or **lofty**. *The city was full of towering buildings.*
grand	**Grand** can mean of great or impressive size. *What a grand house you live in!*
elevated	**Elevated** means raised up, generally above the ground. *The stage was elevated so that the whole audience could see.*

task *noun*

a piece of work you are expected to do. *Everyone was given their own **task** so we would be ready to leave on time.*

chore	A **chore** is a task you have to do that is not very exciting or that you don't like much. *I have to finish my chores before I can come and play.*
errand	An **errand** is a small task you are sent to do. *Dad sent me into town on an errand for him.*
assignment	An **assignment** is a particular task you are given to do. *Our assignment was to make a model of our solar system.*
duty	A **duty** is something you have to do because of your position. *It is your duty as captain to decide the batting order.*
mission	A **mission** is a special task someone is sent to carry out. *Your mission is to discover their secret hide-out.*

tasteless *adjective*

lacking in taste. *The food at that restaurant is **tasteless.***

plain	**Plain** means not rich or strong in taste. *She believes in cooking old-fashioned, plain meals.*
bland	**Bland** means pleasant and easy to digest but lacking a strong or interesting taste. *I always put a lot of salt and pepper on the meals she cooks because they are too bland for me.*
mild	**Mild** can mean not strong or sharp in taste and easy to digest. *He was put on a diet of mild food after his illness.*
insipid	**Insipid** means too tasteless to be pleasant. *I think this cup of tea is insipid.*
flat	**Flat** can mean disappointingly tasteless. *I used all the ingredients in the recipe but the meal was flat.*

contrasting words: **tasty**

tasty *adjective*

full of flavour. *This meat needs a **tasty** sauce.*

savoury	**Savoury** means having a delicious taste, usually not sweet. *There are many savoury meals on the menu to choose from.*
spicy	**Spicy** means strong-tasting because of being flavoured with a spice, such as pepper or cinnamon. *Do you like spicy food?*
sharp	**Sharp** can mean having a strong biting taste. *This lemon drink is too sharp for me.*
pungent	**Pungent** means having a biting taste. *This is a pungent wine.*
piquant	**Piquant** means having a pleasantly strong, biting taste. *This sauce should be more piquant.*

contrasting words: **tasteless**

teach *verb*

to give a skill to someone, or to give knowledge of something. *She **teaches** our class. He **teaches** music.*

instruct To **instruct** means to teach someone or tell them something they don't know. *The dentist instructed us on how to care for our teeth.*

train To **train** means to teach a person or animal to know or do something. *She trained us to speak loudly and clearly.*

drill To **drill** can mean to **train** someone by giving them repeated exercises. *She drilled us until we knew all our lines for the play.*

coach To **coach** means to **train** or teach people in small groups or on their own. *He coached me in maths so I could understand the new work.*

educate To **educate** means to teach or **instruct** someone in order to increase their knowledge and skills. *She also educates her class in skills such as judo and debating.*

contrasting words: **learn**

teacher *noun*

someone who instructs other people. *The **teacher** showed us how to mix the paints to make a new colour.*

tutor A **tutor** is someone who is hired to teach people in small groups or on their own. *Mum hired a tutor to help me with my reading.*

governess A **governess** was a woman who used to teach children in their own homes. *The governess taught the children their manners as well as reading, writing and arithmetic.*

lecturer A **lecturer** teaches very large groups of people. *When the hall was full the lecturer began telling us about her new discovery.*

coach A **coach** is someone who teaches people privately to help them get ready for an exam, or someone who trains athletes. *Did the coach say we have to do a hundred push-ups?*

trainer A **trainer** is someone who helps athletes stay fit and teaches them the skills they need for their sport. *His trainer made out a programme he had to follow to get ready for the big race.*

similar words: **adviser**

tear *verb*

to pull something apart leaving rough edges. *She* ***tore*** *the paper in two.*

rip — To **rip** means to tear something in a rough way. *He ripped his shirt on the barbed-wire fence.*

slash — To **slash** means to cut something violently and unevenly. *Vandals have slashed the train seats.*

slit — To **slit** means to make a long straight cut or opening in something. *He slit the envelope open and took out the letter.*

gash — To **gash** means to make a long deep cut in something. *She gashed her hand with the knife.*

lacerate — To **lacerate** means to cut or tear something roughly. *The broken glass lacerated his foot.*

similar words: **cut, scratch**

tease *verb*

to make fun of or pester someone in a light-hearted but embarrassing way. *Leah's friends* ***tease*** *her about her red hair and freckles.*

taunt — To **taunt** means to insult or tease someone in a cruel way. *The louts taunted the lame boy for not running faster.*

mock — To **mock** means to make fun of someone, especially by imitating them. *It was unkind of them to laugh when Mary mocked Kathy's lisp.*

rib — To **rib** can mean to tease, **ridicule** or make fun of someone. It is more suited to everyday language. *Andrew's friends ribbed him about Clare being his girlfriend.*

heckle — To **heckle** means to torment and bother a speaker with annoying questions and comments. *The man in the audience heckled the politician at the election meeting.*

ridicule — To **ridicule** means to make fun of someone or something in a scornful way. *John ridiculed Robert's attempt to row the boat.*

similar words: **insult**

tell *verb*

to give someone an account or description of something. ***Tell** us the old tale of 'The Hare and the Tortoise'.*

narrate To **narrate** means to tell a particular story in speech or writing. *On my record of 'Peter and the Wolf' a famous actor narrates the story.*

relate To **relate** means to tell or **narrate** something, usually a story. *He related the story of how he had found the lost goldmine.*

recount To **recount** means to tell about something, giving as much information as you can. *Recount everything that happened after I left you.*

describe To **describe** means to tell about something or someone in a way that gives a very clear picture or idea of it. *She described the strawberry cream cake so well we could almost taste it.*

outline To **outline** means to tell about something briefly, giving only the main points. *He outlined the plan for us again.*

similar words: **inform**

temporary *adjective*

lasting for a short time. *Adam had a **temporary** job during the holidays delivering newspapers.*

provisional **Provisional** means temporary or just for the time being. *A provisional government was appointed only until a new election could be held.*

interim **Interim** means temporary or lasting for a short time. *We had to obey the interim orders until a new plan was thought up.*

casual **Casual** can mean employed occasionally. *The manager hired a casual labourer when we were busy.*

makeshift **Makeshift** means used for a short time in place of something else. *She could only find a brick to use as a makeshift hammer.*

contrasting words: **permanent**

test *noun*

a set of questions to answer or some other method of evaluation, designed to show how much you know about something or what your abilities are. *We had a maths **test** on all the work we've learned this term.*

exam An **exam** is a test of knowledge or skill which often has to be passed before the next stage of learning begins. *If I don't pass my exams at the end of the year, I will be upset.*

trial A **trial** can be an experiment or test carried out in order to prove something. *The scientist ran several trials on the new cream to make sure that it was safe to use.*

audition An **audition** is a special test or hearing to see how suitable an actor or performer is for a particular job. *Elsa is having an audition for a part in the new play.*

checkup A **checkup** is a test designed to make sure that all is in order, especially your health. *She went to the doctor for her yearly checkup.*

test *verb*

to attempt to find out a particular thing about something or someone. *I **tested** the water to see how cold it was.*

try To **try** can mean to test something, often by using it yourself. *I am going to try my new ballpoint pen today.*

sample To **sample** means to test or judge something by eating or using some of it. *The judges sampled all the cakes before they announced the winner of the competition.*

check To **check** means to find out the correctness of something. *Dominic checked the car battery before we set off on our trip.*

screen To **screen** means to examine or test a number of people or things. *Jasper screened the rock samples for signs of gold.*

assay To **assay** means to give something a test or trial. *The Health Department assayed the new drug before it was put on the market.*

similar words: **examine, investigate**

the country *noun*

the less developed land outside the towns and cities. *Many people who live in* ***the country*** *are farmers.*

countryside The **countryside** is the rural part of a country, often the scenery of a particular country area. *The countryside was so pretty that we stopped for a picnic.*

hinterland The **hinterland** is the country lying just inland from the coast. *The Norwegian hinterland is mountainous.*

wilderness A **wilderness** is a wild, uninhabited and uncultivated region. *The Bible tells how Jesus spent forty days and forty nights wandering in the wilderness.*

moorlands **Moorlands** are areas of open ground usually covered with heather, coarse grass and bracken. *New Forest ponies run wild on the moorlands.*

the sticks **The sticks** means country areas with small populations, particularly the remote parts which are regarded as lacking some of the comforts of city life. It is more suited to everyday language. *We were bored living out in the sticks.*

contrasting words: **city**

thick *adjective*

measuring rather a lot from one surface to another. *I have a lovely,* ***thick*** *blanket on my bed in winter.*

dense **Dense** means thick or closely packed. *The tropical rainforest was very dense and hard to walk through.*

heavy **Heavy** can mean thicker or greater than usual. *She drew a heavy line under the title of her story.*

solid **Solid** can mean thick or **dense**. *Solid fog filled the valley and progress was impossible.*

chunky **Chunky** can mean thick or bulky. *The chunky sweater was suitable to wear skiing.*

contrasting words: **thin**

thicken *verb*

to become thicker or more dense. *The recipe says to stir the egg and milk mixture until it **thickens**.*

clot — To **clot** means to thicken by forming solid lumps. *After you have been bleeding for a while, your blood clots and stops flowing.*

coagulate — To **coagulate** means to change from a liquid into thick lumps. *The gravy became cold and coagulated in the bottom of the pan.*

congeal — To **congeal** means to thicken by becoming solid. It is similar to **coagulate**. *Cooking fat congeals as it cools.*

curdle — To **curdle** means to go lumpy. It is used particularly about milk that has been treated with an acid or has not been refrigerated. *The milk curdled when it was left out in the sun.*

condense — To **condense** means to become thicker and less in volume. *The steam condensed and formed drops of water when it hit the cold windscreen.*

thief *noun*

someone who steals. *A **thief** must have taken my school bag.*

robber — A **robber** is a thief, often one who uses force or violence. *A robber attacked the old lady and stole her money.*

burglar — A **burglar** is someone who steals by breaking into a house or building. *Our house has an alarm to scare away burglars.*

shoplifter — A **shoplifter** is someone who steals from a shop while pretending to be shopping. *Shoplifters will be reported to the police.*

pickpocket — A **pickpocket** is someone who steals from people's pockets or handbags while they are in public places. *My father's wallet was stolen by a pickpocket on the train.*

kleptomaniac — A **kleptomaniac** is someone who feels an uncontrollable urge to steal things, even though they do not need them. *So many things have been disappearing that I think there must be a kleptomaniac in the school.*

similar words: **bandit, criminal**

thin *adjective*

measuring very little from one surface to the other. *I like nice, **thin** toast.*

slim — **Slim** means pleasantly thin. This can be used about people or things. *He was reading a slim volume of poetry.*

slender — **Slender** is so similar to **slim** you can usually choose either of them. *She has a very slender figure.*

skinny — **Skinny** means very thin. This is usually only used about people or animals. *The poor, skinny old horse was pulling a heavy cart.*

lean — **Lean** can mean thin, but usually also fit and strong. *The lean cowboy mounted his horse and galloped away.*

spindly — **Spindly** means long or tall and **slender**, but usually also weak or frail. *The spindly young shrubs needed plenty of care to make them grow strong and thick.*

---

similar words: **slight**
contrasting words: **thick, stocky**

---

think *verb*

to form or have an idea of something in your mind. ***Think** what you would say if you saw a Martian.*

imagine — To **imagine** means to form a picture of something in your mind. *Imagine his spaceship and that you are walking up to it.*

suppose — To **suppose** can mean to think or believe something without having any actual knowledge. *Do you suppose the Martian would be able to understand you?*

suspect — To **suspect** can mean to think that something is very likely to be true. *I suspect I would be too surprised to be able to say anything.*

reckon — To **reckon** can mean to think or **suppose**. It is more suited to everyday language. *I reckon the Martian would be just as surprised to see me.*

guess — To **guess** can mean to think or believe something. *I guess the Martian would have some interesting stories to tell.*

---

similar words: **believe, conclude, ponder**

---

thorough *adjective*

complete, careful or without missing anything. *We gave our holiday house a **thorough** cleaning before we left.*

comprehensive — **Comprehensive** means including nearly everything. *The newspaper gave a comprehensive report of the opening of the school's new building.*

detailed — **Detailed** means looking at every little part of something. *The scientist made a detailed examination of the sample of blood.*

exhaustive — **Exhaustive** means dealing with something in detail. *The police made an exhaustive search for the missing man.*

intensive — **Intensive** means done with a lot of attention or work. *The nurses and doctors gave him intensive care after his accident.*

in-depth — **In-depth** means thorough or dealing with something completely. *They had an in-depth discussion about how to prevent vandalism.*

similar words: **whole**
contrasting words: **incomplete**

thought *noun*

something that has come into your mind as a result of thinking. *I suddenly had the **thought** that a swim would make me cooler.*

idea — An **idea** is a thought or a picture in your mind. *Our idea grew clearer until we knew exactly what we should do.*

brainstorm — A **brainstorm** is a sudden brilliant thought. *His brainstorm gave us the solution to the whole problem.*

notion — A **notion** is an **idea,** often not very clear in your mind. *I have a notion of what travelling through space may be like.*

theory — A **theory** is a thought or opinion about something that cannot be supported by facts. *I have a different theory about how the planets were formed.*

concept — A **concept** is a general **idea** or understanding of something. *I do not have a very clear concept of computer programming.*

thrash *verb*

to beat someone soundly as a punishment. *He **thrashed** us when he saw what we had done.*

whip To **whip** means to beat something or someone with a whip. *The jockey whipped the racehorse to make it gallop faster.*

cane To **cane** means to strike someone with a cane. *Many years ago teachers caned their pupils if they didn't know the correct answer.*

flog To **flog** means to beat someone hard with a whip or stick, usually as a punishment. *The soldier flogged the convict caught trying to escape.*

lash To **lash** means to strike someone or something hard with a whip or long stick, usually to keep them working or moving. *The slave driver lashed the men cruelly whenever they began to slow down.*

scourge To **scourge** means to strike someone severely with a whip, usually as a punishment or method of torture. This is a rather old-fashioned word. *The enemy scourged their prisoners before they started to question them.*

similar words: **beat**

threaten *verb*

to warn someone, using words or some other sign, that you intend to rob or hurt them. *The leader of the gang **threatened** the bank teller with a revolver.*

menace To **menace** means to take a threatening attitude towards someone. *The thug menaced the old lady and took her jewellery.*

intimidate To **intimidate** means to frighten someone in order to make them do something. *The spy tried to intimidate the ambassador's secretary into giving him the secret code.*

cow To **cow** can mean to frighten someone with threats. *The giant's loud voice did not cow Jack.*

blackmail To **blackmail** means to demand money from someone by threatening to reveal secrets about them. *He was able to blackmail me because he knew I had cheated in the exam.*

similar words: **frighten, force**

thrifty *adjective*

carefully managing or looking after your money or supplies. *The **thrifty** woman always kept a record of how she spent her money.*

frugal — **Frugal** means being very careful not to waste anything. *We must be frugal with our supplies or we won't have enough for the whole journey.*

economical — **Economical** means not wasting anything. *She was such an economical housekeeper that her groceries lasted a long time.*

provident — **Provident** means carefully managing things like money so that you are prepared for the future. *She was so provident that she had enough money for her retirement.*

careful — **Careful** can mean managing your money and possessions so well that people think you are mean and stingy. This is more suited to everyday language. *He's so careful with his money that he won't even buy us some bubblegum.*

similar words: **mean**
contrasting words: **generous**

thrive *verb*

to grow strong or to do well. *Our new business is **thriving**.*

prosper — To **prosper** means to be successful. *The farmers have prospered this year because of the regular rain.*

benefit — To **benefit** means to get better or gain an advantage. *We will all benefit from a holiday in the mountains.*

boom — To **boom** means to suddenly do very well. *During the gold rush business in the country towns was booming.*

blossom — To **blossom** can mean to develop or turn out well. *He has blossomed into a fine athlete.*

bloom — To **bloom** can mean to be healthy and full of life. *When she gave up eating junk food she bloomed.*

similar words: **succeed**
contrasting words: **fail**

throb *verb*

to beat regularly and strongly. *The engine of the boat* ***throbbed*** *as we made our way up the river.*

pulsate To **pulsate** means to throb or beat like your heart. *We could hear the native drums pulsating in the distance.*

palpitate To **palpitate** means to beat much faster than usual. *Our hearts palpitated at the eerie sounds of the forest.*

drum To **drum** can mean to make a thumping sound like a drum. *The blood drummed in his ears as he ran up the steep hill.*

whirr To **whirr** means to make a low vibrating sound while moving or working. *The helicopter whirred over our heads as it followed our progress.*

buzz To **buzz** means to make a low humming sound. *His stream of words buzzed in my head.*

throw *verb*

to send something through the air. *Felicity* ***threw*** *the ball to Elsie.*

toss To **toss** means to throw something, often in a casual way. *She tossed her bag on the bed.*

fling To **fling** means to throw something, usually forcefully or impatiently. *He flung the book angrily onto the table.*

hurl To **hurl** means to throw something with great force or strength. *The huge man hurled the hammer over the boundary in the Highland Games.*

pitch To **pitch** means to throw something, often taking careful aim. *Pitch the ball low so that the little girl can catch it.*

chuck To **chuck** means to throw something carelessly. It is more suited to everyday language. *He chucked the rubbish in the bin.*

tidy *adjective*

having everything in its right place. *If you have a **tidy** room it is easy to find things.*

neat — **Neat** means tidy and well-ordered. *Her homework was neat and easy to read.*

trim — **Trim** means **neat** and smart. *John was very trim in his school uniform.*

orderly — **Orderly** means arranged in a tidy manner. *The books were in orderly rows on the shelves.*

shipshape — **Shipshape** means **neat** and tidy. *We made the house shipshape before Mum came home from hospital with our baby brother.*

methodical — **Methodical** means acting or done in a careful, **orderly** way. *She was methodical in her habits and always hung her clothes in the cupboard.*

contrasting words: **untidy, scruffy**

tire *verb*

to reduce someone's strength and make them sleepy or weak. *The long walk **tired** the children.*

fatigue — To **fatigue** means to tire someone in their body or mind. *The strain of looking after the tiny twins fatigued their mother.*

weary — To **weary** is so similar to **tire** and **fatigue** that you can usually use any of these. *The constant noise and bustle of his office wearies Dad.*

exhaust — To **exhaust** means to tire or wear someone out to a great extent. *Digging in the garden exhausts me.*

tax — To **tax** means to burden or **exhaust** someone or something. *Nursing taxed her much more than she had expected.*

strain — To **strain** can mean to make too many demands upon something or someone. *Having all her relations staying with her at once has strained her resources.*

similar words: **weaken**

tired *adjective*

weak from effort or hard work and needing sleep. *The children were **tired** and ready for bed by the end of sports day.*

weary — **Weary** means tired out in your mind or body by hard work, or something similar. *Mum was very weary after spending all night with the sick baby.*

worn — **Worn** can mean made very tired. *The old lady's shoulders were stooped and worn after her busy day gardening.*

exhausted — **Exhausted** means greatly tired or drained of strength and energy. *The runners were all exhausted after the cross country race.*

bushed — **Bushed** means very tired or **exhausted**. It is usually used in rather informal language. *I was bushed when I had finished cleaning the bathroom.*

fatigued — **Fatigued** means very tired or drained of energy due to effort of your mind or body. *The student was fatigued after the three hour examination.*

similar words: **lethargic**
contrasting words: **energetic**

toast *verb*

to brown something by a flame or heat. *We sat around the campfire and **toasted** marshmallows.*

grill — To **grill** means to cook something under or in a griller. *For breakfast we grilled some sausages and bacon.*

barbecue — To **barbecue** means to cook meat outdoors over an open fire in a specially built fireplace or metal frame. *In summer Dad barbecues chops and sausages and we eat them on paper plates and then play games.*

bake — To **bake** means to cook something in an oven. *Turn the oven to 200° and bake the pie for 40 minutes.*

roast — To **roast** means to cook something over a fire or **bake** it in an oven. *When you roast a chicken the delicious smell spreads all through the house.*

similar words: **boil**

top *noun*

the highest point or surface of anything. *Sir Edmund Hillary climbed to the **top** of Mt Everest in 1953.*

peak A **peak** is the pointed top of anything, usually a mountain. *Many climbers want to reach the peak of Mount Everest.*

pinnacle A **pinnacle** is the highest point of anything, usually a mountain. *No-one has ever climbed that treacherous rocky pinnacle.*

summit A **summit** is the top or highest point of something. *We reached the summit of the hill after a steep climb.*

apex An **apex** is the tip, point or highest part of anything. *Only one tree grew on the apex of the mountain.*

crest A **crest** is the very top of something. *There is a wonderful view from the crest of the hill.*

contrasting words: **bottom**

touch *verb*

to put your hand or finger on something. *I **touched** the book with dirty hands and left a mark on it.*

feel To **feel** means to examine something by touching. *I felt the grass to see how wet it was.*

handle To **handle** means to use your hands to examine or touch something. *The vet handled the injured puppy gently to find any broken bones.*

finger To **finger** means to touch something lightly. *She fingered the lucky charm in her pocket while waiting for the exam to start.*

stroke To **stroke** means to pass your hand gently over something. *The rider stroked the frightened horse to calm it.*

pat To **pat** means to stroke something lightly with your hand. *He patted the chair to show me where to sit.*

touchy *adjective*

irritable or easily offended. *He's so **touchy** you have to be careful what you say to him.*

thin-skinned — **Thin-skinned** means touchy. They are so similar you can usually choose either word. *She's too thin-skinned to listen to any criticism of her work.*

moody — **Moody** means changeable in mood or feelings. *She's so moody you don't know whether to speak to her or not.*

prickly — **Prickly** means easily made angry. *He's always prickly when he's tired.*

sensitive — **Sensitive** means easily affected by something. *He has a sensitive nature and is easily hurt.*

similar words: **grumpy**

trace *noun*

a very small amount. *We found **traces** of gold in the sand from the river bed.*

drop — A **drop** can be a very small amount of something, especially a liquid. *Only a drop of water was left to ease their thirst.*

dash — A **dash** can be a small unmeasured amount of something. It is often used in cooking. *Add just a dash of pepper to the stew.*

pinch — A **pinch** can be the very small amount of something you can hold between your thumb and first finger. *The recipe says to add only a pinch of salt.*

hint — A **hint** can be such a tiny amount of something that you can hardly tell it is there. *There was just a hint of warmth in the air.*

scrap — A **scrap** is a very small amount of something. *Goldilocks did not leave a scrap of the baby bear's porridge.*

similar words: **piece**

transparent *adjective*

allowing light to pass through so that you can see through. *I traced the map using **transparent** paper.*

clear — **Clear** can mean transparent or able to be seen through. *I covered my book with clear plastic so that I could still see the title.*

sheer — **Sheer** means so thin that you can see through. *We could see our visitors through the sheer curtains.*

limpid — **Limpid** means transparent and **clear**. *We could see the shellfish on the sandy bottom of the limpid pools of water.*

translucent — **Translucent** means allowing some light to come through. *Soft light came through the translucent stained-glass window and shone on the crucifix behind the altar.*

contrasting words: **opaque**

trap *noun*

a cage or some kind of device used to catch wild animals. *The farmer set a **trap** to catch the fox.*

snare — A **snare** is a kind of trap with a noose, used to catch small animals or birds. *We took the dead rabbit from the snare.*

net — A **net** can be a type of open fabric made of cord or rope, used to catch fish, large insects, or other animals. *We got out our nets and went to look for butterflies.*

booby trap — A **booby trap** is an object that has been carefully placed so as to fall on, or trip up an unsuspecting person. *She refused to babysit those children as long as they set booby traps for her.*

lure — A **lure** is a device a fisherman uses to attract fish to the hook on his line. *The angler trailed the lure behind the slowly moving boat.*

travel *verb*

to go from one place to another. *We had only **travelled** a little way when we had a flat tyre.*

journey — To **journey** means to travel, usually a long way. *We journeyed right around Australia with our caravan.*

voyage — To **voyage** means to travel by sea or air, usually to somewhere quite far away. *It took many months for the first settlers to voyage to Australia by ship.*

roam — To **roam** can mean to travel with no special purpose. *He spent his youth roaming in the wilds of Africa.*

wander — To **wander** means to go about with no special purpose or place in mind. *I wandered a long way from the farm trying to decide where to go.*

rove — To **rove** is very similar to **roam** and **wander**. *She roved around the world visiting any place that sounded interesting.*

traveller *noun*

someone who goes about from place to place. *After they retired they became world **travellers** for a year.*

tourist — A **tourist** is someone who travels or tours for pleasure. *The tourists bought many souvenirs of their holiday in Fiji.*

sightseer — A **sightseer** is someone who travels to see places of interest or beauty. *The Tower of London is a popular place for sightseers.*

tripper — A **tripper** is someone who goes on short journeys or outings. *The trippers on the ferry enjoyed the views of the harbour.*

pilgrim — A **pilgrim** is someone who travels to a holy place especially to carry out a religious duty. *Every Muslim hopes to be a pilgrim to Mecca at least once in his life.*

commuter — A **commuter** is someone who travels regularly between their home and work place. *The buses are filled with commuters every morning and evening.*

trick *noun*

something done to deceive someone. *Let's play a **trick** on Mum and hide under the bed.*

hoax A **hoax** is a trick or practical joke. *We didn't really mean it — it was only a hoax!*

prank A **prank** is a playful trick. *She is full of pranks and mischief.*

ruse A **ruse** is a dishonest trick or scheme. *Very carefully they planned a ruse to make everyone think they were still in bed.*

swindle A **swindle** is a trick that cheats someone out of something that belongs to them. *The swindle was discovered when they found pieces of paper instead of money in the envelope.*

con A **con** is a trick or a **swindle**. It is a shortened form of 'confidence trick' and is more suited to everyday language. *We didn't know it was a con until we got home and found the bag was empty.*

similar words: **plot**

trick *verb*

to outwit, deceive or cheat someone. *We managed to **trick** Dad on April Fool's Day when we made him believe we had been given a holiday from school.*

fool To **fool** means to trick someone or make them think or believe something that isn't true. *Chris fooled her by pretending to be asleep and then began reading under the bedclothes.*

bluff To **bluff** means to trick someone by pretending to be very bold. *They bluffed the guards by walking straight past them talking and laughing.*

hoax To **hoax** means to deceive someone by playing a trick on them. *Leonie even hoaxed her family with her clever disguise.*

kid To **kid** can mean to trick or tease someone. *We bandaged Craig's arm and kidded his friends into believing he'd had an accident.*

similar words: **deceive, cheat**

trickery *noun*

the tricking, cheating or fooling of someone. *We were so used to Uncle Jack's **trickery** that we never knew when to believe him.*

monkey business — **Monkey business** is trickery or secret and crafty dealing. *It is so quiet I know they are up to some monkey business.*

subterfuge — **Subterfuge** means something, such as a trick or plan, aimed to hide or avoid something. *Our subterfuge worked when they followed the false trail down to the river.*

deceit — **Deceit** means something aimed at tricking or deceiving someone. *Because of their deceit we were blamed and punished.*

cunning — **Cunning** means the use of a clever plan to trick or deceive someone. *His cunning was rewarded when he escaped without being seen.*

guile — **Guile** means cleverness or cunning in the way you deceive someone. *The wily fox used guile to trick the gingerbread man.*

trudge *verb*

to tread or walk heavily and slowly. *We **trudged** through the mud in our gumboots.*

tramp — To **tramp** means to tread or walk heavily and steadily. *Hour after hour the soldiers tramped through the jungle.*

plod — To **plod** means to walk or move in a slow, steady and unexciting way. *Every morning I plod off to school.*

toil — To **toil** can mean to walk or move with difficulty. *We toiled through thick mud and reeds before we finally reached the river.*

slog — To **slog** can mean to keep trudging along. *The weary hikers slogged up yet another long, steep hill.*

lumber — To **lumber** means to move clumsily or heavily, especially because of great size or weight. *The elephants lumbered along the road carrying their huge loads.*

similar words: **walk, march, limp**
contrasting words: **frisk, dart**

true *adjective*

full of truth or not false. *Her story about the bank robbery was **true**.*

right — **Right** can mean free from error or agreeing with the truth or the facts. *I'm sure your information about budgies is right.*

correct — **Correct** means free from mistakes. *All the answers she gave were correct.*

accurate — **Accurate** can mean free from error. *The police said that her account of the accident was accurate.*

valid — **Valid** means made with good reasons. *The teacher thought that he had a valid reason for being late for school.*

certain — **Certain** can mean accepted as true or sure. *It is certain that he tried to be friends with you.*

contrasting words: **incorrect**

turn *verb*

to make something move around or partly around in a circle. *Very slowly Rod **turned** the handle and peered through the doorway.*

rotate — To **rotate** means to turn something around in a circle. *Rotate the handle in a clockwise direction.*

wind — To **wind** means to tighten something, usually a spring, by turning it around. *Every morning I wind my watch.*

screw — To **screw** means to turn something, usually to tighten or seal it. *I poured myself a glass of lemonade then screwed the lid back on the bottle.*

twist — To **twist** can mean to combine two or more things by **winding** them together. *Louise twisted pieces of string together to make a thick, strong rope.*

reel — To **reel** means to **wind** something on a reel or on a cylinder or wheel. *As soon as I felt a bite I reeled in my fishing line.*

similar words: **spin, bend**

twisted *adjective*

curved or bent. *The **twisted** old tree was just right for climbing.*

coiled — **Coiled** means curled around into loops. *The snake was coiled ready to strike.*

winding — **Winding** means turning first one way and then another. *Dad had to drive slowly along the winding road through the mountains.*

squiggly — **Squiggly** means having many short twists and curves. *I thought the squiggly line looked like a snake.*

wavy — **Wavy** means curving first one way and then the other. *Jason has thick wavy hair.*

sinuous — **Sinuous** means winding or having many curves and bends. *We followed the sinuous path up and down and round about till we ended up where we started from.*

---

tyrannical *adjective*

severely cruel or harsh. *The people hated their **tyrannical** king.*

oppressive — **Oppressive** means unjustly cruel. *The oppressive laws of the time allowed people to be sent to Australia as convicts for committimg only petty crimes.*

repressive — **Repressive** means forcefully keeping people under control. *Some repressive governments use armies to stop the people standing up for their rights.*

domineering — **Domineering** means commanding or governing without considering the wishes of others. *The domineering general took no notice of the opinions of his advisors.*

despotic — **Despotic** means like a ruler who has total power, especially one who is cruel and unjust. *The despotic manager made his workers do overtime even if they didn't want to.*

totalitarian — **Totalitarian** means having to do with a government which has complete control and does not allow any opposition. *People who live in a totalitarian state have every aspect of their lives directed and find it difficult to leave if they want to.*

---

similar words: **bossy**
contrasting words: **submissive**

ugly *adjective*

unpleasant to look at. *I was scared by the **ugly** sneer on his face.*

hideous — **Hideous** means extremely ugly. *The film was about a hideous monster.*

repulsive — **Repulsive** can mean so unpleasant to look at that you feel sick or disgusted. *She had a repulsive sore on her arm.*

grotesque — **Grotesque** means ugly in a way that is odd or unnatural. *A grotesque creature stepped out of the flying saucer.*

monstrous — **Monstrous** can mean very ugly. It is similar to **grotesque**. *I dreamt a monstrous two-headed bull was chasing me.*

foul — **Foul** can mean very ugly or nasty. This is rather an unusual way of using this word today. *Some artists in medieval times painted pictures of the foul demons that were supposed to live in Hell.*

contrasting words: **beautiful, pretty**

unashamed *adjective*

not feeling shame or sorrow. *She was **unashamed** of her support for the illegal squatters who were homeless.*

impenitent — **Impenitent** means not feeling sorry for doing wrong and unwilling to put things right. *The judge sentenced the impenitent thug to ten years in jail.*

unrepentant — **Unrepentant** means not showing regret or sorrow for doing wrong. It is very similar to **impenitent**. *She was unrepentant in spite of the unhappiness her naughtiness caused her parents.*

unremorseful — **Unremorseful** means not feeling any regret for doing wrong. *Dad was angry because I was unremorseful when I hit my sister.*

unapologetic — **Unapologetic** means not wanting to say sorry. *The car accident was the fault of the other driver but he was quite unapologetic.*

unregenerate — **Unregenerate** means showing no wish to reform or amend wicked behaviour. *He had so many convictions we were convinced he was unregenerate.*

similar words: **bold**
contrasting words: **sorry**

unbelievable *adjective*

not able to be believed or accepted as true. *I find that what you say is **unbelievable**.*

incredible — **Incredible** can be so similar to **unbelievable** that you can usually use either. *This book is full of incredible tales.*

unlikely — **Unlikely** means not likely to be true. *I'm not tricked by your unlikely story.*

improbable — **Improbable** means probably not true. It is very similar to **unlikely**. *I've never heard such an improbable excuse.*

implausible — **Implausible** means seeming not to be true or reasonable. It is similar to **unlikely** and **improbable**. *His explanation was implausible.*

far-fetched — **Far-fetched** means seeming to be too exaggerated to be true. *I prefer a story to be realistic rather than far-fetched.*

similar words: **impossible**
contrasting words: **believable, possible, likely**

uncertain *adjective*

not known for sure. *The time of the train's arrival is still **uncertain**.*

doubtful — **Doubtful** can mean causing doubt or uncertainty. *He gave a doubtful answer and I wondered if he had really read the book.*

dubious — **Dubious** means open to doubt or suspicion. *He told a dubious tale explaining the whereabouts of his sister.*

questionable — **Questionable** means open to doubt or argument. *It is questionable whether this is true.*

debatable — **Debatable** means open to argument. It is very similar to **questionable**. *Your explanation as to how the world began is debatable.*

open — **Open** can mean not completed or decided. *The question is still open and we will consider it again tomorrow.*

similar words: **vague**
contrasting words: **sure**

unconscious *adjective*

having fainted or lost consciousness. *She tumbled down the hill and was lying **unconscious** at the bottom.*

comatose — **Comatose** means in a coma or unconscious because of sickness or an injury. *After her accident she was comatose for two days.*

stunned — **Stunned** can mean being unconscious or unaware of your surroundings for a short time. *He was stunned for a moment by the blow to his head.*

dazed — **Dazed** means made stupid or almost unconscious. *She was dazed by the crash and tried to remember how it had happened.*

drugged — **Drugged** means unconscious or only partly conscious because you have taken or been given drugs. *He couldn't stand or think clearly in his drugged state.*

out cold — **Out cold** means unconscious. This is more suited to everyday language. *The boxer was out cold after the heavy blow to his head.*

unconventional *adjective*

not according to usual or accepted ways of behaviour. *Her wedding dress was **unconventional** because it was black.*

nonconformist — **Nonconformist** means refusing to accept the usual or expected ideas, customs or ways of living. *My parents think I'm nonconformist because I want to leave school earlier than my brothers did.*

bohemian — **Bohemian** means living and acting without any interest in the usual or accepted ways of behaviour.This word is often used to describe an artist or a writer. *The group of artists led a bohemian life in which their art was all they thought about.*

alternative — **Alternative** can mean offering the types of behaviour or values of a smaller group within, but opposed to, an established society or community, particularly a Western society. *Some people who don't like city living lead alternative lifestyles in the country and grow their own food.*

radical — **Radical** means being in favour of extreme social or political reforms. *The radical group demonstrated outside Parliament.*

similar words: **strange**
contrasting words: **usual**

understand *verb*

to take the idea of something into your mind. *I tried to **understand** his explanation.*

grasp To **grasp** can mean to understand or take something into your mind. *She grasped the idea of the game very quickly.*

comprehend To **comprehend** means to understand the meaning of something. *We tried hard to comprehend our parents' reasons for not wanting us to watch that TV programme.*

perceive To **perceive** can mean to understand or become aware of something with your mind. *The wise teacher perceived that John was unhappy about something.*

fathom To **fathom** means to understand something completely. *I couldn't fathom the instructions for building the model until Maurice helped me.*

make out To **make out** means to see or understand something. *I can't make out the handwriting on this note.*

similar words: **realise**

undertaking *noun*

a task or piece of work you promise to do. *Moving all the books from the old library to the new one will be a huge **undertaking**.*

enterprise An **enterprise** is something that requires effort or courage. *Running the school fete was quite an enterprise.*

venture A **venture** is something you do that is risky or dangerous. *Both companies were involved in the oil exploration venture.*

job A **job** is a piece of work you have to do. *Painting the house was a big job.*

project A **project** is a plan or scheme for a piece of work. *This is a project which should make a lot of money.*

engagement An **engagement** can mean something you are hired to do, especially only once. *The band had an engagement to play at the fete.*

uneven *adjective*

not being equally balanced with something else. *The competition between the Infants' and Primary Schools was **uneven**.*

unequal — **Unequal** means not being of the same quantity, amount, quality and so on. *The children always get upset if they are given unequal servings of dessert.*

unbalanced — **Unbalanced** means not equal or properly balanced. *The teams were unbalanced because two of our players were sick.*

lopsided — **Lopsided** means larger or heavier on one side than the other. *The cake was lopsided so I had to put more icing on one side.*

irregular — **Irregular** means not even or regular. *The sick man's pulse was irregular.*

contrasting words: **equal**

unfair *adjective*

showing favouritism or not treating everyone the same. *It was **unfair** of her to give Peter the best book.*

unjust — **Unjust** can mean unfair and is usually used to describe the actions of someone in authority. It is rather a formal word. *It was unjust of the judge not to listen to all the accused man's witnesses.*

inequitable — **Inequitable** means not fair or even-handed. *The crowd booed the referee for his inequitable treatment of the two teams.*

discriminatory — **Discriminatory** means treating one person or group unfairly because you prefer another. *The discriminatory laws of that country forbid black people and white people to eat at the same restaurants.*

partial — **Partial** can mean showing unfair support for or favouritism towards someone. *We thought that the umpire was being partial towards the other team because his son played in it.*

prejudiced — **Prejudiced** means behaving unfairly because you have formed an opinion without good reason or evidence. *The sports teacher was prejudiced against the new boy even though she had never seen him play.*

contrasting words: **fair, neutral**

unfaithful *adjective*

not staying true to someone or to what you have promised. *The knight was **unfaithful** to his vow to save the king.*

disloyal — **Disloyal** means not faithful or true. *It was disloyal of you not to take my side in the argument.*

false — **False** can mean not faithful or loyal. *He turned out to be a false friend.*

treacherous — **Treacherous** means **disloyal** or likely to betray someone who has trusted you. *The treacherous soldier sold guns to the enemy.*

traitorous — **Traitorous** means betraying a person, a cause or a country. *The traitorous spy plotted to overthrow the government of his country.*

slippery — **Slippery** can mean not to be depended on. This is a rather informal word. *He was such a slippery businessman that no-one wanted to buy things from him.*

similar words: **fickle**
contrasting words: **faithful**

unfriendly *adjective*

not showing friendship or being kind. *She snatched the book from me in an **unfriendly** way.*

cold — **Cold** can mean lacking friendliness or interest. *His cold greeting showed he didn't like me.*

aloof — **Aloof** means not joining in with other people in a friendly way. *People think she is aloof but I know she is only shy.*

stand-offish — **Stand-offish** means unfriendly or keeping your distance from other people. It is rather similar to **aloof**. *She is stand-offish with people she doesn't know well.*

antisocial — **Antisocial** means not wanting to join in with other people. *He has been antisocial since his face was so badly scarred.*

inhospitable — **Inhospitable** means not welcoming or showing people kindness, especially in your own home. *The family next door is quite inhospitable and never ask us in to swim in their pool.*

contrasting words: **friendly**

ungrateful *adjective*

not showing or feeling gratitude or thanks. *How can you be so **ungrateful** when I spent all afternoon cooking you this special dinner?*

unappreciative **Unappreciative** means not showing or feeling appreciation or gratitude. *The band was upset when the unappreciative audience left the concert before the end.*

thankless **Thankless** is usually used to describe unrewarding jobs. *Cleaning the cowshed was a thankless task.*

grudging **Grudging** means unwillingly expressing appreciation or gratitude. *I'd rather have no thanks at all than her grudging thanks.*

heedless **Heedless** can mean not noticing or being aware of someone else's kindness. *She was quite heedless of our efforts to help her.*

similar words: **selfish**

unkind *adjective*

not very friendly, warm-hearted or wanting the best for other people. *Don't be **unkind** and leave me alone when I'm afraid.*

nasty **Nasty** can mean unkind or cruel. *She was nasty to her little brother and often took his favourite toys.*

mean **Mean** can mean unkind or **nasty**. *I think you are mean not to let me play too.*

shabby **Shabby** can mean unfair or **mean**. *That's a shabby way to treat a good friend.*

contemptible **Contemptible** means disgraceful and mean. *Tripping the other runner was a contemptible thing to do.*

despicable **Despicable** means disgraceful and deserving contempt and scorn. *We thought it was despicable of you to treat your mother that way.*

similar words: **resentful**
contrasting words: **kind**

unlucky *adjective*

ill-fated or not having good luck. *We were rather **unlucky** these holidays because we all caught chickenpox.*

unfortunate — **Unfortunate** is so similar to **unlucky** that you can usually use either. *It was unfortunate that we couldn't get any tickets for the film we wanted to see.*

hapless — **Hapless** means unlucky and without much hope. *The old man sleeping in the park looked like a hapless fellow.*

wretched — **Wretched** can mean very unlucky or miserable. *What a wretched thing to happen just when you were doing so well.*

cursed — **Cursed** can mean so unlucky that it's as if someone has wished evil or misfortune to come to you. *I think that racehorse is cursed because it never wins a race.*

star-crossed — **Star-crossed** means having a great deal of bad luck, once thought to be caused by the influence of the stars. *Romeo and Juliet were star-crossed lovers.*

contrasting words: **lucky**

unmarried *adjective*

not married. *Our **unmarried** aunt spends her holidays with us every year.*

unwed — **Unwed** is so similar to **unmarried** you can usually use either. *Uncle Jack is still unwed at 65 and we don't think he will get married now.*

single — **Single** can mean unmarried. *Mum's youngest sister is single and goes to university.*

unattached — **Unattached** can mean not engaged or married. *He was going out with a nice girl for two years but now he is unattached.*

celibate — **Celibate** means being unmarried and never having sexual intercourse. *Roman Catholic priests are celibate.*

lone — **Lone** can mean living without a husband or wife. It is usually used about a parent. *Lone parents have to work hard to bring up their children.*

unrelated *adjective*

having no particular relationship or connection. *His question about space travel was quite* ***unrelated*** *to the road safety talk we listened to.*

irrelevant **Irrelevant** means having nothing to do with the matter being discussed or thought about. *The speaker made so many irrelevant remarks it was hard to understand what he was trying to tell us.*

unconnected **Unconnected** can mean not thought of as related or connected. *His hobby of stamp-collecting is quite unconnected with his ambition to be a professional golfer.*

immaterial **Immaterial** means unimportant, often especially to the matter being discussed. *Where the shoes were made was immaterial to him as long as they were comfortable.*

foreign **Foreign** can mean not belonging. *That comment about India is completely foreign to our discussion of politics in Wales.*

independent **Independent** can mean not depending on something else for its existence, working and so on. *Your argument is independent of anything we have heard so far.*

contrasting words: **related**

untidy *adjective*

not tidy or neat. *Mum made us fix up our* ***untidy*** *rooms before we went to bed.*

messy **Messy** means in an untidy and dirty state. *The kitchen was very messy when we finished cooking dinner.*

chaotic **Chaotic** means in total disorder. *The house was chaotic when we were unpacking after our holiday.*

disorganised **Disorganised** means in confusion or disorder. *My desk was so disorganised I couldn't start my homework.*

haywire **Haywire** can mean in disorder. *Everything was haywire in the house after the party.*

higgledy-piggledy **Higgledy-piggledy** means jumbled. This is more suited to everyday language. *We packed in such a hurry everything was higgledy-piggledy.*

similar words: **scruffy**
contrasting words: **tidy**

unusual *adjective*

not usual, common or ordinary. *She is generally a punctual person so it is **unusual** for her to be late.*

uncommon — **Uncommon** means not likely to be found or encountered. *Seagulls are uncommon away from the coast.*

extraordinary — **Extraordinary** means beyond what is ordinary. *He is a boy of extraordinary strength.*

rare — **Rare** means unusual, **uncommon** or occurring infrequently. *This stamp is valuable because it is rare.*

remarkable — **Remarkable** means worthy of notice because it is so unusual. *Climbing Mount Everest was a remarkable achievement.*

singular — **Singular** means out of the ordinary or **remarkable**. *Her career as an actress has been a singular success.*

similar words: **strange, scarce**
contrasting words: **ordinary, usual**

unwilling *adjective*

not eager or agreeing quite happily. *I am **unwilling** to spend such a lot of money on a toy that could break so easily.*

reluctant — **Reluctant** means unwilling or not prepared. *Fifth formers are always eager to do pottery but often reluctant to clean up afterwards.*

disinclined — **Disinclined** means not feeling a wish or inclination. *I'm disinclined to go out on such a hot day.*

hesitant — **Hesitant** means waiting or pausing because you are not sure what you should do. *Mum said she was hesitant about letting us go to the movie on our own.*

loath — **Loath** means unwilling or not inclined. *I am loath to lend her money because she's always so slow to pay it back.*

averse — **Averse** means opposed or very unwilling. *Luckily for us our teacher is averse to giving us homework every night.*

contrasting words: **enthusiastic**

upset *adjective*

feeling anxious or unhappy. *I was **upset** when I wasn't chosen for the team.*

agitated — **Agitated** means feeling anxious and unable to be still. *Mum was very agitated when they had not come home by dark.*

disturbed — **Disturbed** means feeling troubled or unsettled. *We were quite disturbed by the news reports about the earthquakes.*

flustered — **Flustered** means confused, usually because you are nervous. *Paul was flustered and forgot what to say when he stood up to give his speech.*

uptight — **Uptight** means anxious and unsettled. It is more suited to everyday language. *He was uptight about his piano exam.*

het-up — **Het-up** means anxious or worried. It is more suited to everyday language. *Don't be so het-up over such an unimportant mistake.*

similar words: **nervous**
contrasting words: **calm**

upset *verb*

to make someone feel sad or disturbed. *His insults **upset** me.*

distress — To **distress** means to cause someone great pain, anxiety or sorrow. *Her plan to sail round the world single-handed distressed her parents.*

hurt — To **hurt** can mean to harm someone or cause them to have painful feelings. *Her thoughtlessness hurt him and he turned and walked away.*

worry — To **worry** can mean to make someone feel anxious or uneasy. *It worries our parents if we stay out late.*

trouble — To **trouble** means to disturb or bother someone. *It's a shame to trouble him when he's tired.*

sadden — To **sadden** means to make someone feel sad or upset. *The news of his illness saddened me.*

similar words: **annoy**
contrasting words: **comfort**

use *verb*

to put something into action for some purpose. *Let's **use** our fingers to eat with on the picnic.*

employ To **employ** means to use something. *I'd rather employ my spare time reading than watching television.*

ply To **ply** means to use something, especially in a busy way. *Ply the oars, lads, and we'll soon be home.*

wield To **wield** means to use something as a powerful tool. *She wields her influence with the parents to raise money for the school.*

exploit To **exploit** can mean to put something to good use. *They exploited the land well, growing crops for food.*

utilise To **utilise** means to put something into use. *Many people utilise the sun's energy to make electricity for their homes.*

contrasting words: **discard**

useful *adjective*

of use or service. *Don't throw away anything that might be **useful** for craft.*

handy **Handy** can mean useful or convenient. *That brick made a handy hammer!*

helpful **Helpful** means able or likely to help or be of use. *The dictionary is helpful when I'm not sure what something means.*

valuable **Valuable** can mean of great use or service. *It would be a valuable help if you washed up for me.*

beneficial **Beneficial** means **helpful** or of benefit. *After a long tiring hike we longed for the beneficial effects of a hot bath.*

advantageous **Advantageous** means **helpful** or of advantage to you. *It would be advantageous to get your tickets early so you don't miss out.*

similar words: **possible**
contrasting words: **useless**

useless *adjective*

of no use or serving no purpose. *It was **useless** to try to help her because she wouldn't do what we told her.*

vain — **Vain** can have a meaning so similar to **useless** you can usually use either word. *He made a vain attempt to stop the runaway car before it crashed.*

futile — **Futile** means not able to produce any result. *The dog made futile leaps at the cat in the tree.*

ineffective — **Ineffective** means not producing or giving the expected result. *She made an ineffective attempt to mend the broken chair.*

ineffectual — **Ineffectual** means not able to produce an intended result. *He was an ineffectual spokesman for us in our protest against weekend homework.*

similar words: **impossible**
contrasting words: **useful, possible**

usual *adjective*

most frequently occurring. *We went to school in the **usual** way, forgetting that today was a public holiday.*

normal — **Normal** means standard, common or regular. *It is normal to have rain at this time of the year.*

conventional — **Conventional** means relating to standards or rules, often unwritten, which everyone accepts. *There is a conventional way to dress to play tennis.*

orthodox — **Orthodox** means accepted or approved. *At a formal occasion, the orthodox dress for a man is a suit.*

customary — **Customary** means according to custom or the usual way of acting or doing things. *Shaking hands when you meet someone is customary.*

traditional — **Traditional** means according to the beliefs, customs and stories that have been handed down from one generation to another. *Eating turkey and plum pudding at Christmas time is traditional.*

contrasting words: **unusual, unconventional, strange**

vague *adjective*

not clear or certain. *We saw **vague** shapes in the mist. I had a **vague** feeling of fear.*

indefinite — **Indefinite** means doubtful or not definite. *He was indefinite about his future plans.*

hazy — **Hazy** can mean confused or not distinct. *As I was coming out of the anaesthetic, everything was hazy.*

faint — **Faint** can mean not clear or distinct. *I have only a faint idea of how to get there.*

woolly — **Woolly** can mean not clear or firm. *That was very woolly thinking, so please try again.*

approximate — **Approximate** can mean rough or not exact. *I can't even give you an approximate answer.*

similar words: **uncertain**
contrasting words: **precise, clear**

various *adjective*

different from one another. *Simon earned pocket money doing **various** jobs during the holidays.*

diverse — **Diverse** means of many different kinds or forms. *The castaways found that they had diverse abilities and they soon built a shelter between them.*

mixed — **Mixed** can mean made up of different sorts. *I brought a plate of mixed sandwiches to the picnic.*

assorted — **Assorted** means made up of different kinds. It is similar to **mixed** and you can usually choose either word. *I asked for a box of assorted chocolates.*

miscellaneous — **Miscellaneous** means made up of a mixture of different things. *He had a miscellaneous collection of pens, pencils, rubber bands and paper clips in his desk.*

motley — **Motley** means made up of different types or kinds. *It was a motley group of people who answered the Red Cross appeal for help.*

contrasting words: **similar**

view *noun*

whatever you can see from a particular place. *We all looked at the spectacular **view** from the top of the skyscraper.*

landscape A **landscape** is a view of country scenery. *The landscape consisted of a beautiful green valley with a river running through it.*

vista A **vista** is a view, especially one seen through an opening or passage. *From the farmhouse veranda we gazed at the vista of rolling hills.*

outlook An **outlook** is what you see when looking out from a place. *The outlook from my bedroom window is onto the park.*

scene A **scene** can be a view, especially one in which something is happening. *The main street of our town was a colourful scene on New Year's Eve.*

prospect A **prospect** can be a view or **scene**. *Dad took a photo of the prospect from the front steps of our holiday hotel.*

---

violence *noun*

rough, powerful or damaging force. *The **violence** of his anger over such a small thing surprised us.*

severity **Severity** can mean violence or sharpness. *The severity of the pain caused him to cry out.*

fury **Fury** can mean violence or fierceness. *The hurricane raged with such fury that roofs were ripped off houses.*

vehemence **Vehemence** can mean violence or unusual force. *He slammed the door with such vehemence that all the glasses rattled.*

ferocity **Ferocity** is savage or cruel violence. *The ferocity of the attack on the defenceless man stunned the bystanders.*

brutality **Brutality** is savage cruelty. *The captain of the convict ship refused to allow any brutality on the voyage.*

---

similar words: **force**

violent *adjective*

powerful and causing damage. *The **violent** earthquake killed many people and wrecked all the buildings in the city.*

fierce — **Fierce** can mean violent in force or strength. *Fierce winds buffeted the ship.*

furious — **Furious** means strong and violent. *A furious storm damaged crops over a wide area of land.*

ferocious — **Ferocious** can mean cruel in a violent way. *The overseer dealt out ferocious punishment to the slaves under his control.*

wild — **Wild** can mean violent or **fierce**. *Wild fighting broke out between the fans of the opposing football teams.*

forceful — **Forceful** can mean full of strength or power. *His forceful blow knocked her to the ground.*

similar words: **intense, cruel**
contrasting words: **peaceful**

VIP *noun*

short for very important person. *We had to wear full school uniform when the **VIP** visited our school.*

magnate — A **magnate** is someone who is very powerful and successful, especially in business. *He is one of the magnates of the city and has great influence with members of parliament.*

big shot — A **big shot** is a very important person. This is more suited to everyday language. *She is a big shot in a successful accountancy firm.*

bigwig — A **bigwig** is rather like a **big shot**. It is more suited to everday language. *My uncle is a bigwig in the police force.*

big wheel — A **big wheel** is someone of great importance and influence. It is more suited to everyday language. *He soon became a big wheel in his family's business.*

similar words: **star**

visible *adjective*

able to be seen. *The lighthouse was **visible** a long way out to sea.*

noticeable — **Noticeable** means able to be seen easily. *His scar was noticeable when he first came out of hospital but it soon faded.*

conspicuous — **Conspicuous** means very **noticeable**. *She was conspicuous in her red dress.*

prominent — **Prominent** means standing out. *Their house was so prominent because it was the only one in the street with two storeys.*

exposed — **Exposed** can mean open to view or not hidden. *Did you know that your foot was exposed in our game of hide-and-seek?*

overt — **Overt** means not concealed. *He wore many gold chains and other expensive jewellery in an overt display of his wealth.*

similar words: **obvious**
contrasting words: **invisible**

visit *verb*

to go to see someone or something. *I'm coming to **visit** on Sunday.*

call — To **call** can mean to make a short visit. *We called at Daisy's house on our way home from school.*

drop in — To **drop in** means to visit someone in an informal or casual way. *We dropped in to see why you didn't come to football practice.*

stop by — To **stop by** means to call somewhere for a short visit on your way to another place. *We drove from Melbourne to Adelaide and stopped by to see our cousins in Mt Gambier.*

blow in — To **blow in** means to make an unexpected visit. This is more suited to everyday language. *My friend blew in to borrow a record.*

look in — To **look in** means to come or go in for a short visit. *I decided to look in when I heard you were sick.*

vulgar *adjective*

ill-mannered, rude and badly behaved. *He apologised for his **vulgar** manners during the concert.*

common — **Common** can mean vulgar or impolite. *It is very common to wear all that make-up and such a short skirt.*

uncouth — **Uncouth** means behaving in an ill-mannered or rough way. *I wish those uncouth louts wouldn't push past us like that.*

tasteless — **Tasteless** can mean not showing any sense of what is accepted as polite or correct behaviour. *That is a tasteless way to talk about another person's sorrow.*

crude — **Crude** can mean rude or in such bad taste that some people might be upset. *Nobody laughed at her crude joke.*

coarse — **Coarse** can mean offensive or so rude that it disgusts you. *Such coarse behaviour does not belong in the classroom.*

similar words: **rude**
contrasting words: **polite**

vulnerable *adjective*

likely or able to be hurt or wounded. *The injured bird was **vulnerable** to attack from other animals because it couldn't fly away.*

insecure — **Insecure** can mean not safe from danger. *I'm in an insecure position at the top of this ladder.*

exposed — **Exposed** means not safe from danger, attack or injury. *We were in an exposed position on the cliff face and the winds howled around us.*

susceptible — **Susceptible** means easily affected by something, especially something dangerous or harmful. *Because Mark was so weak after his long illness he was very susceptible to colds.*

open — **Open** can mean likely to be affected by danger or harm. *The goal was open to attack when the goalie left to chase the ball.*

contrasting words: **safe**

walk *verb*

to go about by moving one foot after the other. *I missed the bus so I had to* ***walk*** *to school.*

amble To **amble** means to walk at a relaxed comfortable pace. *It was still early so we ambled along.*

saunter To **saunter** means to walk in an unhurried carefree way. *I sauntered down to the swimming pool munching an apple.*

stroll To **stroll** means to walk in a slow enjoyable way. *We strolled along the path listening to the birds and crickets.*

pad To **pad** means to walk very softly. *I padded around in my bare feet so I wouldn't wake anyone.*

pace To **pace** means to walk with regular steps. *The lion paced up and down inside his cage.*

similar words: **march, limp, trudge**
contrasting words: **frisk, dart, hurry, speed**

want *verb*

to wish for or have need of something. ***I want*** *money to buy my lunch.*

desire To **desire** means to wish for something very much. This is a rather formal word. *The war-weary nation desired peace above all else.*

long for To **long for** means to have a strong wish for something. *He longed for a canoe.*

crave To **crave** means to want or need something desperately. *The day was so hot he craved a cool drink.*

covet To **covet** means to want to have something very much, especially something that belongs to someone else. *She covets that car of yours.*

fancy To **fancy** can mean to feel you want or would like something. *I fancy fish for tea.*

warlike *adjective*

being ready or eager for fighting or conflict. *The early settlers in North America believed the Red Indians were a **warlike** people.*

martial — **Martial** means having to do with fighting or war. *Some people learn Chinese martial arts as a form of exercise.*

militant — **Militant** means fighting or ready to fight, especially for a cause. *They are militant supporters of Aboriginal land rights.*

bellicose — **Bellicose** means warlike or ready to fight. *The bellicose tribes began fighting at the slightest dispute over their hunting grounds.*

bloodthirsty — **Bloodthirsty** means wanting to kill. *The bloodthirsty pirates made all the prisoners walk the plank.*

hawkish — **Hawkish** means favouring a militant attitude towards other nations. It is mostly used about politicians. *We were worried by the prime minister's hawkish attitude at the summit conference.*

similar words: **aggressive**

warn *verb*

to tell someone or to signal to them that there may be danger ahead. *They **warned** us that the road was icy.*

caution — To **caution** is so similar to **warn** that you can usually use either word. *Dad cautioned us not to get into cars with strangers.*

forewarn — To **forewarn** means to warn beforehand. *The weather centre forewarned us about the approaching gale.*

alert — To **alert** means to warn someone of a possible attack or danger. *The scout alerted the general about the planned raid on his camp.*

alarm — To **alarm** can mean to give someone notice of danger to them. *The sentries alarmed the camp when they saw the approaching enemy.*

tip off — To **tip off** can mean to warn someone about trouble they are likely to have. This is more suited to everyday language. *The dishonest policeman tipped off the illegal gamblers about the police raid.*

similar words: **advise**

wary *adjective*

on your guard against danger or trouble. *I was **wary** of the barking dog before I realised he was friendly.*

watchful — **Watchful** means looking out carefully for danger or trouble. *I was rescued by the watchful lifesaver.*

cautious — **Cautious** means being very wary when there is danger. *Be cautious when you cross a busy street.*

careful — **Careful** means taking care to avoid risks. *A careful driver never causes accidents.*

deliberate — **Deliberate** means carefully thought out. *My deliberate movements calmed the frightened horse.*

discreet — **Discreet** means taking trouble not to upset people. *Her discreet behaviour made people trust her.*

contrasting words: **rash**

waste *verb*

to spend or use up something without much result. *Don't **waste** your time being silly when you should be doing your homework.*

squander — To **squander** means to spend or use something wastefully. *The man had squandered all his money on gambling.*

fritter away — To **fritter away** means to waste something gradually. *She fritters away her money on useless things.*

blow — To **blow** can mean to waste something or **squander** it, usually all at one time. It is more suited to everyday language. *He blew all his money at the races and didn't have enough to catch the train home.*

splurge — To **splurge** means to spend money extravagantly or wastefully. *He splurged all his money on taking his friends out to dinner.*

weak *adjective*

not strong or healthy. *She is still very **weak** from her illness.*

frail — **Frail** means weak and delicate. *He helped the frail old lady cross the road.*

feeble — **Feeble** means weak in body or mind. *Grandma became so feeble she had to use a walking stick.*

invalid — **Invalid** means weak and sick. *She has to look after her invalid father.*

helpless — **Helpless** means so weak that you are unable to do anything. *I was helpless from laughter.*

weedy — **Weedy** can mean having a thin weak body. *They made fun of him for being weedy.*

contrasting words: **strong, hardy**

weaken *verb*

to make someone or something weaker. *Old age has **weakened** him.*

sap — To **sap** means to weaken or destroy something gradually. *Worry has sapped her health.*

disable — To **disable** means to make someone unfit or unable to use part of their body. *A car accident disabled him for life.*

incapacitate — To **incapacitate** is so similar to **disable** that you can usually use either. *Illness has incapacitated him.*

cripple — To **cripple** means to make someone unable to use one or more of their limbs. *Polio crippled him when he was only five.*

paralyse — To **paralyse** means to make part of your body unable to move. *The old lady had a stroke which paralysed her left side.*

similar words: **tire**
contrasting words: **strengthen**

wealth *noun*

a large store of money and property. *His main **wealth** comes from his huge cattle station.*

money — **Money** can mean a person's wealth. *He made his money by inventing a robot to do the housework.*

fortune — A **fortune** is a great amount of **money** or property. *Anyone who invented a robot to do homework would make a fortune.*

riches — **Riches** means wealth or many and valuable possessions. *We stared at all the king's riches displayed before us.*

treasure — **Treasure** means a store of wealth or **riches**, especially precious metals or money. *We found the stolen treasure hidden in a cave.*

capital — **Capital** means the amount of money owned by a business or person. *They used nearly all their capital to buy the wine bar.*

contrasting words: **poverty**

wealthy *adjective*

having a lot of money and valuable belongings. *My friends are **wealthy** enough to live in a large house and travel overseas every year.*

rich — **Rich** means having a lot of money. *The rich lady could buy expensive sports cars.*

prosperous — **Prosperous** means successful and wealthy. *The prosperous businessman worked hard to make his company grow.*

well-off — **Well-off** can mean wealthy enough to live a comfortable life. It is usually used in less formal language. *Most of the well-off people in our town have large homes near the water.*

affluent — **Affluent** means wealthy and **prosperous**. It can describe things as well as people. *Switzerland is an affluent country.*

loaded — **Loaded** can mean very wealthy. It is more suited to everyday language. *They were so loaded that they went to Disneyland for Christmas.*

contrasting words: **broke, poor**

weight *noun*

a heavy object or mass. *I put a **weight** on the pile of papers so that they wouldn't blow away.*

burden A **burden** can be something which is carried. *He lifted his heavy burden onto his back.*

load A **load** is something carried on a cart or something similar. *The truck groaned under its load of bricks.*

ballast **Ballast** is the heavy material carried by a ship to keep it steady, or by a balloon to control its height. *The cargo of iron bars acted as ballast for the ship.*

encumbrance An **encumbrance** is a **burden** or something useless which weighs you down. *Please don't bring all those books because they'll just be an encumbrance.*

well-behaved *adjective*

behaving properly. *All her children are **well** -behaved.*

good **Good** is so similar to **well-behaved** that you can usually use either. *Please be good when Grandma arrives.*

as good as gold **As good as gold** means being as well-behaved as possible. It is more suited to everyday language. *It was an enjoyable outing because everyone was as good as gold.*

well-mannered **Well-mannered** means polite or courteous. *Show that you are well-mannered by giving your seat to that old man.*

considerate **Considerate** means behaving properly and thinking about other people's feelings. *It was considerate of you to let me have first choice.*

cooperative **Cooperative** means behaving well and being helpful. *She thanked the class for being so cooperative.*

similar words: **obedient, polite**
contrasting words: **naughty, disobedient**

wet *adjective*

soaked with water or some other liquid. *My clothes were **wet** because I couldn't find shelter from the rain.*

damp — **Damp** means slightly wet. *We took the damp clothes off the line before the rain started.*

moist — **Moist** is so similar to **damp** you can usually choose either word. *His face was moist with perspiration.*

dank — **Dank** means unpleasantly **moist** or **damp**. *The back of the cave was dank from lack of sun and fresh air.*

soggy — **Soggy** means soaked or thoroughly wet. *The ground was soggy after a week of heavy rain.*

sodden — **Sodden** means completely soaked with liquid. *Our shoes were sodden after walking in the rain.*

contrasting words: **dry**

wet *verb*

to soak something with water, or something similar. *We **wet** the ground thoroughly before planting the rosebush.*

dampen — To **dampen** means to make something slightly wet. *I dampened my handkerchief with water and rubbed the dirty mark from my cheek.*

moisten — To **moisten** means to make something moderately wet. *She moistened her lips with her tongue in a nervous way.*

water — To **water** means to pour water on something. *Mum waters her garden every evening during the summer.*

irrigate — To **irrigate** means to supply water to something using a system of canals and pipes. *The farmer irrigated his crops from the river running through his property.*

similar words: **soak**

whisper *noun*

a way of speaking very softly with your breath rather that your voice. *We spoke in a **whisper** so that no one else would hear us.*

murmur A **murmur** is a whispered conversation or whispering sound. *As the curtain rose at the start of the play you could still hear the murmur of the audience.*

sigh A **sigh** is the soft sound you make when you let your breath out slowly, usually when you're tired, sad or relieved about something. *We all gave a sigh of relief when we heard that we had passed the exam.*

tinkle A **tinkle** is a short, light, ringing sound. *We heard the tinkle of the wind chimes hanging on the veranda.*

undertone An **undertone** can be a low quiet sound when it refers to speech. *He was hard to hear because he spoke in an undertone.*

rustle A **rustle** is the very soft sound made when leaves, papers, or something similar rub gently together. *We heard a rustle amongst the leaves and a hedgehog appeared.*

contrasting words: **noise**

white *adjective*

having a colour like milk. *Some soft, **white** clouds drifted across the blue summer sky.*

cream **Cream** means of a yellowish-white colour. *We chose white for the ceiling and a rich, cream paint for the walls.*

pale **Pale** means having a whitish or colourless appearance. *There was no colour in her pale face after her long illness.*

lily-white **Lily-white** means as white as the flower of the same name. *My skin was lily-white after the long, cold winter.*

ivory **Ivory** means of a creamy white colour. *All we could see were huge, ivory teeth as the shark opened its mouth wide.*

snowy **Snowy** means white like snow. *The old man stroked his snowy beard.*

whole *adjective*

making up the maximum, or proper quantity, number or amount of anything. *She gave me the **whole** box of chocolates.*

complete **Complete** means having all its parts. *She has a complete set of those stamps.*

full **Full** can mean whole or **complete**. *We will probably never know the full story of what happened.*

entire **Entire** means whole or without a break. *We played cards the entire evening.*

total **Total** means making up, or having to do with the whole of something. *They all put in enough money to pay the total cost of the farewell gift.*

similar words: **thorough**

contrasting words: **incomplete**

wide *adjective*

having a large size from side to side. ***Wide** roads are much safer for motorists to drive on.*

broad **Broad** means very wide. *The river is broad when it gets nearer the sea.*

extensive **Extensive** means large in size. *The Sahara is the most extensive desert in Africa.*

deep **Deep** can mean going far in or back. *The cupboard was so deep that all our crockery fitted in it.*

outspread **Outspread** means stretched out wide. *She stood to welcome us with outspread arms.*

contrasting words: **narrow**

winner *noun*

someone who wins something or gains a victory. *She was the **winner** of the prize for the best painting.*

victor — A **victor** can be the winner in any game, fight and so on. *Andrew was the victor in the tennis match against Donald.*

champion — A **champion** is someone who holds first place in a sport or contest. *She is the school's chess champion.*

master — A **master** can be someone who has a special skill at a game, like chess or bridge, and has won a certain number of formal competitions. *He is a golf master and competes in international tournaments.*

hit — A **hit** can be a great success. *She has been a hit at parties since she learned to play the guitar.*

wintry *adjective*

cold and stormy like the season of winter. *It was a **wintry** day with lots of snow left on the mountains.*

chilly — **Chilly** means causing you to shiver or feel cold. *The water was chilly when we first dived in.*

chill — **Chill** means moderately cold. It is very similar to **chilly**. *A chill wind blew down from the mountains.*

raw — **Raw** can mean damp and cold. *The air was raw as we climbed higher.*

bleak — **Bleak** means cold or harsh. *It was a bleak, grey day outside.*

glacial — **Glacial** means icy or as cold as ice. *The glacial weather and blizzards made a rescue mission impossible.*

similar words: **cold**
contrasting words: **fine, hot**

wipe *verb*

to rub lightly in order to dry or clean. *We **wiped** the dishes and put them away.*

mop To **mop** means to clean or rub something. *I mopped the floor with a floor cloth.*

blot To **blot** means to dry or soak something up. *Mum blotted the spilt tea with a cloth.*

sponge To **sponge** means to wash or wipe something with a sponge, or something similar. *She sponged her little boy's dirty hands and face before lunch.*

swab To **swab** means to clean or wipe with a large mop, or a piece of sponge, cloth or cottonwool. *Go and swab the deck! The nurse swabbed the deep cut in my leg before putting a bandage on it.*

towel To **towel** means to dry or wipe something with a towel. *I towelled my soaking hair until water stopped dripping down my neck.*

wisecrack *noun*

a smart or amusing remark. *Her **wisecracks** are sometimes hurtful.*

quip A **quip** is a clever or sarcastic remark. *I laughed at his quip that my room looked as though a hurricane had hit it.*

gibe A **gibe** is a taunting or sarcastic remark. *He made a cruel gibe about my lisp.*

in-joke An **in-joke** is a joke which only the people who are involved in a particular situation can understand. *Every family has its in-jokes.*

pun A **pun** is a play on words which sound alike but are different in meaning. *The baker who was short of money made a pun when he said he would need some dough.*

witticism A **witticism** is a joke or witty remark. *If you have to make a speech, try to include a few witticisms so people don't get bored.*

similar words: **joke**

wish *noun*

something that you long for. *It is my **wish** to finish school and become a plumber.*

desire — A **desire** is a strong wish or need for something. *Her main desire is to help others less lucky than herself.*

craving — A **craving** is an eager or urgent **desire**. *Mountain climbers usually have a craving for excitement in their lives.*

will — Your **will** can be your wish or **desire**. *He was forced to sell his house against his will.*

yen — A **yen** is a strong wish or longing. *Many migrants have a yen to return to their homelands for a visit.*

inclination — **Inclination** means a preference or tendency for something. *My inclination was to go to the beach rather than the farm for our holiday.*

wonderful *adjective*

causing surprise and excitement. *It was a **wonderful** sight to see the rocket taking off.*

marvellous — **Marvellous** means wonderful and surprising. *It was marvellous to see the pictures of earth taken from space.*

fabulous — **Fabulous** means wonderful and very pleasing.It is more suited to everyday language. *We had a fabulous time looking over the space museum.*

incredible — **Incredible** means hard to believe because it is so surprising. *It is incredible to think that people have walked on the moon.*

extraordinary — **Extraordinary** means unusual or remarkable. *Sending rockets into space is an extraordinary achievement.*

phenomenal — **Phenomenal** is very similar to **extraordinary** and means beyond what is ordinary or everyday. *What a phenomenal feeling it would be to travel through space!*

similar words: **astonishing, excellent, great**

work *noun*

something that needs to be done using your muscles or mind. *Farming is hard **work**.*

labour	**Labour** is hard tiring work. *The people were sweating after their labour in the fields.*
drudgery	**Drudgery** is hard boring work. *She hated the drudgery of scrubbing the floors.*
effort	**Effort** is the use of physical strength. *He put a lot of effort into building the wall.*
exertion	**Exertion** is similar to **effort** and you can often use either word. *The exertion of her long swim tired her.*
industry	**Industry** is hard, careful, conscientious work. *His success in the exam was due to his industry.*

contrasting words: **rest**

work *verb*

to do something that needs an effort of your body or mind. *You should **work** when you're in class.*

labour	To **labour** means to do hard or tiring work. *They laboured for four months building the house.*
toil	To **toil** means to work hard for a long time. *Each day the people toiled in the fields.*
slave	To **slave** means to work very hard, like a slave. *The farmer slaved to get his crops planted before sunset.*
slog	To **slog** means to work very hard. *We slogged all day but there was so much rubbish we couldn't clear it all away.*
pull your weight	To **pull your weight** means to do your full share of the work. *Everyone has to pull their weight or we won't finish this project on time.*

contrasting words: **rest, laze**

worry *verb*

to feel anxious or uneasy. *I **worry** when I am running late for school.*

bother To **bother** means to worry or give yourself trouble. *Don't bother about making your bed this morning.*

fret To **fret** means to be worried or annoyed. *Don't fret, I'll show you how to fix it!*

fuss To **fuss** means to worry or be anxious about unnecessary things. *That's too silly to fuss about.*

flap To **flap** can mean to become anxious or to panic. It is more suited to everyday language. *Although there was a lot of blood, the cut was too small to flap about.*

sweat out To **sweat out** means to feel worried or impatient about something. It is more suited to everyday language. *We sweated out the time until our results arrived.*

similar words: **fear**

worship *verb*

to feel love, esteem and veneration for someone or something, sometimes in a religious way. *The children **worshipped** their granny. Christians **worship** God.*

revere To **revere** means to feel deep admiration or a high regard for someone. *Jews revere Moses and all their prophets.*

respect To **respect** means to hold someone or something in high regard. *Aboriginal children are taught to respect their tribal elders.*

honour To **honour** means to show admiration or esteem for someone or something. *We honour our country by singing the national anthem.*

venerate To **venerate** means to pay honour to someone or something that you respect very much. *Roman Catholics venerate the Pope.*

idolise To **idolise** means to worship someone or regard them with devotion, despite their faults. *She idolised her children but often didn't correct them when they were naughty.*

similar words: **love**
contrasting words: **insult, slander, hate**

write *verb*

to form letters or words with a pen, pencil or similar thing. *Karen said she would* ***write*** *the sum on the blackboard with chalk.*

print — To **print** means to write something in separate letters rather than cursive writing. *I printed the names of the towns on my map.*

scribble — To **scribble** means to write something hastily or carelessly. *I scribbled a note to Lisa to remind her to buy the comics, but she couldn't read it.*

scrawl — To **scrawl** means to write something untidily. *He scrawled his name in my autograph book.*

doodle — To **doodle** means to draw something or **scribble** while you are thinking about something else. *I doodled a pattern of triangles and circles while waiting for the lesson to begin.*

scratch — To **scratch** can mean to draw a line through something with a pen or pencil. *I scratched the mistake from the word because I didn't have a rubber.*

---

yak *verb*

to talk on and on without saying anything very important. *My sister* ***yaks*** *on the phone for hours every evening.*

gas — To **gas** means to talk too much and too often. It is more suited to everyday language. *They gas all the time in class and our teacher gets annoyed.*

chatter — To **chatter** means to talk quickly, often without making sense. *At camp the children chattered long after they should have been asleep.*

gush — To **gush** can mean to express yourself in a rush of emotional talk. *Our neighbour gushes about her children and how clever they are.*

harp on — To **harp on** means to continue to speak or write in an annoying way. *He harps on how good things were before we moved here.*

rant — To **rant** can mean to speak for a long time in a loud and angry voice. *He was ranting for hours and saying all sorts of nasty things.*

---

similar words: **rave, talk**

yellow *adjective*

having a bright colour like butter. *The sun was like a big, **yellow** ball in the sky.*

lemon — **Lemon** means having a clear light-yellow colour. *My favourite roses are the lemon ones.*

canary — **Canary** can mean having a very bright, clear yellow colour. *You can see my sister's new canary car from a long way off.*

tawny — **Tawny** means having a yellowish-brown colour. *I would love to stroke the lion's rich, tawny coat.*

buff — **Buff** means having a light-yellow colour. *Pass me the buff folder, please.*

saffron — **Saffron** means having a yellow-orange colour. *The Buddhist monks in India wear saffron robes.*

young *adjective*

being in the early stage of life or growth. *The **young** koalas cling to their mothers' backs until they are old enough to care for themselves.*

juvenile — **Juvenile** can be very similar to **young**. It is usually used in more formal language. *Juvenile swans are known as cygnets.*

adolescent — **Adolescent** means being older than a child but not yet an adult. *We spend most of our adolescent years at secondary school.*

junior — **Junior** means younger. *Heats for the junior club members will be held first.*

youthful — **Youthful** means being young, or looking or behaving as you did when you were young. *Their youthful high spirits led them into a lot of trouble.*

childish — **Childish** means belonging to, or like a child. *I'd rather ride my new bike than play with my childish old toys.*

contrasting words: **adult**

Index

Aa

abandon *verb* **quit** 325
abate *verb* **decrease** 97
abbreviate *verb* **shorten** 373
abduct *verb* 1
abhor *verb* **hate** 190
able *adjective* **competent** 70
abnormal *adjective* **strange** 402
abolish *verb* **cancel** 49
abominable *adjective* **bad** 26
abominate *verb* **hate** 190
abridge *verb* **shorten** 373
abridged *adjective* **brief** 42
abrupt *adjective* 1
abrupt *adjective* **sudden** 408
abscond *verb* **flee** 157
absconder *noun* **escapee** 134
absent-minded
adjective **dreamy** 120
absorb *verb* **learn** 237
absurd *adjective* **ridiculous** 347
abundant *adjective* 2
abuse *verb* **maltreat** 251
abysmal *adjective* **bad** 26
accentuate *verb* **emphasise** 126
accept *verb* **believe** 32
acceptable *adjective* **nice** 276
accident *noun* **misfortune** 262
accidental *adjective* 2
accident-prone *adjective* **clumsy** 63
acclaim *verb* 3
accommodating
adjective **helpful** 193
accompanist *noun* **musician** 268
accompany *verb* 3
accomplish *verb* 4
accomplishment
noun **achievement** 5
accumulate *verb* **gather** 173
verb **increase** 209
accurate *adjective* **precise** 310
adjective **true** 438
accuse *verb* 4
ace *adjective* **great** 182
noun **expert** 141
ache *noun* **pain** 290
achieve *verb* **accomplish** 4
achievement *noun* 5
acid *adjective* **sour** 392
acknowledge *verb* **admit** 6
acknowledgment *noun* **reaction** 328
acquaintance *noun* **friend** 167
acquire *verb* **get** 175
acquittal *noun* **pardon** 290
acquit yourself *verb* **behave** 31
act *noun* **deed** 98
action *noun* **deed** 98
active *adjective* **busy** 46
actual *adjective* 5
act up *verb* **misbehave** 260
adage *noun* **saying** 357
adamant *adjective* **stubborn** 404
adapt *verb* **change** 53
add *verb* 6
add up *verb* **count** 82
adequate *adjective* **sufficient** 408
adhesive *noun* **glue** 178
adjacent *adjective* **near** 272
adjourn *verb* **defer** 100
adjudicate *verb* **judge** 228
administrator *noun* **manager** 252
admit *verb* 6
admonish *verb* **scold** 359
adolescent *adjective* **young** 473
adopt *verb* **take** 415
adore *verb* **love** 247
adult *adjective* 7
advance *verb* 7
advance *verb* **further** 171
advantageous *adjective* **useful** 451
adversary *noun* **enemy** 130
advertise *verb* **publish** 321
advise *verb* 8
advise *verb* **inform** 214
advise against *verb* **discourage** 112

adviser *noun* 8
advocate *noun* **lawyer** 235
verb **advise** 8
verb **approve** 17
affected *adjective* **pompous** 304
affectionate *adjective* **loving** 248
affluent *adjective* **wealthy** 462
affront *verb* **insult** 220
afraid *adjective* **frightened** 168
aged *adjective* **adult** 7
aggravate *verb* **annoy** 14
aggressive *adjective* 9
agile *adjective* 9
agitated *adjective* **upset** 450
agnostic *noun* **heathen** 191
agrarian *adjective* **country** 83
agree *verb* 10
agreeable *adjective* 10
aid *noun* **help** 192
verb **help** 192
aide *noun* **helper** 193
ailing *adjective* **sick** 377
air *noun* **appearance** 17
air-condition *verb* **cool** 79
akin *adjective* **similar** 379
alarm *verb* **frighten** 168
verb **warn** 459
alert *adjective* 11
alert *verb* **warn** 459
alias *noun* **name** 269
alien *adjective* **foreign** 163
alight *verb* **land** 233
alike *adjective* **similar** 379
allege *verb* **accuse** 4
alleviate *verb* **comfort** 68
allied *adjective* **related** 334
allocate *verb* **distribute** 118
allocation *noun* **share** 369
allot *verb* **distribute** 118
allotment *noun* **share** 369
allow *verb* 11
all the rage *adjective* **chic** 55
all thumbs *adjective* **clumsy** 63
allude to *verb* **hint** 196
alms *noun* **gift** 176
alone *adjective* **lonely** 246
aloof *adjective* **unfriendly** 445
alter *verb* **change** 53
altercation *noun* **argument** 18
alternative
adjective **unconventional** 442
noun **choice** 56
amalgamate *verb* **combine** 67
amass *verb* **gather** 173
amateur
adjective **inexperienced** 212
amateurish
adjective **incompetent** 208
amazed *adjective* **astonished** 21
amazing *adjective* **astonishing** 22
amber *adjective* **orange** 285
ambiguous *adjective* **confusing** 77
ambivalent *adjective* **confused** 77
amble *verb* **walk** 458
ambush *noun* **attack** 22
verb **catch** 51
amend *verb* **correct** 81
amiable *adjective* **agreeable** 10
amnesty *noun* **pardon** 290
ample *adjective* **abundant** 2
adjective **big** 34
amplify *verb* **enlarge** 131
verb **expand** 139
amusing *adjective* **funny** 171
analyse *verb* **examine** 135
analysis *noun* **inquiry** 216
ancestor *noun* 12
ancient *adjective* **old** 282
anger *noun* 12
anger *verb* 13
angry *adjective* 13
anguish *noun* **misery** 261
animosity *noun* **dislike** 113
annex *verb* **take** 415
annihilate *verb* **destroy** 105
announce *verb* **inform** 214
annoy *verb* 14
annoyed *adjective* 14
annoying *adjective* 15
annul *verb* **cancel** 49

answer *verb* 15
answer *noun* **reaction** 328
antagonist *noun* **enemy** 130
antagonistic *adjective* **defiant** 101
antecedents *noun* **ancestor** 12
anthem *noun* **song** 391
anthology *noun* **book** 38
anticipate *verb* **expect** 140
anticlimax *noun* **disappointment** 109
antipathy *noun* **dislike** 113
antiquated *adjective* **old-fashioned** 282
antique *adjective* **old** 282
antisocial *adjective* **unfriendly** 445
antithetical *adjective* **opposite** 284
anxious *adjective* **enthusiastic** 132
adjective **nervous** 274
apathetic *adjective* 16
ape *verb* **mimic** 259
aperture *noun* **hole** 197
apex *noun* **top** 432
appal *verb* **shock** 372
apparel *noun* **clothing** 61
apparent *adjective* **obvious** 280
apparition *noun* **ghost** 175
appeal to *verb* **please** 301
appear *verb* 16
appearance *noun* 17
appease *verb* **pacify** 289
append *verb* **add** 6
appetising *adjective* **delicious** 102
applaud *verb* **acclaim** 3
appointment *noun* **meeting** 256
noun **position** 306
appraise *verb* **judge** 228
appreciate *verb* **like** 241
appreciative *adjective* **grateful** 182
apprehend *verb* **capture** 49
apprehensive *adjective* **nervous** 274
approach *noun* **method** 258
appropriate *verb* **take** 415
approval *noun* **permission** 296
approve *verb* 17
approximate *adjective* **vague** 453
apt *adjective* **likely** 242
aquamarine *adjective* **blue** 36
arbitrary *adjective* **irrational** 224
arbitrate *verb* **negotiate** 274
archaic *adjective* **old-fashioned** 282
arduous *adjective* **difficult** 106
argue *verb* 18
argument *noun* 18
argumentative *adjective* 19
arid *adjective* **dry** 122
arise *verb* **happen** 187
aristocratic *adjective* **distinguished** 117
aroma *noun* **smell** 386
arrange *verb* 19
arrange *verb* **plan** 301
arrest *verb* **capture** 49
arrive *verb* **come** 67
arrogant *adjective* **proud** 319
artful *adjective* **cunning** 90
articulate *adjective* **fluent** 160
verb **pronounce** 317
ascend *verb* **climb** 60
ascertain *verb* **realise** 329
as good as gold *adjective* **well-behaved** 463
ashamed *adjective* **sorry** 391
ask *verb* 20
ask *verb* **demand** 103
aspect *noun* **appearance** 17
asphyxiate *verb* **suffocate** 409
assassinate *verb* **kill** 230
assault *noun* **attack** 22
verb **attack** 23
assay *verb* **test** 422
assemble *verb* 20
assemble *verb* **combine** 67
assembly *noun* **club** 62
assent *verb* **agree** 10
assess *verb* **examine** 135
assets *noun* **property** 318
assignation *noun* **meeting** 256
assignment *noun* **task** 417
assimilate *verb* **learn** 237
assist *verb* **help** 192

assistance *noun* **help** 192
assistant *noun* **helper** 193
associate *noun* 21
associated *adjective* **related** 334
associate with *verb* **accompany** 3
association *noun* **club** 62
assorted *adjective* **various** 453
assortment *noun* **mixture** 264
assume *verb* **believe** 32
astonished *adjective* 21
astonishing *adjective* 22
astounded *adjective* **astonished** 21
astounding *adjective* **astonishing** 22
astute *adjective* **shrewd** 375
asylum *noun* **refuge** 333
atheist *noun* **heathen** 191
athletic *adjective* **agile** 9
atonal *adjective* **discordant** 111
atrocious *adjective* **bad** 26
atrophy *verb* **shrink** 376
attach *verb* **add** 6
attack *noun* 22
attack *verb* 23
attack *verb* **attempt** 24
attain *verb* **accomplish** 4
attempt *noun* 23
attempt *verb* 24
attendant *noun* **helper** 193
attend to *verb* **concentrate on** 73
attentive *adjective* **alert** 11
adjective **careful** 50
attire *noun* **clothing** 61
attitude *noun* **manner** 252
noun **opinion** 283
attorney *noun* **lawyer** 235
attract *verb* 24
attract *verb* **please** 301
attractive *adjective* 25
attractive *adjective* **pretty** 312
auction *verb* **sell** 364
audition *noun* **test** 422
augment *verb* **enlarge** 131
auspicious *adjective* **lucky** 248
austere *adjective* **strict** 403
authentic *adjective* **genuine** 174
authorise *verb* **allow** 11
authorised *adjective* **legal** 238
authoritarian *adjective* **bossy** 40
authority *noun* **expert** 141
autocratic *adjective* **bossy** 40
autonomous
adjective **independent** 210
avant-garde *adjective* **new** 275
avaricious *adjective* **greedy** 183
average *adjective* **ordinary** 286
averse *adjective* **unwilling** 449
aversion *noun* **dislike** 113
avid *adjective* **enthusiastic** 132
avoid *verb* 25
awake *adjective* **alert** 11
award *noun* **prize** 315
verb **give** 176
awareness *noun* **feeling** 151
awful *adjective* **nasty** 271
awkward *adjective* **clumsy** 63
azure *adjective* **blue** 36

Bb

babble *verb* **rave** 327
back *verb* **reverse** 346
backing *noun* **help** 192
backlog *noun* **excess** 137
backward *adjective* **ignorant** 203
bad *adjective* 26
badly-behaved
adjective **naughty** 271
baffle *verb* **puzzle** 324
bake *verb* **toast** 431
balance *verb* **steady** 399
bald *adjective* **bare** 28
ball *noun* 26
ballad *noun* **song** 391
ballast *noun* **weight** 463
balmy *adjective* **fine** 155
bamboozle *verb* **confuse** 76
ban *verb* 27
banal *adjective* **mediocre** 255

band *noun* **group** 185
noun **layer** 235
bandit *noun* 27
bang *verb* **beat** 29
banish *verb* **expel** 140
bank *verb* **store** 402
bankrupt *adjective* **broke** 44
bar *verb* **ban** 27
verb **block** 36
barbaric *adjective* **cruel** 89
barbecue *verb* **toast** 431
bare *adjective* 28
bargain for *verb* **expect** 140
barricade *verb* **block** 36
barrier *noun* **obstacle** 280
barrister *noun* **lawyer** 235
base *noun* **bottom** 41
noun **support** 411
bash *noun* **attempt** 23
bashful *adjective* **shy** 376
basin *noun* **lake** 233
bat *verb* **hit** 196
battle *noun* **fight** 153
bawl *verb* **cry** 90
verb **shout** 373
bay *noun* 28
be *verb* **live** 245
beam *verb* **shine** 370
bear *verb* **produce** 315
bearing *noun* **manner** 252
bear out *verb* **prove** 320
beat *verb* 29
beat *noun* **rhythm** 346
verb **defeat** 99
verb **pass** 291
beat up *verb* **attack** 23
beautiful *adjective* 29
become extinct *verb* 30
bed *noun* **bottom** 41
bedraggled *adjective* **scruffy** 361
beefy *adjective* **stocky** 400
beeline *noun* **course** 84
be foolish *verb* **misbehave** 260
befriend *verb* 30
befuddle *verb* **confuse** 76
beg *verb* **ask** 20
begin *verb* 31
begin *verb* **start** 397
beginning *noun* **start** 397
beguile *verb* **charm** 53
behave *verb* 31
beholden *adjective* **grateful** 182
beige *adjective* **brown** 44
belief *noun* **religion** 335
believable *adjective* 32
believe *verb* 32
belittle *verb* **insult** 220
bellicose *adjective* **warlike** 459
belligerent *adjective* **aggressive** 9
bellow *verb* **shout** 373
belly *noun* **inside** 218
bellyful *noun* **excess** 137
belongings *noun* **property** 318
be lost in thought
verb **daydream** 95
belt out *verb* **shout** 373
bemused *adjective* **dreamy** 120
bend *verb* 33
beneficial *adjective* **useful** 451
benefit *verb* **thrive** 428
be no more *verb* **become extinct** 30
bent *adjective* **crooked** 87
berth *verb* **come** 67
beseech *verb* **ask** 20
best *adjective* 33
betray *verb* 34
betray *verb* **admit** 6
better *verb* **improve** 206
bewilder *verb* **puzzle** 324
bewildering *adjective* **confusing** 77
bewitch *verb* **charm** 53
bias *verb* **influence** 213
biased *adjective* **narrow-minded** 270
bicker *verb* **disagree** 108
bid *noun* **offer** 281
big *adjective* 34
big-headed *adjective* **conceited** 73
bight *noun* **bay** 28
bigoted *adjective* **narrow-minded** 270
big shot *noun* **VIP** 455

big smoke *noun* **city** 57
big wheel *noun* **VIP** 455
bigwig *noun* **VIP** 455
billow *verb* **protrude** 319
bistro *noun* **restaurant** 343
bitter *adjective* **resentful** 340
adjective **sour** 392
bizarre *adjective* **strange** 402
blab *verb* 35
black *adjective* 35
black *adjective* **evil** 135
blackmail *verb* **threaten** 427
bland *adjective* **tasteless** 418
blank *adjective* **empty** 127
blanket *verb* **cover** 84
blaring *adjective* **loud** 247
blasé *adjective* **bored** 39
blasphemous *adjective* **sacrilegious** 352
blaze *verb* **shine** 370
blazing *adjective* **hot** 200
bleached *adjective* **colourless** 66
bleak *adjective* **dreary** 120
adjective **wintry** 467
blend *verb* **combine** 67
bless *verb* **approve** 17
blessed *adjective* **holy** 198
blissful *adjective* **joyful** 228
blithe *adjective* **happy** 188
blitz *noun* **attack** 22
block *verb* 36
blockade *verb* **block** 36
bloke *noun* **male** 250
bloodshot *adjective* **rosy** 348
bloodthirsty *adjective* **warlike** 459
bloom *verb* **flourish** 158
verb **thrive** 428
blossom *verb* **flourish** 158
verb **thrive** 428
blot *verb* **wipe** 468
blow *noun* **disappointment** 109
noun **misfortune** 262
verb **gasp** 172
verb **waste** 460
blow in *verb* **visit** 456
blow your own trumpet *verb* **boast** 37
blubber *verb* **cry** 90
blue *adjective* 36
bluff *verb* **trick** 436
blunder *noun* **mistake** 263
blunt *adjective* **abrupt** 1
blurt out *verb* **admit** 6
bluster *verb* **boast** 37
board *noun* **council** 81
verb **reside** 341
boast *verb* 37
boaster *noun* **show-off** 374
bog *noun* **swamp** 413
bogus *adjective* **fake** 145
bohemian *adjective* **unconventional** 442
boil *verb* 37
boil *verb* **swelter** 414
bold *adjective* 38
bold *adjective* **brave** 41
bonus *noun* **profit** 316
boob *verb* **err** 133
boo-boo *noun* **mistake** 263
booby trap *noun* **trap** 434
book *noun* 38
book *verb* **accuse** 4
boom *verb* **thrive** 428
boost *verb* **enlarge** 131
booty *noun* **loot** 246
border *noun* **edge** 125
bored *adjective* 39
boring *adjective* 39
borrow *verb* **take** 415
boss *noun* 40
bossy *adjective* 40
botch *verb* **bungle** 45
bother *verb* **worry** 471
bottom *noun* 41
boulder *noun* **stone** 401
bouncy *adjective* **elastic** 126
bound *verb* **jump** 229
boundary *noun* **outskirts** 287
bountiful *adjective* **abundant** 2

bouquet *noun* **smell** 386
bout *noun* **competition** 71
bowl over *verb* **overturn** 288
verb **shock** 372
box in *verb* **enclose** 127
boycott *verb* **ban** 27
brace *verb* **strengthen** 403
brag *verb* **boast** 37
brainstorm *noun* **thought** 426
brainwash *verb* **influence** 213
brainy *adjective* **clever** 60
braise *verb* **boil** 37
brand *verb* **label** 232
brave *adjective* 41
brawl *noun* **fight** 153
brawny *adjective* **strong** 404
brazen *adjective* **bold** 38
break *noun* 42
break *noun* **rest** 342
breakable *adjective* **fragile** 165
break off *verb* **cancel** 49
verb **separate** 366
breathe *verb* **live** 245
breathe your last *verb* **die** 106
breathtaking *adjective* **exciting** 138
breed *verb* **produce** 315
bridge *verb* **cross** 88
brief *adjective* 42
brief *adjective* **momentary** 265
noun **report** 340
brigand *noun* **bandit** 27
bright *adjective* 43
bright *adjective* **clever** 60
adjective **colourful** 66
brighten *verb* **recover** 331
brilliant *adjective* **bright** 43
adjective **clever** 60
brim *noun* **edge** 125
bring off *verb* **accomplish** 4
brink *noun* **edge** 125
bristly *adjective* **rough** 349
brittle *adjective* **fragile** 165
broad *adjective* **wide** 466
broadcast *verb* **publish** 321
broad-minded *adjective* 43
broke *adjective* 44
broker *noun* **seller** 364
brood *verb* **grieve** 184
brown *adjective* 44
browned off
adjective **dissatisfied** 116
browse through *verb* **read** 328
brunette *adjective* **brown** 44
brusque *adjective* **abrupt** 1
brutal *adjective* **cruel** 89
brutality *noun* **violence** 454
buccaneer *noun* **bandit** 27
buckled *adjective* **crooked** 87
budge *verb* **move** 266
buff *adjective* **yellow** 473
verb **polish** 303
bug *verb* **irritate** 224
build *verb* 45
build *noun* **shape** 369
bulge *verb* **protrude** 319
bulky *adjective* **big** 34
bulldoze *verb* **force** 162
bulletin *noun* **report** 340
bully *verb* **force** 162
bump into *verb* **meet** 256
bumpy *adjective* **rough** 349
bunch *noun* **group** 185
bungle *verb* 45
bunkum *noun* **nonsense** 277
buoyant *adjective* **optimistic** 284
burden *noun* **weight** 463
burglar *noun* **thief** 424
burly *adjective* **stocky** 400
burn *verb* **shine** 370
verb **swelter** 414
burnish *verb* **polish** 303
bursting *adjective* **full** 170
bushed *adjective* **tired** 431
business *noun* **job** 226
busker *noun* **entertainer** 132
bust-up *noun* **conflict** 76
busy *adjective* 46
butter up *verb* **flatter** 156
butt in *verb* **intrude** 222
buy *verb* 46

buyer *noun* 47
buzz *verb* **throb** 429
bygone *adjective* **past** 292

Cc

cackle *verb* **laugh** 234
cacophonous
adjective **discordant** 111
cafe *noun* **restaurant** 343
cafeteria *noun* **restaurant** 343
cagey *adjective* **secretive** 362
calamity *noun* **disaster** 110
calculate *verb* 47
call *noun* **demand** 102
verb **name** 269
verb **visit** 456
callous *adjective* 48
callow *adjective* **inexperienced** 212
calm *adjective* 48
calm *verb* **pacify** 289
camouflage *verb* **hide** 194
canary *adjective* **yellow** 473
cancel *verb* 49
candid *adjective* **frank** 165
candied *adjective* **sweet** 414
cane *verb* **thrash** 427
canny *adjective* **shrewd** 375
cantankerous
adjective **argumentative** 19
canteen *noun* **restaurant** 343
capable *adjective* **competent** 70
caper *verb* **frisk** 169
capital *noun* **city** 57
noun **wealth** 462
capital punishment
noun **homicide** 198
capitulate *verb* **give in** 177
capricious *adjective* **fickle** 152
capsize *verb* **overbalance** 288
captive *noun* **prisoner** 314
capture *verb* 49
carcinogenic
adjective **poisonous** 303
career *noun* **job** 226
care for *verb* **love** 247
careful *adjective* 50
careful *adjective* **thrifty** 428
adjective **wary** 460
careless *adjective* 50
caricature *verb* **mimic** 259
carol *noun* **song** 391
carriage *noun* **manner** 252
carry *verb* 51
carry through *verb* **accomplish** 4
carry yourself *verb* **behave** 31
casual *adjective* **careless** 50
adjective **informal** 214
adjective **temporary** 421
catastrophe *noun* **disaster** 110
catch *verb* 51
cause *verb* 52
caution *verb* **warn** 459
cautious *adjective* **wary** 460
cease *verb* **end** 129
celebrate *verb* **rejoice** 334
celebrated *adjective* **famous** 147
celebrity *noun* **star** 396
celibate *adjective* **unmarried** 447
cell *noun* **room** 348
cement *noun* **glue** 178
censor *verb* **ban** 27
censure *verb* **fault** 150
centre *noun* 52
ceremonial *adjective* **formal** 164
cerise *adjective* **purple** 323
certain *adjective* **sure** 412
adjective **true** 438
chafe *verb* **roughen** 350
chain *noun* **series** 367
chamber *noun* **room** 348
champion *noun* **winner** 467
verb **befriend** 30
championship *noun* **competition** 71
chance *adjective* **accidental** 2
noun **fate** 149
change *verb* 53

changeable *adjective* **fickle** 152
change your tune
verb **fluctuate** 159
channel *noun* **groove** 185
chaotic *adjective* **untidy** 448
chap *verb* **roughen** 350
chaperone *verb* **accompany** 3
chaplain *noun* **clergyman** 59
charcoal *adjective* **grey** 184
charge *noun* **price** 313
verb **accuse** 4
verb **attack** 23
charisma *noun* **influence** 213
charismatic *adjective* **attractive** 25
charitable *adjective* **generous** 174
charity *noun* **help** 192
charm *verb* 53
charm *verb* **please** 301
charming *adjective* **agreeable** 10
chase *verb* **follow** 161
chastise *verb* **punish** 322
chat *verb* **talk** 416
chatter *verb* **yak** 472
chatty *adjective* **talkative** 416
cheap *adjective* 54
cheat *verb* 54
cheat *noun* **crook** 87
check *verb* **test** 422
checkup *noun* **test** 422
cheeky *adjective* **rude** 351
cheer *verb* **acclaim** 3
cheerful *adjective* **happy** 188
cheerless *adjective* **dreary** 120
cherish *verb* **love** 247
chew *verb* 55
chic *adjective* 55
chicken *noun* **coward** 85
chicken out *verb* **cower** 85
chief *adjective* **main** 249
noun **boss** 40
childish *adjective* **young** 473
chill *adjective* **wintry** 467
verb **cool** 79
chilly *adjective* **wintry** 467
chime *verb* **ring** 347
chink *noun* **hole** 197
chip in *verb* **intrude** 222
chivalrous *adjective* **polite** 304
choice *noun* 56
choke *verb* **suffocate** 409
chomp *verb* **chew** 55
choose *verb* 56
choose *verb* **intend** 220
chop and change *verb* **fluctuate** 159
chore *noun* **task** 417
chorister *noun* **singer** 381
chortle *verb* **laugh** 234
chow *noun* **food** 161
christen *verb* **name** 269
chuck *verb* **throw** 429
chuckle *verb* **laugh** 234
chunky *adjective* **thick** 423
city *noun* 57
civic *adjective* 57
claim *noun* **demand** 102
clamber *verb* **climb** 60
clap *verb* **acclaim** 3
clarify *verb* **explain** 142
clash *verb* **argue** 18
clasp *verb* **hold** 197
class *noun* **grade** 181
classified *adjective* **secret** 361
classify *verb* **arrange** 19
classy *adjective* **distinguished** 117
clay *noun* **earth** 123
clean *adjective* 58
clean *verb* 58
cleanse *verb* **clean** 58
clear *adjective* 59
clear *adjective* **obvious** 280
adjective **sure** 412
adjective **transparent** 434
verb **forgive** 164
clearance *noun* **permission** 296
clergyman *noun* 59
clever *adjective* 60
climb *verb* 60
climb down *verb* **descend** 104
cling to *verb* **hold** 197

clink *noun* **prison** 314
clip *verb* **cut** 91
verb **hit** 196
close *adjective* **humid** 202
adjective **narrow** 270
adjective **near** 272
noun **end** 128
verb **block** 36
verb **finish** 155
clot *verb* **thicken** 424
cloth *noun* 61
clothing *noun* 61
cloudy *adjective* 62
cloudy *adjective* **opaque** 283
clout *noun* **influence** 213
club *noun* 62
clue *noun* **indicator** 211
clumsy *adjective* 63
clutch *verb* **hold** 197
clutter *noun* **mess** 257
coach *noun* **teacher** 419
verb **teach** 419
coagulate *verb* **thicken** 424
coarse *adjective* **rough** 349
adjective **vulgar** 457
coarsen *verb* **roughen** 350
coast *verb* **descend** 104
coat *verb* 63
coating *noun* 64
coax *verb* **persuade** 298
cobble *noun* **stone** 401
coddle *verb* **boil** 37
cocky *adjective* **bold** 38
coerce *verb* **force** 162
coherent *adjective* **sane** 355
coil *noun* 64
coiled *adjective* **twisted** 439
coin *verb* **invent** 222
coincidental *adjective* **accidental** 2
cold *adjective* 65
cold *adjective* **unfriendly** 445
cold-blooded *adjective* **callous** 48
cold-shoulder *verb* **isolate** 225
collaborate *verb* **cooperate** 79
collaborator *noun* **associate** 21
collapse *verb* **fail** 143
verb **sag** 354
colleague *noun* **associate** 21
noun **helper** 193
collect *verb* **gather** 173
collective *adjective* **public** 320
collude *verb* **plot** 302
colonise *verb* **inhabit** 215
colossal *adjective* **huge** 201
colour *verb* 65
colourful *adjective* 66
colourless *adjective* 66
comatose *adjective* **unconscious** 442
combat *noun* **fight** 153
combative *adjective* **aggressive** 9
combine *verb* 67
combine *verb* **cooperate** 79
come *verb* 67
come *verb* **appear** 16
come about *verb* **happen** 187
come across *verb* **meet** 256
comedian *noun* **entertainer** 132
come to blows *verb* **fight** 154
comfort *noun* 68
comfort *verb* 68
comfortable *adjective* **satisfied** 356
comical *adjective* **funny** 171
command *noun* **order** 285
verb **rule** 352
commence *verb* **begin** 31
commencement *noun* **start** 397
commend *verb* **praise** 310
comment *noun* 69
commission *noun* **pay** 293
commissioner *noun* **manager** 252
committee *noun* **council** 81
commodious
adjective **spacious** 393
common *adjective* **public** 320
adjective **subordinate** 406
adjective **vulgar** 457
commotion *noun* 69
communal *adjective* **public** 320
communicative
adjective **talkative** 416

communiqué *noun* **message** 257
commuter *noun* **traveller** 435
companion *noun* **friend** 167
company *noun* **organisation** 286
comparable *adjective* **similar** 379
compartment *noun* **room** 348
compassion *noun* **pity** 299
compassionate *adjective* **lenient** 239
compel *verb* **force** 162
compensate *verb* **repay** 338
compete *verb* 70
competent *adjective* 70
competition *noun* 71
complacent *adjective* **satisfied** 356
complain *verb* 71
complete *adjective* **perfect** 295
adjective **whole** 466
verb **finish** 155
complex *adjective* **difficult** 106
noun **obsession** 279
complexion *noun* **appearance** 17
compliant *adjective* **obedient** 278
complicated *adjective* 72
compliment *verb* **praise** 310
comply with *verb* **obey** 279
compose *verb* 72
compose *verb* **create** 86
composed *adjective* **calm** 48
compound *noun* **prison** 314
comprehend *verb* **understand** 443
comprehensive
adjective **thorough** 426
compress *verb* **press** 312
comprise *verb* **include** 207
compromise *verb* **endanger** 129
compute *verb* **calculate** 47
comrade *noun* **associate** 21
con *noun* **trick** 436
conceal *verb* **hide** 194
concealed *adjective* **invisible** 223
conceited *adjective* 73
conceivable *adjective* **believable** 32
conceive *verb* **invent** 222
concentrate on *verb* 73
concept *noun* **thought** 426
concert *noun* 74
concise *adjective* **brief** 42
conclude *verb* 74
conclude *verb* **finish** 155
conclusion *noun* **end** 128
noun **result** 344
concoct *verb* 75
concrete *adjective* **actual** 5
concrete jungle *noun* **city** 57
concur *verb* **agree** 10
condemn *verb* **fault** 150
condense *verb* **shorten** 373
verb **thicken** 424
condensed *adjective* **brief** 42
condition *verb* **influence** 213
conduct yourself *verb* **behave** 31
confer *verb* **give** 176
verb **talk** 416
confess *verb* **admit** 6
confident *adjective* **optimistic** 284
adjective **sure** 412
confidential *adjective* **secret** 361
confine *verb* 75
confine *verb* **enclose** 127
confined *adjective* **narrow** 270
confirm *verb* **prove** 320
confiscate *verb* **take** 415
conflict *noun* 76
conflict *verb* **argue** 18
conflicting *adjective* **opposite** 284
confound *verb* **puzzle** 324
confuse *verb* 76
confused *adjective* 77
confusing *adjective* 77
congeal *verb* **thicken** 424
congregate *verb* **assemble** 20
congregation *noun* **club** 62
congress *noun* **council** 81
connect *verb* **join** 226
connected *adjective* **related** 334
connive *verb* **plot** 302
conquer *verb* **defeat** 99
conscientious *adjective* **careful** 50
adjective **reliable** 335
consent *noun* **permission** 296

courier *noun* **messenger** 258
course *noun* 84
course *noun* **lesson** 239
noun **series** 367
court *verb* **love** 247
courteous *adjective* **polite** 304
cove *noun* **bay** 28
cover *verb* 84
cover *verb* **hide** 194
verb **include** 207
covet *verb* **want** 458
covetous *adjective* **jealous** 225
cow *verb* **threaten** 427
coward *noun* 85
cowardly *adjective* **fearful** 151
cower *verb* 85
coy *adjective* **shy** 376
crack *noun* **attempt** 23
noun **break** 42
noun **joke** 227
verb **solve** 390
crack up *verb* **laugh** 234
cradle *verb* **hug** 200
craft *noun* **profession** 316
crafty *adjective* **cunning** 90
crammed *adjective* **full** 170
cramp *noun* **pain** 290
cramped *adjective* **narrow** 270
crave *verb* **want** 458
craving *noun* **wish** 469
craze *noun* **fashion** 147
crazy *adjective* **mad** 249
cream *adjective* **white** 465
creamy *adjective* **smooth** 387
create *verb* 86
credible *adjective* **believable** 32
credit *verb* **believe** 32
creepy *adjective* **frightening** 169
crest *noun* **top** 432
crevice *noun* **break** 42
criminal *noun* 86
criminal *adjective* **illegal** 204
crimson *adjective* **red** 332
cripple *verb* **weaken** 461
critical *adjective* **significant** 378
criticise *verb* **fault** 150
crone *noun* **female** 152
crook *noun* 87
crooked *adjective* 87
crooked *adjective* **dishonest** 113
crooner *noun* **singer** 381
cross *verb* 88
cross *adjective* **grumpy** 186
verb **extend** 142
crotchety *adjective* **grumpy** 186
adjective **annoyed** 14
crow *verb* **boast** 37
crowd *noun* 88
crowded *adjective* **full** 170
crucial *adjective* **necessary** 273
crude *adjective* **vulgar** 457
cruel *adjective* 89
cruise *verb* **sail** 354
crumble *verb* **crush** 89
crumbling *adjective* **decrepit** 98
crummy *adjective* **inferior** 212
crush *verb* 89
crust *noun* **coating** 64
cry *verb* 90
cry-baby *noun* **coward** 85
cubicle *noun* **room** 348
cuddle *verb* **hug** 200
cultivated *adjective* **educated** 125
cunning *adjective* 90
cunning *noun* **trickery** 437
curb *verb* **limit** 242
curdle *verb* **thicken** 424
curious *adjective* **inquisitive** 217
curl *noun* **coil** 64
verb **bend** 33
current *adjective* **modern** 265
cursed *adjective* **unlucky** 447
curt *adjective* **abrupt** 1
curtail *verb* **subtract** 407
curve *verb* **bend** 33
customary *adjective* **usual** 452
customer *noun* **buyer** 47
cut *noun* 91
cut *verb* 91
cut *noun* **share** 369

cut back *verb* **reduce** 332
cut off *verb* **interrupt** 221
cut up *adjective* **miserable** 261
cycle *noun* **series** 367

Dd

dainty *adjective* **slight** 383
dally *verb* **dawdle** 94
dam *noun* **lake** 233
damage *verb* 92
damn *verb* **fault** 150
damp *adjective* **wet** 464
dampen *verb* **wet** 464
dance *verb* **frisk** 169
dangerous *adjective* 92
dank *adjective* **wet** 464
dapper *adjective* **chic** 55
dark *adjective* 93
dark *adjective* **black** 35
darken *verb* 93
darn *verb* **sew** 367
dart *verb* 94
dash *noun* **trace** 433
verb **hurry** 202
dash off *verb* **compose** 72
date *noun* **meeting** 256
daub *verb* **coat** 63
dawdle *verb* 94
daydream *verb* 95
dazed *adjective* **unconscious** 442
dazzling *adjective* **bright** 43
dead *adjective* 95
deadlock *noun* **halt** 186
deadly *adjective* **fatal** 149
deafening *adjective* **loud** 247
dealer *noun* **seller** 364
dear *adjective* 96
dearth *noun* **lack** 232
debacle *noun* **disaster** 110
debatable *adjective* **uncertain** 441
debate *noun* **talk** 415
debris *noun* **rubbish** 350
decay *verb* **rot** 349
deceased *adjective* **dead** 95
deceit *noun* **trickery** 437
deceitful *adjective* **dishonest** 113
deceive *verb* 96
decent *adjective* 97
decent *adjective* **sufficient** 408
decide *verb* **choose** 56
verb **negotiate** 274
declare *verb* **publish** 321
decline *verb* **deteriorate** 105
verb **refuse** 333
decompose *verb* **rot** 349
decrease *verb* 97
decrease *verb* **reduce** 332
decree *noun* **order** 285
decrepit *adjective* 98
deduce *verb* **conclude** 74
deduct *verb* **subtract** 407
deed *noun* 98
deep *adjective* **wide** 466
defame *verb* **slander** 382
defeat *verb* 99
defective *adjective* 99
defence *noun* 100
defend *verb* **befriend** 30
verb **protect** 318
defer *verb* 100
defiant *adjective* 101
deficiency *noun* **lack** 232
deficient
adjective **incomplete** 208
adjective **insufficient** 219
deficit *noun* **lack** 232
definite *adjective* **precise** 310
adjective **sure** 412
deflect *verb* **bend** 33
defraud *verb* **cheat** 54
defuse *verb* **pacify** 289
defy *verb* **disobey** 114
verb **resist** 341
degenerate *adjective* **indecent** 210
verb **deteriorate** 105
dehydrated *adjective* **dry** 122

delay *verb* **dawdle** 94
verb **defer** 100
delete *verb* **exclude** 139
deliberate *adjective* 101
deliberate *adjective* **wary** 460
delicate *adjective* **fragile** 165
adjective **light** 241
adjective **slight** 383
delicious *adjective* 102
delight *verb* **please** 301
delighted *adjective* **glad** 177
delinquent
adjective **disobedient** 114
deliver *verb* **carry** 51
verb **free** 166
delude *verb* **deceive** 96
deluxe *adjective* **superior** 411
delve into *verb* **investigate** 223
demand *noun* 102
demand *verb* 103
demanding *adjective* **difficult** 106
dematerialise *verb* **disappear** 109
demolish *verb* **destroy** 105
verb **disprove** 116
demonstrate *verb* **show** 374
demonstration *noun* **display** 115
demure *adjective* **shy** 376
den.*noun* **room** 348
denomination *noun* **religion** 335
denounce *verb* **accuse** 4
dense *adjective* **opaque** 283
adjective **stupid** 405
adjective **thick** 423
depart *verb* **leave** 237
departed *adjective* **dead** 95
dependable *adjective* **reliable** 335
dependant *noun* 103
depict *verb* **describe** 104
deport *verb* **expel** 140
deposit *noun* **layer** 235
verb **place** 300
depraved *adjective* **indecent** 210
depressed *adjective* **miserable** 261
depressing *adjective* **dreary** 120
adjective **pessimistic** 298
depression *noun* **misery** 261
deprivation *noun* **poverty** 307
deputy *noun* **helper** 193
derision *noun* **scorn** 360
derive *verb* **calculate** 47
descend *verb* 104
descendant *noun* **offspring** 281
describe *verb* 104
describe *verb* **tell** 421
desert *verb* **quit** 325
deserted *adjective* **empty** 127
desiccated *adjective* **dry** 122
design *noun* **shape** 369
verb **create** 86
desire *noun* **wish** 469
verb **want** 458
despicable *adjective* **unkind** 446
despise *verb* **hate** 190
despondent *adjective* **miserable** 261
despotic *adjective* **tyrannical** 439
destiny *noun* **fate** 149
destitute *adjective* **broke** 44
destitution *noun* **poverty** 307
destroy *verb* 105
detach *verb* **separate** 366
detached *adjective* **neutral** 275
detailed *adjective* **thorough** 426
detect *verb* **find** 154
deter *verb* **discourage** 112
deteriorate *verb* 105
determined *adjective* **persistent** 297
detest *verb* **hate** 190
develop *verb* **create** 86
verb **expand** 139
devious *adjective* **cunning** 90
devise *verb* **invent** 222
devoted *adjective* **faithful** 145
adjective **loving** 248
devotion *noun* **respect** 342
devour *verb* **eat** 124
devout *adjective* **religious** 336
dialect *noun* **language** 234
dialogue *noun* **talk** 415
diary *noun* **book** 38
dicey *adjective* **dangerous** 92

dictatorial *adjective* **bossy** 40
die *verb* 106
die out *verb* **become extinct** 30
differ *verb* **disagree** 108
difference *noun* **argument** 18
difficult *adjective* 106
diffident *adjective* **shy** 376
dig *verb* 107
digest *verb* **learn** 237
digit *noun* **number** 277
dignified *adjective* **grand** 181
digress *verb* **ramble** 326
dilemma *noun* **choice** 56
diligent *adjective* **careful** 50
dim *adjective* **dark** 93
verb **darken** 93
diminish *verb* **decrease** 97
verb **subtract** 407
din *noun* **noise** 276
dingy *adjective* **drab** 119
dip *verb* **drop** 122
direct *adjective* **frank** 165
verb **manage** 251
director *noun* **manager** 252
dirt *noun* **earth** 123
dirt-cheap *adjective* **cheap** 54
dirty *adjective* 107
dirty *verb* 108
disable *verb* **weaken** 461
disadvantaged *adjective* **poor** 305
disagree *verb* 108
disagreement *noun* **conflict** 76
disappear *verb* 109
disappointment *noun* 109
disapprove of *verb* 110
disaster *noun* 110
disaster *noun* **failure** 144
disbelieve *verb* **doubt** 119
discard *verb* 111
discipline *verb* **punish** 322
disclose *verb* **reveal** 345
disconnect *verb* **interrupt** 221
verb **separate** 366
discontented
adjective **dissatisfied** 116
discordant *adjective* 111
discount *adjective* **cheap** 54
discourage *verb* 112
discouraging
adjective **pessimistic** 298
discover *verb* **find** 154
verb **realise** 329
discreet *adjective* **wary** 460
discriminatory *adjective* **unfair** 444
discussion *noun* **talk** 415
disdain *noun* **scorn** 360
disembark *verb* **land** 233
disentangle *verb* **simplify** 380
disgruntled
adjective **dissatisfied** 116
disguise *verb* **hide** 194
disgust *verb* 112
dishevelled *adjective* **scruffy** 361
dishonest *adjective* 113
disinclined *adjective* **unwilling** 449
disinterested *adjective* **neutral** 275
disjointed *adjective* **inarticulate** 207
dislike *noun* 113
dislodge *verb* **remove** 337
disloyal *adjective* **unfaithful** 445
dismal *adjective* **dreary** 120
adjective **pathetic** 292
dismount *verb* **land** 233
disobedient *adjective* 114
disobey *verb* 114
disobey *verb* **rebel** 330
disorganise *verb* 115
disorganised *adjective* **untidy** 448
dispatch *noun* **message** 257
verb **send** 365
dispel *verb* **repel** 339
dispensable
adjective **insignificant** 218
dispensation *noun* **permission** 296
dispense *verb* **distribute** 118
disperse *verb* **scatter** 358
display *noun* 115
display *verb* **show** 374
displeased *adjective* **dissatisfied** 116
disprove *verb* 116

dispute *noun* **argument** 18
verb **disagree** 108
disqualify *verb* **ban** 27
disregard *verb* **neglect** 273
disrespect *noun* **scorn** 360
disrupt *verb* **disorganise** 115
dissatisfied *adjective* 116
dissent *verb* **disagree** 108
dissident *adjective* **defiant** 101
dissipate *verb* **scatter** 358
dissolve *verb* **cancel** 49
verb **disappear** 109
dissonant *adjective* **discordant** 111
dissuade *verb* **discourage** 112
distant *adjective* 117
distinct *adjective* **obvious** 280
distinguished *adjective* 117
distort *verb* **misrepresent** 262
distorted *adjective* **crooked** 87
distract *verb* **confuse** 76
distress *noun* **poverty** 307
verb **upset** 450
distribute *verb* 118
distribute *verb* **scatter** 358
distrust *verb* **doubt** 119
disturb *verb* **disorganise** 115
verb **interrupt** 221
disturbed *adjective* **upset** 450
ditch *noun* **groove** 185
verb **discard** 111
dive *verb* **dart** 94
diverge *verb* **ramble** 326
diverse *adjective* **various** 453
divide *verb* **separate** 366
verb **share** 370
dividend *noun* **profit** 316
divine *verb* **predict** 311
docile *adjective* **obedient** 278
dock *verb* **subtract** 407
document *noun* **report** 340
dogged *adjective* **persistent** 297
dole out *verb* **share** 370
dominant *adjective* **powerful** 308
dominate *verb* **rule** 352
verb **subdue** 405
domineering
adjective **tyrannical** 439
donate *verb* **give** 176
donation *noun* **gift** 176
doodle *verb* **write** 472
dope *noun* **information** 215
dossier *noun* **report** 340
dote on *verb* **love** 247
dotty *adjective* **mad** 247
double *adjective* 118
doublecross *verb* **betray** 34
doubt *verb* 119
doubtful *adjective* **uncertain** 441
dour *adjective* **solemn** 390
down-to-earth
adjective **practical** 309
downtrodden
adjective **submissive** 406
downy *adjective* **soft** 389
doze *verb* **sleep** 383
drab *adjective* 119
draft *verb* **compose** 72
drag *verb* **pull** 322
draw *verb* **attract** 24
verb **pull** 322
drawback *noun* **obstacle** 280
dreadful *adjective* **horrible** 199
dream *verb* **imagine** 205
dreamy *adjective* 120
dreary *adjective* 120
drench *verb* **soak** 388
dress *noun* **clothing** 61
dribble *verb* **drip** 121
drift *noun* **meaning** 254
drill *noun* **practice** 309
verb **teach** 419
drink *verb* 121
drip *verb* 121
drive *verb* **force** 162
verb **push** 323
drive someone up the wall
verb **anger** 13
drizzle *verb* **rain** 326
droll *adjective* **funny** 171
droop *verb* **sag** 354

drop *verb* 122
drop *noun* **trace** 433
verb **descend** 104
verb **exclude** 139
drop in *verb* **visit** 456
drowse *verb* **sleep** 383
drudgery *noun* **work** 470
drugged
adjective **unconscious** 442
drum *verb* **throb** 429
dry *adjective* 122
dry *adjective* **sour** 392
dual *adjective* **double** 118
dub *verb* **name** 269
dubious *adjective* **uncertain** 441
dud *adjective* **inferior** 212
noun **failure** 144
dull *adjective* 123
dull *adjective* **boring** 39
adjective **cloudy** 62
adjective **stupid** 405
dumb *adjective* **stupid** 405
dump *verb* **discard** 111
dupe *verb* **deceive** 96
duplicate *adjective* **double** 118
noun **copy** 80
verb **copy** 80
durable *adjective* **hardy** 189
dutiful *adjective* **obedient** 278
adjective **reliable** 335
duty *noun* **task** 417
dwell *verb* **reside** 341
dwindle *verb* **shrink** 376
dye *verb* **colour** 65
dynamic *adjective* **energetic** 131
adjective **moving** 266

Ee

eager *adjective* **enthusiastic** 132
earth *noun* 123
ease *noun* **comfort** 68
verb **comfort** 68
verb **further** 171
verb **insert** 217
easy *adjective* 124
easygoing *adjective* **informal** 214
eat *verb* 124
ebb *verb* **reverse** 346
ebony *adjective* **black** 35
eclipse *verb* **darken** 93
economical *adjective* **thrifty** 428
ecstatic *adjective* **joyful** 228
edge *noun* 125
edgy *adjective* **nervous** 274
educate *verb* **teach** 419
educated *adjective* 125
effect *noun* **result** 344
effigy *noun* **copy** 80
effort *noun* **achievement** 5
noun **attempt** 23
noun **work** 470
effortless *adjective* **easy** 124
egotistic *adjective* **conceited** 73
eisteddfod *noun* **concert** 74
elaborate *adjective* **complicated** 72
elastic *adjective* 126
elated *adjective* **joyful** 228
elderly *adjective* **adult** 7
elect *verb* **prefer** 311
elegant *adjective* **chic** 55
elevate *verb* **lift** 240
elevated *adjective* **tall** 417
elfin *adjective* **slight** 383
elope *verb* **flee** 157
eloquent *adjective* **fluent** 160
elucidate *verb* **explain** 142
elude *verb* **avoid** 25
emancipate *verb* **free** 166
embark *verb* **begin** 31
embellish *verb* **expand** 139
emblem *noun* **sign** 378
embrace *verb* **hug** 200
verb **include** 207
embroider *verb* **expand** 139
verb **sew** 367

emerald *adjective* **green** 183
emerge *verb* **appear** 16
emigrate *verb* **leave** 237
eminent *adjective* **important** 205
emphasise *verb* 126
employ *verb* **use** 451
empty *adjective* 127
emulsify *verb* **mix** 263
encircle *verb* **enclose** 127
enclose *verb* 127
enclose *verb* **insert** 217
encounter *verb* **meet** 256
encourage *verb* 128
encumbrance *noun* **weight** 463
end *noun* 128
end *verb* 129
end *verb* **finish** 155
endanger *verb* 129
endeavour *noun* **attempt** 23
endless *adjective* **continuous** 78
adjective **countless** 82
endorse *verb* **approve** 17
endurance *noun* **persistence** 297
endure *verb* 130
endure *verb* **continue** 78
enduring *adjective* **steadfast** 398
enemy *noun* 130
energetic *adjective* 131
engagement *noun* **undertaking** 443
engineer *verb* **plan** 301
engulf *verb* **flood** 158
enhance *verb* **improve** 206
enjoy *verb* **like** 241
enjoyable *adjective* **nice** 276
enlarge *verb* 131
enormous *adjective* **huge** 201
enough *adjective* **sufficient** 408
enquiring *adjective* **inquisitive** 217
enrage *verb* **anger** 13
enrich *verb* **improve** 206
enter *verb* **record** 331
enterprise *noun* **undertaking** 443
entertainer *noun* 132
enthusiastic *adjective* 132
entice *verb* **charm** 53
entire *adjective* **whole** 466
entreat *verb* **ask** 20
enumerate *verb* **list** 244
enunciate *verb* **pronounce** 317
envelop *verb* **cover** 84
envious *adjective* **jealous** 225
environment
noun **surroundings** 412
environs *noun* **surroundings** 412
envoy *noun* **messenger** 258
ephemeral *adjective* **momentary** 265
epigram *noun* **saying** 357
epistle *noun* **message** 257
equal *adjective* 133
equipped *adjective* **ready** 329
equivalent *adjective* **equal** 133
eradicate *verb* **destroy** 105
erase *verb* **remove** 337
erect *verb* **build** 45
err *verb* 133
errand *noun* **task** 417
erratic *adjective* 134
erroneous *adjective* **incorrect** 209
error *noun* **mistake** 263
erudite *adjective* **educated** 125
escape *verb* **flee** 157
escapee *noun* 134
escort *verb* **accompany** 3
essence *noun* **meaning** 254
essential *adjective* **necessary** 273
establish *verb* **initiate** 216
verb **position** 306
established *adjective* **formal** 164
esteem *noun* **respect** 342
estimate *verb* **measure** 255
estuary *noun* **bay** 28
eternal *adjective* **permanent** 295
ethereal *adjective* **shadowy** 368
ethical *adjective* **decent** 97
ethnic *adjective* **foreign** 163
euthanasia *noun* **homicide** 198
evacuate *verb* **quit** 325
evade *verb* **avoid** 25
evaluate *verb* **judge** 228
even *adjective* **flat** 156

even-handed *adjective* **neutral** 275
everlasting
adjective **permanent** 295
evict *verb* **expel** 140
evident *adjective* **clear** 59
adjective **obvious** 280
evil *adjective* 135
evil *noun* **misfortune** 262
evoke *verb* **cause** 52
exact *adjective* **precise** 310
exaggerate *verb* **misrepresent** 262
exam *noun* **test** 422
examination *noun* **inquiry** 216
examine *verb* 135
example *noun* 136
exasperate *verb* **annoy** 14
exasperating *adjective* **annoying** 15
excavate *verb* **dig** 107
excellent *adjective* 136
exceptional *adjective* **excellent** 136
excess *noun* 137
excessive *adjective* **extra** 143
exchange *verb* 137
excise *verb* **remove** 337
excited *adjective* 138
exciting *adjective* 138
exclamation *noun* **comment** 69
exclude *verb* 139
exclusive *adjective* **single** 381
excursion *noun* **journey** 227
excuse *verb* **forgive** 164
verb **justify** 229
execute *verb* **kill** 230
exertion *noun* **work** 470
exhaust *verb* **tire** 430
exhausted *adjective* **tired** 431
exhaustive *adjective* **thorough** 426
exhibit *verb* **show** 374
exhibition *noun* **display** 115
exhibitionist *noun* **show-off** 374
exhilarated *adjective* **excited** 138
exhilarating *adjective* **exciting** 138
exile *verb* **expel** 140
exist *verb* **live** 245
exorbitant *adjective* **dear** 96
exotic *adjective* **foreign** 163
expand *verb* 139
expand *verb* **enlarge** 131
verb **increase** 209
expansive *adjective* **spacious** 393
expect *verb* 140
expected *adjective* **likely** 242
expedition *noun* **journey** 227
expel *verb* 140
expend *verb* **pay** 294
expendable
adjective **insignificant** 218
expense *noun* **price** 313
expensive *adjective* **dear** 96
experience *verb* **sense** 365
experienced *adjective* 141
expert *noun* 141
expert *adjective* **competent** 70
expire *verb* **die** 106
verb **end** 129
explain *verb* 142
explain *verb* **justify** 229
explicit *adjective* **clear** 59
exploit *noun* **deed** 98
verb **use** 451
explore *verb* **investigate** 223
expose *verb* **endanger** 129
verb **reveal** 345
exposed *adjective* **bare** 28
adjective **visible** 456
adjective **vulnerable** 457
express *adjective* **fast** 148
verb **describe** 104
exquisite *adjective* **beautiful** 29
extend *verb* 142
extensive *adjective* **wide** 466
exterior *noun* **outside** 287
exterminate *verb* **destroy** 105
extra *adjective* 143
extract *verb* **remove** 337
extraordinary
adjective **unusual** 449
adjective **wonderful** 469
eye-catching
adjective **spectacular** 394

Ff

fabric *noun* **cloth** 61
fabulous *adjective* **wonderful** 469
facade *noun* **outside** 287
face *noun* **outside** 287
facilitate *verb* **further** 171
factual *adjective* **genuine** 174
fad *noun* **fashion** 147
fade *verb* **disappear** 109
faded *adjective* **colourless** 66
fail *verb* 143
failure *noun* 144
faint *adjective* **quiet** 325
adjective **vague** 453
fair *adjective* 144
fair *adjective* **fine** 155
adjective **ordinary** 286
adjective **pretty** 312
faith *noun* **religion** 335
faithful *adjective* 145
fake *adjective* 145
fall *verb* 146
fall *verb* **happen** 187
fallen *adjective* **dead** 95
fall through *verb* **fail** 143
false *adjective* **fake** 145
adjective **incorrect** 209
adjective **unfaithful** 445
falsetto *adjective* **high-pitched** 195
falsify *verb* **misrepresent** 262
faltering
adjective **inarticulate** 207
family *noun* 146
famous *adjective* 147
fan *verb* **cool** 79
fanciful *adjective* **imaginary** 204
fancy *verb* **like** 241
verb **want** 458
fantastic *adjective* **excellent** 136
adjective **imaginary** 204
faraway *adjective* **distant** 117
farcical *adjective* **ridiculous** 347
far-fetched
adjective **unbelievable** 441
fascinate *verb* **charm** 53
fashion *noun* 147
fashion *verb* **build** 45
fashionable *adjective* **chic** 55
fast *adjective* 148
fat *adjective* 148
fatal *adjective* 149
fate *noun* 149
fateful *adjective* **significant** 378
fathom *verb* **understand** 443
fatigue *verb* **tire** 430
fatigued *adjective* **tired** 431
fatuous *adjective* **silly** 379
fault *verb* 150
faultless *adjective* **perfect** 295
faulty *adjective* **defective** 99
favour *verb* **prefer** 311
fawn *adjective* **brown** 44
fear *verb* 150
fearful *adjective* 151
fearless *adjective* **brave** 41
feasible *adjective* **possible** 307
feast *noun* **meal** 253
feat *noun* **achievement** 5
feathery *adjective* **light** 241
fed up *adjective* **annoyed** 14
adjective **bored** 39
fee *noun* **pay** 293
feeble *adjective* **powerless** 308
adjective **weak** 461
feed *noun* **meal** 253
feedback *noun* **reaction** 328
feel *verb* **sense** 365
verb **touch** 432
feeling *noun* 151
feign *verb* **imagine** 205
felon *noun* **criminal** 86
felonious *adjective* **illegal** 204
female *noun* 152
ferocious *adjective* **violent** 455
ferocity *noun* **violence** 454
fester *verb* **rot** 349
fetid *adjective* **smelly** 386

flower *verb* **flourish** 158
fluctuate *verb* 159
fluent *adjective* 160
fluff *verb* **bungle** 45
fluid *adjective* **liquid** 244
fluky *adjective* **accidental** 2
flushed *adjective* **rosy** 348
fluster *verb* **confuse** 76
flustered *adjective* **upset** 450
flutter *verb* **fly** 160
fly *verb* 160
focus *noun* **centre** 52
focus on *verb* **concentrate on** 73
foe *noun* **enemy** 130
fog *verb* **darken** 93
foggy *adjective* **cloudy** 62
fold *verb* **mix** 263
follow *verb* 161
follow *verb* **obey** 279
fond *adjective* **loving** 248
food *noun* 161
fool *verb* **trick** 436
foolhardy *adjective* **rash** 327
foolish *adjective* **silly** 379
foolproof *adjective* **easy** 124
foot *noun* **bottom** 41
foray *noun* **attack** 22
forbid *verb* **prevent** 313
forbidding *adjective* **frightening** 169
force *noun* 162
force *verb* 162
forceful *adjective* **powerful** 308
adjective **violent** 455
ford *verb* **cross** 88
forebear *noun* **ancestor** 12
forecast *noun* 163
forecast *verb* **predict** 311
forefather *noun* **ancestor** 12
foreign *adjective* 163
foreign *adjective* **unrelated** 448
foreman *noun* **boss** 40
foresee *verb* **expect** 140
verb **predict** 311
forewarn *verb* **warn** 459
forge ahead *verb* **advance** 7
forget *verb* **neglect** 273
forgive *verb* 164
forlorn *adjective* **miserable** 261
form *noun* **shape** 369
verb **make** 250
formal *adjective* 164
former *adjective* **past** 292
formula *noun* **rule** 351
forsake *verb* **quit** 325
forthright *adjective* **frank** 165
fortify *verb* **strengthen** 403
fortunate *adjective* **lucky** 248
fortune *noun* **fate** 149
noun **wealth** 462
forward *adjective* **bold** 38
verb **send** 365
foul *adjective* **ugly** 440
verb **spoil** 395
found *verb* **initiate** 216
foundation *noun* **support** 411
founder *verb* **fail** 143
fraction *noun* **number** 277
noun **part** 291
fragile *adjective* 165
fragment *noun* **piece** 299
fragmentary *adjective* **incomplete** 208
fragrance *noun* **smell** 386
frail *adjective* **fragile** 165
adjective **weak** 461
frame *verb* **accuse** 4
framework *noun* **support** 411
frank *adjective* 165
fraud *noun* **crook** 87
fraudulent *adjective* **illegal** 204
fray *noun* **fight** 153
freak out *verb* **fear** 150
free *adjective* 166
free *verb* 166
free *verb* **separate** 366
freelance *adjective* **independent** 210
freeze *verb* **cool** 79
verb **harden** 189
freezing *adjective* **cold** 65
frenzied *adjective* **excited** 138

frequent *adjective* **repeated** 339
fresh *adjective* **new** 275
fret *verb* **worry** 471
friend *noun* 167
friendly *adjective* 167
frighten *verb* 168
frightened *adjective* 168
frightening *adjective* 169
frightful *adjective* **horrible** 199
frigid *adjective* **cold** 65
frisk *verb* 169
frisky *adjective* **lively** 245
fritter away *verb* **waste** 460
frolicsome *adjective* **lively** 245
frontier *noun* **outskirts** 287
frosty *adjective* **cold** 65
frown *verb* 170
frown on
verb **disapprove of** 110
frugal *adjective* **thrifty** 428
frustrate *verb* **hinder** 195
fugitive *noun* **escapee** 134
fulfil *verb* **accomplish** 4
full *adjective* 170
full *adjective* **whole** 466
full of beans
adjective **energetic** 131
fumble *verb* **bungle** 45
fumbling
adjective **incompetent** 208
fundamental *adjective* **main** 249
funny *adjective* 171
furbish *verb* **polish** 303
furious *adjective* **angry** 13
adjective **violent** 455
furrow *noun* **groove** 185
further *verb* 171
furtive *adjective* **secretive** 362
fury *noun* **anger** 12
noun **violence** 454
fuse *verb* **combine** 67
fuss *noun* **commotion** 69
verb **worry** 471
fussy *adjective* **careful** 50
futile *adjective* **useless** 452
future *adjective* 172

Gg

gaffe *noun* **mistake** 263
gag *noun* **joke** 227
gaiety *noun* **happiness** 187
gain *verb* **get** 175
gallant *adjective* **polite** 304
gambol *verb* **frisk** 169
game *noun* **competition** 71
gang *noun* **group** 185
gangling *adjective* **clumsy** 63
gangster *noun* **criminal** 86
gap *noun* **hole** 197
gape *verb* **stare** 396
garb *noun* **clothing** 61
garbage *noun* **rubbish** 350
garish *adjective* **colourful** 66
garrulous *adjective* **talkative** 416
gas *verb* **yak** 472
gash *noun* **cut** 91
verb **tear** 420
gasp *verb* 172
gather *verb* 173
gather *verb* **assemble** 20
verb **conclude** 74
gaudy *adjective* 173
gauge *verb* **measure** 255
gauzy *adjective* **light** 241
gawk *verb* **stare** 396
gay *adjective* **colourful** 66
gaze *verb* **stare** 396
gear *noun* **property** 318
gelatinous *adjective* **gluey** 178
general *adjective* **public** 320
generous *adjective* 174
generous *adjective* **big** 34
genial *adjective* **friendly** 167
genius *noun* **scholar** 359
genteel *adjective* **distinguished** 117

gentle *adjective* **lenient** 239
adjective **peaceful** 294
gentleman *noun* **male** 250
genuine *adjective* 174
genuine *adjective* **frank** 165
geriatric *adjective* **adult** 7
germinate *verb* **flourish** 158
get *verb* 175
get a move on *verb* **hurry** 202
get even *verb* **retaliate** 344
get going *verb* **start** 397
get off *verb* **start** 397
get on someone's nerves *verb* **annoy** 14
ghost *noun* 175
ghostly *adjective* **shadowy** 368
gibe *noun* **wisecrack** 468
gift *noun* 176
gig *noun* **profession** 316
gigantic *adjective* **huge** 201
giggle *verb* **smile** 387
gilt *adjective* **orange** 285
ginger *adjective* **orange** 285
gist *noun* **meaning** 254
give *verb* 176
give away *verb* **blab** 35
give in *verb* 177
give up *verb* **betray** 34
give way *verb* **move** 266
glacé *adjective* **sweet** 414
glacial *adjective* **wintry** 467
glad *adjective* 177
glare *verb* **frown** 170
glaring *adjective* **bright** 43
glassy *adjective* **smooth** 387
glaze *noun* **coating** 64
gleaming *adjective* **shining** 371
glean *verb* **realise** 329
glee *noun* **happiness** 187
gleeful *adjective* **happy** 188
glide *verb* **sail** 354
glimmer *verb* **sparkle** 393
glitter *verb* **sparkle** 393
globe *noun* **ball** 26
globule *noun* **ball** 26
gloom *noun* **misery** 261
gloomy *adjective* **drab** 119
adjective **glum** 179
adjective **pessimistic** 298
glossy *adjective* **shiny** 371
glow *verb* **shine** 370
verb **swelter** 414
glower *verb* **frown** 170
glue *noun* 178
gluey *adjective* 178
glum *adjective* 179
glut *noun* **excess** 137
gnarled *adjective* **rough** 349
goad *verb* **irritate** 224
gobble *verb* **eat** 124
god-fearing *adjective* **religious** 336
goggle *verb* **stare** 396
good *adjective* 179
good *adjective* **well-behaved** 463
good at *adjective* **competent** 70
good-looking *adjective* **pretty** 312
good-natured *adjective* **agreeable** 10
gorgeous *adjective* **beautiful** 29
gossip *noun* 180
gossip *verb* **talk** 416
go to seed *verb* **deteriorate** 105
gouge *verb* **dig** 107
govern *verb* **manage** 251
governess *noun* **teacher** 419
go wrong *verb* **err** 133
grab *verb* 180
gracious *adjective* **polite** 304
grade *noun* 181
grade *verb* **arrange** 19
gradient *noun* **slope** 384
grand *adjective* 181
grand *adjective* **tall** 417
grant *verb* **give** 176
grapple *verb* **fight** 154
grasp *verb* **hold** 197
verb **understand** 443
grasping *adjective* **greedy** 183
grateful *adjective* 182
grave *adjective* **solemn** 390

graze *verb* **scratch** 360
great *adjective* 182
great *adjective* **important** 205
greedy *adjective* 183
green *adjective* 183
green *adjective* **inexperienced** 212
adjective **jealous** 225
adjective **sour** 392
grey *adjective* 184
grey *adjective* **dreary** 120
grieve *verb* 184
grill *verb* **question** 324
verb **toast** 431
grim *adjective* **frightening** 169
grimy *adjective* **dirty** 107
grin *verb* **smile** 387
grind *verb* **crush** 89
verb **smooth** 388
grip *verb* **hold** 197
gripe *verb* **complain** 71
grit *noun* **persistence** 297
groggy *adjective* **sick** 377
groove *noun* 185
grotesque *adjective* **ugly** 440
grotty *adjective* **dirty** 107
ground *noun* **earth** 123
groundless *adjective* **irrational** 224
group *noun* 185
group *verb* **arrange** 19
grow *verb* **increase** 209
verb **produce** 315
grub *noun* **food** 161
grubby *adjective* **dirty** 107
grudging *adjective* **ungrateful** 446
grumble *verb* **complain** 71
grumpy *adjective* 186
guard *verb* **protect** 318
guess *verb* **think** 425
guffaw *verb* **laugh** 234
guide *noun* **adviser** 8
noun **example** 136
noun **indicator** 211
verb **advise** 8
guile *noun* **trickery** 437
gulf *noun* **bay** 28
gullible *adjective* **naive** 268
gulp *verb* **eat** 124
gum *noun* **glue** 178
guru *noun* **adviser** 8
gush *verb* **flow** 159
verb **yak** 472
gutless *adjective* **fearful** 151
adjective **powerless** 308
guts *noun* **inside** 218
guy *noun* **male** 250
guzzle *verb* **drink** 121
gyrate *verb* **spin** 395

Hh

habitat *noun* **surroundings** 412
hairy *adjective* **frightening** 169
half-asleep *adjective* **dreamy** 120
half-hearted *adjective* **apathetic** 16
hallowed *adjective* **holy** 198
halt *noun* 186
halt *verb* **stop** 401
hammer *verb* **beat** 29
hamper *verb* **hinder** 195
handicap *noun* **obstacle** 280
handle *verb* **touch** 432
handsome *adjective* **pretty** 312
handy *adjective* **useful** 451
hang around with
verb **accompany** 3
hanger-on *noun* **dependant** 103
hang-up *noun* **obsession** 279
haphazard *adjective* **accidental** 2
hapless *adjective* **unlucky** 447
happen *verb* 187
happiness *noun* 187
happy *adjective* 188
happy *adjective* **lucky** 248
happy-go-lucky
adjective **optimistic** 284
harakiri *noun* **homicide** 198
hard *adjective* 188

hard *adjective* **difficult** 106
harden *verb* 189
hard-hearted *adjective* **callous** 48
hardship *noun* **misfortune** 262
hard up *adjective* **poor** 305
hard-working *adjective* **busy** 46
hardy *adjective* 189
harebrained *adjective* **rash** 327
harm *verb* **hurt** 203
harmonious *adjective* **peaceful** 294
harp on *verb* **yak** 472
harsh *adjective* **strict** 403
hassle *verb* **annoy** 14
hasten *verb* **hurry** 202
hasty *adjective* **rash** 327
hatch *verb* **concoct** 75
hate *verb* 190
hatred *noun* **dislike** 113
haughty *adjective* **proud** 319
haul *verb* **pull** 322
have all to yourself *verb* **own** 289
have in mind *verb* **intend** 220
haven *noun* **refuge** 333
hawk *verb* **sell** 364
hawkish *adjective* **warlike** 459
haywire *adjective* **untidy** 448
hazardous *adjective* **dangerous** 92
hazel *adjective* **green** 183
hazy *adjective* **cloudy** 62
adjective **vague** 453
head *adjective* **best** 33
headstrong *adjective* **disobedient** 114
healthy *adjective* 190
hearsay *noun* **gossip** 180
heart *noun* **centre** 52
heart-broken *adjective* **miserable** 261
heathen *noun* 191
heave *verb* **gasp** 172
heavy *adjective* 191
heavy *adjective* **thick** 423
heavy-duty *adjective* **hardy** 189
heavy-handed *adjective* **clumsy** 63
heckle *verb* **tease** 420
hectic *adjective* **busy** 46
heed *verb* **obey** 279
heedless *adjective* **ungrateful** 446
hefty *adjective* **heavy** 191
heinous *adjective* **evil** 135
help *noun* 192
help *verb* 192
helper *noun* 193
helpful *adjective* 193
helpful *adjective* **useful** 451
helping *noun* **share** 369
helpless *adjective* **weak** 461
herald *noun* **messenger** 258
herd *noun* **crowd** 88
hermit *noun* 194
hero *noun* **star** 396
heroic *adjective* **brave** 41
hesitant *adjective* **inarticulate** 207
adjective **unwilling** 449
hesitate *verb* **stop** 401
het-up *adjective* **upset** 450
hidden *adjective* **invisible** 223
hide *verb* 194
hideous *adjective* **ugly** 440
higgledy-piggledy *adjective* **untidy** 448
high *adjective* **high-pitched** 195
adjective **smelly** 386
adjective **tall** 417
high class *adjective* **superior** 411
highlight *verb* **colour** 65
verb **emphasise** 126
high-pitched *adjective* 195
high spirits *noun* **happiness** 187
highwayman *noun* **bandit** 27
hijack *verb* **capture** 49
hilarious *adjective* **funny** 171
hinder *verb* 195
hindrance *noun* **obstacle** 280
hint *verb* 196
hint *noun* **trace** 433
hinterland *noun* **the country** 423
hire *verb* **buy** 46
hit *verb* 196
hit *noun* **winner** 467

immaterial *adjective* **unrelated** 448
imminent *adjective* **future** 172
immobile *adjective* **still** 400
immoral *adjective* **indecent** 210
immortal *adjective* **permanent** 295
immune *adjective* **safe** 353
impartial *adjective* **fair** 144
impeccable *adjective* **perfect** 295
impecunious *adjective* **broke** 44
impede *verb* **hinder** 195
impending *adjective* **future** 172
impenitent *adjective* **unashamed** 440
imperative *adjective* **necessary** 273
imperceptible *adjective* **invisible** 223
imperious *adjective* **bossy** 40
impersonate *verb* **mimic** 259
impetuous *adjective* **rash** 327
impious *adjective* **sacrilegious** 352
implausible *adjective* **unbelievable** 441
implore *verb* **ask** 20
imply *verb* **hint** 196
impolite *adjective* **rude** 351
important *adjective* 205
imported *adjective* **foreign** 163
impossible *adjective* 206
impotent *adjective* **powerless** 308
impoverished *adjective* **poor** 305
impracticable *adjective* **impossible** 206
impression *noun* **feeling** 151
imprison *verb* **confine** 75
improbable *adjective* **unbelievable** 441
impromptu *adjective* **sudden** 408
improve *verb* 206
improvise *verb* **create** 86
impudent *adjective* **rude** 351
impulsive *adjective* **sudden** 408
inaccurate *adjective* **incorrect** 209
inadequate *adjective* **insufficient** 219
inane *adjective* **silly** 379
inarticulate *adjective* 207
inattentive *adjective* **dreamy** 120
incandescent *adjective* **shining** 371
incapacitate *verb* **weaken** 461
incapacitated *adjective* **powerless** 308
incense *verb* **anger** 13
incision *noun* **cut** 91
inclination *noun* **wish** 469
incline *noun* **slope** 384
include *verb* 207
income *noun* **pay** 293
incompetent *adjective* 208
incomplete *adjective* 208
inconsiderate *adjective* **selfish** 363
inconsistent *adjective* **irrational** 224
inconspicuous *adjective* **invisible** 223
incorporate *verb* **include** 207
incorrect *adjective* 209
incorrigible *adjective* **naughty** 271
increase *verb* 209
increase *verb* **enlarge** 131
incredible
adjective **unbelievable** 441
adjective **wonderful** 469
indebted *adjective* **grateful** 182
indecent *adjective* 210
indefinite *adjective* **vague** 453
independent *adjective* 210
independent *adjective* **unrelated** 448
in-depth *adjective* **thorough** 426
index *verb* **list** 244
indicator *noun* 211
indifferent *adjective* **apathetic** 16
adjective **mediocre** 255
indignant *adjective* **angry** 13
indigo *adjective* **purple** 323
indisposed *adjective* **sick** 377
indistinct *adjective* **quiet** 325
indolent *adjective* **lazy** 236
induce *verb* **cause** 52
verb **persuade** 298
indulgent *adjective* **broad-minded** 43

industrious *adjective* **busy** 46
industry *noun* **work** 470
inedible *adjective* 211
ineffective *adjective* **useless** 452
ineffectual *adjective* **useless** 452
inept *adjective* **incompetent** 208
inequitable *adjective* **unfair** 444
inert *adjective* **lethargic** 240
inexpensive *adjective* **cheap** 54
inexperienced *adjective* 212
infer *verb* **conclude** 74
inferior *adjective* 212
infidel *noun* **heathen** 191
infinite *adjective* **countless** 82
infirm *adjective* **decrepit** 98
inflamed *adjective* **rosy** 348
inflexible *adjective* **stubborn** 404
influence *noun* 213
influence *verb* 213
inform *verb* 214
informal *adjective* 214
information *noun* 215
infrequent *adjective* **scarce** 358
infringe *verb* **disobey** 114
infuriate *verb* **anger** 13
infuriated *adjective* **annoyed** 14
infuriating *adjective* **annoying** 15
inhabit *verb* 215
inhibit *verb* **hinder** 195
verb **limit** 242
inhospitable
adjective **unfriendly** 445
initiate *verb* 216
in-joke *noun* **wisecrack** 468
injure *verb* **hurt** 203
inky *adjective* **black** 35
inlet *noun* **bay** 28
inmate *noun* **prisoner** 314
innocent *adjective* **naive** 268
innovate *verb* **invent** 222
innovative *adjective* **new** 275
innumerable
adjective **numerous** 278
innumerate *adjective* **ignorant** 203
inquiry *noun* 216
inquisitive *adjective* 217
insane *adjective* **mad** 249
insatiable *adjective* **greedy** 183
insecure *adjective* **vulnerable** 457
insensitive *adjective* **callous** 48
insert *verb* 217
inside *noun* 218
insignificant *adjective* 218
insinuate *verb* **hint** 196
verb **insert** 217
insipid *adjective* **tasteless** 418
insist *verb* **demand** 103
insolent *adjective* **rude** 351
insolvent *adjective* **broke** 44
inspect *verb* 219
inspire *verb* **cause** 52
verb **encourage** 128
install *verb* **position** 306
institute *verb* **initiate** 216
instruct *verb* **inform** 214
verb **teach** 419
instrumentalist *noun* **musician** 268
insubordinate
adjective **disobedient** 114
insufficiency *noun* **lack** 232
insufficient *adjective* 219
insult *verb* 220
insulting *adjective* **rude** 351
intangible *adjective* **shadowy** 368
integer *noun* **number** 277
intellectual *noun* **scholar** 359
intelligence *noun* **information** 215
intelligent *adjective* **clever** 60
intend *verb* 220
intense *adjective* 221
intensive *adjective* **thorough** 426
intentional *adjective* **deliberate** 101
intercede *verb* **negotiate** 274
interfere *verb* **intrude** 222
interim *adjective* **temporary** 421
interior *noun* **inside** 218
interject *verb* **intrude** 222
interjection *noun* **comment** 69
interminable
adjective **continuous** 78

intermittent *adjective* **erratic** 134
intern *verb* **confine** 75
internee *noun* **prisoner** 314
interpret *verb* **explain** 142
interrogate *verb* **question** 324
interrupt *verb* 221
intervene *verb* **negotiate** 274
interview *noun* **talk** 415
verb **question** 324
intimidate *verb* **threaten** 427
intolerant *adjective* **narrow-minded** 270
intricate *adjective* **complicated** 72
intrigue *noun* **plot** 302
verb **plot** 302
introduce *verb* **insert** 217
introvert *noun* **hermit** 194
intrude *verb* 222
inundate *verb* **flood** 158
verb **soak** 388
invalid *adjective* **weak** 461
invalidate *verb* **disprove** 116
invent *verb* 222
invert *verb* **overturn** 288
invest *verb* **pay** 294
investigate *verb* 223
investigation *noun* **inquiry** 216
invisible *adjective* 223
involve *verb* **include** 207
involved *adjective* **complicated** 72
irate *adjective* **angry** 13
ire *noun* **anger** 12
iron *verb* **smooth** 388
irrational *adjective* 224
irregular *adjective* **erratic** 134
adjective **uneven** 444
irrelevant *adjective* **unrelated** 448
irresistible *adjective* **attractive** 25
irresponsible *adjective* **careless** 50
irreverent *adjective* **sacrilegious** 352
irrigate *verb* **wet** 464
irritable *adjective* **grumpy** 186
irritate *verb* 224
irritating *adjective* **annoying** 15
isolate *verb* 225
isolated *adjective* **distant** 117
issue *noun* **offspring** 281
verb **distribute** 118
itemise *verb* **list** 244
ivory *adjective* **white** 465

Jj

jabber *verb* **rave** 327
jack up *verb* **lift** 240
jail *noun* **prison** 314
verb **confine** 75
jam *verb* **press** 312
jamb *noun* **side** 377
jam session *noun* **concert** 74
jargon *noun* **language** 234
jaunt *noun* **journey** 227
jaunty *adjective* **lively** 245
jealous *adjective* 225
jeopardise *verb* **endanger** 129
jest *noun* **joke** 227
jester *noun* **entertainer** 132
jet-black *adjective* **black** 35
jettison *verb* **discard** 111
jittery *adjective* **nervous** 274
job *noun* 226
job *noun* **undertaking** 443
join *verb* 226
join up with *verb* **meet** 256
joke *noun* 227
jolly *adjective* **happy** 188
journal *noun* **publication** 321
journey *noun* 227
journey *verb* **travel** 435
joyful *adjective* 228
jubilant *adjective* **joyful** 228
judge *verb* 228
jumble *noun* **mess** 257
noun **mixture** 264
jump *verb* 229
jumpy *adjective* **nervous** 274

junior *adjective* **subordinate** 406
adjective **young** 473
junk *noun* **rubbish** 350
just *adjective* **fair** 144
justify *verb* 229
jut *verb* **protrude** 319
juvenile *adjective* **young** 473

Kk

keel over *verb* **overbalance** 288
keen *adjective* **enthusiastic** 132
keep *verb* 230
keepsake *noun* **souvenir** 392
key *adjective* **main** 249
keyed up *adjective* **excited** 138
kick the bucket *verb* **die** 106
kid *verb* **trick** 436
kidnap *verb* **abduct** 1
kill *verb* 230
kin *noun* **family** 146
kind *adjective* 231
kinetic *adjective* **moving** 266
kingdom *noun* **country** 83
kitsch *adjective* **gaudy** 173
kleptomaniac *noun* **thief** 424
knave *noun* **crook** 87
knell *verb* **ring** 347
knit *verb* **join** 226
knock *verb* **hit** 196
knock off *verb* **steal** 399
know-all *noun* **show-off** 374
knowing *adjective* **shrewd** 375
knowledgeable
adjective **educated** 125

Ll

label *noun* 231
label *verb* 232
labour *noun* **work** 470
verb **emphasise** 126
verb **work** 470
lacerate *verb* **tear** 420
lack *noun* 232
lacking *adjective* **insufficient** 219
lacklustre *adjective* **dull** 123
laconic *adjective* **reticent** 345
lad *noun* **male** 250
laden *adjective* **full** 170
la-di-da *adjective* **pompous** 304
lady *noun* **female** 152
lagoon *noun* **lake** 233
lake *noun* 233
lament *verb* **grieve** 184
lance *verb* **scratch** 360
land *verb* 233
landscape *noun* **view** 454
language *noun* 234
languid *adjective* **lethargic** 240
lap *verb* **pass** 291
lapse *verb* **misbehave** 260
large *adjective* **big** 34
lash *verb* **thrash** 427
lass *noun* **female** 152
last *verb* **continue** 78
last the distance *verb* **persist** 296
late *adjective* **dead** 95
adjective **modern** 265
adjective **past** 292
laugh *verb* 234
laugh *noun* **joke** 227
laugh off *verb* **minimise** 259
launch *verb* **initiate** 216
lavish *adjective* **generous** 174
law *noun* **rule** 351
law-abiding *adjective* **obedient** 278
lawful *adjective* **legal** 238
lawyer *noun* 235
lax *adjective* **careless** 50
layer *noun* 235
laze *verb* 236
lazy *adjective* 236
lazy *adjective* **slow** 385

leading *adjective* **best** 33
leading light *noun* **star** 396
leaf through *verb* **read** 328
lean *adjective* **thin** 425
verb **slope** 384
leap *verb* **jump** 229
learn *verb* 237
learn *verb* **realise** 329
learned *adjective* **educated** 125
leave *verb* 237
leave *noun* **permission** 296
leave out *verb* **exclude** 139
verb **neglect** 273
lecture *noun* **lesson** 239
lecturer *noun* **teacher** 419
leftovers *noun* **remains** 336
legacy *noun* **gift** 176
legal *adjective* 238
legion *adjective* **numerous** 278
legitimate *adjective* **genuine** 174
adjective **legal** 238
leisure *noun* **rest** 342
leisurely *adjective* **slow** 385
lemon *adjective* **yellow** 473
lengthy *adjective* 238
lenient *adjective* 239
lessen *verb* **minimise** 259
verb **reduce** 332
lesson *noun* 239
let down *verb* **drop** 122
letdown *noun* **disappointment** 109
let fly *verb* **attack** 23
lethal *adjective* **fatal** 149
lethargic *adjective* 240
let off *verb* **forgive** 164
let out *verb* **blab** 35
let slip *verb* **blab** 35
let your thoughts wander
verb **daydream** 95
level *adjective* **equal** 133
adjective **flat** 156
noun **grade** 181
level-headed *adjective* **sensible** 366
lever *verb* **lift** 240
levy *noun* **demand** 102
liable *adjective* **likely** 242
libel *verb* **slander** 382
liberal *adjective* **broad-minded** 43
adjective **generous** 174
liberate *verb* **free** 166
license *verb* **allow** 11
lick *verb* **defeat** 99
lifeless *adjective* **dead** 95
adjective **dull** 123
lift *verb* 240
light *adjective* 241
light *adjective* **agile** 9
adjective **bright** 43
lighten *verb* **comfort** 68
like *verb* 241
likeable *adjective* **agreeable** 10
likely *adjective* 242
likeness *noun* **copy** 80
lilac *adjective* **purple** 323
lily-white *adjective* **white** 465
lime *adjective* **green** 183
limit *verb* 242
limit *noun* **outskirts** 287
limp *verb* 243
limpid *adjective* **transparent** 434
line *noun* 243
linger *verb* **dawdle** 94
link *verb* **join** 226
liquid *adjective* 244
lisp *verb* **mumble** 267
list *verb* 244
list *verb* **slope** 384
listless *adjective* **lethargic** 240
litter *noun* **mess** 257
little *adjective* **small** 385
live *verb* 245
live *verb* **reside** 341
live it up *verb* **rejoice** 334
lively *adjective* 245
lively *adjective* **energetic** 131
livid *adjective* **angry** 13
load *noun* **weight** 463
loaded *adjective* **wealthy** 462
loaf *verb* **laze** 236

loam *noun* **earth** 123
loath *adjective* **unwilling** 449
loathe *verb* **hate** 190
lobby *noun* **club** 62
verb **persuade** 298
locate *verb* **find** 154
verb **position** 306
location *noun* **place** 300
lock up *verb* **confine** 75
lockup *noun* **prison** 314
lodge *verb* **place** 300
verb **reside** 341
lofty *adjective* **grand** 181
adjective **tall** 417
log *verb* **record** 331
logical *adjective* **sane** 355
loiter *verb* **dawdle** 94
loll *verb* **laze** 236
verb **sag** 354
lollop *verb* **jump** 229
lone *adjective* **lonely** 246
adjective **unmarried** 447
lonely *adjective* 246
loner *noun* **hermit** 194
long-drawn-out *adjective* **lengthy** 238
long for *verb* **want** 458
long-suffering *adjective* **patient** 293
longwinded *adjective* **lengthy** 238
look down on *verb* **disapprove of** 110
look forward to *verb* **expect** 140
look in *verb* **visit** 456
look over *verb* **inspect** 219
loom *verb* **appear** 16
loop *noun* **coil** 64
verb **bend** 33
loot *noun* 246
lopsided *adjective* **uneven** 444
loquacious *adjective* **talkative** 416
lordly *adjective* **grand** 181
lose *verb* **pass** 291
lose your nerve *verb* **fear** 150
loud *adjective* 247
loud *adjective* **gaudy** 173
love *verb* 247
lovely *adjective* **beautiful** 29
adjective **nice** 276
loving *adjective* 248
low *adjective* **quiet** 325
adjective **sad** 353
low-down *noun* **information** 215
lower *verb* **drop** 122
verb **reduce** 332
lowly *adjective* **humble** 201
adjective **subordinate** 406
loyal *adjective* **faithful** 145
luck *noun* **fate** 149
lucky *adjective* 248
ludicrous *adjective* **ridiculous** 347
lug *verb* **pull** 322
lukewarm *adjective* **apathetic** 16
lullaby *noun* **song** 391
lumber *verb* **trudge** 437
luminous *adjective* **shining** 371
lurch *verb* **sway** 413
lure *noun* **trap** 434
verb **attract** 24
luscious *adjective* **delicious** 102
lustrous *adjective* **shiny** 371
lyrical *adjective* **musical** 267

Mm

mad *adjective* 249
maddening *adjective* **annoying** 15
made-up *adjective* **imaginary** 204
magazine *noun* **publication** 321
magenta *adjective* **purple** 323
magnanimous *adjective* **generous** 174
magnate *noun* **VIP** 455
magnetic *adjective* **attractive** 25
magnetise *verb* **attract** 24
magnify *verb* **emphasise** 126
maiden *noun* **female** 152
maim *verb* **hurt** 203
main *adjective* 249

maintain *verb* **keep** 230
majestic *adjective* **grand** 181
major *adjective* **main** 249
make *verb* 250
make *verb* **calculate** 47
make a slip *verb* **err** 133
make believe *verb* **imagine** 205
make headway *verb* **advance** 7
make light of *verb* **minimise** 259
make mischief *verb* **misbehave** 260
make out *verb* **understand** 443
makeshift *adjective* **temporary** 421
make the grade *verb* **succeed** 407
make up *verb* **concoct** 75
make up to *verb* **flatter** 156
male *noun* 250
malicious *adjective* **resentful** 340
malign *verb* **slander** 382
malignant *adjective* **fatal** 149
malleable *adjective* **flexible** 157
maltreat *verb* 251
manage *verb* 251
manager *noun* 252
maniacal *adjective* **mad** 249
manipulate *verb* **influence** 213
manner *noun* 252
manoeuvrable *adjective* **moving** 266
manslaughter *noun* **homicide** 198
manual *noun* **book** 38
manufacture *verb* **make** 250
mar *verb* **damage** 92
march *verb* 253
margin *noun* **edge** 125
marine *noun* **sailor** 355
mariner *noun* **sailor** 355
maritime *adjective* **nautical** 272
mark *verb* **label** 232
marker *noun* **indicator** 211
market *noun* **shop** 372
maroon *adjective* **red** 332
marsh *noun* **swamp** 413
martial *adjective* **warlike** 459
marvellous *adjective* **wonderful** 469
mash *verb* **mix** 263
verb **soften** 389
mask *verb* **hide** 194
massive *adjective* **huge** 201
master *noun* **boss** 40
noun **winner** 467
mastermind *noun* **scholar** 359
verb **plan** 301
masticate *verb* **chew** 55
match *noun* **competition** 71
verb **copy** 80
mate *noun* **friend** 167
material *adjective* **actual** 5
noun **cloth** 61
materialise *verb* **appear** 16
matt *adjective* **dull** 123
matter-of-fact
adjective **practical** 309
mature *adjective* **adult** 7
mauve *adjective* **purple** 323
maxim *noun* **saying** 357
meagre *adjective* **scant** 357
meal *noun* 253
mean *adjective* 254
mean *adjective* **unkind** 446
verb **intend** 220
meaning *noun* 254
means *noun* **method** 258
measly *adjective* **scant** 357
measure *verb* 255
medal *noun* **prize** 315
meddle *verb* **intrude** 222
mediate *verb* **negotiate** 274
mediocre *adjective* 255
meditate on *verb* **ponder** 305
medley *noun* **mixture** 264
meek *adjective* **humble** 201
meet *verb* 256
meet *verb* **assemble** 20
meeting *noun* 256
melancholy *noun* **misery** 261
mellow *adjective* **musical** 267
melodious *adjective* **musical** 267
melt *verb* **disappear** 109
memento *noun* **souvenir** 392
memorable *adjective* **significant** 378
memorise *verb* **learn** 237

menace *verb* **threaten** 427
mend *verb* **repair** 338
mentor *noun* **adviser** 8
merchant *noun* **seller** 364
merciful *adjective* **lenient** 239
mercurial *adjective* **fickle** 152
mercy *noun* **pity** 299
merge *verb* **combine** 67
merriment *noun* **happiness** 187
merry *adjective* **happy** 188
mesmerise *verb* **charm** 53
mess *noun* 257
message *noun* 257
mess around *verb* **misbehave** 260
messenger *noun* 258
mess up *verb* **disorganise** 115
messy *adjective* **untidy** 448
meteoric *adjective* **sudden** 408
method *noun* 258
methodical *adjective* **tidy** 430
metropolis *noun* **city** 57
metropolitan *adjective* **civic** 57
middle-of-the-road
adjective **moderate** 264
middling *adjective* **mediocre** 255
might *noun* **force** 162
mighty *adjective* **powerful** 308
migrant *adjective* **foreign** 163
mild *adjective* **fine** 155
adjective **lenient** 239
adjective **tasteless** 418
militant *adjective* **defiant** 101
adjective **warlike** 459
mill *verb* **crush** 89
mimic *verb* 259
mind *verb* **concentrate on** 73
mine *verb* **dig** 107
mingy *adjective* **mean** 254
miniature *adjective* **small** 385
minimise *verb* 259
minimise *verb* **reduce** 332
minister *noun* **clergyman** 59
minor *adjective* 260
minstrel *noun* **singer** 381
minute *adjective* **small** 385
mire *noun* **swamp** 413
mirth *noun* **happiness** 187
misbehave *verb* 260
miscalculate *verb* **err** 133
miscarry *verb* **fail** 143
miscellaneous *adjective* **various** 453
miscellany *noun* **mixture** 264
mischievous *adjective* **naughty** 271
miserable *adjective* 261
miserable *adjective* **pathetic** 292
miserly *adjective* **mean** 254
misery *noun* 261
misfortune *noun* 262
mishap *noun* **misfortune** 262
mislead *verb* **deceive** 96
misrepresent *verb* 262
miss *verb* **avoid** 25
mission *noun* **task** 417
mistake *noun* 263
misty *adjective* **cloudy** 62
mix *verb* 263
mixed *adjective* **various** 453
mixture *noun* 264
mix up *verb* **disorganise** 115
mob *noun* **crowd** 88
mobile *adjective* **moving** 266
mock *verb* **tease** 420
model *noun* **copy** 80
noun **example** 136
moderate *adjective* 264
moderate *verb* **decrease** 97
modern *adjective* 265
modest *adjective* **humble** 201
adjective **moderate** 264
adjective **shy** 376
moist *adjective* **wet** 464
moisten *verb* **wet** 464
mollify *verb* **pacify** 289
molten *adjective* **liquid** 244
momentary *adjective* 265
momentous
adjective **significant** 378
money *noun* **wealth** 462
monk *noun* **hermit** 194
monkey business *noun* **trickery** 437

monopolise *verb* **own** 289
monotonous *adjective* **boring** 39
monstrous *adjective* **bad** 26
adjective **ugly** 440
moody *adjective* **glum** 179
adjective **touchy** 433
moorlands *noun* **country** 423
mop *verb* **wipe** 468
mope *verb* **grieve** 184
mop up *verb* **clean** 58
moral *adjective* **decent** 97
more-ish *adjective* **delicious** 102
morose *adjective* **glum** 179
morsel *noun* **piece** 299
mortar *noun* **glue** 178
moth-eaten *adjective* **decrepit** 98
motionless *adjective* **still** 400
motivate *verb* **encourage** 128
motley *adjective* **various** 453
motto *noun* **saying** 357
mount *verb* **climb** 60
verb **increase** 209
mourn *verb* **grieve** 184
mousy *adjective* **drab** 119
mouth-watering
adjective **delicious** 102
move *verb* 266
move *noun* **deed** 98
moving *adjective* 266
mow *verb* **cut** 91
muck up *verb* **bungle** 45
mucous *adjective* **gluey** 178
muddle *noun* **mess** 257
verb **confuse** 76
muddy *adjective* **opaque** 283
muff *verb* **bungle** 45
muffled *adjective* **quiet** 325
mug *verb* **attack** 23
muggy *adjective* **humid** 202
multiple *adjective* **numerous** 278
multiply *verb* **increase** 209
multitudinous
adjective **numerous** 278
mumble *verb* 267
mumbo jumbo *noun* **nonsense** 277
munch *verb* **chew** 55
mundane *adjective* **mediocre** 255
murder *verb* **kill** 230
murky *adjective* **dark** 93
murmur *noun* **whisper** 465
muscle *noun* **force** 162
muscly *adjective* **strong** 404
muse *verb* **daydream** 95
musical *adjective* 267
musician *noun* 268
mutilate *verb* **hurt** 203
mutiny *noun* **rebellion** 330
verb **rebel** 330
mutter *verb* **mumble** 267
myriad *adjective* **countless** 82
mysterious *adjective* **confusing** 77
mystify *verb* **puzzle** 324
mythical *adjective* **imaginary** 204

Nn

nab *verb* **grab** 180
nag *verb* **complain** 71
nail *verb* **grab** 180
naive *adjective* 268
naked *adjective* **bare** 28
name *noun* 269
name *verb* 269
nap *verb* **sleep** 383
narcissistic *adjective* **conceited** 73
narrate *verb* **tell** 421
narrow *adjective* 270
narrow-minded *adjective* 270
nasty *adjective* 271
nasty *adjective* **unkind** 446
nation *noun* **country** 83
natural *adjective* **simple** 380
naughty *adjective* 271
nauseate *verb* **disgust** 112
nautical *adjective* 272
naval *adjective* **nautical** 272
navy *adjective* **blue** 36
near *adjective* 272

neat *adjective* **tidy** 430
nebulous *adjective* **shadowy** 368
necessary *adjective* 273
need *noun* **poverty** 307
needy *adjective* **poor** 305
neglect *verb* 273
negligent *adjective* **careless** 50
negotiate *verb* 274
neighbouring *adjective* **near** 272
neighbourly *adjective* **friendly** 167
nervous *adjective* 274
net *noun* **trap** 434
neutral *adjective* 275
neutral *adjective* **colourless** 66
new *adjective* 275
news *noun* **information** 215
newspaper *noun* **publication** 321
next *adjective* **future** 172
adjective **near** 272
nibble *verb* **chew** 55
nice *adjective* 276
nice *adjective* **kind** 231
nick *verb* **scratch** 360
verb **steal** 399
nickname *noun* **name** 269
nimble *adjective* **agile** 9
nippy *adjective* **cold** 65
noble *adjective* **distinguished** 117
no-frills *adjective* **cheap** 54
noise *noun* 276
non-committal *adjective* **neutral** 275
nonconformist
adjective **unconventional** 442
nondescript *adjective* **ordinary** 286
nonplussed *adjective* **confused** 77
nonsense *noun* 277
nonsensical *adjective* **ridiculous** 347
normal *adjective* **usual** 452
nosh *noun* **food** 161
nosy *adjective* **inquisitive** 217
notable *adjective* **famous** 147
notch *noun* **cut** 91
note *noun* **message** 257
verb **record** 331
noted *adjective* **famous** 147
notice *verb* **see** 362
noticeable *adjective* **visible** 456
notify *verb* **inform** 214
notion *noun* **thought** 426
notorious *adjective* **famous** 147
not pull your weight *verb* **laze** 236
novel *adjective* **new** 275
noxious *adjective* **poisonous** 303
nucleus *noun* **centre** 52
nude *adjective* **bare** 28
number *noun* 277
number *verb* **count** 82
numeral *noun* **number** 277
numerous *adjective* 278
nurse *verb* **help** 192
verb **hug** 200
nutty *adjective* **mad** 249

Oo

oath *noun* **promise** 317
obedient *adjective* 278
obese *adjective* **fat** 148
obey *verb* 279
objective *adjective* **fair** 144
obligatory *adjective* **necessary** 273
oblige *verb* **help** 192
obliged *adjective* **grateful** 182
obliging *adjective* **helpful** 193
obscure *adjective* **dark** 93
verb **darken** 93
observant *adjective* **alert** 11
observation *noun* **comment** 69
observe *verb* **obey** 279
verb **see** 362
obsession *noun* 279
obsolete
adjective **old-fashioned** 282
obstacle *noun* 280
obstinate *adjective* **stubborn** 404
obstruct *verb* **block** 36
verb **resist** 341
obvious *adjective* 280

obvious *adjective* **clear** 59
occasional *adjective* **scarce** 358
occupation *noun* **job** 226
occupy *verb* **inhabit** 215
verb **own** 289
occur *verb* **happen** 187
odd *adjective* **strange** 402
odds and ends *noun* **remains** 336
odds-on *adjective* **likely** 242
odour *noun* **smell** 386
off *adjective* **inedible** 211
off beam *adjective* **incorrect** 209
off-colour *adjective* **sick** 377
offend *verb* **disgust** 112
offended *adjective* **angry** 13
offender *noun* **criminal** 86
offer *noun* 281
office *noun* **position** 306
official *adjective* **formal** 164
noun **manager** 252
officiate *verb* **rule** 352
off-putting *adjective* **pessimistic** 298
offspring *noun* 281
old *adjective* 282
old-fashioned *adjective* 282
olive *adjective* **green** 183
omen *noun* **forecast** 163
omit *verb* **neglect** 273
only *adjective* **single** 381
onset *noun* **start** 397
onslaught *noun* **attack** 22
ooze *verb* **drip** 121
opaque *adjective* 283
open *adjective* **free** 166
adjective **spacious** 393
adjective **uncertain** 441
adjective **vulnerable** 457
verb **begin** 31
opinion *noun* 283
opponent *noun* **enemy** 130
oppose *verb* **prevent** 313
verb **resist** 341
opposite *adjective* 284
oppress *verb* **subdue** 405
oppressive *adjective* **humid** 202
adjective **tyrannical** 439
opt for *verb* **prefer** 311
optimistic *adjective* 284
option *noun* **choice** 56
opulent *adjective* **spectacular** 394
orange *adjective* 285
orb *noun* **ball** 26
orbit *noun* **course** 84
order *noun* 285
order *verb* **demand** 103
orderly *adjective* **tidy** 430
ordinary *adjective* 286
organisation *noun* 286
organise *verb* **plan** 301
origin *noun* **start** 397
original *adjective* **new** 275
originate *verb* **invent** 222
orthodox *adjective* **usual** 452
ostentatious *adjective* **spectacular** 394
ostracise *verb* **isolate** 225
out cold *adjective* **unconscious** 442
outcome *noun* **result** 344
outfit *noun* **organisation** 286
outgoing *adjective* **friendly** 167
outlaw *noun* **criminal** 86
verb **ban** 27
outlay *noun* **price** 313
outlet *noun* **shop** 372
outline *noun* **summary** 410
verb **tell** 421
outlook *noun* **opinion** 283
noun **view** 454
outlying *adjective* **distant** 117
out-of-date *adjective* **old-fashioned** 282
outset *noun* **start** 397
outside *noun* 287
outskirts *noun* 287
outspread *adjective* **wide** 466
outstanding *adjective* **excellent** 136
outstrip *verb* **pass** 291
overbalance *verb* 288

overbearing *adjective* **bossy** 40
overcast *adjective* **cloudy** 62
overlook *verb* **neglect** 273
overpower *verb* **subdue** 405
overseer *noun* **boss** 40
oversupply *noun* **excess** 137
overt *adjective* **visible** 456
overtake *verb* **pass** 291
overturn *verb* 288
overwhelm *verb* **flood** 158
own *verb* 289

Pp

pace *verb* **walk** 458
pacify *verb* 289
pack *noun* **crowd** 88
packed *adjective* **full** 170
pact *noun* **promise** 317
pad *verb* **expand** 139
verb **walk** 458
pagan *noun* **heathen** 191
pageant *noun* **display** 115
pain *noun* 290
paint *verb* **colour** 65
pal *noun* **friend** 167
pale *adjective* **colourless** 66
adjective **white** 465
palpitate *verb* **throb** 429
paltry *adjective* **scant** 357
pamphlet *noun* **publication** 321
pandemonium *noun* **noise** 276
panic *verb* **fear** 150
panicky *adjective* **frightened** 168
pant *verb* **gasp** 172
parade *noun* **display** 115
verb **march** 253
verb **show** 374
paralyse *verb* **weaken** 461
paraphernalia *noun* **property** 318
parasite *noun* **dependant** 103
parched *adjective* **dry** 122
pardon *noun* 290
pardon *verb* **forgive** 164
park *verb* **place** 300
parliament *noun* **council** 81
parson *noun* **clergyman** 59
part *noun* 291
partial *adjective* **incomplete** 208
adjective **unfair** 444
particle *noun* **piece** 299
partner *noun* **associate** 21
verb **accompany** 3
pass *verb* 291
pass *verb* **become extinct** 30
pass away *verb* **die** 106
passing *adjective* **momentary** 265
passionate *adjective* **intense** 221
passive *adjective* **apathetic** 16
pass on *verb* **send** 365
past *adjective* 292
paste *noun* **glue** 178
pastel *adjective* **colourless** 66
pastoral *adjective* **country** 83
pat *adjective* **precise** 310
verb **touch** 432
patch up *verb* **repair** 338
path *noun* **course** 84
pathetic *adjective* 292
pathetic *adjective* **powerless** 308
patient *adjective* 293
patron *noun* **buyer** 47
pattern *noun* **example** 136
pause *verb* **stop** 401
pave *verb* **coat** 63
pay *noun* 293
pay *verb* 294
peaceful *adjective* 294
peach *adjective* **orange** 285
peak *noun* **top** 432
peal *verb* **ring** 347
pebble *noun* **stone** 401
peculiar *adjective* **strange** 402
peddle *verb* **sell** 364
pelt *verb* **speed** 394
pen *verb* **compose** 72
penalise *verb* **punish** 322
penitent *adjective* **sorry** 391

penitentiary *noun* **prison** 314
pen-name *noun* **name** 269
pennant *noun* **prize** 315
penny-pinching *adjective* **mean** 254
perceive *verb* **sense** 365
verb **understand** 443
perception *noun* **feeling** 151
perennial *adjective* **permanent** 295
perfect *adjective* 295
perfect *verb* **improve** 206
perforation *noun* **hole** 197
perform *verb* **behave** 31
performer *noun* **entertainer** 132
perilous *adjective* **dangerous** 92
perimeter *noun* **outskirts** 287
periodic *adjective* **repeated** 339
peripheral
adjective **insignificant** 218
periphery *noun* **outskirts** 287
perish *verb* **die** 106
verb **rot** 349
permanent *adjective* 295
permission *noun* 296
permissive
adjective **broad-minded** 43
permit *verb* **allow** 11
permitted *adjective* **legal** 238
perpetual *adjective* **permanent** 295
perplex *verb* **puzzle** 324
perplexing *adjective* **confusing** 77
persecute *verb* **subdue** 405
perseverance *noun* **persistence** 297
persevere *verb* **persist** 296
persevering *adjective* **patient** 293
persist *verb* 296
persist *verb* **continue** 78
persistence *noun* 297
persistent *adjective* 297
persistent *adjective* **continuous** 78
adjective **patient** 293
persuade *verb* 298
pert *adjective* **bold** 38
perverse *adjective* **naughty** 271
perverted *adjective* **indecent** 210
pessimistic *adjective* 298
peter out *verb* **decrease** 97
petite *adjective* **slight** 383
petrified *adjective* **frightened** 168
petrify *verb* **frighten** 168
verb **harden** 189
petty *adjective* **minor** 260
petulant *adjective* **grumpy** 186
phantom *noun* **ghost** 175
phenomenal
adjective **wonderful** 469
philosopher *noun* **scholar** 359
phobia *noun* **obsession** 279
phoney *adjective* **fake** 145
phosphorescent
adjective **shining** 371
photocopy *verb* **copy** 80
physical *adjective* **actual** 5
pick *verb* **choose** 56
pickings *noun* **loot** 246
pickpocket *noun* **thief** 424
pick to pieces *verb* **fault** 150
pick up *verb* **capture** 49
verb **recover** 331
pidgin *noun* **language** 234
piece *noun* 299
piecemeal *adjective* **incomplete** 208
piece of advice
noun **suggestion** 409
piffle *noun* **nonsense** 277
pig-headed *adjective* **stubborn** 404
pile up *verb* **gather** 173
pilfer *verb* **steal** 399
pilgrim *noun* **traveller** 435
pinch *noun* **trace** 433
verb **steal** 399
pine away *verb* **grieve** 184
pink *adjective* **red** 332
pinnacle *noun* **top** 432
pioneer *verb* **initiate** 216
pious *adjective* **religious** 336
piquant *adjective* **tasty** 418
pique *verb* **irritate** 224
pirate *noun* **bandit** 27
pitch *noun* **slope** 384
verb **throw** 429

pitch-black *adjective* **black** 35
pitch-dark *adjective* **dark** 93
pitch forward *verb* **fall** 146
pitiful *adjective* **pathetic** 292
pity *noun* 299
place *noun* 300
place *verb* 300
place *verb* **remember** 337
placid *adjective* **calm** 48
plain *adjective* **clear** 59
adjective **obvious** 280
adjective **simple** 380
adjective **tasteless** 418
plan *verb* 301
plan *noun* **summary** 410
verb **intend** 220
plane *verb* **smooth** 388
planned *adjective* **deliberate** 101
plaster *verb* **coat** 63
plausible *adjective* **believable** 32
play down *verb* **minimise** 259
player *noun* **entertainer** 132
playful *adjective* **lively** 245
playmate *noun* **friend** 167
pleasant *adjective* **nice** 276
please *verb* 301
pleased *adjective* **glad** 177
pledge *noun* **promise** 317
plentiful *adjective* **abundant** 2
pliable *adjective* **flexible** 157
plod *verb* **trudge** 437
plodding *adjective* **slow** 385
plot *noun* 302
plot *verb* 302
plump *adjective* **fat** 148
plunder *noun* **loot** 246
ply *verb* **use** 451
poach *verb* **abduct** 1
verb **boil** 37
pointer *noun* **indicator** 211
noun **suggestion** 409
poised *adjective* **calm** 48
poisonous *adjective* 303
polish *verb* 303
polished *adjective* **smooth** 387
polite *adjective* 304
poll *noun* **inquiry** 216
pollute *verb* **spoil** 395
polluted *adjective* **dirty** 107
pompous *adjective* 304
ponder *verb* 305
ponderous *adjective* **heavy** 191
poor *adjective* 305
poor *adjective* **inferior** 212
popular *adjective* **public** 320
populate *verb* **inhabit** 215
pore over *verb* **ponder** 305
portion *noun* **part** 291
portly *adjective* **fat** 148
portray *verb* **describe** 104
position *noun* 306
position *verb* 306
position *noun* **place** 300
positive *adjective* **optimistic** 284
adjective **sure** 412
possess *verb* **own** 289
possessions *noun* **property** 318
possessive *adjective* **jealous** 225
adjective **selfish** 363
possible *adjective* 307
possible *adjective* **believable** 32
post *noun* **position** 306
postman *noun* **messenger** 258
postpone *verb* **defer** 100
posture *noun* **manner** 252
potent *adjective* **powerful** 308
pound *verb* **crush** 89
pour *verb* **rain** 326
pout *verb* **frown** 170
poverty *noun* 307
power *noun* **country** 83
noun **force** 162
noun **influence** 213
powerful *adjective* 308
powerless *adjective* 308
practicable *adjective* **possible** 307
practical *adjective* 309
practice *noun* 309
practised *adjective* **experienced** 141
pragmatic *adjective* **practical** 309

praise *verb* 310
prance *verb* **frisk** 169
prank *noun* **trick** 436
precarious *adjective* **dangerous** 92
precept *noun* **rule** 351
precis *noun* **summary** 410
precise *adjective* 310
preclude *verb* **exclude** 139
predecessor *noun* **ancestor** 12
predict *verb* 311
prediction *noun* **forecast** 163
pre-eminent
adjective **important** 205
prefer *verb* 311
preference *noun* **choice** 56
prehistoric *adjective* **old** 282
prejudice *verb* **influence** 213
prejudiced
adjective **narrow-minded** 270
adjective **unfair** 444
premeditated
adjective **deliberate** 101
preoccupied *adjective* **dreamy** 120
prepare *verb* **make** 250
prepared *adjective* **ready** 329
preposterous
adjective **ridiculous** 347
presence *noun* **appearance** 17
present *noun* **gift** 176
verb **give** 176
preserve *verb* **keep** 230
verb **save** 356
preside *verb* **rule** 352
press *verb* 312
press *verb* **hug** 200
press on *verb* **persist** 296
prestigious *adjective* **important** 205
pretend *verb* **imagine** 205
pretentious *adjective* **pompous** 304
pretty *adjective* 312
prevent *verb* 313
preview *noun* **display** 115
price *noun* 313
pricey *adjective* **dear** 96
prickly *adjective* **touchy** 433
priest *noun* **clergyman** 59
primary *adjective* **main** 249
principal *adjective* **best** 33
print *verb* **write** 472
prison *noun* 314
prisoner *noun* 314
private *adjective* **secret** 361
prize *noun* 315
prize *adjective* **superior** 411
probable *adjective* **believable** 32
adjective **likely** 242
probe *verb* **investigate** 223
procedure *noun* **method** 258
proceed *verb* **advance** 7
proceeds *noun* **profit** 316
proclaim *verb* **publish** 321
procure *verb* **get** 175
prodigy *noun* **expert** 141
produce *verb* 315
produce *verb* **cause** 52
verb **make** 250
profane *adjective* **sacrilegious** 352
profession *noun* 316
professional
adjective **experienced** 141
proficient *adjective* **competent** 70
profile *noun* **side** 377
profit *noun* 316
profound *adjective* **intense** 221
progeny *noun* **offspring** 281
prognosis *noun* **forecast** 163
progress *verb* **advance** 7
prohibit *verb* **prevent** 313
project *noun* **undertaking** 443
verb **protrude** 319
prolific *adjective* **abundant** 2
prolong *verb* **keep** 230
promenade concert
noun **concert** 74
prominent *adjective* **important** 205
adjective **visible** 456
promise *noun* 317
promising *adjective* **lucky** 248
promote *verb* **further** 171

pronounce *verb* 317
propaganda *noun* **information** 215
propel *verb* **push** 323
proper *adjective* **decent** 97
adjective **legal** 238
property *noun* 318
prophesy *verb* **predict** 311
proportion *noun* **part** 291
proposal *noun* **offer** 281
propose *verb* **advise** 8
proposition *noun* **offer** 281
prop up *verb* **strengthen** 403
prospect *noun* **view** 454
prospective *adjective* **future** 172
prosper *verb* **thrive** 428
prosperous *adjective* **wealthy** 462
protect *verb* 318
protected *adjective* **safe** 353
protection *noun* **defence** 100
protégé *noun* **dependant** 103
protrude *verb* 319
proud *adjective* 319
prove *verb* 320
proven *adjective* **genuine** 174
proverb *noun* **saying** 357
providence *noun* **fate** 149
provident *adjective* **thrifty** 428
provisional *adjective* **temporary** 421
provisions *noun* **food** 161
provoke *verb* **cause** 52
verb **irritate** 224
prudent *adjective* **sensible** 366
pseudonym *noun* **name** 269
public *adjective* 320
publication *noun* 321
publish *verb* 321
puff *verb* **gasp** 172
pugnacious *adjective* **aggressive** 9
pull *verb* 322
pull in *verb* **attract** 24
pull your weight *verb* **work** 470
pulp *verb* **soften** 389
pulsate *verb* **throb** 429
pulverise *verb* **crush** 89
pun *noun* **wisecrack** 468
punch *verb* **beat** 29
punctuate *verb* **interrupt** 221
pungent *adjective* **tasty** 418
punish *verb* 322
puny *adjective* **slight** 383
puppet *noun* **slave** 382
purchase *verb* **buy** 46
purchaser *noun* **buyer** 47
pure *adjective* **clean** 58
purple *adjective* 323
purposeful *adjective* **deliberate** 101
pursue *verb* **follow** 161
verb **seek** 363
push *verb* 323
push on *verb* **advance** 7
put a damper on
verb **discourage** 112
put at risk *verb* **endanger** 129
put down *verb* **kill** 230
put in the picture *verb* **inform** 214
putrefy *verb* **rot** 349
putrid *adjective* **smelly** 386
put up *verb* **build** 45
put up with *verb* **endure** 130
put your feet up *verb* **rest** 343
puzzle *verb* 324
puzzled *adjective* **confused** 77
puzzle out *verb* **solve** 390
puzzling *adjective* **confusing** 77

Qq

quaff *verb* **drink** 121
quagmire *noun* **swamp** 413
quail *verb* **cower** 85
quake *verb* **shake** 368
qualified *adjective* **experienced** 141
qualify *verb* **suit** 410
quality *adjective* **superior** 411
quarantine *verb* **isolate** 225
quarrel *noun* **argument** 18
verb **argue** 18

quarrelsome
adjective **argumentative** 19
quavery *adjective* **inarticulate** 207
querulous *adjective* **dissatisfied** 116
query *verb* **doubt** 119
question *verb* 324
question *verb* **doubt** 119
questionable
adjective **uncertain** 441
questioning
adjective **inquisitive** 217
queue *noun* **line** 243
quick *adjective* **fast** 148
quiet *adjective* 325
quiet *adjective* **peaceful** 294
adjective **reticent** 345
adjective **simple** 380
quieten *verb* **pacify** 289
quip *noun* **wisecrack** 468
quit *verb* 325
quit *verb* **stop** 401
quiz *verb* **question** 324
quota *noun* **share** 369

Rr

race *noun* **competition** 71
verb **compete** 70
verb **speed** 394
racket *noun* **noise** 276
noun **profession** 316
radical
adjective **unconventional** 442
rage *noun* **anger** 12
noun **fashion** 147
rain *verb* 326
raise *verb* **lift** 240
rake in *verb* **gather** 173
rally *verb* **assemble** 20
verb **recover** 331
ram *verb* **push** 323
ramble *verb* 326
rambling *adjective* **lengthy** 238
rancid *adjective* **inedible** 211
random *adjective* **accidental** 2
rank *adjective* **inedible** 211
adjective **smelly** 386
noun **grade** 181
noun **line** 243
rant *verb* **yak** 472
rapacious *adjective* **greedy** 183
rapid *adjective* **fast** 148
rapturous *adjective* **joyful** 228
rare *adjective* **scarce** 358
adjective **unusual** 449
rash *adjective* 327
rasp *verb* **roughen** 350
rate *noun* **price** 313
ration *verb* **distribute** 118
raucous *adjective* **loud** 247
rave *verb* 327
raw *adjective* **inexperienced** 212
adjective **wintry** 467
reach *verb* **come** 67
react *verb* **answer** 15
reaction *noun* 328
read *verb* 328
ready *adjective* 329
real *adjective* **actual** 5
realise *verb* 329
realistic *adjective* **practical** 309
realm *noun* **country** 83
reason *verb* **conclude** 74
reasonable *adjective* **moderate** 264
adjective **sensible** 366
rebel *verb* 330
rebellion *noun* 330
rebellious *adjective* **defiant** 101
rebound *verb* **reverse** 346
rebuff *verb* **refuse** 333
verb **repel** 339
rebuke *verb* **scold** 359
rebut *verb* **disprove** 116
recalcitrant *adjective* **defiant** 101
recall *verb* **remember** 337
recede *verb* **reverse** 346
receive *verb* **get** 175
recent *adjective* **modern** 265

reciprocate *verb* **retaliate** 344
reckless *adjective* **rash** 327
reckon *verb* **calculate** 47
verb **think** 425
recluse *noun* **hermit** 194
reclusive *adjective* **lonely** 246
recognise *verb* **remember** 337
verb **sense** 365
recollect *verb* **remember** 337
recommend *verb* **advise** 8
recommendation
noun **suggestion** 409
recompense *verb* **repay** 338
reconnoitre *verb* **inspect** 219
record *verb* 331
recount *verb* **tell** 421
recover *verb* 331
rectify *verb* **correct** 81
recuperate *verb* **recover** 331
recurrent *adjective* **repeated** 339
red *adjective* 332
redeem *verb* **buy** 46
reduce *verb* 332
reduced *adjective* **cheap** 54
redundant *adjective* **extra** 143
reel *verb* **sway** 413
verb **turn** 438
refined *adjective* **distinguished** 117
reflect on *verb* **ponder** 305
reform *verb* **correct** 81
refrigerate *verb* **cool** 79
refuge *noun* 333
refugee *noun* **escapee** 134
refund *verb* **repay** 338
refuse *verb* 333
refuse *noun* **rubbish** 350
refute *verb* **disprove** 116
regard *noun* **respect** 342
register *verb* **record** 331
regular *adjective* **repeated** 339
regulation *noun* **rule** 351
rehearsal *noun* **practice** 309
reign *verb* **rule** 352
reimburse *verb* **repay** 338
reinforce *verb* **strengthen** 403
reject *verb* **refuse** 333
rejoice *verb* 334
relate *verb* **tell** 421
related *adjective* 334
relations *noun* **family** 146
relatives *noun* **family** 146
relax *verb* **rest** 343
relaxed *adjective* **calm** 48
adjective **informal** 214
relay *verb* **send** 365
release *noun* **pardon** 290
verb **free** 166
relevant *adjective* **related** 334
reliable *adjective* 335
relief *noun* **comfort** 68
noun **help** 192
relieve *verb* **comfort** 68
religion *noun* 335
religious *adjective* 336
relish *verb* **like** 241
reluctant *adjective* **unwilling** 449
remain *verb* **live** 245
remains *noun* 336
remark *noun* **comment** 69
remarkable *adjective* **astonishing** 22
adjective **unusual** 449
remedy *verb* **correct** 81
remember *verb* 337
remnants *noun* **remains** 336
remorseful *adjective* **sorry** 391
remote *adjective* **distant** 117
remove *verb* 337
remove *verb* **subtract** 407
rendezvous *noun* **meeting** 256
renounce *verb* **refuse** 333
renovate *verb* **repair** 338
renowned *adjective* **famous** 147
rent *verb* **buy** 46
repair *verb* 338
repast *noun* **meal** 253
repay *verb* 338
repeal *verb* **cancel** 49
repeated *adjective* 339
repel *verb* 339
repentant *adjective* **sorry** 391

replace *verb* **exchange** 137
replica *noun* **copy** 80
reply *noun* **reaction** 328
verb **answer** 15
report *noun* 340
report *verb* **betray** 34
verb **publish** 321
represent *verb* **describe** 104
repress *verb* **subdue** 405
repressive *adjective* **tyrannical** 439
reprieve *noun* **pardon** 290
reprimand *verb* **scold** 359
reproduce *verb* **copy** 80
republic *noun* **country** 83
repulse *verb* **repel** 339
repulsive *adjective* **nasty** 271
adjective **ugly** 440
request *verb* **ask** 20
require *verb* **demand** 103
requisition *noun* **demand** 102
rescue *verb* **free** 166
verb **save** 356
research *verb* **investigate** 223
resentful *adjective* 340
reserve *verb* **buy** 46
reserved *adjective* **reticent** 345
reservoir *noun* **lake** 233
reside *verb* 341
residue *noun* **remains** 336
resilient *adjective* **elastic** 126
resist *verb* 341
resolve *verb* **solve** 390
resonant *adjective* **loud** 247
respect *noun* 342
respect *verb* **worship** 471
respectable *adjective* **decent** 97
resplendent
adjective **spectacular** 394
respond *verb* **answer** 15
response *noun* **reaction** 328
responsible *adjective* **reliable** 335
rest *noun* 342
rest *verb* 343
rest *verb* **place** 300
restaurant *noun* 343
restless *adjective* **excited** 138
restore *verb* **repair** 338
restrain *verb* **confine** 75
restrained *adjective* **moderate** 264
restrict *verb* **limit** 242
result *noun* 344
résumé *noun* **summary** 410
retailer *noun* **seller** 364
retain *verb* **keep** 230
retaliate *verb* 344
retard *verb* **hinder** 195
reticent *adjective* 345
retire *verb* **leave** 237
retort *verb* **answer** 15
retreat *noun* **refuge** 333
verb **leave** 237
return *noun* **profit** 316
verb **answer** 15
reveal *verb* 345
revel *verb* **rejoice** 334
revere *verb* **worship** 471
reverent *adjective* **religious** 336
reverse *verb* 346
review *verb* **examine** 135
revise *verb* **correct** 81
revolt *noun* **rebellion** 330
verb **disgust** 112
verb **rebel** 330
revolting *adjective* **nasty** 271
revolution *noun* **rebellion** 330
reward *verb* **repay** 338
rhythm *noun* 346
rhythmical *adjective* **repeated** 339
rib *verb* **tease** 420
rich *adjective* **colourful** 66
adjective **wealthy** 462
riches *noun* **wealth** 462
ridicule *noun* **scorn** 360
verb **tease** 420
ridiculous *adjective* 347
rift *noun* **break** 42
rigged out *adjective* **ready** 329
right *adjective* **decent** 97
adjective **fair** 144
adjective **true** 438

Ss

sailor *noun* 355
saintly *adjective* **holy** 198
salary *noun* **pay** 293
salvage *verb* **save** 356
sample *noun* **example** 136
verb **test** 422
sanction *verb* **approve** 17
sanctuary *noun* **refuge** 333
sand *verb* **smooth** 388
sane *adjective* 355
sap *verb* **weaken** 461
sapphire *adjective* **blue** 36
satellite *noun* **dependant** 103
satiated *adjective* **satisfied** 356
satin *adjective* **shiny** 371
satisfactory *adjective* **good** 179
adjective **sufficient** 408
satisfied *adjective* 356
satisfy *verb* **please** 301
saucy *adjective* **bold** 38
saunter *verb* **walk** 458
savage *adjective* **cruel** 89
save *verb* 356
save *verb* **store** 402
savoury *adjective* **tasty** 418
saying *noun* 357
scale *verb* **climb** 60
scamper *verb* **dart** 94
scan *verb* **inspect** 219
scant *adjective* 357
scarce *adjective* 358
scare *verb* **frighten** 168
scared *adjective* **frightened** 168
scaredy-cat *noun* **coward** 85
scare off *verb* **repel** 339
scarlet *adjective* **red** 332
scarper *verb* **flee** 157
scary *adjective* **frightening** 169
scatter *verb* 358
scene *noun* **surroundings** 412
noun **view** 454
scent *noun* **smell** 386
scheme *noun* **plot** 302
verb **plot** 302
scholar *noun* 359
scold *verb* 359
scoop *verb* **dig** 107
scoot *verb* **dart** 94
score *noun* **cut** 91
verb **scratch** 360
scorn *noun* 360
scourge *verb* **thrash** 427
scowl *verb* **frown** 170
scramble *verb* **dart** 94
scrap *noun* **piece** 299
noun **trace** 433
verb **discard** 111
scrappy *adjective* **incomplete** 208
scratch *verb* 360
scratch *verb* **write** 472
scrawl *verb* **write** 472
scream *verb* **shriek** 375
screech *verb* **shriek** 375
screen *verb* **protect** 318
verb **test** 422
screw *verb* **turn** 438
scribble *verb* **write** 472
scrub *verb* **clean** 58
scruffy *adjective* 361
scrumptious *adjective* **delicious** 102
scrupulous *adjective* **honest** 199
scrutinise *verb* **investigate** 223
scuffle *verb* **fight** 154
scurry *verb* **dart** 94
seafarer *noun* **sailor** 355
seafaring *adjective* **nautical** 272
seagoing *adjective* **nautical** 272
seam *noun* **layer** 235
seaman *noun* **sailor** 355
search *verb* **inspect** 219
search for *verb* **seek** 363
seaworthy *adjective* **nautical** 272
secondary *adjective* **minor** 260
second-rate
adjective **mediocre** 255
secret *adjective* 361
secretive *adjective* 362
secretive *adjective* **reticent** 345
section *noun* **part** 291

secure *adjective* **safe** 353
adjective **steady** 398
verb **protect** 318
verb **steady** 399
security *noun* **defence** 100
sedentary *adjective* **still** 400
seductive *adjective* **attractive** 25
see *verb* 362
see eye to eye *verb* **agree** 10
seek *verb* 363
seep *verb* **drip** 121
segment *noun* **part** 291
seize *verb* **grab** 180
select *verb* **choose** 56
selection *noun* **choice** 56
self-centred *adjective* **selfish** 363
self-effacing *adjective* **humble** 201
selfish *adjective* 363
self-sufficient *adjective* **independent** 210
sell *verb* 364
seller *noun* 364
sell out *verb* **betray** 34
seminar *noun* **lesson** 239
senate *noun* **council** 81
send *verb* 365
send up *verb* **mimic** 259
senile *adjective* **adult** 7
sensation *noun* **feeling** 151
sensational *adjective* **excellent** 136
sense *verb* 365
sense *noun* **feeling** 151
noun **meaning** 254
senseless *adjective* **silly** 379
sensible *adjective* 366
sensitive *adjective* **touchy** 433
separate *verb* 366
separate *adjective* **independent** 210
sepia *adjective* **brown** 44
sequel *noun* **result** 344
sequence *noun* **series** 367
serene *adjective* **peaceful** 294
serf *noun* **slave** 382
series *noun* 367
serious *adjective* **significant** 378
adjective **solemn** 390
sermon *noun* **lesson** 239
servant *noun* **slave** 382
serve *verb* **suit** 410
servile *adjective* **submissive** 406
set *verb* **harden** 189
verb **place** 300
set about *verb* **begin** 31
set an example to *verb* **encourage** 128
setback *noun* **disappointment** 109
set down *verb* **compose** 72
set out *verb* **start** 397
setting *noun* **surroundings** 412
settle *verb* **inhabit** 215
settle a score *verb* **retaliate** 344
set up *verb* **plan** 301
severe *adjective* **intense** 221
severity *noun* **violence** 454
sew *verb* 367
shabby *adjective* **unkind** 446
shade *verb* **darken** 93
shadow *verb* **follow** 161
shadowy *adjective* 368
shadowy *adjective* **dark** 93
shady *adjective* **dishonest** 113
shaggy *adjective* **rough** 349
shake *verb* 368
shake a leg *verb* **hurry** 202
shake hands *verb* **agree** 10
sham *adjective* **fake** 145
shambles *noun* **mess** 257
shanghai *verb* **abduct** 1
shape *noun* 369
shape *verb* **build** 45
share *noun* 369
share *verb* 370
shark *noun* **crook** 87
sharp *adjective* **cold** 65
adjective **discordant** 111
adjective **shrewd** 375
adjective **tasty** 418
shear *verb* **cut** 91

shed *verb* **discard** 111
sheer *adjective* **transparent** 434
shelter *noun* **refuge** 333
sheltered *adjective* **safe** 353
shelve *verb* **defer** 100
shield *noun* **defence** 100
verb **protect** 318
shift *verb* **move** 266
shifty *adjective* **dishonest** 113
shimmer *verb* **sparkle** 393
shin *verb* **climb** 60
shine *verb* 370
shine *verb* **polish** 303
verb **succeed** 407
shining *adjective* 371
shiny *adjective* 371
shipshape *adjective* **tidy** 430
shirk *verb* **avoid** 25
shock *verb* 372
shoddy *adjective* **defective** 99
adjective **inferior** 212
shop *noun* 372
shoplifter *noun* **thief** 424
shopper *noun* **buyer** 47
shore up *verb* **strengthen** 403
short *adjective* **abrupt** 1
adjective **brief** 42
adjective **insufficient** 219
adjective **small** 385
shortage *noun* **lack** 232
shorten *verb* 373
shout *verb* 373
shove *verb* **push** 323
show *verb* 374
show *verb* **reveal** 345
show-off *noun* 374
show up *verb* **appear** 16
showy *adjective* **gaudy** 173
shrewd *adjective* 375
shriek *verb* 375
shrill *adjective* **high-pitched** 195
adjective **loud** 247
shrink *verb* 376
shrivel *verb* **shrink** 376
shroud *verb* **cover** 84
shudder *verb* **fear** 150
verb **shake** 368
shuffle *verb* **limp** 243
shut away *verb* **isolate** 225
shy *adjective* 376
sick *adjective* 377
sicken *verb* **disgust** 112
sickly *adjective* **sweet** 414
sick of *adjective* **bored** 39
side *noun* 377
sidepiece *noun* **side** 377
side with *verb* **befriend** 30
sigh *noun* **whisper** 465
sightseer *noun* **traveller** 435
sign *noun* 378
sign *noun* **indicator** 211
significance *noun* **meaning** 254
significant *adjective* 378
silken *adjective* **smooth** 387
silky *adjective* **shiny** 371
adjective **soft** 389
silly *adjective* 379
silver *adjective* **grey** 184
silver-tongued *adjective* **fluent** 160
similar *adjective* 379
simmer *verb* **boil** 37
simple *adjective* 380
simple *adjective* **easy** 124
adjective **naive** 268
simplify *verb* 380
sincere *adjective* **honest** 199
sinful *adjective* **evil** 135
singer *noun* 381
single *adjective* 381
single *adjective* **unmarried** 447
single-minded
adjective **persistent** 297
single out *verb* **prefer** 311
sing someone's praises
verb **praise** 310
singular *adjective* **unusual** 449
sink *verb* **descend** 104
verb **drop** 122
sinuous *adjective* **twisted** 439
sip *verb* **drink** 121

sissy *noun* **coward** 85
site *noun* **place** 300
verb **position** 306
situation *noun* **position** 306
size up *verb* **judge** 228
skeleton *noun* **support** 411
skim *verb* **read** 328
verb **sail** 354
skimpy *adjective* **scant** 357
skin *noun* **coating** 64
skinny *adjective* **thin** 425
skip *verb* **exclude** 139
verb **frisk** 169
skirmish *noun* **fight** 153
skittle *verb* **overturn** 288
skive *verb* **laze** 236
slack *adjective* **lazy** 236
slander *verb* 382
slang *noun* **language** 234
slant *noun* **slope** 384
verb **misrepresent** 262
verb **slope** 384
slash *verb* **tear** 420
slate *adjective* **grey** 184
slave *noun* 382
slave *verb* **work** 470
slay *verb* **kill** 230
sleazy *adjective* **scruffy** 361
sleek *adjective* **shiny** 371
sleep *verb* 383
slender *adjective* **thin** 425
slick *adjective* **fluent** 160
slight *adjective* 383
slight *adjective* **minor** 260
verb **insult** 220
slim *adjective* **thin** 425
slimy *adjective* **gluey** 178
slip *noun* **mistake** 263
verb **fall** 146
verb **insert** 217
slippery *adjective* **smooth** 387
adjective **unfaithful** 445
slit *noun* **cut** 91
noun **hole** 197
verb **tear** 420
sliver *noun* **piece** 299
slog *verb* **trudge** 437
verb **work** 470
slope *noun* 384
slope *verb* 384
sloppy *adjective* **liquid** 244
adjective **scruffy** 361
slothful *adjective* **lazy** 236
slouch *verb* **sag** 354
slow *adjective* 385
slow *adjective* **stupid** 405
sluggish
adjective **lethargic** 240
slumber *verb* **sleep** 383
slump *verb* **sag** 354
sly *adjective* **cunning** 90
smack *verb* **beat** 29
small *adjective* 385
small *adjective* **narrow** 270
small-time
adjective **insignificant** 218
smart *adjective* **chic** 55
adjective **clever** 60
smart alec *noun* **show-off** 374
smear *verb* **coat** 63
verb **dirty** 108
verb **slander** 382
smell *noun* 386
smelly *adjective* 386
smile *verb* 387
smirk *verb* **smile** 387
smooth *adjective* 387
smooth *verb* 388
smooth *adjective* **flat** 156
adjective **fluent** 160
smother *verb* **flood** 158
verb **suffocate** 409
smudge *verb* **dirty** 108
smug *adjective* **proud** 319
snack *noun* **meal** 253
snap *adjective* **sudden** 408
snappy *adjective* **grumpy** 186
snap up *verb* **grab** 180
snare *noun* **trap** 434
verb **catch** 51

snatch *verb* **grab** 180
sneak *verb* **betray** 34
snigger *verb* **smile** 387
snip *verb* **cut** 91
snobbish *adjective* **proud** 319
snoopy *adjective* **inquisitive** 217
snooty *adjective* **pompous** 304
snooze *verb* **sleep** 383
snowy *adjective* **white** 465
snub *verb* **insult** 220
soak *verb* 388
soar *verb* **fly** 160
sob *verb* **cry** 90
sober *adjective* **solemn** 390
sociable *adjective* **friendly** 167
sodden *adjective* **wet** 464
soft *adjective* 389
soft *adjective* **quiet** 325
soften *verb* 389
soft-soap *verb* **flatter** 156
soggy *adjective* **wet** 464
soil *noun* **earth** 123
verb **dirty** 108
soiree *noun* **concert** 74
solace *noun* **comfort** 68
sole *adjective* **single** 381
solemn *adjective* 390
solicitor *noun* **lawyer** 235
solid *adjective* **heavy** 191
adjective **thick** 423
solidify *verb* **harden** 189
solitary *adjective* **lonely** 246
soloist *noun* **musician** 268
solve *verb* 390
sombre *adjective* **drab** 119
somersault *verb* **overbalance** 288
sometime *adjective* **past** 292
song *noun* 391
soothe *verb* **comfort** 68
soprano
adjective **high-pitched** 195
sorrow *noun* **misery** 261
sorry *adjective* 391
sort *verb* **arrange** 19
sort out *verb* **simplify** 380
sound *adjective* **healthy** 190
adjective **sane** 355
verb **measure** 255
verb **pronounce** 317
sour *adjective* 392
souvenir *noun* 392
spacious *adjective* 393
span *verb* **cross** 88
spare *verb* **forgive** 164
sparkle *verb* 393
sparse *adjective* **scant** 357
spasm *noun* **pain** 290
spasmodic *adjective* **momentary** 265
speak well of *verb* **praise** 310
specialist *noun* **expert** 141
specimen *noun* **example** 136
spectacular *adjective* 394
spectre *noun* **ghost** 175
speed *verb* 394
speedy *adjective* **fast** 148
spell out *verb* **explain** 142
spend *verb* **pay** 294
sphere *noun* **ball** 26
spick-and-span *adjective* **clean** 58
spicy *adjective* **tasty** 418
spill the beans *verb* **blab** 35
spin *verb* 395
spindly *adjective* **thin** 425
spineless *adjective* **fearful** 151
spiral *noun* **coil** 64
spirited *adjective* **energetic** 131
spit *verb* **rain** 326
spiteful *adjective* **resentful** 340
splendid *adjective* **great** 182
split *noun* **break** 42
verb **share** 370
splurge *verb* **waste** 460
splutter *verb* **mumble** 267
spoil *verb* 395
spoils *noun* **loot** 246
spoilt *adjective* **selfish** 363
sponge *verb* **wipe** 468
spongy *adjective* **soft** 389
spontaneous *adjective* **free** 166
spook *noun* **ghost** 175

stipulate *verb* **demand** 103
stir *verb* **mix** 263
verb **move** 266
stitch *noun* **pain** 290
verb **sew** 367
stockpile *verb* **store** 402
stocky *adjective* 400
stodgy *adjective* **heavy** 191
stoical *adjective* **patient** 293
stone *noun* 401
stony *adjective* **callous** 48
stop *verb* 401
stop *verb* **end** 129
verb **prevent** 313
stop by *verb* **visit** 456
stoppage *noun* **halt** 186
store *verb* 402
store *noun* **shop** 372
stout *adjective* **fat** 148
stout-hearted
adjective **steadfast** 398
stow *verb* **store** 402
straightforward *adjective* **clear** 59
adjective **frank** 165
strain *verb* **tire** 430
straitlaced *adjective* **strict** 403
strange *adjective* 402
strangle *verb* **suffocate** 409
stratagem *noun* **plot** 302
stratum *noun* **layer** 235
stray *verb* **ramble** 326
streak *verb* **speed** 394
stream *verb* **flow** 159
streamline *verb* **simplify** 380
strength *noun* **force** 162
strengthen *verb* 403
stress *verb* **emphasise** 126
stretch *verb* **extend** 142
stretchy *adjective* **elastic** 126
strew *verb* **scatter** 358
strict *adjective* 403
stride *verb* **march** 253
strike *verb* **hit** 196
string *noun* **line** 243
strive for *verb* **seek** 363
stroke *verb* **touch** 432
stroll *verb* **walk** 458
strong *adjective* 404
strong *adjective* **powerful** 308
stroppy *adjective* **argumentative** 19
structure *noun* **shape** 369
struggle *verb* **fight** 154
strut *verb* **march** 253
stubborn *adjective* 404
stuck-up *adjective* **conceited** 73
study *verb* **examine** 135
verb **read** 328
stuff *noun* **cloth** 61
stumble *verb* **fall** 146
stumpy *adjective* **stocky** 400
stunned *adjective* **astonished** 21
adjective **unconscious** 442
stunning *adjective* **beautiful** 29
stupendous
adjective **astonishing** 22
stupid *adjective* 405
sturdy *adjective* **hardy** 189
adjective **steadfast** 398
stutter *verb* **mumble** 267
subdue *verb* 405
subject *noun* **slave** 382
submerge *verb* **drop** 122
submissive *adjective* 406
submit *verb* **give in** 177
subordinate *adjective* 406
subservient
adjective **submissive** 406
subsidiary
adjective **subordinate** 406
substandard *adjective* **defective** 99
substantial *adjective* **big** 34
substantiate *verb* **prove** 320
substitute *verb* **exchange** 137
subterfuge *noun* **trickery** 437
subtract *verb* 407
suburb *noun* **city** 57
suburban *adjective* **civic** 57
succeed *verb* 407
success *noun* **achievement** 5
succession *noun* **series** 367

succumb *verb* **give in** 177
suck up to *verb* **flatter** 156
sudden *adjective* 408
suffer *verb* **allow** 11
verb **endure** 130
suffice *verb* **suit** 410
sufficient *adjective* 408
suffocate *verb* 409
sugary *adjective* **sweet** 414
suggest *verb* **advise** 8
verb **hint** 196
suggestion *noun* 409
suicide *noun* **homicide** 198
suit *verb* 410
sullen *adjective* **glum** 179
sultry *adjective* **humid** 202
summarise *verb* **shorten** 373
summary *noun* 410
summit *noun* **top** 432
summons *noun* **order** 285
sum up *verb* **shorten** 373
sunny *adjective* **fine** 155
super *adjective* **great** 182
superb *adjective* **great** 182
supercilious *adjective* **proud** 319
superfluous *adjective* **extra** 143
superintendent
noun **manager** 252
superior *adjective* 411
supermarket *noun* **shop** 372
supervise *verb* **manage** 251
supervisor *noun* **boss** 40
supple *adjective* **flexible** 157
supplement *verb* **add** 6
support *noun* 411
support *verb* **help** 192
verb **steady** 399
supportive *adjective* **helpful** 193
suppose *verb* **think** 425
suppress *verb* **prevent** 313
sure *adjective* 412
surface *noun* **outside** 287
verb **come** 67
surge *verb* **flow** 159
surly *adjective* **glum** 179
surplus *adjective* **extra** 143
noun **excess** 137
noun **remains** 336
surprised *adjective* **astonished** 21
surrender *verb* **give in** 177
surreptitious
adjective **secretive** 362
surround *verb* **enclose** 127
surroundings *noun* 412
survey *noun* **inquiry** 216
verb **inspect** 219
verb **measure** 255
survive *verb* **continue** 78
verb **live** 245
susceptible *adjective* **vulnerable** 457
suspect *verb* **think** 425
suspend *verb* **defer** 100
sustain *verb* **keep** 230
swab *verb* **wipe** 468
swagger *verb* **march** 253
swallow *verb* **drink** 121
swamp *noun* 413
swamp *verb* **flood** 158
verb **soak** 388
swap *verb* **exchange** 137
sway *verb* 413
sway *noun* **influence** 213
sweat out *verb* **worry** 471
sweet *adjective* 414
sweet *adjective* **musical** 267
sweet-talk *verb* **flatter** 156
swell *verb* **protrude** 319
swelter *verb* 414
sweltering *adjective* **hot** 200
swift *adjective* **fast** 148
swindle *noun* **trick** 436
verb **cheat** 54
swing *noun* **rhythm** 346
swirl *verb* **spin** 395
switch off *verb* **daydream** 95
symbol *noun* **sign** 378
symmetrical *adjective* **equal** 133
sympathy *noun* **pity** 299
syndicate *noun* **organisation** 286

Tt

termination *noun* **end** 128
terracotta *adjective* **orange** 285
terrible *adjective* **horrible** 199
terrific *adjective* **excellent** 136
adjective **good** 179
terrify *verb* **frighten** 168
terrorise *verb* **frighten** 168
terse *adjective* **abrupt** 1
test *noun* 422
test *verb* 422
textbook *noun* **book** 38
textile *noun* **cloth** 61
thankful *adjective* **grateful** 182
thankless *adjective* **ungrateful** 446
thaw *verb* **soften** 389
the country *noun* 423
theology *noun* **religion** 335
theory *noun* **thought** 426
the sticks *noun* **the country** 423
thick *adjective* 423
thick *adjective* **gluey** 178
adjective **opaque** 283
adjective **stupid** 405
thicken *verb* 424
thickset *adjective* **stocky** 400
thief *noun* 424
thieve *verb* **steal** 399
thin *adjective* 425
think *verb* 425
thin-skinned *adjective* **touchy** 433
thorough *adjective* 426
thought *noun* 426
thoughtful *adjective* **kind** 231
thoughtless *adjective* **careless** 50
thrash *verb* 427
thrash *verb* **defeat** 99
threadbare *adjective* **decrepit** 98
threaten *verb* 427
threaten *verb* **endanger** 129
thrifty *adjective* 428
thrilled *adjective* **excited** 138
adjective **glad** 177
thrilling *adjective* **exciting** 138
thrive *verb* 428
throb *verb* 429
throng *noun* **crowd** 88
throw *verb* 429
throw in *verb* **add** 6
throw out *verb* **expel** 140
thrust *verb* **push** 323
thump *verb* **beat** 29
ticket *noun* **label** 231
tickled pink *adjective* **glad** 177
tick off *verb* **scold** 359
tidy *adjective* 430
tight *adjective* **mean** 254
adjective **narrow** 270
tilt *noun* **slope** 384
verb **slope** 384
time *noun* **rhythm** 346
timeworn *adjective* **decrepit** 98
timid *adjective* **fearful** 151
tinkle *noun* **whisper** 465
tint *verb* **colour** 65
tiny *adjective* **small** 385
tip *noun* **forecast** 163
noun **suggestion** 409
verb **slope** 384
tip off *verb* **warn** 459
tip over *verb* **overturn** 288
tire *verb* 430
tired *adjective* 431
tired of *adjective* **bored** 39
title *noun* **name** 269
verb **name** 269
titter *verb* **smile** 387
toast *verb* 431
toast *verb* **acclaim** 3
toddle *verb* **limp** 243
toil *verb* **trudge** 437
verb **work** 470
token *noun* **sign** 378
noun **souvenir** 392
tolerant *adjective* **broad-minded** 43
adjective **patient** 293
tolerate *verb* **allow** 11
verb **endure** 130
toll *verb* **ring** 347
tomboy *noun* **female** 152
tongue *noun* **language** 234

tongue-tied
adjective **inarticulate** 207
top *noun* 432
top *adjective* **best** 33
topple *verb* **fall** 146
torment *verb* **maltreat** 251
torture *verb* **maltreat** 251
toss *verb* **throw** 429
toss and turn *verb* **fidget** 153
total *adjective* **whole** 466
verb **count** 82
totalitarian *adjective* **tyrannical** 439
totem *noun* **sign** 378
totter *verb* **limp** 243
touch *verb* 432
touch down *verb* **land** 233
touchy *adjective* 433
tough *adjective* **difficult** 106
adjective **hard** 188
adjective **hardy** 189
tour *noun* **journey** 227
tourist *noun* **traveller** 435
tow *verb* **pull** 322
towel *verb* **wipe** 468
towering *adjective* **tall** 417
toxic *adjective* **poisonous** 303
trace *noun* 433
trace *verb* **copy** 80
verb **find** 154
track *noun* **course** 84
verb **follow** 161
tractable *adjective* **obedient** 278
trade *noun* **profession** 316
traditional *adjective* **usual** 452
tragedy *noun* **disaster** 110
train *verb* **teach** 419
trainer *noun* **teacher** 419
training *noun* **practice** 309
traitorous *adjective* **unfaithful** 445
tramp *verb* **trudge** 437
trample *verb* **press** 312
tranquil *adjective* **peaceful** 294
transfer *verb* **carry** 51
transform *verb* **change** 53
transgress *verb* **disobey** 114
translucent
adjective **transparent** 434
transmit *verb* **send** 365
transparent *adjective* 434
transpire *verb* **happen** 187
transport *verb* **carry** 51
transpose *verb* **exchange** 137
trap *noun* 434
trap *verb* **capture** 49
verb **catch** 51
trash *noun* **rubbish** 350
travel *verb* 435
traveller *noun* 435
traverse *verb* **cross** 88
treacherous *adjective* **unfaithful** 445
treasure *noun* **wealth** 462
treble *adjective* **high-pitched** 195
tremble *verb* **fear** 150
verb **shake** 368
trembly *adjective* **frightened** 168
trench *noun* **groove** 185
trend *noun* **fashion** 147
trial *noun* **test** 422
trick *noun* 436
trick *verb* 436
trickery *noun* 437
trickle *verb* **drip** 121
trifling *adjective* **minor** 260
trim *adjective* **tidy** 430
verb **cut** 91
trip *noun* **journey** 227
verb **fall** 146
tripper *noun* **traveller** 435
trip up *verb* **err** 133
triumph *verb* **succeed** 407
trivial *adjective* **minor** 260
trivialise *verb* **minimise** 259
troop *noun* **group** 185
trophy *noun* **prize** 315
noun **souvenir** 392
troubadour *noun* **singer** 381
trouble *verb* **upset** 450
truant *noun* **escapee** 134
trudge *verb* 437

true *adjective* 438
trust *verb* **believe** 32
trustworthy *adjective* **faithful** 145
trusty *adjective* **faithful** 145
truthful *adjective* **honest** 199
try *verb* **attempt** 24
verb **test** 422
trying *adjective* **annoying** 15
tryst *noun* **meeting** 256
tubby *adjective* **fat** 148
tumble *verb* **overbalance** 288
tumble to *verb* **realise** 329
tumult *noun* **commotion** 69
tuneful *adjective* **musical** 267
turbid *adjective* **opaque** 283
turmoil *noun* **commotion** 69
turn *verb* 438
turn down *verb* **refuse** 333
turn out *verb* **assemble** 20
turn up *verb* **come** 67
turquoise *adjective* **green** 183
tussle *verb* **fight** 154
tutor *noun* **teacher** 419
twin *adjective* **double** 118
twinge *noun* **pain** 290
twinkle *verb* **sparkle** 393
twirl *verb* **spin** 395
twist *noun* **coil** 64
verb **misrepresent** 262
verb **turn** 438
twisted *adjective* 439
twisted *adjective* **crooked** 87
two-piece *adjective* **double** 118
tyrannical *adjective* 439

Uu

ugly *adjective* 440
adjective **nasty** 271
ultimatum *noun* **demand** 102
umpteen *adjective* **countless** 82
unadorned *adjective* **simple** 380
unapologetic
adjective **unashamed** 440
unappreciative
adjective **ungrateful** 446
unashamed *adjective* 440
unattached
adjective **independent** 210
adjective **unmarried** 447
unattainable
adjective **impossible** 206
unbalanced *adjective* **uneven** 444
unbelievable *adjective* 441
unburden *verb* **admit** 6
uncertain *adjective* 441
uncommon *adjective* **unusual** 449
uncomplicated *adjective* **easy** 124
uncompromising
adjective **stubborn** 404
unconnected
adjective **unrelated** 448
unconscious *adjective* 442
unconventional *adjective* 442
unconventional *adjective* **free** 166
uncooperative
adjective **naughty** 271
uncouth *adjective* **vulgar** 457
undecided *adjective* **confused** 77
underhand *adjective* **secretive** 362
understand *verb* 443
undertake *verb* **attempt** 24
undertaking *noun* 443
undertone *noun* **whisper** 465
unearth *verb* **find** 154
uneducated *adjective* **ignorant** 203
unequal *adjective* **uneven** 444
uneven *adjective* 444
unfair *adjective* 444
unfaithful *adjective* 445
unfeeling *adjective* **callous** 48
unflagging *adjective* **persistent** 297
unfold *verb* **reveal** 345
unfortunate *adjective* **unlucky** 447
unfriendly *adjective* 445

ungrateful *adjective* 446
unhappy *adjective* **sad** 353
unhurried *adjective* **slow** 385
uniform *adjective* **equal** 133
unimportant
adjective **insignificant** 218
uninhibited *adjective* **free** 166
unique *adjective* **single** 381
unite *verb* **cooperate** 79
verb **join** 226
unjust *adjective* **unfair** 444
unkempt *adjective* **scruffy** 361
unkind *adjective* 446
unlikely *adjective* **unbelievable** 441
unlucky *adjective* 447
unmarried *adjective* 447
unnecessary *adjective* **extra** 143
unobtrusive *adjective* **simple** 380
unofficial *adjective* **informal** 214
unpalatable *adjective* **inedible** 211
unravel *verb* **simplify** 380
unreasonable
adjective **irrational** 224
unregenerate
adjective **unashamed** 440
unrelated *adjective* 448
unremorseful
adjective **unashamed** 440
unrepentant
adjective **unashamed** 440
unruly *adjective* **disobedient** 114
unseen *adjective* **invisible** 223
unselfish *adjective* **kind** 231
unskilful *adjective* **incompetent** 208
unsophisticated *adjective* **naive** 268
unsound *adjective* **defective** 99
unsteady *adjective* **erratic** 134
unthinkable
adjective **impossible** 206
untidy *adjective* 448
untold *adjective* **countless** 82
untrained
adjective **inexperienced** 212
untrue *adjective* **incorrect** 209
unusual *adjective* 449
unwed *adjective* **unmarried** 447
unwilling *adjective* 449
unworldly *adjective* **naive** 268
upgrade *verb* **improve** 206
uppity *adjective* **pompous** 304
upright *adjective* **honest** 199
uprising *noun* **rebellion** 330
uproar *noun* **noise** 276
upset *adjective* 450
upset *verb* 450
upset *adjective* **sad** 353
verb **disorganise** 115
verb **overturn** 288
uptight *adjective* **upset** 450
up-to-date *adjective* **modern** 265
urban *adjective* **civic** 57
urge *verb* **encourage** 128
use *verb* 451
useful *adjective* 451
useful *adjective* **helpful** 193
useless *adjective* 452
usual *adjective* 452
utilise *verb* **use** 451
utter *verb* **pronounce** 317

Vv

vacant *adjective* **empty** 127
vacate *verb* **quit** 325
vacillate *verb* **fluctuate** 159
vague *adjective* 453
vain *adjective* **conceited** 73
adjective **useless** 452
valiant *adjective* **brave** 41
valid *adjective* **true** 438
valuable *adjective* **useful** 451
value *verb* **judge** 228
vandalise *verb* **damage** 92
vanish *verb* **become extinct** 30
verb **disappear** 109
vanquish *verb* **defeat** 99
various *adjective* 453
vary *verb* **change** 53

vassal *noun* **slave** 382
vast *adjective* **huge** 201
vault *verb* **jump** 229
vehemence *noun* **violence** 454
vein *noun* **layer** 235
velvet *adjective* **soft** 389
vendor *noun* **seller** 364
veneer *noun* **coating** 64
venerate *verb* **worship** 471
veneration *noun* **respect** 342
vengeful *adjective* **resentful** 340
venomous *adjective* **poisonous** 303
venture *noun* **undertaking** 443
venue *noun* **place** 300
verify *verb* **prove** 320
vet *verb* **examine** 135
veteran *adjective* **experienced** 141
vex *verb* **irritate** 224
vexed *adjective* **annoyed** 14
viable *adjective* **possible** 307
vibrate *verb* **shake** 368
vicar *noun* **clergyman** 59
vicious *adjective* **cruel** 89
victimise *verb* **maltreat** 251
victor *noun* **winner** 467
victuals *noun* **food** 161
vie *verb* **compete** 70
view *noun* 454
view *verb* **see** 362
viewpoint *noun* **opinion** 283
vigorous *adjective* **energetic** 131
vigour *noun* **force** 162
vile *adjective* **nasty** 271
villainous *adjective* **evil** 135
vindicate *verb* **justify** 229
vindictive *adjective* **resentful** 340
vintage *adjective* **old** 282
violate *verb* **disobey** 114
violence *noun* 454
violent *adjective* 455
violent *adjective* **intense** 221
VIP *noun* 455
virtuoso *noun* **musician** 268
viscous *adjective* **gluey** 178
visible *adjective* 456
visit *verb* 456
vista *noun* **view** 454
vital *adjective* **necessary** 273
vivacious *adjective* **lively** 245
vivid *adjective* **colourful** 66
adjective **intense** 221
vocalist *noun* **singer** 381
vocation *noun* **job** 226
vogue *noun* **fashion** 147
voice *verb* **pronounce** 317
void *adjective* **empty** 127
voluble *adjective* **talkative** 416
volume *noun* **book** 38
voracious *adjective* **greedy** 183
vow *noun* **promise** 317
verb **intend** 220
voyage *verb* **travel** 435
vulgar *adjective* 457
vulnerable *adjective* 457

Ww

waddle *verb* **sway** 413
wade through *verb* **read** 328
waffle *verb* **rave** 327
wage *noun* **pay** 293
wail *verb* **cry** 90
walk *verb* 458
wander *verb* **ramble** 326
verb **travel** 435
wane *verb* **decrease** 97
want *verb* 458
want *noun* **poverty** 307
wanting *adjective* **insufficient** 219
ward *noun* **dependant** 103
wardrobe *noun* **clothing** 61
warlike *adjective* 459
warm *adjective* **friendly** 167
adjective **hot** 200
adjective **near** 272
warm-up *noun* **practice** 309
warn *verb* 459
warn *verb* **predict** 311

warped *adjective* **crooked** 87
warrant *noun* **order** 285
verb **justify** 229
wary *adjective* 460
wash *verb* **clean** 58
verb **flow** 159
washout *noun* **disappointment** 109
waste *verb* 460
waste away *verb* **deteriorate** 105
watch *verb* **see** 362
watchful *adjective* **alert** 11
adjective **wary** 460
water *verb* **wet** 464
wave *verb* **sway** 413
waver *verb* **cower** 85
verb **fluctuate** 159
wavy *adjective* **twisted** 439
wax *verb* **polish** 303
waylay *verb* **catch** 51
weak *adjective* 461
weaken *verb* 461
weak-willed
adjective **submissive** 406
wealth *noun* 462
wealthy *adjective* 462
weary *adjective* **tired** 431
verb **tire** 430
weedy *adjective* **weak** 461
weigh *verb* **ponder** 305
weight *noun* 463
weighty *adjective* **heavy** 191
weird *adjective* **strange** 402
welcome *adjective* **nice** 276
verb **like** 241
well *adjective* **healthy** 190
well-balanced *adjective* **sane** 355
adjective **steady** 398
well-behaved *adjective* 463
well-informed
adjective **educated** 125
well-mannered
adjective **well-behaved** 463
well-meaning *adjective* **kind** 231
well-off *adjective* **wealthy** 462
wet *adjective* 464
wet *verb* 464
wheeze *verb* **gasp** 172
whimper *verb* **cry** 90
whine *verb* **complain** 71
whinge *verb* **complain** 71
whip *verb* **thrash** 427
whip up *verb* **make** 250
whirl *verb* **spin** 395
whirr *verb* **spin** 395
verb **throb** 429
whisper *noun* 465
whisper *noun* **gossip** 180
white *adjective* 465
whole *adjective* 466
wholesale *verb* **sell** 364
whoop it up *verb* **rejoice** 334
wicked *adjective* **evil** 135
wide *adjective* 466
wide *adjective* **spacious** 393
wield *verb* **use** 451
wild *adjective* **free** 166
adjective **violent** 455
wilderness *adjective* **country** 83
noun **the country** 427
wilful *adjective* **disobedient** 114
will *noun* **wish** 469
willing *adjective* **enthusiastic** 132
wily *adjective* **cunning** 90
win *verb* **get** 175
verb **succeed** 407
wind *verb* **turn** 438
wind down *verb* **rest** 343
winding *adjective* **twisted** 439
wing *noun* **side** 377
winner *noun* 467
wintry *adjective* 467
wipe *verb* 468
wipe out *verb* **destroy** 105
wiry *adjective* **strong** 404
wise *adjective* **sensible** 366
wisecrack *noun* 468
wish *noun* 469
withdraw *verb* **leave** 237
verb **remove** 337
wither *verb* **shrink** 376

withstand *verb* **resist** 341
witness *verb* **see** 362
witticism *noun* **wisecrack** 468
wobble *verb* **sway** 413
woeful *adjective* **pathetic** 292
wonderful *adjective* 469
woolly *adjective* **vague** 453
word *noun* **message** 257
word of honour *noun* **promise** 317
wordy *adjective* **lengthy** 238
work *noun* 470
work *verb* 470
work *noun* **job** 226
verb **sew** 367
workable *adjective* **possible** 307
work out *verb* **solve** 390
work towards *verb* **attempt** 24
worn *adjective* **tired** 431
worry *verb* 471
worry *verb* **upset** 450
worsen *verb* **deteriorate** 105
worship *verb* 471
worthless *adjective* **inferior** 212
wound *verb* **hurt** 203
wraith *noun* **ghost** 175
wrangle *verb* **disagree** 108
wrap *verb* **cover** 84
wrath *noun* **anger** 12
wreathe *verb* **cover** 84
wreck *verb* **damage** 92
wretched *adjective* **pathetic** 292
adjective **unlucky** 447
wriggle *verb* **fidget** 153
writ *noun* **order** 285
write *verb* 472
write *verb* **compose** 72
write-off *noun* **failure** 144
writhe *verb* **fidget** 153

yak *verb* 472
yarn *verb* **talk** 416
yell *verb* **shout** 373
yellow *adjective* 473
yellow *adjective* **fearful** 151
yelp *verb* **shriek** 375
yen *noun* **wish** 469
yield *verb* **give in** 177
verb **produce** 315
young *adjective* 473
young *noun* **offspring** 281
youth *noun* **male** 250
youthful *adjective* **young** 473

Guide to the index

What do you do when you want to describe a recent holiday and the only word you can think of is 'nice'?

. . . Simple! Start at the INDEX, the back section of the book. The Index lists all the words in the Thesaurus in alphabetical order. At the top of the pages you will find the first and last words on those pages.

Look at the sample of the index on the opposite page. You will find 'nice' listed twice. These two entries direct you to two different meanings of this word.

The first time 'nice' is listed it is printed in bold (darker) type along with its part of speech and the page it is on. The bold type tells you that **nice** is a keyword. This means that it is the first word in a word group which has the overall meaning 'nice'. This word group can be found on page 276 and includes the other adjectives *pleasant, enjoyable, lovely, acceptable, welcome.* 'Pleasant' and 'enjoyable' would both be better words than 'nice' to describe your holiday.

The second time 'nice' is listed it is printed in normal type along with its part of speech, the keyword **kind** in bold type, and its page number. Obviously, you would not want to describe your holiday as 'kind' so you would not bother to look up this word group to find other useful words. However, if you wanted to describe a nice person you met on your holiday, you could look up **kind** on page 231. Here you will find other words with the overall meaning 'kind'. These are *thoughtful, considerate, unselfish, well-meaning.* Any one of these words could be used to describe your friend.

So, when you look up a word in the index it guides you to the right meaning of the word as well as to the page on which you will find it.